ENERGY AND CHANGE

INSURRECTIONS: CRITICAL STUDIES IN RELIGION,
POLITICS, AND CULTURE

INSURRECTIONS: CRITICAL STUDIES IN RELIGION,
POLITICS, AND CULTURE

Slavoj Žižek, Clayton Crockett, Creston Davis, Jeffrey W. Robbins, Editors

The intersection of religion, politics, and culture is one of the most discussed areas in theory today. It also has the deepest and most wide-ranging impact on the world. Insurrections: Critical Studies in Religion, Politics, and Culture will bring the tools of philosophy and critical theory to the political implications of the religious turn. The series will address a range of religious traditions and political viewpoints in the United States, Europe, and other parts of the world. Without advocating any specific religious or theological stance, the series aims nonetheless to be faithful to the radical emancipatory potential of religion.

For a complete list of titles see page 293

ENERGY AND CHANGE

A NEW MATERIALIST COSMOTHEOLOGY

CLAYTON CROCKETT

Columbia University Press
New York

Columbia University Press
Publishers Since 1893
New York   Chichester, West Sussex
cup.columbia.edu
Copyright © 2022 Columbia University Press
All rights reserved

Library of Congress Cataloging-in-Publication Data
Names: Crockett, Clayton, 1969– author.
Title: Energy and change : a new materialist cosmotheology / Clayton Crockett.
Description: New York: Columbia University Press, 2022. | Series: Insurrections: critical studies in religion, politics, and culture | Includes bibliographical references and index.
Identifiers: LCCN 2021058017 | ISBN 9780231206105 (hardback) | ISBN 9780231206112 (trade paperback) | ISBN 9780231556323 (ebook)
Subjects: LCSH: Religion—Philosophy. | Materialism. | Change.
Classification: LCC BL51 .C6977 2022 | DDC 210—dc23/eng20220314
LC record available at https://lccn.loc.gov/2021058017

Cover design: Noah Arlow
Cover image: Getty Images

TO STEPHANIE, AND TO OUR SKELETONS . . .
I O U ETERNITY

CONTENTS

Acknowledgments ix

INTRODUCTION: NEW MATERIALISM AND ENERGY TRANSFORMATION 1

1. ENERGY AND THE DYNAMICS OF NATURE 26

2. VITAL MATTERS: BIOENERGETICS AND LIFE 76

3. POLITICAL ECONOMY AND POLITICAL ECOLOGY: ENERGY, GENERAL ECONOMY, AND EXCHANGE 132

4. OF SPIRIT IN AMERINDIAN, VODOU, AND CHINESE TRADITIONS 185

5. RADICAL THEOLOGY AND THE NATURE OF GOD 228

Notes 261
Index 285

ACKNOWLEDGMENTS

I would like to acknowledge everyone who has been part of and supported, engaged, challenged, and/or criticized me along this extraordinary fifteen-year journey. The list of people is far too numerous to set out, but includes Wendy Lochner, my editor at CUP, whose help and support for this project has been extraordinary; two anonymous readers for the Press whose criticisms and suggestions for revision have been invaluable for improving the book; my coeditors of Insurrections, Jeffrey W. Robbins, Creston Davis, and Slavoj Žižek—colleagues, friends and cocreators of this extraordinary book series; Catherine Keller, for being such a wonderful, careful, generous and enthusiastic reader; and the late Kevin Mequet for his technical education and his enthusiasm for scientific and theological ideas—your energy is deeply missed and yet lives on in me and many others.

The University of Central Arkansas has been my home for almost twenty years, and I deeply appreciate so many of my colleagues at UCA, including Charlie Harvey, Taine Duncan, Jesse Butler, Nick Brasovan, Guo-ou Zhuang, Sharon Mason, Mary Ruth Marotte, Benjamin Rider, Kim Newman, and Tierra Underwood; I am also tremendously grateful for students and former students including Tim Snediker, Sarah Harvey, Jeff Lambert, Keith Witty, Clem Johnson, Alex Cannon, Mason Brothers, Alex Waitkus, Alex Velte, Julia Dani Pistole, Oscar Albert Garcia Delgado, Cat Hicks, and Elaina Taylor. Finally, I want to acknowledge a sabbatical that was awarded by the University Research Council of UCA in spring 2017 that allowed me the time to begin writing this book.

I am also profoundly grateful to so many friends, colleagues, mentors and peers, including Noëlle Vahanian, Mary-Jane Rubenstein, Catherine Malabou, Jack Caputo, the late Charles Long, Saitya Brata Das, Anindya Sekhar Purkayastha, Dai Zhaoguo, Chen Xudong, Lv Hui (吕惠) aka Norah—and all of my dear friends from Anhui Normal University in Wuhu, as well as Katerina Kolozova, Mike Grimshaw, Ward Blanton, Malik Saafir, Kalvin Graham, Stacy Lettman, Mary Keller, Wilson Dickinson, Michael W. Wilson, Jordan Miller, Karen Bray, Tad Delay, David Galston, Alan Richard, George Schmitt, Bo Eberle, An Yountae, Lisa Gasson-Gardner, Philip Goodchild, Shelley Denis, Petra Carlsson Rendel, Dan Miller, Carol Wayne White, Chris Satoor, Bill Connolly, Gil Anidjar, Santiago Slabodsky, Lowell Frye, Carl Raschke, LeRon Shults, Dan Colucciello Barber, Elijah Pruitt-Davis, Jay Carter, John Reader, Hollis Phelps, Lewis Gordon, Luke Higgins, Peter Rollins, Robyn Henderson-Espinoza, Saswat Das, Rustam Singh, Jane Gordon, Devin Singh, Russell Re Manning, Matt Baker, Eric Bourdelieu, Elaine Charry, Elias Ortega-Aponte, Giovanni Tusa, Terra Rowe, Michael Marder, and Santiago Zabala for their influence, engagement, and inspiration. My apologies to everyone I missed!

INTRODUCTION

New Materialism and Energy Transformation

> *All that you touch*
> *You Change.*
> *All that you Change*
> *Changes You.*
> *The only lasting truth*
> *is Change.*
> *God*
> *is Change.*
>
> —OCTAVIA E. BUTLER, *PARABLE OF THE SOWER*

OVERVIEW

In traditional Western metaphysics, Plato establishes an opposition between two pre-Socratics, Heraclitus and Parmenides. Parmenides denies that anything can change, whereas Heraclitus is the philosopher of ceaseless flux. Plato wants to set his philosophy up as the dialectical solution to these two opposed views, so he exaggerates them, especially Heraclitus. Plato argues that there is both movement, flux and change, but there must be something eternal and unchanging that exists in some way behind these transitory appearances, which he calls *eidos*, or forms.

Aristotle adopts this view, although he situates the forms more directly in the midst of a changing world. Still, there must be something that does not change, which is a prime mover, or God.

Christianity inherits Greek philosophy, situating an eternal changeless God beyond the world. The main difference is that this God is personal and becomes incarnated in human form as the Christ. Still, most of what we call Western metaphysics leans toward the Platonic valuation of that which does not change over that which does. *But what if there is nothing that does not change?*

Energy is a way to measure change. Energy becomes a scientific concept in the nineteenth century with the development of thermodynamics. Thermodynamics in turn appears as a way to account for the new heat engines, such as the steam engine, that drive the Industrial Revolution in Britain and then everywhere else. Energy is a philosophical word coined by Aristotle, *energeia*, as an active principle in his *Physics* and *Metaphysics*. Energeia is associated with the word *ergon*, or work, and it involves the actualizing of something in its work. For Aristotle, this actuality of energy exceeds its potentiality, which is different from the modern conception of energy, where potential energy is at least as important as, if not more important than, kinetic energy.

We actualize something by making it productive, by making it work. We use energy to do things, and we require energy to live and work and think and love. Energy cuts across multiple thresholds of existence, and it is always dynamic, always changing. Being is energy transformation. This book is a philosophy of energy, drawing on various scientific, theoretical, and spiritual understandings of energy across multiple traditions. It instantiates a vision, whereby energy is how we talk about change, and change is what is ultimately real. This vision is also a spiritual vision, because energy also cuts across the opposition between spirit and matter, and offers new ways to think about spirit in physical terms.

Energy and change work across multiple levels of existence. These levels are not hierarchical, however, insofar as one level is more valuable or more fundamental compared to others. We should understand levels more like how Gilles Deleuze and Félix Guattari understand plateaus in *A Thousand Plateaus*. They take the word *plateau* from Gregory Bateson and they offer a perspectival account of various plateaus, including how they are constituted and how they operate.

This book posits energy as an immanent and spiritual process that is nonetheless physical or material, particularly since Albert Einstein's special relativity views mass and energy as convertible at the square of the speed of light. Energy cuts across traditional oppositions like soul and body, time and eternity, idealism and materialism, even as they often emphasize one of these terms more than the other. In this book I privilege conceptions of energy and its concomitant change and I examine their interactions across multiple plateaus: physics and thermodynamics; biology and life; political economy and political ecology; and spirit and religion or theology. None of these plateaus necessarily supersedes the others or renders them insignificant.

As thinking humans, we are facing an energy crisis that is also an ecological crisis. It involves the anthropogenic warming of the planet to temperatures that threaten human flourishing and, at a certain point, even existence. Global warming is one symptom of an ecological situation that sets our technologies over against a planet that possesses abundant but not infinite resources to be exploited and utilized. We have used, and used up, many natural resources, and we are facing real limits. We have also used human beings as material resources in brutal and immoral ways.

The best name for our contemporary condition is neoliberal capitalism, because it represents a metastasis of liberal capitalism. Neoliberalism is a desperate attempt to perpetuate economic and financial growth so as to ward off catastrophe, a catastrophe that modern liberal capitalism along with its attendant colonialism and slavery, have caused. We are facing this catastrophe, even as we want to deny it or imagine fantastic ways to resolve it.

Energy and change are at the heart of existence, including but not only our existence. Many scholars in the humanities have been taking up the study of energy in the past few years, as part of what is called "energy humanities." In addition to scientific, technical, and economic energy studies, many of which are focused on alternative energies as a way to supplement or replace fossil fuels, we need new ways to think about energy systems and how they are integrated into our lives in a broad sense. According to Cara New Daggett, energy humanities analyzes energy not just in terms of science, technology, fuel, or machines, but "as a sociomaterial apparatus that flows through political and cultural life."[1] *Energy and Change* constitutes a philosophy of energy that is also a contribution to this nascent field of energy humanities, even as it sometimes draws upon scientific concepts.

Classical materialism as it emerges in European modernity criticizes vitalist and spiritual explanations as superstitious and nonscientific. Matter is viewed as inert stuff that obeys deterministic laws, and there is no need to posit any other force or substance to explain our world. Of course we know that matter is not inert; it is dynamic even if that is not apparent at human scales of awareness. In the early twenty-first century, a new philosophy of matter, a new materialism, emerges as a better theoretical way to account for the intrinsic dynamism of matter. This new materialism does not often explicitly treat energy, perhaps because energy has been associated too closely with a crude positivist thermodynamics or alternatively a naïve vitalism. However, my approach to understanding energy in this book is best described as new materialist.

WHAT IS NEW MATERIALISM?

New materialism is a new theoretical perspective that emerges in the early twenty-first century with roots in the philosophies of Alfred North Whitehead, Maurice Merleau-Ponty, and Deleuze. New materialism draws upon the work of these three thinkers to challenge the linguistic constructivism that dominated much of late twentieth-century philosophy. Deleuze, Merleau-Ponty, and Whitehead each delineate a dynamic ontology of material existence.

In 1929, Whitehead's Gifford Lectures were published as *Process and Reality*. This book forges a new philosophical vision that takes into account some of the revolutionary findings of quantum physics. Here Whitehead affirms "the displacement of the notion of static stuff by the notion of fluent energy. Such energy has its structure of action and flow, and is inconceivable apart from such structure. It is also conditioned by 'quantum' requirements."[2] *Process and Reality*'s very uniqueness and complexity, however, makes it difficult to harmonize with other works in twentieth-century philosophy.

Building on Henri Bergson's groundbreaking analysis in *Matter and Memory*, and incorporating the phenomenology of Edmund Husserl,

Merleau-Ponty published his *Phenomenology of Perception* in 1945. Merleau-Ponty grounds perception in the body, most famously with his example of two hands touching each other. Even though he casts his analysis in terms of transcendental philosophy, Merleau-Ponty affirms that "there is a logic of the world to which my body in its entirety conforms, and through which things of inter-sensory experience become possible for us."[3] The senses of and the sensing through the body open onto an intersubjective world that is not split between rational thought and felt physical sensation.

This phenomenology of the body inspires later philosophers, including feminist philosophers like Rosi Braidotti and Luce Irigaray, to think with rather than against the body. As Diana Coole explains, Merleau-Ponty presages a new materialism that "is achieved by recognizing the body as 'the pivot of the world' and nature as a phenomenal field inhabited by bodies as beings-in-the-world."[4] And Deleuze explains that for Merleau-Ponty consciousness is not a hole in being but rather a fold of being. This folding is a material capacity of body, of being, and of flesh.[5]

Deleuze is the third major influence on new materialism. In his philosophy, Deleuze advances an ontological becoming based on differential intensity. In *Difference and Repetition*, Deleuze works out a philosophy of difference that rejects the logics of identity and representation. The fundamental problem for Deleuze is how difference can relate to difference without a prior sameness. The key idea is that of a differentiator, which he takes from Martin Heidegger, a *Sich-unterscheidende*. The differentiator works because "a system must be constituted on the basis of two or more series, each series being defined by the differences between the terms which compose it. If we suppose that the series communicate under the impulse of a force of some kind, then it is apparent that this communication relates differences to differences."[6] This impulsive force is called intensity, which brings the constituents of the series together and allows them to interact so that a new difference can emerge. An example of this is a moiré pattern, where one pattern is superimposed over another pattern and what emerges is the differences between the two patterns.

Intensity brings together differences and further differentiates them; this the repetition of difference that Deleuze works out in his masterwork. Beneath the apparent identity and the cancellation of differences in extensity, there is a remainder of intensity or difference that continues to be available for other transformations. Deleuze's work along with that of Guattari inspires many contributors to new materialism, even those who are critical of some of their specific concepts.

In the mid-1990s, Rosi Braidotti used the term "neo-materialism" to indicate an affirmation of and engagement with material reality beyond the linguistic constructivism of much twentieth-century philosophy. This neomaterialism becomes new materialism in the early twenty-first century. According to Braidotti, the hegemony of the linguistic branch of poststructuralism was dominant in the 1990s; therefore for her, "neo-materialism emerges as a method, a conceptual frame and a political stand, which refuses the linguistic paradigm, stressing instead the concrete yet complex materiality of bodies immersed in social relations of power."[7] Braidotti's materialism is strongly influenced by Deleuze and Irigaray. In her 2002 book *Metamorphoses* she contrasts her neomaterialist feminism with a more traditional "essentialist feminism" and the opposition to this that sees sex and gender as constructed and performative, as in the work of Monique Wittig and Judith Bulter. Braidotti claims that her philosophy of radical immanence is materialist without being essentialist and involves "a deeply embedded vision of the embodied subject."[8]

In addition to Braidotti, other theorists associated with new materialism include Manuel DeLanda, Jane Bennett, William Connolly, Karen Barad, Diana Coole, Elizabeth Grosz, Pheng Cheah, Rick Dolphijn, Sarah Ahmed, Brian Massumi, and Mel Chen. There is a family resemblance with some elements of speculative realism, including the speculative materialism of Quentin Meillassoux. Finally, there is the biological materialism of Catherine Malabou, who is more influenced by Hegel, Heidegger, and Derrida. This is not an exhaustive summary, but more of an overview to provide background for readers who are less familiar with new materialism.[9]

This new materialism differs from the classical expressions of materialism in early modern Europe. Classical materialism develops out of the emergence of modern science that culminates in the great synthesis of Isaac Newton. Newtonian mechanics presupposes material forces that act on bodies in a framework of objective space and linear time. The discovery of atoms in the early twentieth century consolidates the assumption of tiny units that compose everything else that exists, although this occurs at the same time as the dissolution of the Newtonian worldview. The new discoveries of relativity and quantum physics destroy the premises of any reductionist atomic materialism, although philosophy was slow to respond to this situation, with the notable exception of Whitehead.

James K. Feibleman explains in a book titled *The New Materialism*, published in 1970, in anticipation of later expressions, that "matter is no longer considered a simple, inert stuff which resists analysis and has to be reckoned with only in the round, but has been acknowledged to be a highly dynamic agent capable of sustaining the most complex activities."[10] This early articulation of new materialism conveys the central thesis of the inherent dynamism of matter, and it argues that what we call spirit is "a property of matter" rather than a separate phenomenon or an unreal presupposition.[11]

New materialists stress the dynamism of matter, as opposed to its apparently static qualities. This affirmation of a dynamic material existence resists the need to resort to idealist or vitalist qualities that need to be added onto matter. We do not need to posit something in addition to the workings of material reality to get novelty and change. As Cheah argues, "for Deleuze, materiality is nothing other than the plane of immanence."[12] The plane of immanence, or the plane of consistency, is a way for Deleuze to avoid the trap of transcendence, or the need to import meaning and significance from elsewhere to provide value to a thing.

New materialism conjoins complex philosophies of material things with scientific theories of chaos, complexity, and self-organization. As DeLanda explains, Deleuze works with many of the ideas of chaos and complexity theory, even though he does not use the language of physics. In *Intensive Science and Virtual Philosophy*, DeLanda extracts a realist ontology from Deleuze that is consonant with theories of chaotic complexity and self-organization. He argues that our focus on linear processes obscures the way that the world actually works, and that attention to "nonlinear models and their multiple attractors, as well as nonlinear causes and their complex capacities to affect and be affected, define a world capable of surprising us through the emergence of unexpected novelty."[13]

New materialists attend to the intrinsic dynamism of matter. What many of these theorists leave out, however, is an explicit engagement with the concept of energy. *This book centers new materialism around energy transformations across multiple thresholds of being.* What is being? I claim that being is energy transformation. Energy is never static; it is constantly changing because energy is dynamics; it is how we measure change. Furthermore, change is always exchange, because it exists in complex relationship with everything else, including itself. This exchange is something that Barad calls intra-activity that is just as fundamental as interactivity. We have to confront reality in new ways, spurred on not only by the findings of twentieth-century physics but also the philosophies of dynamic material reality.

What about Marx? Often Marx and Marxism are seen as examples of the crude materialism that new materialism is supposed to overcome. And certainly many examples of Marxism conform to this representation. At the same time, there is a new materialist Marx, and perhaps this Marx is closer to Marx than most would presume. In 2000, John Bellamy Foster published *Marx's Ecology: Materialism and Nature*, which shows how Marx's philosophy foreshadowed contemporary ecological thinking. Foster shows how Marx's doctoral thesis on Epicurus supplied him with a complex nondeterministic materialism. We mostly know Epicurus's ideas through *On the Nature of Things*, by Lucretius, but Epicurus was one of the most prolific philosophers of ancient Greece. He established his Garden in Athens in 306 BCE. Although he adopts an atomic materialism inspired by Democritus and Leucippus, he saw these atoms as subject to chance and indeterminacy. This is the famous notion of the "swerve," or *clinamen*, that exposes material reality to chance and freedom. As Foster explains, "Epicurus opposed all teleology and all absolute determinism in the treatment of nature," anticipating much of modern and contemporary science.[14] For Epicurus, life is emergent from matter, and this understanding allows Marx to affirm a dialectical materialism that evades the deterministic mechanical materialism of his day.

Marx separates Epicurus from Democritus, because "Epicurus' swerve—a swerve that was a slight deviation—created the realm of chance (in the sense of contingency) and hence possibility free from determinism. It made the world itself possible, as Lucretius had written, since otherwise there would be no collision of atoms and 'the world would never have been created.'"[15] This complex materialism drawn from Epicurus allows Marx to oppose both mechanical materialism and Hegelian idealism in his philosophy. In a section titled "The New Materialism," Foster explains that Marx supplements Epicurus's speculative materialism with a more practical historical materialism in his break with Ludwig

Feuerbach.[16] He wants to shift the focus from nature to human society and history and ground both in a complex indeterminate materialism. Rather than merely interpret the world, Marx wants to *change* it.

Change works by means of contradictions and oppositions; these rifts are challenges and opportunities for a dialectical historical materialism committed to human flourishing. Marx analyzes the historical development of the European economy based fundamentally on the opposition between town and country that opens up during the instantiation of capitalism. The most profound historical and social contradiction exists within the framework of the relegation of country to non-historical existence in favor of the city. It is under capitalism that "the antagonism of town and country becomes fully developed, 'the most important division of material and mental labor.'"[17] At the same time, this rift between town and country exacerbates and exposes the "metabolic rift" between humanity and nature.

Foster shows how deeply relevant Marx's thought is for both ecology and new materialism. At the same time, his reliance on Marx in a way that suggests a harmonious natural relation between human and natural metabolism indicates a residual idealism in how we perceive that nature works, which also pervades many ecological perspectives. Metabolism only works by means of rifts, even if the rift that is created by capitalism between humanity and the earth is one of the largest rifts in planetary history. There is no metabolic process without rift, without chance or change.

Foster directly engages Marx's philosophy, and he critiques much of twentieth century Marxist thought that treats his ideas mainly in social terms. He does praise Marxist scientists, however, such as Richard Levins, Stephen Jay Gould, and R. C. Lewontin, who combine Marx's materialism with a sophisticated Darwinism. Interestingly enough, Foster fails to mention Louis Althusser, perhaps the most influential French Marxist of the second half of the twentieth century. The later writings of Althusser are another significant influence on new materialism, among them his essay "The Underground Current of the Materialism of the Encounter."

In 1980 Althusser, who suffered from depression, strangled his wife in an episode that he claims not to remember. Absolved of legal guilt, he was institutionalized in clinics, although after a few years he began writing sporadically, including his memoir *The Future Lasts a Long Time*. His last writings are included in a volume called *Philosophy of the Encounter*. Here

Althusser reconsiders his entire work and sets off in a new direction, one that he is unable to complete before his death in 1990. In the essay on the materialism of the encounter, extracted from his writings, he announces *"the existence of an almost completely unknown materialist tradition in the history of philosophy: the 'materialism' of the rain, the swerve, the encounter."*[18] Althusser links his aleatory materialism to that of Epicurus and Lucretius, whose "swerve" provides Marx his own conception of materialism, which avoids the prevalent mechanical materialism of modern Europe.

For Althusser, the rain is a rain of chance. It is the chance of rain, the swerve or clinamen of where and when rain will fall, atoms will come together and decay, beings and societies will rise and fall and come apart. He links "the rain" of "Epicurus' atoms that fall parallel to each other in the void" to "the 'rain' of the parallelism of the infinite attributes in Spinoza and many others: Machiavelli, Hobbes, Rousseau, Marx, Heidegger too, and Derrida." This aleatory materialism is contrasted to the materialism of determinate necessity or teleology, which is "a transformed, disguised form of idealism."[19] Althusser refuses the alternatives of determinism and freedom, especially the efforts to preserve human freedom in a world of apparent necessity. Foster shows how Marx reads Epicurus to avoid deterministic materialism and preserve human freedom, but Althusser radicalizes this Epicureanism to emphasize the contingency of any encounter by means of the swerve.

We are not here by necessity, by fate, or by the will of God. An almost unfathomable series of chance encounters produced us and everything we see. According to Althusser, "Swerve, not Reason or Cause, is the origin of the world."[20] Chance implies randomness; it implies indeterminacy. We perceive patterns and regularities that we call laws, but these regularities are themselves the result of chance encounters. Freedom and necessity are both freighted with what Whitehead calls a "misplaced concreteness" because they are defined in absolute terms in opposition to each other. Chance is swerve of the necessity of logic and nature together with the freedom of choice and will. Chance is always already overdetermined, but it is the only chance for meaningful existence. Chance represents the possibility for change. Althusser's aleatory materialism is a subterranean influence on new materialism, and it is due to the chance of his own ability to articulate something important near the end of his difficult life.

WHAT IS TO BE DONE IN THE ANTHROPOCENE?

In 1902 V. I. Lenin published a pamphlet called "What Is to Be Done?" This essay outlines the task and project of Communist revolution, which culminates in the Russian Revolution of 1919. According to Lenin, "We are passing from the sphere of history to the sphere of the present and, partly, of the future. But we firmly believe that the fourth period will lead to the consolidation of militant Marxism, that Russian Social-Democracy will emerge from the crisis in the full flower of manhood, that the opportunist rearguard will be 'replaced' by the genuine vanguard of the most revolutionary class."[21] This fourth period begins in promise and devolves into terror with the Stalinist purges. Early in the twenty-first century, we cannot believe in a Communist political revolution in the way Lenin and other radicals did, but his question is still relevant. In his work, Lenin combined a theoretical and practical focus, and while this book is more intensively theoretical, it is concerned with urgent practical issues.

In evaluating Lenin, we cannot avoid the possibility that the desire to create the best change can end up bringing about the worst, although even the worst is relative so long as we are alive and can imagine alternatives. For most observers, Hitler, Nazism, and the Holocaust comprise the worst scenario of the twentieth century, although the horrific excesses of Stalin and Mao also led to the deaths of millions of people, in addition to the ongoing impoverishment and destruction wrought in the name of free-market capitalism. Here is no equivocation but simply recognition that there is no simple and pure righteousness at the level of human being and society.

In the present century, we are witnessing the final gasps of neoliberalism, led by the declining economic power but still unavoidable military might of the United States. The European Union is straining and coming apart because of sovereign debt crises and nationalist protests, including the vote by Britain to leave the Union, or Brexit. China is surging forward in economic terms, while Russia attempts to compete militarily and economically with the U.S. and China, respectively. In 2020 the global economy and society as we have mostly experienced it plunged into an abyss from which we desperately want to recover, even though we know that things will never be the same. We know that change is unavoidable, but dread and fear often outweigh optimism and hope.

The 2016 election of Donald Trump reveals the surface of that fear, both for supporters and opponents, and it indicates a partial transition from neoliberalism to neofascism, although these should not be seen simply in oppositional terms. White Christian nationalism becomes more prevalent in political and social terms, and this is largely a reaction to economic decline and distress. The election of Joe Biden in 2020 constitutes a pivot back toward neoliberalism, although neofascism remains a vital element in American society, as indicated in the failed attempted coup of January 6, 2021.

The United States and most of the world did not really recover from the global recession of 2008; what occurred was a financial stabilization and then a resumption of business as usual, which continues to shift wealth from the poor to the rich. Religious extremism and terrorism frightens many Westerners, but this situation is also the result of a desperate struggle for resources, including oil and oil pipelines. The development of North American shale has staved off some of the imminent crises of declining oil reserves, but this is a temporary measure that cannot be indefinitely sustained.

In the spring of 2020, the global pandemic of COVID-19 struck most of the world, upending life as we know it. The global economy ground to a near halt, and the U.S. politicized its response in disastrous ways, as Trump attempted desperately to cling to power. On May 25, the brutal killing of George Floyd in Minneapolis sparked renewed protests and riots across the country that were met with the militarized violence of the police and other agents of state control. These outcries in the name of Black Lives Matter against racist police brutality also went global, and were sustained by President Trump's racially coded support for law and order. Under the surface, massive transfers of wealth were accelerated as Jeff Bezos and Elon Musk vied for richest human and many people worked from home, lost their jobs, or were exposed to the virus as essential frontline workers.

All these phenomena must be analyzed and reconsidered in light of the increasing effects of large-scale climate change. Global warming is occurring as the result of the concentration of carbon dioxide, methane, and other greenhouse gases in our atmosphere, although, ironically, the levels of carbon emissions plunged significantly with the economic shutdown in 2020. These processes are raising temperatures, melting ice, elevating sea levels, increasing ocean acidity, and contributing to extreme and intense weather events. Despite the dire warnings of scientists and environmentalists, most countries and organizations are doing little to decrease carbon emissions. We lack the will and the authority to act in any significant way, even as the effects are becoming more and more undeniable.

The Intergovernmental Panel on Climate Change (IPCC) released its *Sixth Assessment Report* in 2021. The conclusions are sobering and dire, even in best-case scenarios, with a current estimate of atmospheric carbon dioxide at 420 parts per million. Climate change is already affecting every part of the planet and will continue even if global emissions are halted. According to the report's "Summary for Policy Makers," our likely temperature increase *over the next twenty years* is a 1.5 degrees Celsius hotter average temperature compared to recorded global temperatures between 1850 and 1900. Between 2041 and 2060, the average increase in temperature increase is estimated between 1.6 and 2.4 degrees Celsius, and finally, 2081–2100 predicts a range of between 2.1 and 3.5 degrees Celsius.[22] Even a 2 degrees Celsius increase is an enormous challenge to human civilization and its workings, and it is almost certain that the global temperature increase will be above 2 degrees by 2100.

Reports show that 2016 was the hottest year on record;. 2017 and 2018 declined slightly from this peak, coming in fourth and fifth, respectively, while 2019 was the second hottest year on record, just slightly cooler than 2016. Although the destruction of the global economy and slowdown of manufacturing, consumption, and emissions led to a slightly cooler 2020, many of the processes contributing to global warming cannot be stopped, only mitigated slightly, and these same processes are being amped back up. July 2021 was officially declared the planet's hottest month on record by the National Oceanic and Atmospheric Administration.[23] And the concentration of atmospheric gas corresponds to a concentration of wealth in the world, where less than one hundred corporations are responsible for two-thirds of greenhouse gas emissions.[24]

Due to human activities on a global scale, we are undergoing what some observers are calling the "Sixth Extinction," following five other massive extinction events in Earth's history.[25] The difference is that this event appears to be primarily connected to the actions of human beings on the planet. According to Vandana Shiva, writing in 2012, humans are undertaking numeral planetary wars against the Earth, with the result that "humans have driven 75 of agricultural biodiversity to extinction because of industrial farming, and between three to 300 species are being pushed to extinction every day."[26] The irony of this situation is that humans may themselves undergo extinction in a worst-case scenario as a result of ecological and environmental devastation.

We do need to be a little careful about comparing the present extinction to previous mass extinctions. The current extinction rate is about one hundred times that of the "normal" background rate of extinction of species, and that is pretty much all due to the activities and effects of humans. But we are still very far from a mass extinction of life along the lines of the Permian, Devonian, Triassic, Cretaceous, or Pleistocene mass extinctions. Compared to those mass extinctions, we are still very much in a background extinction rate, but it is possible that circumstances could create a tipping point that would unleash a truly mass extinction event.[27]

Climate change is already affecting everyone and everything, but it harms the most vulnerable most and first. In our understanding of human existence and its technological civilization, as well as our practices of economic capitalism, everything has to change. We live in a world that appears stable, at least in terms of the trajectory of technological development and human consumption, but this apparent stability is a lie. Every organism, every species, and every society is caught up in a dynamic process that exists in a metastable state, namely, a state that is not at equilibrium.

On the one hand, we need as much human solidarity as possible to confront the urgent environmental situation we face, one that can and may destroy us sooner or later. As Naomi Klein's book puts it, *This Changes Everything*. According to Klein, "our economic system and our planetary system are now at war."[28] We all need to recognize that the greatest threat to human existence in large-scale civilizational terms is fossil-fueled corporate capitalism, and organize against it however we can. On the other hand, even if our world is crumbling ecologically, we can be sure that the people who are suffering and will continue to suffer the least will be people who are male, who are white, and who are rich. And we can already see that the people who are most exposed to environmental devastation are poor, are nonwhite, and are women.

In very general terms, we are coming up against real physical limits in terms of planetary resources, including cheap energy reserves, fresh water, arable land, rare earth metals, and atmospheric absorption capacity. As Michael T. Klare explains in *The Race for What's Left*, we face an extraordinary combination of factors: "A lack of any unexplored resource preserves beyond those now being eyed for development; the sudden emergence of rapacious new consumers; technical and environmental limitations on the exploitation of new deposits; and the devastating effects of climate change. In many cases, the commodities procured during this new round of extraction will represent the final supplies of their type."[29]

Contemporary capitalist economics and social processes obfuscate and confuse our perception of these realities. At the most basic level there is the insistence of physical reality: you cannot have infinite (or indefinite) growth with a finite resource base. We have been indoctrinated to believe in growth, and in the impossibility of reversal or decline. But according to some studies, we would need more than five Earths to supply the resources for every person in the world to achieve the living standard of the average American or first-world consumer.

The unbelievable technological progress of the last few centuries, including the Industrial Revolution, is fueled by the burning of fossilized forms of carbon—coal, gas, and oil. Our incredible civilization is not the result of really clever European minds, but rather was built on the exploitation of cheap energy. The steam engine was both the result of and the solution for the mining of coal, and the combustion engine was developed to make use of burgeoning oil supplies. The twentieth century witnessed what scholars call the Great Acceleration, the almost constant increase in the rate of economic growth from 1945 until around 1970. In the wake of the Great Depression and World War II, the Bretton Woods financial agreements shaped the postwar monetary and economic system and enabled the financialization of oil flows from giant and supergiant oil fields. The greatest supergiant oil fields were and are in Saudi Arabia, including the largest, Ghawar.

This unprecedented acceleration accustomed humans to expect permanent growth and gave rise to the theory of development whereby poorer countries would develop incrementally and eventually take their place as first-world wealthy nations. Of course, this underlying economic premise of modern liberalism clashes with the doctrines of revolutionary class struggle of Marxist Communism, unevenly adopted and intermittently endorsed by the USSR and Communist China. Despite the Cold War, the capitalist economic system flourished through much of the middle of the twentieth century, driven and sustained by supplies of cheap oil.

According to theorists like Christian Marrazi, the global economy shifted from a productive economy to a financialized debt-based economy in the early 1970s.[30] Production was outsourced to third-world nations, mainly China, in a desperate attempt to save labor costs. What happened around 1970 is a kind of shock as the world began to hit the first limits to growth. As David Harvey explains, in the early 1970s "capital began to experience an inflexion point in the trajectory of exponential growth."[31] Once the rate of growth starts to slow down, the only way to keep growing at the same rate is to accumulate a higher percentage of the growth. This means that wealth is concentrated among fewer and fewer people, countries, and corporations. The ongoing massive concentration of wealth simultaneously impoverishes more and more people. The rich get richer and the poor get poorer, and this phenomenon has been increasing since the early 1970s.

We are reaching real limits to growth in planetary terms. Humans are straining to grow, to sustain, to ward off economic decline and keep hope alive for progress or a return to progress. There are pockets of incredible affluence and unbelievable devastation, but many of the elements that underlie our current conflicts are related to resource scarcity and climate change. This situation is not new, but it has been intensifying over the last few decades. Human population has exceeded seven billion and is expected to grow to over eleven billion by 2100, barring a catastrophic die-off. There exist real limits to the energy, food, water, and land available for our use, and we are running up against them.[32]

Many people are unable to imagine any genuine alternative to global capitalism, even though we understand that it is destroying the planet. We are conditioned to envisage and expect more and more growth. We are unwilling to change because we are unable to change. We are unable to imagine and live as a society and as a species without consuming our dwindling resources and discounting the future.

What is to be done? What can we do? One thing we can do is to attempt to understand and define the problem, which is both simple and obvious as well as incredibly complex. But what can ultimately be done to solve it? Nothing. There is nothing to be done. Why not? Because it is our nature. We are fulfilling our nature as living beings and we cannot do otherwise.

We maximize our resources, we reproduce to fill all available niches, and we emit waste products until our environment is no longer hospitable and we collapse. We have seen this story of collapse play itself out in specific locations many times, as Jared Diamond points out, and now we are seeing it happen in global terms.[33]

ENERGY AND CHANGE

We cannot change our nature. It is fixed, immutable, a death sentence; just like life. We have to change our nature, but that is impossible. *But what if our nature is change?* That is the thesis of this book. We talk about change, but what if we do not really understand change? In material terms, change and transformation are connected to the flow of energy. Our lives and our activities depend on energy, but what is energy?

According to Richard Feynman, in his 1963 *Lectures on Physics*: "It is important to realize that in physics today, we have no knowledge of what energy *is*. We do not have a picture that energy comes in little blobs of a definite amount. It is not that way. However, there are formulas for calculating some numerical quantity . . . [but] it is an abstract thing in that it does not tell us the mechanism or the *reasons* for the various formulas."[34] In a more recent overview of energy by Vaclav Smil, he claims that "energy is not a single, easily definable entity, but rather an abstract collective concept, adopted by nineteenth-century physicists to cover a variety of natural and anthropogenic (generated by humans) processes."[35] We do not really know what energy is, but we have found ways to define and describe what it does. In physical terms, energy lies at the center of everything that exists.

Being is energy transformation. Energy is convertible with mass at the square of the speed of light, which is 186,000 miles per second. Material form is an incredible concentration of energy in the form of mass, but energy is itself physical, that is fully material. New materialism is dynamic and energetic as well as embodied. I am trying to reorient new materialism more explicitly around energy to take account of this reality. We do not really know what energy is, only something about what it does and how it can be measured. Energy is always conserved; it can neither be created nor destroyed. This is the First Law of Thermodynamics. The Second Law, however, says that in any closed system the amount of useful energy degrades or breaks down; this is the Law of Entropy.

Energy appears at once infinite and directional; it progresses from an ordered to a disordered state. It is the directionality of energy that allows us to harness it for productive purposes because we can set up a thermal gradient between hot and cold that generates a powerful force. At the same time, it is this progression from order to disorder that supplies a limit to amount of work that any machine or system can accomplish, due to the constraint of entropy. Energy is defined scientifically in terms of work. Energy is the amount of force required to move a certain mass a certain distance. And this modern conception of energy is forged in the furnace of nineteenth-century thermodynamics with its emphasis on heat engines.

Our modern understanding of energy is very different from that of Aristotle, as noted at the beginning of this introduction. In the *Metaphysics*, energeia is a working, an actuality, in contrast with *dunamis*, which is only potential energy. Energeia is associated with, and also distinguished from, *entelechia*, or entelechy. Entelechia is a kind of optimal working, a complete reality or an ideal actuality that is accomplished when something works the way that it is supposed to. This entelechy conjoins the matter of something with its essential form in a productive way. In modern science, this opposition between actual and potential energy is overcome, so that all energy is essentially potential, or dynamic.

Since Aristotle's word and philosophy are so important for all of these later changes in how we think about energy, I start by examining Aristotle's *Physics* and *Metaphysics* in some detail in chapter 1. For Aristotle, all material things that are in motion seek their goal in rest. However, it is important to keep in mind that modern and contemporary science dispenses with any goal or telos of physical processes. Furthermore, the law of inertia means that there is no natural state of rest; a thing will only come to a halt if acted on by another object or force. Science is concerned with energy as a measure of how things work and how much work processes are able to accomplish.

In the 1800s, the laws of thermodynamics were developed as a way to explain the workings of machines, and entropy provided a limit to the ability of a thermodynamic machine to work. Sadi Carnot elaborated the initial principles of thermodynamics, and these laws were later formalized by Rudolf Clausius and Ludwig Boltzmann. Machinic work is a new form of labor, supplementing and in some cases replacing human labor, as Marx and others have analyzed. The new machines were developed to exploit new resources of energy, or old resources in new ways, by burning stored carbon in the form of coal, oil, and gas. Energy transformations are at the heart of the Industrial Revolution and European modernity.

Today we face an energy crisis that is also an environmental crisis, as it is getting more and more expensive and destructive to tap into remaining resources of fossil fuels, and the emissions from burning these fuels is driving global warming. Energy is at the heart of the problem because it is at the heart of everything. Energy cuts across diverse thresholds and transformations, changing itself and the terms in which anything may be done.

One of the most important measures of energy is called EROI, or EROEI, that is, energy return on (energy) investment. Put simply, this means that you need to get more work out of an activity than you put into it in the form of raw materials and effort for it to be viable. In absolute terms, this is impossible due to entropy, but in relative terms it is possible, at least temporarily, for at least two reasons. One is that you discount certain external costs, that is, the time and energy it took for the Earth to compress biomatter into usable forms of carbon for fuel. The second is that you find a productive gradient, or a difference, that allows for a more efficient and productive use of whatever material or resources.

Human beings are not machines, but they do work in thermodynamic terms, because we oxidize food as fuel. The oxygen burns up the fuel and converts it into usable energy. At the level of the cell, this is called ATP; ATP allows the mitochondria in our cells to push a proton across a membrane, giving us energy to do work. Life requires energy flow to exist. Humans require sources of food and energy to work and to live. Our brains require large inputs of fuel to function. Thinking is also work, and it takes energy to accomplish. Energy works on all levels, but it takes different forms. Energy changes.

In 1998, cosmologists discovered that the expansion of the universe is accelerating rather than remaining constant or slowing down. We do not know what is causing this acceleration, but this force has been given a name, *dark energy*. Although we do not understand dark energy, it is estimated that dark energy makes up nearly three-quarters of the entire matter-energy in the universe. Most of the rest is dark matter, while our conventional baryonic matter constitutes less than 5 percent of what exists. Dark energy indicates that there is a positive cosmological constant, Λ, that acts as a kind of antigravity, driving against and exceeding the force of gravity that is pulling things together. We do not know what energy in itself is, especially if it is "dark," and we do not fully understand how it is related to the energy that we can measure. At the most macroscopic scale, as at the most microscopic, things are a more than a little strange. In the middle where we are is energy transformation. Energy changes form.

In a closed system, energy tends toward entropy and static equilibrium. But no system is completely closed off from the rest of the universe. Systems are more or less open systems, and they exist as dissipative systems, taking in energy and emitting information, usually in the form of heat. Most actual systems, including living ones, are nonlinear systems. These systems are metastable, and they coalesce around attractors. Fundamental changes in the system are called singularities. A singularity occurs when a system is subject to perturbation; when it is changed in a significant way that changes the very nature and function of the system. Most of the time, when a singularity takes place within a system, a bifurcation occurs. A bifurcation splits the system around a point and changes the locus of an attractor.

I am drawing on language developed and applied to mathematics and physics to describe how physical, biological, ecological, and economic systems operate in dynamic and nonlinear ways, which is how these systems actually operate in the world. Energy flow generates structures and composes systems, and as these structures interact with energy flow they change their nature. This process takes place across living and nonliving systems. In chapter 1, I explain why I think that energy comes first, prior to structure and form, how it generates form and then alters it. I begin by way of reconsidering the way in which Aristotle's *Physics* explains how material things change and how energy works for his philosophy. Here I suggest that physics *is* metaphysics, because we are forced to experiment on and speculate about the world, however formal or rigorous our language and our formulas.

I then take up theoretical aspects of, thermodynamics, systems theory, and quantum physics to think about how energy works and how it changes systems in profound and important ways. Energy flow through a system organizes that system, and this organization persists as long as the energy flow continues. Nonequilibrium thermodynamics is a crucial advance over classical thermodynamics, because it considers systems that are open and dynamic rather than closed. In addition, the thermal gradient is relativized, becoming one among many gradients rather than the primary gradient.

We need to change how we think about energy and we need to think about how energy effects change. In chapter 2, I consider living systems more explicitly, to reflect on life and what it means for us. Some philosophers are criticizing certain conceptions of life in an attempt to overcome the vestiges of vitalism, but I think we need to understand life in terms of energy and change rather than seek to eliminate life as an fundamental category. Here evolution and natural selection are the major drivers of change, but we need an understanding of how bioenergetics works at the level of the cell and the organism and some sense of how genetic and epigenetic changes occur.

Here I draw on the philosophy of Catherine Malabou, whose biological materialism informs my thinking about living systems. Along with Malabou, I draw on the work of Lynn Margulis and Stephen Jay Gould as well as Marion Lamb and Eva Jablonka to help fashion a poststructural evolutionary thinking. For Malabou, as informed by biologists and neuroscientists, life is fundamentally about change, metamorphosis, and the changing of difference that takes place as trans-differentiation. We tend to think about identity and difference as opposites, and one way to look at French poststructuralism is to view it as a philosophy of difference. But the problem is that difference in itself is often viewed as incoherent, despite the extraordinary efforts of Deleuze and Derrida to explain how difference is primary to identity. For Malabou, both difference and identity are grounded in change, and it is the question of change that animates her work.

Biology forces us to reflect on life and death, but human life and death takes place in society. In chapter 3, I take up a thinking of energy and change at the level of politics, economics, and civilization. Here the work of anthropologists, economists, political philosophers, and ecologists informs an emergent political ecology. Nicolas Georgescu-Roegen connects energy and entropy with economic processes in important ways in the early 1970s, and every political economy is organized around energy exploitation and use, including contemporary capitalism. Georges Bataille centers his understanding of a general economy around energy expenditure in his extraordinary work on *The Accursed Share*. Kojin Karatani shifts our thinking about political economy from systems of production to systems of exchange, and he helps us focus specifically on the reciprocal forms of exchange that constitute a clan society. This economy of the gift is crucial for us to understand and in some ways recuperate today, and Malabou again helps us philosophically rethink being as exchange.

Questions about the Anthropocene, including the significance and value of the human, resurface as we come up against real planetary limits. Every question of philosophy and politics involves the ecological situation of the environment and the climate; this is the horizon for any serious theoretical and practical work in the twenty-first century. *Change* is also a political term, and new materialism carries a political charge, informed by a nondogmatic Marxist analysis. We cannot simply understand the world, we need to change it. But we cannot effect change without understanding, and that means understanding how energy works. We have exploited energy in the form of natural resources for our technological machines and our political power, including the exploitation of other human beings, not to mention other life forms. We need a new orientation to energy and energy transformation to survive as a political animal, that is a social being who operates as part of a polis, or city.

Everything must change. It is changing, all the time, but some changes are singular transformations, while others are more apparently conservative. We want to conserve ourselves and what we cherish, but we are not permanent either. It's not that there is no stability, but the rate of change has been increasing. Everything in the universe, including the universe itself as a result of dark matter, is accelerating, coming apart. We know this, but we do not want to know it, and we do not even necessarily know who or what we are. Everything is at stake, including spirit. According to Buddhist teachings, the most real aspect of existence is change, which in Sanskrit is *anicca*, or impermanence. Buddhism argues that there is no substantial permanent identity, whether of the self, the world, or even God. We need to embrace rather than disavow this insight, and our religious traditions offer resources to contend with this situation.

Chapter 4 concerns spirit. Religion is contested, but from this new materialist perspective humans are essentially spiritual beings at the same time as they are material beings. We cannot avoid religious and spiritual questions, including the question of ultimate reality. Energy understood as fully material and fully spiritual avoids the dualism that often characterizes discussions of materialism and religion, and this is the crucial argument of this book. In this context, our new materialism is not new, but it is a better philosophical perspective than classical reductive materialism because it views nature as intrinsically dynamic. This new materialism attends to non-Christian spiritual traditions that are often mistakenly understood as nonmaterial, such that we could also speak of re*new*able materialisms. In a renewable materialist context, there is no opposition between what we call matter and what we call spirit because energy is what cuts across both these phenomena.

This fourth chapter engages three nonmodern traditions—Amerindian, Haitian Vodou, and neo-Confucian qi philosophy—and sets up what Deleuze calls an effects series among them. It's not the essence of these traditions, and certainly not an exhaustive knowledge of them, that is important here. They compose what Barad calls a diffraction pattern where their similarities and differences resonate against and across each other. Each diffracts a distinct but relevant conception of spirit in energetic and new materialist terms.

In order to think about spirit, I engage indigenous and nonmodern peoples whose perspectives are shaped by clan organizations of reciprocity, as initially discussed in chapter 3. In his work on Amerindians, Eduardo Viveiros de Castro develops a multinaturalism that does not conform to our more familiar multiculturalism, and this is a crucial exchange that opens up a new conception of spirit in the form of material anthropomorphic agents.

After engaging the spiritual nature of Amerindians, including the Haudenosaunee, I then consider resources from Haitian Vodou, in which the *lwa* are personal manifestations of vital energy forces that manifest political and spiritual power in their transformational possession of practitioners. These spirits, like indigenous spirits, are often described in animist terms, but they should be better understood as agential, following Bruno Latour and Barad. Furthermore, we can analyze a Vodou performance as what Deleuze calls a time-image in his revolutionary books on cinema, *Cinema 1* and, more important, *Cinema 2*.

Finally, chapter 4 engages another non-Western understanding of spirit expressed by Chinese neo-Confucian philosophy. Here, most powerfully in the work of Zhang Zai, *qi* is a concept that is best comprehended as dynamic energy transformation. The qi philosophy of Zhang and others refuse the bifurcation of reality into material and spiritual forces, which is often the result of Western metaphysics. Qi is a material and vital force that when refined produces spirit, which is less anthropomorphic and more subtly thought as something "inscrutable" by Zhang Zai. These traditions are often distorted, marginalized, and dismissed by Euromodernity, but they open up new perspectives onto reality that contest any opposition between matter and spirit, and they are more compatible with philosophies of new materialism.

As a way to name the source of energy, we have inherited the word God. However, to understand God in traditional monotheistic terms is to confront the reality of the death of this God. In the twentieth century, a radical death of God theology emerged, in some ways as a strange echo of Friedrich Nietzsche's announcement of the death of God in the late nineteenth century. In the final chapter, I trace the development of radical theology from the death of God to contemporary reflections to see where and how it opens up to these issues of energy and change in theological terms. From the perspective of twenty-first century, radical theology includes and incorporates insights of liberation and process theologies in addition to the death of God theologies. We can see how particular expressions of panentheism in the theology of Catherine Keller, and pantheism or pantheology in the work of Mary-Jane Rubenstein, converge with the insights of de Castro as well as the perspectives of other nonmodern and nonmonotheistic traditions. Change involves chance, the possibility of a swerve of existence that we may or may not have or take. We may resist or we can affirm the inescapable reality of change. The affirmation of change, and even of God as the All of Change, is a form of love. Love can be considered a form of spiritual energy that radiates liberating transformations. The future, if there is one for humans and related beings, is open. We may not survive, but energy is conserved, infinitely, in its irreducible multiplicity.

It is necessary to stress here that I am not a scientist and this is not a book of science; it is a book of philosophy that attempts to think with and about scientific ideas without getting too caught up in the technical terms or mathematic equations. Despite its pretensions to objective truth, modern science is always implicated in broader philosophical and political frameworks, as the philosopher of science Isabelle Stengers demonstrates in her multivolume *Cosmopolitics*.[36] Science is fundamentally about developing and testing ideas as empirically as possible, often in mathematical terms. Philosophical thinking is not derivative of scientific explanation; both are a distinct kind of change that "repeats" the change nature performs. Here I am drawing on new materialist philosophies as well as various conceptions of energy and change to fashion a contemporary cosmology that accounts for the world in which we live. We need to better comprehend this situation if we want to continue to have a world in which to live and think.

1

ENERGY AND THE DYNAMICS OF NATURE

ARISTOTLE'S *PHYSIS*

What is nature? I begin with Aristotle, because his conceptual categories ground so much of our philosophical thinking about the world, even where we no longer view his conclusions as credible. Nature is the translation of *physis*, which we also call physics. The *Physics* is Aristotle's treatise on how natural things change. To understand nature, we have to understand how things change. At the start of book 1, Aristotle says that "natural things are some or all of them subject to change."[1] Later, at the beginning of book 3, he asserts that, "Since nature is a principle of change and alteration, and our inquiry is about nature, it must not escape us what change is: for if it is not known, it must be that nature is not known either."[2] The only way to comprehend nature is to understand change.

The Greek word for change is *metabolē*. Aristotle qualifies his assertion that everything in nature changes, because he says that change must be understood in relation to that which does not change. The infinite does not change; it is changeless. But this changelessness illuminates what it means to change. Nature for Aristotle is a subset of being, that which is and exists. Being includes nature, the soul, and the infinite and goes all the way up to the Unmoved Mover, who is called God. The way we read Aristotle and the way we understand physics leads us to contrast nature as physics with the supernatural or spiritual as metaphysics. *Metaphysics* is the name given to Aristotle's treatise concerning "First Things." This work is placed *after the physics* in the collection of Aristotle's works, which are really detailed lecture notes rather than published books.

Here I want to collapse nature and what is beyond nature, including human and spiritual realities. Nature is all-encompassing, but since it is so often viewed in distinction to other realities, such as human culture, it has become a deeply problematic term. Some ecologists and philosophers like Timothy Morton and Bruno Latour have called for an end to any useful meaning of the word *nature*. Whether or not we hold onto the specific term, we have to change our understanding of what we call nature and natural processes, because we cannot reasonably conceive of human being outside of or beyond the sphere of nature in a broader ecological sense. Latour uses the findings of contemporary anthropology concerning nonmodern societies as evidence for his claim that the modern Western division between society and nature is uncommon and unnatural. Culture and nature are not separate realms, but two distinct ways of thinking about the same phenomena. We cannot maintain a concept of nature as bounded, cut off from the rest of reality.

For Aristotle, nature is a delimited sphere, which is a problem that persists through European modernity, but we can still gain insights from his treatment of nature or physis. For my purposes, physics *is* metaphysics. That is, our understandings of nature and natural phenomena are already metaphysical because they ask fundamental questions about the nature and origin of physical reality. We cannot ground life, consciousness, society, and culture in nature in a crude reductionist or sociobiological way, but we have to grasp the basic material reality of all of these phenomena and processes. I am intentionally conflating metaphysics with physics, since Aristotle's description of physis is already metaphysical and there is nothing that is not exposed to change. This does not mean nothing is infinite, but infinite does not mean something that continues forever in an unchanging manner, nor does it originate everything in the universe out of some first cause or unmoved mover.

In many ways, the text we call *Metaphysics* is just a more detailed elaboration of the materials he discusses in the *Physics*. For Aristotle to talk about change in nature, in both works, he has to discuss causality, that which causes things to change. He consolidates his understanding of causality around the four fundamental causes: material, formal, efficient, and final (*Metaphysics* book 5, 2). The matter is the material stuff of existence, while the form is its shape as well as its essence. Form for Aristotle is residually Platonic, because these essences or forms are distinguishable from matter even though they exist in material form rather than in some transcendent realm. Efficient causes explain why and how something comes to be, and these are the causes that most scientists focus on, based on principles like the Principle of Least Action and Nature Abhors a Vacuum. Final causes are teleological purposes, and these are rejected by modern science as tautological.

To cause something to change is to alter it, which shows that it is mutable rather than immutable. What is uncaused is unchanged, because it lacks an efficient cause. For Aristotle, natural things are things that change, and natural change occurs when a thing changes something else and is itself changed *in the same process*.[3] I am not denying Aristotle's description of nature so much as his delimitation of it, because for him there are things which do not change and things which cause other things to change without themselves changing, and that is what I deny. Everything is change.

For Aristotle to explain change, he has to explain the concepts of the infinite, place, void, and time, which takes up books 3 and 4 of the *Physics*.[4] I will not go into detail on these important concepts, but rather focus on his discussion of motion and rest. Aristotle conceives causality and change in terms of motion or movement, which is *kinēsis* in Greek. To cause something to change is to act upon it, which is a kind of movement. A thing desires to rest or to come to a state of rest. This desire for rest is a telos, an end or goal intrinsic to a phenomenon. Without any telos, there is no place to come to rest, and the modern scientific notion of inertia states that an object in motion will remain in motion until or unless acted on by another object or force. So movement for Aristotle is in many ways limited, secondary, and provisional, which makes things subject to change less important than things that cannot be moved or changed. This is a Greek prejudice.

Motion is a kind of activity, however, which is preferred by Aristotle over a state of passivity. Here is where things get interesting, because in many respects *kinēsis* replaces and substitutes for *metabolē* in the writing of the *Physics*. That is, he begins with change in the broadest sense, metabolē, but then in his analysis focuses mostly on kinēsis. Change is practically equated with and restricted to movement, and movement is subordinated to what does not move or change. At the same time, in the *Metaphysics*, kinēsis as actual motion contrasts with potential motion, *dunamis*. Dunamis is potency or potentiality, and for Aristotle potentiality is less significant than actuality. In terms of movement, actual movement or kinēsis is better than potential motion, but, in general terms, dunamis is opposed to actuality.

How do things change in actuality? Here Aristotle coins two important words, *entelechia* and *energeia*. Actuality can be an activity, and actual activity is superior to passive or even potential activity. Activity implies change, but it ultimately begins with something that does not change and results in the actualization of this activity in rest, the cessation of change. Potentiality is a kind of capacity, while actuality, "which we connect with 'complete reality,' has, in the main, been extended from movement to other things; for actuality in the strict sense is thought to be identical to movement."[5] Actuality is strictly connected to movement, but it is also expanded to connect up to complete reality for Aristotle.

Aristotle is talking about primary substance, *ousia*, as the definition of "what is" or "what exists" in the *Metaphysics*. This substance is actualized in a kind of movement, kinēsis, whereas dunamis is a potential movement or change. The broader understanding of actuality that Aristotle develops in the *Metaphysics* is actuality understood as energeia. *Energeia* is a term that Aristotle coins from the Greek word *ergon*, or work. Energeia is an actualized working. For Aristotle, the actuality of energeia precedes dunamis as potentiality. He explains that according to every sense in which he uses the word *potentiality*, "actuality is prior both in formula and in substantiality."[6] Actuality precedes potentiality because it gives every potentiality its end, or telos, to which a potency is related. For Aristotle, "actuality is the end, and it is for the sake of this that the potency is acquired."[7] Again, this is all explained according to a paradigm of movement, although he generalizes his ideas of actuality and potentiality beyond movement in a strict sense.

Energy in Aristotelian terms designates actuality, an actual working of a process or situation. Energy is not potential energy, except in derivative terms, as tending toward the actual end or goal. Energeia as actuality is also connected to another word that Aristotle comes up with, *entelechia*, or entelechy. Energeia is a more general principle of actuality, while entelechy involves the specific purpose or function of an actualization. The entelechia is the perfect actualization of a capacity in terms of its given telos. Entelechia includes telos; it incorporates the purpose of whatever is being actualized in an ideal way. Energy is actuality, in a way that is working—the German word *Wirklichkeit* expresses this conception well. The entelechy is the energetic working in relation to a thing's end, which makes it a kind of ideal working or perfection. In *De Anima*, Aristotle characterizes the material part of the human person as the potentiality, whereas the soul, psyche, names the actualization of the person according to the purpose of the human being.

Aristotle develops an initial idea of energy based on actuality and movement, even though he also subordinates movement to rest as the end of a process of movement. This energy is intrinsically related to change, although Aristotle subordinates things that change in nature to things that do not change. We have inherited this Aristotelian terminology and conceptuality even when we have rejected or transformed it. In modern physics and philosophy we can see a correction of the relation of actuality and potentiality in terms of energy. Here energy concerns potential energy (dunamis) just as profoundly as actual energy (kinēsis), because actual or kinetic energy is not any more real than potential or dynamic energy. In addition, as already mentioned, modern science dispenses with the Aristotelian final cause, which means that there is no intrinsic purpose to observed phenomena. Finally, the specific goal of rest is eliminated from modern physics, because inertia shows that an object in motion will remain in motion unless acted upon by something else.

In his *Monadology*, G. W. Leibniz uses the Aristotelian term *entelechy* to describe his monads as souls, although this aspect of Leibniz's metaphysics has been largely discarded. However, Leibniz inaugurates a new understanding of potentiality by calling his science a "dynamics of power and action." Dynamics refers to the fact that energy as force, power, or motion can be transferred between and among different phenomena, and this potential energy can be both actualized and *conserved*. The conservation of energy will become a fundamental law of the science of thermodynamics. Leibniz wanted to retain the idea of final causes in nature, and the emphasis on actual forces rather than merely potential ones, but the effect of his work on science and mathematics along with his use of the word *dynamics* ends up contributing to the modern shift from actual energeia toward potential dunamis. Later both Thomas Hobbes and John Locke will frame their thinking about energy in terms of force or power as the interpretation of the Latin word *potentia*, which translates dunamis as potency or potentiality. Modern philosophy and modern physics adopts this shift in orientation from viewing energy mainly in terms of actuality to thinking about energy as comprised of potential and kinetic energy.

DREAMING OF ENERGY

For the Australian Aborigines, *dreamtime* names the primordial state of humanity prior to the disruption of history that renders it distant, but dreamtime can be reencountered in sacred rituals. According to Gilles Deleuze, whose expression converges with the dreamtime of indigeneity, "dreams are our eggs, our larvae and our properly psychic individuals."[8] Dreams contain their own intensity and their own individuating difference for us to actualize. Many modern people associate dreaming with the wishful thinking of a utopia, a no-place that may become actualized if we work hard enough. We are not sure whether dreaming is an energy for a potential actuality, which is more along the lines of utopian dreaming or daydreaming, or instead dreaming constitutes an actuality in itself. Are dreams real or illusory, and do they matter?

Today, many people dream of a technological fix to the problems of our planet. We long for a new form of powerful, clean energy that could fuel our civilization beyond war, struggle, poverty, and even launch us further into outer space. This dream of a new source of energy sustains much science fiction literature and film. Another form of technodream is the hope for a mechanism to counteract global warming and cool our planet. Geoengineering could either suck carbon and methane out of the atmosphere or shoot particles into the atmosphere to reflect some of the sunlight heading to Earth back into space, reducing the amount of heat that reaches the planet. The latter is called solar radiation management, and it has some serious implications when we consider the effects of volcanic eruptions that emit sulfuric acid droplets into the air that then seriously cool down the planet. This is what happened in 1991 when Mount

Pinatubo erupted in the Philippines, reducing global temperatures by half a degree Celsius. Such geoengineering schemes are incredibly risky but may be seen as viable options if global warming continues to rapidly increase. One problem with solar radiation management is that this sulfur dioxide appears to cause a significant reduction of rainfall, leading to situations of severe drought.[9] Our dreams can have unintended and unwanted consequences.

At its most extreme, our techno-utopian dreams sometimes foster a fantastic transhumanism in which we imagine we will achieve what Teilhard de Chardin calls the Omega Point, or what Ray Kurzweil calls the singularity, a transformative threshold-shattering event that opens us up beyond our physical, biological, and even mortal constraints.[10] Such an understanding appears incredible, and even unmoored from material reality, despite the impressive technological innovations over the last couple of centuries. My argument is that these technological achievements are only possible due to our exploitation of cheap energy in the form of fossil fuels. We cannot simply attribute them to the cleverness of our minds, and we cannot assume that we may continue to achieve technological breakthroughs without new sources of cheap energy. In fact, energy has gotten more expensive, and the rate of technological innovation is slowing down.[11]

In his book *Energy Dreams*, Michael Marder returns to Aristotle to envision a new relation to actuality beyond our modern obsession with potentiality. For Marder, the reversal of Aristotle in modern philosophy and science is catastrophic, and our insistence on energy as *potentia* leads to a "pyropolitics" in which "the world is burning and, in its blazing finitude, is reducing itself to smoldering ashes."[12] If we want a living future on a living planet, we need to recover a more authentic Aristotelian view of "energetic rest, of energy *as* rest and accomplishment."[13] Our obsession with potential energy and its productive power is destroying the planet, and Marder dreams about restoring energy as actuality without potentiality. Aristotle sees potentiality and actuality as contraries, and the interaction between them as productive and teleological at the same time, but our overemphasis on dynamic energy requires a restoration of energy as energeia. For us, Marder writes, "energy is, precisely, not actuality, unless we are sufficiently sophisticated to detect in what presently exists the storehouses of yet unreleased force."[14] We can only register energy as potential force to be actualized and unleashed. This actualization is a destructive capacity, whereas energeia as actuality without potentiality seeks rest rather than more power.

Energy is fundamentally ambiguous, and we will consider this further in terms of thermodynamics later in the chapter. Here energy shifts from being associated in Aristotle with actuality, with an implicitly purposive working, to a modern view where energy is fundamentally potential and kinetic. Potential energy is stored, transferred, and ultimately unleashed as power. For Aristotle, energy finds its way; it contributes to a proper entelechy of nature and humanity, as mind, body, and soul. For us, energy is a blind power, to be directed to whatever ends. Energy enables consumption, and in turn energy consumes us. This is why Marder attempts to invert our obsession with energy as potentiality and return to Aristotle. But Marder's intervention also transforms Aristotelian energy, because he want to liberate energy as actuality *without potentiality*, which is inconceivable to Aristotle.

Marder dreams of energy as actuality divorced from potentiality, and hopes that such a dream might save us from the nightmare of contemporary pyropolitics that is burning up the Earth. Dunamis is a kind of dynamite, a potential explosion where "energy extraction tears apart actual beings."[15] The equivalence of mass and energy in Einstein's famous equation is destructive because it renders mass and matter into potentiality as pure form. Here energy is the name of an explosive power that is then harnessed for a bomb. This energy-mass equivalence "is highly destructive, to the extent that it literally mobilizes the mass at rest making it into an unimaginably mobile mass, into energy."[16] Energy cycles through infinite transformations without ever being actualized as such, as energeia. Modern and contemporary energy consists of "dunamis cut off from energeia." For this reason, "the law of conservation of energy spurns finality, finitude—indeed, life itself—and so aggravates the crisis of energy."[17]

Energeia is a more peaceful work, a work that works and works out, a pure actuality that arrests the rapacious dynamic force of potentiality, allowing us to rest. Aristotle posits a pure energeia at the origin, an actuality without potentiality, even though in reality everything in nature consists of a mixture of energeia and dunamis. How can we think energeia or actuality as such, beyond potentiality? Marder points to the idea of the unmoved mover, which appears incredible. For Aristotle, the unmoved mover is inserted at the origin of a chain of causes to prevent an infinite regress, which is horrifying to the Greeks. But for Marder, the unmoved mover is a way to think energeia in itself without any potentiality. He imagines that the "unmoved mover is the self-relation of energy, or of energies, just as the soul is the body's relation to itself."[18] Energeia is an active, ongoing self-relation that excludes potentiality. This is an actuality that is paradoxically at rest. At the end of the book, Marder considers quantum physics, particularly as described by Karen Barad, as a better way to think about matter and energy. Both Aristotle and quantum physics "share the presupposition that matter is the energy of energy needed for any putting-to-work"; it is the restful intra-activity of quantum field theory as articulated by Barad. Marder suggests that Barad's quantum field theory–informed agential realism and its understanding of the world's intra-activity can be understood as "a contemporary designation for Aristotle's unmoved mover as the world's self-relation."[19] I will return to Barad's work toward the end of the chapter, but for Marder this vision of energeia allows us to conceive a pure actuality that is nonetheless at rest, and this is the very self-relation that makes the world exist as unmoved mover. We need to return to this origin to avoid the excesses of potential energy and its destructive power.

As brilliant and appealing as Marder's work is, it remains just a dream, not a reality. He wishes that it could become actual, but this is impossible. We never have actuality without potentiality, or creation without destruction. Marder, like Aristotle, conceives of pure activity in an idealized manner. Unfortunately, the world doesn't work that way. That doesn't mean we can't think it, however, and we do definitely need to dream about it. We are exhausted, and most of us can never get enough rest. We appear caught in a destructive and ultimately fatal process from which we want to extricate ourselves. One option, as attractive as it is implausible, is to slow down. We need slow food, a slower pace of life, to learn to walk or ride a bicycle rather than speed along in a car or a plane. We need to slow our rate of production and consumption, to make our lives and our world more sustainable, recyclable, and reproducible. I don't see how this is possible at a general social, political, or species level, although it is certainly possible for individuals up to a point.

Another possibility, which is attractive in different ways, is to speed up. This is the philosophy of accelerationism, which is based on an interpretation of Georges Bataille and Deleuze and Guattari's work, especially

Anti-Oedipus. What if we push capitalism beyond its limits so that it falls apart and breaks down? Following this logic of Bataille and Deleuze, Nick Land characterizes "the revolutionary task as one of pushing capitalism to the point of its auto-dissolution via the complete dis-inhibition of productive synthesis."[20] Unfortunately, the end result of such a dissolution is to realize that capitalism already envisages this disinhibition of productive synthesis and demands that we consume to excess precisely to keep the system going. Ultimately Land and others "arrive at the admission that there is no 'foreseeable 'beyond' to the 'infinite' expansion of capitalism (since capitalism is 'beyondness' as such)."[21]

In his book, Marder claims that Bataille's energy is "an overreaction to the classical fixation on production and depth," and a form of exergy, "an extravagant spending that leaves no room and no time for energetic rest."[22] I think this is good criticism of accelerationism, but I don't think it is a very good interpretation of Bataille. I will return to Bataille's idea of a general economy in chapter 3, but here I want to note the contrast between speeding up and slowing down.

Given the choice between speeding up, accelerating, and decelerating or slowing down, we would have to prefer the latter, but it is more important to refuse this as a false choice, assuming we have a choice. For Aristotle and for Marder, there is a problematic logic of contraries at work, and Deleuze helps us see this in *Difference and Repetition*. Actuality and potentiality are contraries, oppositions that are understood and defined in relation to each other. Aristotle thinks about things in terms of these contrary notions. Something is only large in relation to something small, and vice versa. For any particular situation, there is an ideal state that lies between the contraries. For a person, there is a point of growth that is neither too large nor too small.

Aristotle defines energeia as actuality and downgrades dunamis as potentiality, so that kinēsis or kinetic energy becomes the model for energy. In the modern world, we shift our understanding so that kinetic energy is one form of energy while potential energy is the other, but in many ways potential energy as dynamic force frames our thinking about energy. Aristotle uses the distinction between genera and species to articulate his understanding of how contraries work, how they are related to the ideas of the one and the many. The one is opposed to the plurality as contrary, on the one hand, but the one is also the generic category, on the other. "To the one belong," he explains in the *Metaphysics*, "the same and the like and the equal, and to plurality belong the other and the unlike and the unequal."[23] Difference occurs by way of a contrary opposite, and a thing differs from another thing within the context of this contrary relationship, which involves a likeness and an unlikeness.

Aristotle says that the greatest difference is "contrariety," which is "the complete difference ... between two things."[24] This difference is expressed in contrary terms, but, as Deleuze says, this operation captures difference and renders it subordinate to the identical or the same. For Aristotle, "all things which are generated from their contraries involve an underlying subject; a subject then, much be present in the case of contraries, if anywhere."[25] A contrary has to refer to a subject that underlies it, that grounds it in an identity. According to Deleuze, "contrariety alone expresses the capacity of a subject to bear opposites while remaining substantially the same (in matter or in genus)."[26] A contrary is a generic difference insofar as it involves the modification of an underlying subject, while specific differences, which Aristotle calls the "greatest difference," is further subordinated to the logic of generic unity. What Deleuze is saying is that, although Aristotle claims that specific differences constitute the greatest difference, they are really only present as a way to establish the unity or sameness of the concept (or species or genera). A genera is a higher-order concept that subsumes species, and both generic differences and specific differences are subordinated to a logic of unity and identity.

This is a very abstract discussion, but the point is that for Aristotle contraries are always grounded in a unity that privileges one of the terms. In the case of the contrary pair of actuality and potentiality, both are mixed in matter and changing nature, but they are grounded epistemologically in a prior actuality. Energeia is a process of actuality that is connected to the original actuality of the prime mover and the ideal actualization of entelechia. Here energy is constrained as actual work in contrast with the lesser potency of dunamis. We cannot avoid using forms of these words, but we also need to understand what is going on conceptually. Energy has become more associated with dynamic force as potential energy, and Marder intervenes into this situation by liberating a new understanding of energy as actuality-at-rest by revisiting and rereading Aristotle. This is a valuable and important interpretation, but it is caught in a problematic opposition between actuality and potentiality because Marder downgrades and dismisses potentiality. I agree with his pragmatic desire to correct our thinking about energy, and his corresponding valorization of energy as rest, but I think that the terms in which he expresses his book are too Aristotelian.

In terms of modern and contemporary thermodynamics, Marder is not quite accurate about the overemphasis on potential energy, as both potential and kinetic energy are equally fundamental. In terms of kinetic energy, an individual particle has energy on its own terms, whereas for potential energy, this energy must be understood as an "energy of configuration, or, more generally, an energy of interaction with other parts of the system."[27] Of course, Marder is right in practical, technological, and political ways about the effects of our orientation to energy as power. At the same time, the rest energy, which is the zero point for kinetic—actual—energy, is extremely large compared to our human scales of energy interaction. Jennifer Coopersmith explains that "the rest energy in a gram of matter is 90 trillion Joules, about the same as the energy released in the bomb at Nagasaki."[28]

Deleuze's philosophy of difference offers a better epistemology of being and energy than Aristotle's. In *Difference and Repetition*, Deleuze wants to think difference in itself, freed from the four iron shackles of representation: "the identity of the concept," "the opposition of the predicate," "the analogy of judgement," and "the resemblance of perception."[29] *Difference and Repetition* is not simply a book about difference, however; just as importantly, it is a book about repetition. Repetition is a repetition of difference rather than identity. Identity is produced as individuation as a result of this repetition of difference. And, as we will see, this repetition has to do with energy, which Deleuze calls intensity.

In *Difference and Repetition*, Deleuze criticizes Aristotle's logic of contrariety and counters with the proposition that being is univocal. Here, starting with Duns Scotus and then stretching back to incorporate Parmenides and Heidegger, with particular reference to Spinoza and Nietzsche, being, "even if it absolutely common, is nevertheless not a genus."[30] According to Deleuze, what we call being, which Aristotle refers to as that which is, is a "common designated, in so far as it expresses itself, [and it] is said in turn in a single and same sense of all the numerically distinct designators and expressors."[31] Being expresses itself and is said in "a single and same sense," which appears to return that which exists to a prior identity. Alain Badiou and others accuse Deleuze of being a secret philosopher of the One, based on this designation of being, but that is not what univocity means.³² For Deleuze, univocity establishes what he later calls a plane of immanence, a zone of consistency that works against the separation of any type of two-worlds theory of dualistic philosophy. This is primarily a logical and epistemological concept, even if it is expressed in ontological terms. The univocity of being undermines our logics of identity, opposition, analogy, and resemblance because it undercuts the basis of what is being compared or represented. Univocity of being grounds difference because it says that being can only be said of what differs, what becomes differently, which is how Deleuze understands Nietzsche's idea of the eternal return.

The last sentence of *Difference and Repetition* reads: "A single and same voice for the whole thousand-throated multiple, a single and same Ocean of all the drops, and single clamour of Being for all beings: on condition that each being, each drop and each voice has reached the state of excess—in other words, the difference which displaces and disguises them and, in returning upon its mobile cusp, causes them to return."³³ Being is univocal only so that it can be different, so that there can be real difference. The problem with contrariety and analogy is that it constrains and fixes difference between the contraries or beneath what is being analogized. Aristotle expresses energy in terms his contraries of actuality and potentiality, but energy is ideally actuality, as entelechy is in turn ideal and complete actuality. And it is the logic of the opposition between actuality and potentiality as they are constructed and rendered into a genus that needs to be overcome.

I am using energy as a name for what is called being. Being is energy transformation, because energy is always in transformation, even when it is at rest. This is a univocity of energy, because we don't know what energy is, only how it works and how it is expressed in different forms. Energy constitutes a plane of immanence, not because everything is reduced to energy, but because the complexity of energy transformation across thresholds of singularity creates novelty. This novelty is not pre-given or pre-established according to a definite blueprint or plan. Transcendence for Deleuze is the *plan* that determines the working out of being, energy or reality according to established laws. In his book *Spinoza: Practical Philosophy*, Deleuze says that "any organization that comes from above and refers to a transcendence, be it a hidden one, can be called a theological plan: a design in the mind of a god, but also an evolution in the supposed depths of nature, or a society's organization of power."[34] The rejection of a transcendent plan does not mean that what we experience or value is diminished; it means that how we think, act, and live occurs along an open line of existence, even if this line is not linear.

THERMODYNAMIC LAW

The concept of energy in the modern world results from the scientific development of thermodynamics in the nineteenth century. As Cara Daggett explains in *The Birth of Energy*, thermodynamics is the energy science that "arose at the moment when a handful of things collided: fossil fuels, steam engines, global capitalism, human terraforming, the slave trade, climate systems, empires."[35] This constellation of phenomena produces thermodynamics in the latter half of the nineteenth century, in the wake of the Industrial Revolution. In this chapter I focus more on the scientific aspects of thermodynamics compared to Daggett's attention to political, cultural, and even religious implications surrounding the production of thermodynamics. I want to sketch the classical version of nineteenth-century thermodynamics in somewhat technical terms so that we can see what happens in the twentieth century. In the twentieth century, this classical understanding of thermodynamics breaks apart due to the displacement of the *thermal* gradient as the primary gradient as well as the emphasis on open rather than closed systems. This downgrading of the thermal gradient occurs as the result of Einstein's work and the emergence of quantum physics generally. The shift from closed to open systems takes place later in the century, with the development of systems theory, dissipative systems, and nonequilibrium thermodynamics. I return to some of the broader economic and political aspects of this picture in chapter 3.

Leibniz is an important precursor to thermodynamics because he coins the term *dynamics*, although he uses the word, dunamis, that for Aristotle means potential energy. Leibniz understands dynamics to refer to what we call actual or kinetic energy. For Leibniz, actual energy is *vis viva*, which is a living force that animates nature. On the other hand, his idea of a dead force, *vis mortua*, is closer to what we call potential energy. Dead force is the propensity to motion, which can become actual force or *vis viva*. For Leibniz, the formula for this dead force is mv, or mass times velocity, whereas *vis viva* is mv^2. This is incorrect in modern scientific terms, although mv^2 is closer to our contemporary understanding of the formula of kinetic energy, which is ½ mv^2.[36]

Until the 1800s, most physicists, including Isaac Newton, thought about energy in terms of force. It was the understanding of force in relation to heat that produced thermodynamics, and this connection is something that Leibniz and Newton both lacked. Heat emerges as the key concept due to the development of heat engines, primarily the steam engine of Thomas Newcomen that was later perfected by James Watt. The steam engine was invented mainly to pump water out of the coal mines in Great Britain as coal was being developed as a resource. It is only then that coal became the primary fuel for this steam engine, which touched off the Industrial Revolution in the early 1800s.

The two most important precursors to thermodynamics in the 1700s were Joseph Black and Daniel Bernoulli. Black discovered the concepts of latent heat and specific heat, as well as the relation between heat and temperature. He realized the significance that "different bodies, left to themselves, will all acquire the same temperature."[37] This is the basic insight into equilibrium, that is, the tendency of bodies to all move toward the same general temperature. Black did not understand that bodies are trying to cool down rather than to heat up, however. It is this directionality to heat that becomes crucial for an understanding of thermodynamics, primarily in the work of Sadi Carnot.

Bernoulli is the first scientist to really advance the idea of potential energy in a modern form. He applied the idea of the motion theory of heat to gases, and he "managed to derive a quantitative expression of the live force contained within the gas.[38] Bernoulli equated the actual live force of Leibniz and Newton with potential energy, as two aspects of one basic force, and he gave it the correct formula of ½ mv^2. As Coopersmith explains, "Daniel Bernoulli was the only one of his contemporaries who saw kinetic and potential energy in a wider context, outside the confines of mechanics, and in the real world of engines and machines."[39] Although he did not fully correlate them, he started scientists along the path of seeing energy in terms of work. Work is the action of force across distance, so, as already discussed, it is equivalent to live force, *vis viva*, or kinetic energy. Energy is then conceptualized primarily in terms of *work*. Eventually, in 1807, Thomas Young introduces the term *energy*, derived from Aristotle's *energeia*, to replace the phrase *living force*.

Energy is divided into two fundamental forms, kinetic and potential, and it concerns the ability to do work. The reason that energy is correlated with heat is for two reasons: first, the fact that heat engines are invented as an incredible new technology to perform work; second, the fact that heat, and temperature as a measure of heat, is discovered to be the most fundamental property of energy. Prior to the mid-1800s, heat was understood not as a dynamic theory of particles but as a subtle fluid, or caloric. While many investigators were encountering compelling evidence for molecules/atoms, it would not be until 1905 that an analytical framework for their broader acceptance was produced that confirmed them as real entities. Before these concepts were jettisoned, the caloric was thought to be the stuff of heat, just as phlogiston was the stuff of air and ether was the stuff of everything. Part of what makes this discovery of science possible is the incredibly powerful technology that is being developed to enable measurement, observation, and experimentation at extremely precise levels. Another part of this process is the progressive complexification of things like stuff, matter, force, energy, and eventually atoms and subatomic particles.

Why is temperature so important? Early modern scientists were able to invent thermometers to measure temperature according to scales, like Fahrenheit and Celsius. But temperature was discovered to be not simply a relative relation, but an absolute one. Absolute zero is a real, natural limit. Heat is the motion of small particles, and the complete lack of motion corresponds with absolute zero, which is calculated on the Kelvin scale. The movement of tiny particles generates heat, and temperature allows us to measure that activity. There is a tendency for things and processes, furthermore, to achieve equilibrium, and this equilibrium is primarily understood in terms of temperature rather than pressure, volume, or weight.[40] Temperature is primary, at least in the nineteenth century; it is the way we can ultimately describe how things work.

The establishment of temperature as a fundamental category with an absolute limit at zero is what is called the third law of thermodynamics. The third law is sometimes seen as less important than the first two, but it essentially grounds them in the phenomenon of temperature and heat. I will return to the third law, but first I want to acknowledge the weird fact that thermodynamics has a zeroth law. This is odd, but it is because the laws of thermodynamics were articulated after their discovery, and the first three laws were viewed as depending on the zeroth law. The zeroth law, however, seems like a very basic and uninteresting phenomenon. But it is the basis for everything to do with thermodynamics, at least in the nineteenth century, and it is the displacement of that zero in both the zeroth law *and* the third law that is so important for twentieth-century thermodynamics.

Thermodynamics is intrinsic to any adequate understanding of energy. And we cannot understand *non*equilibrium thermodynamics as it emerges in the twentieth century unless we have some sort of grasp of classical equilibrium thermodynamics. The zeroth law is the basis of equilibrium thermodynamics because it establishes the relationship of equilibrium across systems. It is also related to temperature, but in a more relative fashion. As Peter Atkins expresses it, the zeroth law of thermodynamics reads:

Law 0: "if A is in thermal equilibrium with B, and B is in thermal equilibrium with C, then C will be in thermal equilibrium with A."[41]

This law reads as a simple application of the logical rule of a transitive property: if A is to B and B is to C, then A is to C. Yes, but it is more than that given the idea of thermal equilibrium. Thermal equilibrium is *how* the systems A, B, and C are being related.

First of all, each of these systems should be considered closed systems. The technical term is *adiabatic*. Adiabatic means that "no heat is transferred between the system and its surroundings—in other words, the system is enclosed by insulating walls."[42] An adiabatic system is not completely closed, but it is understood as insulated in terms of its heat, or the measure of its heat as temperature. An adiabatic system, A is then brought into contact with another adiabatic system, B. This means that A and B are no longer adiabatic in relation to each other. What occurs is a process whereby the systems achieve thermal equilibrium. The temperatures equalize. What the zeroth law tells us is that any system that is brought into contact thermally will achieve this thermal equilibrium. And it gives us a way to measure the relative temperature between and among discrete systems with a thermometer. This all sounds commonplace and basic, but the point is not the fact of the relationship; it is, what is the medium of relationship between and among these systems?

The fact that the systems can be related in terms of thermal equilibrium means that equilibrium is not based primarily on anything else, like the size, weight, volume or pressure of the system. That is why heat is so important and why temperature is such a fundamental measure. We understand and conceive of equilibrium as based on temperature, or thermal equilibrium. Temperature is the basis of the third law as well, so it bookends the other two laws. The other two laws, however, are where things get really interesting.

We all know that energy is conserved, but we don't necessarily know what exactly that means. The first law of thermodynamics expresses the conservation of energy. One way to express this law, again using Atkins:

Law 1: "the internal energy of an isolated system is constant."[43]

It is the constancy of energy that is conserved, and that is why the first law concerns the conservation of energy overall, even though it is expressed here in terms of an isolated system. An isolated system is an adiabatic (closed) system, although for the purposes of generalization we can view the entire universe as an isolated system, because it is not in thermal equilibrium with anything else that we can know anything about.

The fact that internal energy is constant also means that it is impossible to construct a machine of perpetual motion. A perpetual motion machine could do work internally in a closed system, without adding anything to it, and that would raise the level of internal energy. Internal energy, written as U, measures the work that is done in any system in a particular state. One of the discoveries of thermodynamics is that *"the same amount of work, however it is performed, brings about the same change of state of the system."*[44] Energy is the capacity of a system to do work, and the transfer of energy takes place as heat. This is the connection to the zeroth law, because temperature measures heat as the transfer of energy from one state of a system to another. The transfer of energy is then calculated as work, so energy, heat, and work are all interrelated.

At the same time, there is a tension between heat and work, because heat is how we describe the random motion of atoms and molecules. This random motion generates heat, and this heat tends toward equilibrium, that is, the thermal equilibrium of a system in relation to its surroundings. Work, however, gives the atoms and molecules a uniform motion that resists or works against the random motion of particles. This work is what we measure as energy, the internal energy of a given system, U. We have to do something; we have to act upon a system if we want to get it to do work.

Every action has an equal and opposite reaction, according to Newton. In thermodynamic terms, this means that any energy that is used to act on a system to make it work does not create this energy out of nothing; it has to utilize whatever energy exists in whatever form. There is no spontaneous generation of energy, which means that it is conserved. Energy is conserved, but not always or necessarily as heat. This is one reason that thermodynamics was so difficult to work out, because until the mid-1800s many scientists confused the conservation of *energy* with the conservation of *heat*. There were three problems that had to be resolved: first, it had to be understood in terms of dynamic motion of particles rather than as a subtle fluid or caloric; second, the intrinsic conservation of nature had to be expressed in terms of energy rather than just in terms of conservation of heat; finally, physicists had to understand the direction in which energy flows. Actually these understandings took place in reverse order from my listing of them.

The first and in many ways most important breakthrough of thermodynamics, was made by Sadi Carnot in his 1824 treatise *Reflections on the Motive Power of Fire*. Carnot is considered the father of thermodynamics because he was able to generalize what is going on in steam engines not only for all heat engines but for all natural processes. Carnot remained committed to the caloric notion of heat, and he also confused the conservation of energy with the conservation of heat, but he was able to grasp the fundamental nature of a heat engine by means of what is still called a Carnot cycle. According to Carnot, "In order to consider in a general way the principle of the production of motion as heat, it must be considered independently of any mechanism or particular agent. It is necessary to establish principles applicable not only to steam engines but to all imaginable heat-engines, whatever the working substance and whatever the mechanism by which it is operated."[45] There is something universal to the working of any and all heat engines.

Carnot understood what Watt and others had accomplished in their development of the steam engine. The work, or the motive power of force that was accomplished by the engine, depends on the temperature difference between the heat of the boiler and the cold of the surrounding reservoir. The greater the temperature difference, the greater the work that can be done. The transfer of temperature from hot to cold does work due to the destruction and then reestablishment of thermal equilibrium. Therefore, heat as a measure of the transfer of energy goes from hot to cold, or hot to less hot. Things never spontaneously go from cold to hot. Heat is a measure of the motion of atomic particles, but Carnot adhered to the caloric fluid theory of heat. "The production of motive power is then due in steam-engines not to an actual consumption of caloric," which Carnot erroneously thought was conserved, in addition to being a fluid, "but to its transportation from a warm body to a cold body."[46] Heat is a measure of this transfer of energy from warm to cool, and the greater the temperature difference, the more work that can be produced.[47]

Carnot also envisioned a heat engine based on air, which anticipates the internal combustion engine. He realized that any engine had to follow the same basic law and function. We now know that energy is conserved in that transfer, but not necessarily as heat. The maximum amount of motive power, or work, that a steam engine can do is at the same time the maximum of work that can be done by any engine whatsoever. This is a crucial insight into machines, but for physicists it is also an insight into the nature of reality that is captured by the first law of thermodynamics. The conservation of energy means that there can never be a perpetual motion machine, and the directionality of energy from hot to cold explains how a system does work and anticipates the second law.

With Carnot's treatise, as Coopersmith states, "direction (of a process) came into physics for the first time."[48] This direction is more implicit in the first law, and becomes more explicit in the second law. The first law establishes something called internal energy, U, of a system, and states that absent of any outside action, this internal energy will remain forever constant. Energy as a whole, as well as in particular any closed system, is conserved.

Energy that does work, however, results from a change in the system. The first law is a conservation law, and every conservation law presupposes a fundamental symmetry. In the case of the first law of thermodynamics, that symmetry is the symmetry of time. As Atkins states, "energy is conserved because time is uniform."[49] But the second law calls into question the symmetry and uniformity of time. According to Atkins, the second law of thermodynamics "provides a foundation for understanding why *any* change occurs."[50] If internal energy, U, measures a quantity in a system, entropy (S), which is essentially connected to the second law, is a measure of the *quality* of a system.

The two main figures responsible for the formulation of the laws of thermodynamics are Rudolf Clausius and William Thomson. It is Thomson, later known as Lord Kelvin, who supplies the theoretical framework for thermodynamics in the middle of the nineteenth century. While in Paris in the late 1840s, Thomson found Carnot's 1824 treatise and recognized its significance, which most scientists failed to comprehend at the time. When he studied Carnot's cycle of an ideal heat engine, Thomson realized two things, which are the basis for the second and third laws of thermodynamics. First, he understood that Carnot's work enables the elaboration of a temperature scale that is absolute, which is the third law.

> **Law 3**: "no finite sequence of cyclic processes can succeed in cooling a body to absolute zero."[51]

Absolute zero is the limit of physical cooling, because it is the state where all atomic movement ceases, all electrical spin aligns, and there is no entropy. The temperature of absolute zero is a limit that cannot be reached in actual finite processes. In two papers from 1849 and 1854, Thomson derived the temperature scale that we still use today.[52] It is called the Kelvin scale, where 0 Kelvin corresponds to -459.67 degrees Fahrenheit and -273.15 degrees Celsius.

The third law grounds temperature in absolute terms, whereas the zeroth law establishes the reality of temperature as a physical relationship, but only in relative terms. The second law, however, is the most difficult and the most complex. In terms of what became the third law, Thomson realized that the ideal efficiency of any engine can never be less than absolute zero. But in the late 1840s he was unable to reconcile the conservation of energy, as based on and confirmed by James Prescott Joule's experiments, with Carnot's claim that *heat* is conserved. Thomson also continued to hold onto the idea of heat as a caloric, or fluid.

Then lightning struck, in the form of Clausius's 1850 paper "On the Motive Power of Heat, and the Laws That Can Be Deduced from It for the Theory of Heat." Clausius reconciled Joule and Carnot and affirmed the conservation of energy by doing away with the conservation of heat while preserving the central insights of the Carnot cycle. Clausius also dispensed finally with the caloric theory of heat, establishing the dynamic theory of heat. When Thomson read Clausius's paper, he finally and fully understood that Joule and Clausius were right, that heat is not conserved and that heat is not a caloric. Oh, and Clausius also invented or discovered entropy, which is the basis of the second law.

There are two alternative formulations of the second law of thermodynamics, one by Thomson and one by Clausius.

> **Law 2 (Thomson/Kelvin):** "no cyclic process is possible in which heat is taken from a hot source and converted completely into work."[53]
> **Law 2 (Clausius):** "heat does not pass from a body at low temperature to one at high without an accompanying change elsewhere."[54]

Both of these statements are equivalent. The accompanying change is what Clausius calls entropy. Basically, Clausius and then Thomson realized that "heat cannot flow from a low temperature to a higher temperature unless aided by work."[55] This means that heat naturally flows from hot to cold, and not just in the case of a steam engine. Thomson generalized Clausius's insight to apply to all of nature.

How do things work? Things go from hot to cold, naturally and spontaneously. If we want things to go the other way, we have to work on them. This work is never perfect or free, because something is lost in the effort—there is a cost. Clausius recognized "an asymmetry in Nature," and he "introduce[d] a new thermodynamic function, the *entropy*, S," to account for it.[56] The change is entropy is an effect of the heat supplied reversibly divided by the temperature, and it measures the *quality* of stored energy in a system.

Entropy is derived from a Greek word that means "turning in," or transforming. Energy turns as it flows, becoming less apparently ordered or structured. In natural and mechanical processes, energy goes from lower to higher entropy or from hotter to cooler states. We have to be careful how we apply these terms, order and disorder, however, because they are somewhat subjective and misleading. Thomson used the term *dissipation*, which is better, because cycles, engines, processes, and things tend to dissipate, and this dissipation is what we call entropy. In an 1852 paper, he says that "there is at present in the material world a universal tendency to the dissipation of mechanical energy.... Any restoration of mechanical energy, without more than an equivalent of dissipation, is impossible."[57] Everything, not just mechanical energy but every form of energy, tends toward dissipation. This is what the second law means, and it is the most important insight into the nature of reality in the nineteenth century, with the exception of Charles Darwin's theory of natural selection.

The second law of thermodynamics introduces an asymmetry into nature, and it establishes a direction of time, sometimes called an arrow. Entropy naturally or spontaneously increases, and if you work to reduce entropy, the amount of work that you perform must be greater than the amount of entropy you reduce. That is, in order to overcome the effects of entropy temporarily, you have to introduce energy from outside a system. That is why entropy applies mainly to systems that are closed, or adiabatic.

When these laws were discovered in the mid-1800s, scientists had not fully accepted the existence of atoms. John Dalton proposed the modern atomic theory in the early 1800s, but this theory was not confirmed until one of Einstein's 1905 papers, the one on Brownian motion, theoretically established the existence of atoms, and this was experimentally confirmed three years later by Jean Perrin. As physicists established the existence of molecules, atoms, and subatomic particles, thermodynamics was reconceptualized in the early 1900s by Ludwig Boltzmann and Josiah Willard Gibbs. Boltzmann understood that the laws of thermodynamics applied to distributions, not individual particles, and he applied these laws in statistical terms. An individual particle might or might not obey the second law, but at macroscopic scales large numbers of particles act thermodynamically and entropically. Boltzmann adapted James Clerk Maxwell's kinetic theory of gases, expressed in terms of a statistic (or stochastic) distribution. Maxwell described molecules in terms of their velocity, but Boltzmann realized that they could be better described in terms of energy, and he expressed these distributions in thermodynamic terms. He showed that energy has a kind of statistical weight based on the number of molecules and atoms in a given amount of a gas. Instead of following the trajectory of one particle across a period of time, he switched "to looking at *all the molecules at one time*."[58] Boltzmann's efforts went underappreciated during his lifetime and contributed to his suicide in 1906.

Statistical thermodynamics is necessary for thinking about energy in atomic and molecular terms, because it has to work with probabilities and tendencies rather than the actions of individual molecules. Gibbs then completed this transformation to statistical thermodynamics in the later 1800s, as he extended Boltzmann's work on gases to other thermodynamic systems. Gibbs also identified what is called Gibbs free energy, which is the internal energy of a system that is available to do work. This free energy is not free in absolute terms, and it does not negate the law of entropy, but it is a measure of relative freedom or ability to do work while taking the requisite entropy into account.[59]

Most histories and discussions of thermodynamics culminate with Gibbs's statistical thermodynamics. There is also the matter of a demon, called Maxwell's demon. Maxwell invented the idea of a demon that could rearrange particles in such a way that they could evade the second law. He did this as a thought experiment, not a real hypothesis, and he used this to show that it is not in fact possible to avoid or invalidate the law of entropy. The reason is because even if we imagine such a demon, the information required for us to know the work that the demon does would cost more than the information that we could acquire from it. That is, there would still be entropy, but here it is expressed in terms of information, which becomes a crucial term later in the twentieth century.

NONEQUILIBRIUM THERMODYNAMICS

In the twentieth century, entropy is understood more in terms of information than energy. The problem is that this trajectory loses sight of what happens in thermodynamics in this century and how thermodynamics shifts from a focus on closed systems at equilibrium to open, nonequilibrium systems. Nonequilibrium thermodynamics is a newer understanding of how energy works, but it is grounded in developments that occurred during the twentieth century. Energy is dynamic; it is always in transformation. Energy is productive, but there is always a cost, and the cost is named entropy. Entropy is seen as the loss of energy from the standpoint of usable work, but we can also see how the generation of entropy is an intrinsic part of the process of energy becoming itself. Twentieth-century views of thermodynamics suggest that entropy is a much more complex phenomenon, because there is no such thing as a closed system.

Energy flows and it produces what we call entropy as a result of gradient reduction. A gradient is a difference that is set up between two things, for example a temperature difference between a hot room and a cold one. The flow of molecules from a hot room into a cold environment reduces the temperature gradient and eventually produces a state of thermal equilibrium. For thermodynamics, temperature is the fundamental measure, and temperature gradients are preferred over other gradients like pressure and chemical reactions. But nonequilibrium (thermo-) dynamics relativizes this emphasis on heat.

Most of the time this reduction of gradient differentials appears destructive as it produces a homogeneous equilibrium. However, in special cases in systems that are not in a state of equilibrium, the flow of energy and the reduction of gradients produces and sustains patterns, forms, and structures. Nonequilibrium systems, or what Ilya Prigogine calls dissipative systems, actually produce structures. One example of a dissipative system is a "storm in a bottle," where two plastic soda bottles are taped together with one side filled with a liquid. If you just turn the bottle over and let the liquid fall from one bottle into the other, it will slowly and inefficiently fill the other bottle. But if you give the bottle a twist, it will organize into a vortex that empties the bottle much more quickly. A bottle that is rotated organizes the liquid flow and allows it to empty at a much faster rate, because this organization allows for the more efficient reduction of gradients.

A system is a way to talk about organic and inorganic processes in a way that does not make a strong division or dualism between the two, although here we are simply describing physical, inorganic processes. A dissipative system that is not at equilibrium means that there is a continuous source of energy flow into the system. A nonequilibrium system is an open system, whereas a system that is in or tends to a state of equilibrium is a closed system. In a closed system, the increase of entropy tends to a state of disorder, homogeneity, and "heat death." But in an open system, with constant inputs of energy, things look very different. Living organisms are also open systems, and they require continuous sources of nutrition, air, and water to survive.

The ecologist Rod Swenson explains that the apparent incompatibility of thermodynamics and evolution gives the impression of "two incommensurable rivers—the river of physics that flows downhill, and the river of biology, psychology and culture that flows uphill."[60] In his famous book *What Is Life?* Erwin Schrödinger coins the term *negative entropy* to characterize the increasing complexity of biological evolution, and some scientists misleadingly use the phrase negative entropy to mean the opposite of entropy.

What Schrödinger and others call negative entropy, however, is actually just entropy, but understood differently in special conditions. Many nonscientists assume a nineteenth-century view of entropy and thermodynamics and ignore the newer understandings of nonequilibrium thermodynamics that have developed in the twentieth century. Swenson builds on the work of Ilya Prigogine and Ludwig von Bertalanffy, and he argues that nonequilibrium dissipative systems are self-organizing—Swenson uses the technical term *autocatakinetic*, which means a self-catalyzing dynamic system. He claims that when an open, self-organizing system encounters a gradient differential, it will select the path or paths "that minimize potential or maximize the entropy at the fastest rate given the constraints."[61]

This is what Swenson calls the law of maximum entropy production, because it maximizes the efficiency of reducing a gradient. Given a temperature or pressure differential, a difference that forms a gradient between two levels of pressure or temperature, the flow of energy that occurs will work to reduce this gradient differential as quickly and efficiently as possible. Swenson give the example of a warm cabin in cold woods. In a closed cabin, the trapped heat escapes the cabin into the surrounding environment relatively slowly, but if a window is opened, the rate of heat dissipation increases in order to maximize the entropy as quickly as possible. The opening of the window allows nature to reduce the temperature gradient more efficiently.

Organized flow through the window is more efficient at reducing gradient differentials than disordered flow, and this is most clearly seen in a rotating vortex, where organized air or water flow empties a container much more quickly than a slow, disorganized system. This is the "storm in a bottle" I have already described. Swenson draws the conclusion: "the world can be expected to produce order whenever it gets the chance—the world is in the order-production business because ordered flow produces entropy faster than disordered flow."[62] If Swenson is right, the production of order is not an exception to the second law but a consequence of it.

Swenson restates the second law of thermodynamics as the law of maximum entropy production. The law of maximum entropy production means that maximum entropy is the most efficient means of reducing any gradient differential, whether it is a temperature, pressure, or a chemical gradient. In their book *Into the Cool*, Eric D. Schneider and Dorion Sagan provide an overview of this nonequilibrium thermodynamics. Schneider is an environmental scientist who was inspired by the work of a biochemist, Jeffrey Wicken, and he collaborated with a systems engineer, James Kay, to develop his understanding of evolution and nonequilibrium thermodynamics.[63] When Kay died in 2004, Schneider joined with with Dorion Sagan, a science writer and the son of Carl Sagan and Lynn Margulis, to complete the book that Schneider started writing with Kay. In *Into the Cool*, Schneider and Sagan restate the second law of thermodynamics as "nature abhors a gradient."[64] Entropy is gradient reduction rather than the inevitable triumph of disorder over order or the establishment of thermal equilibrium. Usually, what we perceive as order is the establishment and maintenance of gradient differentials, whereas the reduction of gradients leads to static equilibrium. However, in open, self-organizing systems that are not in a state of equilibrium, the flow of energy can take the form of organization, structure, or pattern.

Energy flow organizes a system, maintaining large-scale gradients even while working to reduce smaller-scale gradients more effectively and efficiently. Entropy can produce form in certain situations, even as it works to undermine and destroy forms in other cases. Because entropy gives a direction to the flow of energy, it constitutes a general sense of time, a before and after or a movement from a lower entropy to a higher entropy state. Thermodynamics provides an arrow of time based on heat and temperature, and nonequilibrium thermodynamics helps us understand the arrow of time that organizes life and prevents it from closing in on itself.

This means that there is an irreversibility to nature, which is what the original law of entropy establishes, but time is relative rather than absolute. Many physicists argue that without an absolute time, time does not exist. I think that we should view time as emergent, in terms of change, but that does not mean that time is nonexistent. It is, however, profoundly nonlinear. Life is not an exception to the universe, just as humanity is not an exception to nature. Both are special forms of energetic-entropic production, as we will consider in the following chapter.

In their book, Schneider and Sagan detail some of the scientific advances in understanding entropy and thermodynamics over the course of the twentieth century. Early in the twentieth century, a French physicist named Henri Bénard used a steep temperature gradient to organize sperm whale oil into "completely nonliving, honeycomb-like 'cells.'"[65] Fueled by the temperature gradient of heat, the oil organizes into symmetrical hexagons that endure as long as the gradient remains in place. Bénard observed that "when these systems bifurcate from conduction to convection, from random to organized, the system's heat flow—its entropy production—goes up." Bénard's experiments took place around 1900, and they have been updated and further developed by scientists Lothar Koschmieder, Michel Assenheimer, Victor Steinberg, and John William Strutt (Baron Rayleigh). Another set of experiments undertaken by Geoffrey Ingram Taylor in 1923 involves the spiral flow of a liquid between a rotating inner cylinder and a stationary outer cylinder to form complex vortices. "Beyond a critical stability point," Schneider and Sagan explain, "fluids exposed to a rotational pressure gradient in a Taylor apparatus abruptly transform into pairs . . . of counter-rotating vortices."[66] These vortices are called Taylor vortices, and they are organized by pressure gradients rather than temperature differentials.

Another striking quality of these systems, discovered by fluid dynamicist Donald Coles, is that they contain an implicit memory of previous states. Although initially, "nature displays no intrinsic preference for one rather than another gradient-breaking solution," once an organized system of vortices is established, "in their cyclicity they embody past modes of seeking equilibrium."[67] The past history of a system affects future behavior, because the system demonstrates that it will follow the same pattern once a pattern is established. Here the physical system "remembers" its previous states and is much more likely to repeat the pattern that it previously followed. This memory is called hysteresis, which is a retardation or lagging induced by tendency to repeat previous patterns of organization. Hysteresis is a kind of implicit memory that is expressed by physical systems; it is not conscious but demonstrates that previous states contribute to future states based on their organization and history.

Complex systems like Bénard cells and Taylor vortices do not emerge out of nowhere, or from some mysterious spiritual potential, but they occur in specific contexts of continuous energy flows. Furthermore, while these systems are not totally unpredictable, "no absolute predictability is possible because nature's tendency to organize complex degradation systems, creative destroyers, may be restrained by inadequate materials, inadequate quantities of energy, or insufficient systemic organization to use the energy and materials."[68] The specific situation, including energy flow and gradient differential, leads to the emergence of temporary states and patterns of complex organization. This organization is a self-organization that is made possible by a persistence of thermodynamic flows of energy. There is no self that precedes the organization; the "self" emerges out of the intrinsic organization of the system.

Many of the studies of nonequilibrium systems involve fluid dynamics, and one of the most important consequence is that the distinct gradients are interrelated. In 1931, Lars Onsager published a paper, "Reciprocal Relations in Irreversible Processes," where he shows how nonequilibrium systems can be described as having a "local equilibrium" in which the different gradients interact. For example, if there is a fluid system where both temperature and pressure vary, then pressure differences at constant temperature can cause heat to flow, while temperature changes at constant pressure can produce a flow of matter. Onsager uses statistical mechanics based on the work of Boltzmann and Gibbs to understand how macroscopic irreversible processes can occur based on microscopic, molecular, reversible processes. These Onsager relations were confirmed and extended to other processes, including chemical processes, by D. G. Miller in 1960.

For Onsager's reciprocity relations, forces and fluxes are coupled, and different gradients are correlated. Onsager's work allows scientists to understand how systems that are not at equilibrium achieve a metastable state: "an open system with moderately steep gradients will slow to a steady state of minimum entropy production," maintaining itself within the confines of a continuous gradient.[69] These Onsager relations take place in systems that are not at equilibrium, although they remain close to equilibrium. This state of minimum entropy production refers to the entropy effect on the system itself; in Swenson's terms, it maximizes the entropy that it dissipates into the surrounding environment so that it can minimize its own entropy and maintain its organization. This is again a completely physical process, not a biological one until the invention of life.

Ilya Prigogine was awarded a Nobel Prize for his work on chemical systems, and he popularized the term *dissipative structures*. Prigogine did his work on systems that are farther from equilibrium than the ones that Onsager studied, and he demonstrated that these "dissipative structures become more complex by exporting—dissipating—entropy into their surroundings."[70] When cyclic chemical reactions take place at non- or far-from-equilibrium situations, they produce bifurcations that bring the system to a different state. As the system is pushed farther from equilibrium, the bifurcations become more numerous and more intense, and then turbulence sets in. This is a very volatile situation, but "sometimes the system reaches macroscopic dynamic stable states" as a result of these turbulent bifurcations that work in nonlinear ways according to complex feedback loops.[71]

The reduction of gradient differentials—differences between gradients in the form of temperature, pressure, and other kinds of forces including chemical gradients—explains how (thermo)dynamic energy works. Energy is the excess of being that seeks equilibrium in the form of gradient reduction. In its tendency to reduce gradients, these systems can produce new forms of organization in highly specific situations, which occur in open systems that are not at equilibrium. These systems exist near the edge of chaos and they are sustained by ongoing flows of energy. Energy flow produces structures or patterns that degrade differences more quickly, and these structures are maintained so long as energy flow persists.

In *Difference and Repetition*, Gilles Deleuze articulates a view similar to this nonequilibrium thermodynamics. Deleuze's philosophy explains energy transformation as the repetition of difference, and he uses the term *intensity* to mean what we call energy. *Difference and Repetition* draws on the entire history of Western philosophy as well as much mathematics and physics. Although the book was published in French in 1968, it was not translated into English until 1994. Most scholars recognize the central significance of *Difference and Repetition* for Deleuze's philosophy. However, many readers focus on difference as the pivotal concept of the book and neglect the concept of repetition. I argue, however, that repetition is the key to understanding the book and to appreciating that repetition is a repetition of difference. Repetition of difference occurs based on an energetic intensity, a force that repeats everything differently. What Deleuze calls repetition of difference in *Difference and Repetition* resembles the way that energy flow reduces gradient differentials in nonequilibrium thermodynamics.

The fundamental question of *Difference and Repetition* is how repetition can be understood as a repetition of difference rather than identity. How can difference be repeated? Drawing on Heidegger, Deleuze asserts that it is not enough to assert empirical differences. There must be some way to "relate different to different without any mediation whatsoever by the identical, the similar, the analogous or the opposed."[72] This relation of different to different is accomplished by a *differentiator*. What is a differentiator? Deleuze says that the only way a differentiator can function as an in-itself to difference is if a system is organized into a series, "each series being defined by the differences between the terms which compose it."[73] Series are defined by the differences among their members, and therefore a differentiator is what allows us to compare two series together and see that identity emerges out of difference, rather than vice versa. The differentiator is a second-degree difference because it relates the first-degree differences to one another.

The result of this process of differentiation is similar to what physicists call a diffraction pattern or a moiré, where two waves or patterns are superimposed and the result is generated by the difference between them.[74] Deleuze calls the differentiator a dark precursor; he explains that "given two series of differences, the precursor plays the part of the differentiator of these differences."[75] New identities emerge out of differences based on the operation of a differentiator. This identification of a differentiator, however, is not sufficient to explain repetition, because something must actively relate the series together. The force that propels a series of differences together and makes them interact is intensity, and this intensity is what drives repetition. Deleuze says that "there are intensities, the peculiarity of intensities being to be constituted by a difference which itself refers to other differences."[76] Intensity is a kind of energy flow. Intensity is the force that relates difference to difference that enables the convergence or overlay of two series so that they can be compared and something new can emerge as the product of their differences. This is genuine repetition, as opposed to the false repetition that presumes the replication of a prior identity.

Deleuze calls the intensive relation of difference to difference, "which resonates to infinity[,] *disparity*."[77] Here intensity is more directly correlated with energy and contrasted with extensity, which means the extensive surface on which differences are canceled out. Extensity is the level on which we perceive identity and lack of apparent difference, while intensity is the hidden force that produces difference and the extensity that appears to cancel it out. The problem, according to Deleuze, is that "we only know forms of energy which are already localized and distributed in extensity, or extensities already qualified by forms of energy.[78] Energy in itself is intensity, a repetition of difference, but it manifests itself in forms of extensity, including entropy.

Drawing on the work of Léon Selme, a French theorist who critiqued Clausius's formulation of the second law of thermodynamics as being a kind of transcendental illusion, Deleuze criticizes our general conception of entropy. Intensity is difference, but this difference is hidden underneath and canceled out in extensity. In classical thermodynamics, "intensity defines an objective sense for a series of irreversible states which pass, like an 'arrow of time,' from more to less differentiated, from a productive to a reduced difference, and ultimately to a cancelled difference."[79] Here intensity is correlated with order and extensity with disorder, and the arrow of time runs inexorably from one to the other. But this notion of thermodynamics is outdated, even if it persists in the popular imagination. Energy is the force of intensity, which is the differentiation of differences. Entropic intensity is the force that reduces gradients in the quickest and most efficient way possible. The result in most cases appears to be a loss of organization, but the intensity that drives the process does not simply destroy structure; it also creates it in specific circumstances so long as energy flows through a metastable system. According to Deleuze, in classical thermodynamics "intensity is suspect only because it seems to rush headlong into suicide," but that is the wrong interpretation of intensity.[80] The explication of difference cancels out difference; "to be explicated is to be cancelled or to dispel the inequality which constitutes it."[81] Difference drawn outside itself cancels itself out in extensity, which is how we ordinarily conceive of thermodynamics. But this view is incomplete, because "difference of intensity is cancelled or tends to be cancelled in this system, but it creates the system by explicating itself."[82]

Selme points out that entropy cannot be measured by any "procedure independent of energetics." This means that entropy is paradoxical. On the one hand, it is an extension or explication of a system and the inevitable canceling out of difference as intensity. On the other hand, entropy can only exist as implicated, "because it has the function of *making possible* the general movement by which that which is implicated explicates itself or is extended."[83] The intensity of energy flow makes explication possible, and this revised view of thermodynamics is the result of an expansion of entropy from a specific measure of extensive effects to a more general economy that incorporates intensive difference. Intensive difference cancels itself out, but it reserves itself and persists in driving further repetition. There is always a remainder, and that is what Deleuze calls intensity or intensive difference.

Intensity is a force, which is why Deleuze says that it is a kind of affirmation. He says that "since intensity is already difference, it refers to a series of other differences that it affirms by affirming itself."[84] Sensible form is a product of an asymmetrical synthesis. The title of chapter 5 of *Difference and Repetition* is "Asymmetrical Synthesis of the Sensible," and it refers to the working of energetic intensity. Intensity is the name for the result of this sensible synthesis, and it is an asymmetrical because it is based on gradient reduction. Gradient reduction is directional; it proceeds from the hot *into the cool*, referring to temperature gradients. The reduction of gradient differentials goes only one way, from the more highly structured, less entropic state to the higher entropy state of equilibrium. This directionality is what Deleuze means by asymmetrical. Gradient reduction is an asymmetrical synthesis. Gradients are differential forces, like an atmospheric gradient where a high-pressure mass of air meets a lower-pressure zone. The gradient is reduced as efficiently as possible, which means from the state of higher pressure toward the state of lower pressure. And this example usually results in a dramatic thunderstorm.

Deleuze casts this relation in metaphorical terms of height and depth when he says that gradient reduction, or asymmetrical intensity, goes from high to low. The descent is the reduction of the gradient differential, which is reduced in the most efficient way. This reduction, however, harbors an intensity that can contribute to the setting up and maintaining of other gradients, given the right conditions and the continuous flow of energy. Deleuze says that "intensity affirms even the *lowest*; it makes the lowest an object of affirmation."[85] High and low are not terms of moral value but serve to contrast the gradient differential. Entropy as gradient reduction means that existence goes in one asymmetrical direction; there is no simple symmetry between past and future states. This directionality, however, is not itself simple, because it proceeds along the path of whatever gradients are established, which are the result of previous gradients and their reduction. Here is the path of the dark precursor. "Everything goes from high to low, and by that movement affirms the lowest: asymmetrical synthesis."[86] The affirmation of the low is the force of energetic intensity that is thermodynamic in nonstatic or nonequilibrium terms. The intensity cancels itself out in extensity, where differences are reduced and equilibrium is achieved, but there is also a remainder of intensive difference. This vital remainder of intensity is hidden underneath the extensive quantitative field, but it contributes to the generation of further differences. A symmetrical synthesis cancels out all of the terms, while an asymmetrical synthesis preserves intensive difference as an energetic remainder.

This asymmetrical synthesis means that our laws and systems are neither closed nor static—they evolve. Energy transformation is what is most real about reality, from the Big Bang to stars to planets to ecosystems to humans. Energy is material, but it is not atomic; it cannot simply be reduced to tiny building blocks that make up larger objects. Organization only works with energy flow. Energy flows generate and sustain organization. We need a new cognitive understanding of the world to appreciate this situation, which the philosophy of Deleuze helps us to achieve.

We can affirm, with Manuel DeLanda, that Deleuze theorizes dynamical processes of a realist or material ontology: "Some of these processes are material and energetic, some are not, but even the latter remain immanent to the world of matter and energy."[87] These dynamic processes are described in virtual, or mathematical, terms, as well as in actual, or physical, terms as a way to understand the chaotic complexity of nonlinear systems. Chaos involves a new science and a new mathematics that emerges in the 1960s and 1970s to account for the sensitive dependence on initial conditions, the tiny perturbations that generate large-scale effects. Nature forms patterns due to the complex interactions of different forces of stability and instability. James Gleick explains that a delicate balance between instability and stability is created, in which tiny scales can be crucial, and this "sensitive dependence on initial conditions serves not to destroy but to create."[88] The creation of new patterns is the temporary result of the metastability of these conditions, given continuous energy flow.

In 1984, Ilya Prigogine and Isabelle Stengers published their groundbreaking book *Order Out of Chaos*. They argue that dynamic chemical processes help reconcile the apparent opposition between classical and quantum physics, which is static and reversible, and the irreversible world of thermodynamics. Here the growth of entropy drives evolution, and "this transition leads to a new concept of matter, matter that is 'active,' as matter leads to irreversible processes and as irreversible processes organize matter."[89] The generation of entropy creates an infinite barrier that cannot be crossed, which is why time is real and lies at the heart of reality. Prigogine and Stengers argue that time is reintroduced into nature by means of these dissipative structures and nonequilibrium systems. As dynamic fluid and chemical systems are pushed away from equilibrium, turbulence develops and oscillations occur. These oscillations are the result of perturbations to a system, and, as they are increased, the system moves farther from equilibrium and its behavior becomes less periodic and more strange. A strange attractor, like a Lorenz butterfly, shows how a system behaves chaotically but not deterministically, because it continues to oscillate in a dynamic way, never settling down to a steady state.

As the system is pushed farther from equilibrium, it reaches a threshold of stability, or "thermodynamic branch." This threshold produces a "bifurcation point" where "two new stable solutions emerge."[90] There is an irreducible random element in the system, because this choice between solutions cannot be predicted in advance. Random fluctuation produces new types of behavior, because at certain precise nonequilibrium moments the system is hypersensitive to any tiny fluctuation. Sometimes the random fluctuations will be absorbed, and the system will remain in its previous state, and sometimes, at what is called the edge of chaos, a random fluctuation will achieve criticality and push the system into a new metastable state.

These fluctuations are akin to the *clinamen,* or swerve, described by Lucretius in his poem on Epicurus, the very slight deviation that prevents atoms from being deterministic and predictable. For Prigogine and Stengers, "the clinamen attempts to explain events such as laminar flow ceasing to be stable and spontaneously turning into turbulent flow."[91] These random events construct and constitute irreversibility, which gives a direction to reality in the form of time. They conclude: "At all levels, be it the level of macroscopic physics, the level of fluctuation, or the microscopic level, *nonequilibrium is the source of order. Nonequilibrium brings 'order out of chaos.'* "[92] The flow of energy is what drives these processes, creating entropy as a result, but also creating order. Every system is a nonequilibrium system.

For adiabatic systems at equilibrium, it is easier to measure and calculate the entropy, but for nonequilibrium systems entropy is much more difficult to track. A system requires an energy source as well as an energy sink. Energy flows from the source to the sink. For many nonequilibrium systems, there is not a simple linear relationship from source to sink, because there is an intermediate system between the source and the sink where energy is transferred in a cyclic process that may experience a temporary decrease in entropy. In the Carnot engine cycle, the intermediate region is the piston that drives the engine. The piston lies between the hot fuel and the cold sink, and it operates according to a continuous cycle.

As Harold J. Morowitz explains, "The difference between equilibrium and steady state [or metastable] systems is that in the latter, there is a continuous net flow of either matter or energy through the system from and to external reservoirs. The steady state as well as other nonequilibrium systems are not characterized by entropy maxima and need not be considered within the narrow confines of the second law of thermodynamics."[93] These systems do not break the second law, but they relativize its workings due to their dissipation of entropy into the environment. For an organism, for example, its "existence depends on increasing the entropy to the rest of the universe."[94] Here energy flow organizes a system, and the continual flow through the system sustains its organization. The simultaneous existence of gradients like temperature and pressure and chemical reactions or redox gradients intersect and interact in complex ways to generate structures and patterns in physical as well as biological systems.

These nonequilibrium steady state or metastable systems require an intermediate energy flow, neither too high nor too low in terms of electrical energy. If the total amount is too high, the system becomes too unstable and breaks down. If the amount is too low, the system is unable to maintain its organization. The edge of chaos is a fine line, a "goldilocks" region of not too little and not too much. Any system that is pushed too far from equilibrium will disintegrate, just as any system that is in a state of total equilibrium cannot produce or sustain organization. The point is that it is the flow of energy that generates, organizes, and maintains a system, given certain conditions and ranges of material, sources, and flows.

QUANTUM DYNAMICS

One problem of this nonequilibrium thermodynamics is how to reconcile the irreversibility of macroscopic processes with the apparent reversibility of microscopic, including quantum, processes. This is part of the project of Prigogine and Stengers, although in *Order Out of Chaos* they focus more on chemical reactions and dynamics and less directly on quantum phenomena. The other problem is the role of heat. For classical thermodynamics, temperature is a more fundamental measure than other gradient differentials, because it measures the motion of particles as they tend to an absolute limit of zero, which is absolute rest. Nonequilibrium thermodynamics *relativizes* temperature because it accords just as much significance to other gradients.

In 1905, Einstein wrote five papers during what is called his *annus mirabilis* that established his genius and revolutionized twentieth-century physics. One of these papers established the equivalence of energy and mass at the square of the speed of light, which became the famous equation $E = mc^2$. Another opened up the realm of quantum physics, because Einstein adopted Max Planck's term *quanta* to describe how light exists as discrete packets rather than a wavelike continuum. The most important paper, "On the Electrodynamics of Moving Bodies," is the one that establishes special relativity, which means that time and space are relative to their reference frames, and there is no absolute privileged reference frame. The speed of light is a limit, meaning that time and space cannot be given an absolute definition. It was only later in 1916 that Einstein was able to extend his relativity theory to gravity in what is called general relativity.

One of Einstein's papers that is sometimes overlooked, however, is his paper on "Investigations on the Theory of Brownian Movement," which is actually two papers combined; the first is concerned with statistical analysis (stochastic distributions) of the movement itself, and the second with the calculation of maximum and minimum sizes of molecules/atoms that impart the kinetic movement. Brownian molecular motion was a contested phrase because it assumed the existence of tiny atoms and the agglomeration of atoms into molecules, and, as already mentioned, there were many physicists who were unconvinced that atoms existed. Einstein's paper confirmed the foundations of atomic theory, as inaugurated by John Dalton and experimentally confirmed by Jean Perrin in 1908. Now there is no more question of their existence. In this paper, Einstein utilizes the thermodynamic "molecular-kinetic theory of heat" to derive an osmotic pressure, which is the minimum amount of pressure necessary to prevent the inward flow of water across a permeable membrane.[95] Then he gives an equation for the diffusion based on the movements of these molecular particles.

Einstein accepts the basic distributions of statistical thermodynamics as established by Maxwell and Boltzmann, and he applies them to the molecules that exhibit this molecular motion. What is often missed, however, is that his principle of relativity, which is not explicitly mentioned in this paper, *also* applies to thermodynamics and the average statistical motions of atoms through time. In deriving the pressure from the temperature of these particles, Einstein implies, but does not state, a *relativity* of gradient differentials. That does not make sense in terms of how I just stated it, if pressure is derived from temperature. However, it is possible to understand this conclusion by paying close attention to the connection between this paper on Brownian motion and his paper on electrodynamics.

Electrodynamics has to do with the propagation of electric and magnetic fields at right angles from each other *at the velocity of light*. The constant velocity of the speed of light entails the relativity of length and time. But is also entails a mechanical relativity of moving bodies, and this means that heat does not *ground* motion. Electricity and magnetism involve heat but do not themselves work solely based on temperature. Temperature is a measure of molecular movement, but it is not the only one, because motion is not grounded in absolute rest as measure in terms of zero. This relativity of gradients is developed throughout the twentieth century in nonequilibrium thermodynamics as a relativizing of heat. And heat is displaced from the center of dynamics.

In the nineteenth century, energy emerges as a scientific notion along with thermodynamics. Temperature is the privileged measure, and heat is the fundamental quality. Heat is an effect of the motion of atoms and molecules, and there exists an absolute temperature scale, Kelvin, that attempts to situate thermodynamics in comparison with other elements like time and space within a Newtonian framework. This ground becomes ungrounded in the twentieth century, but the displacement of heat from the core of thermodynamics is not well known, understood, or appreciated. In the twentieth century, energy is dislodged from its essential connection to entropy and thermodynamics, which become more associated with information. I think that we need to rethink what we mean by entropy—and think it along the lines of gradient reduction as suggested by Swenson, Schneider, and Sagan. I also think that we need to refocus our understandings of (thermo)dynamics and physics on energy, and this requires taking into account what happens with quantum physics.

Einstein theorizes light as quantum packets, and this names the further revolution in physics that Einstein opens up. At the same time, Einstein shrinks back from the implications of the worldview he helps inaugurate. In the 1920s, after the development of general relativity, the experiments on the atom reveal some very bizarre and counterintuitive phenomena. Basically, subatomic particles seem to behave very differently from larger-scale things. In the 1920s, Niels Bohr, Werner Heisenberg, and Paul Dirac were able to theorize and mathematize a lot of what was being discovered about these particles. Basically, the claim is that particles exist only as specific instantiations of a field and emerge only when they interact with other things. Subatomic particles do not have permanent existence, and they do not seem to possess any substantial reality until or unless they are measured in some respect.

According to Carlo Rovelli, "quantum mechanics brings probability to the heart of the evolution of things."[96] An electron does not simply exist; it can be described in terms of a range of potential probabilities. Probability at the heart of reality means that there is no determinism at the smallest level. The apparent determinateness of the macroscopic world is composed of an average of an enormous number of microscopic fluctuations that are basically random in individual terms. The random fluctuations are a contemporary way of reenvisioning the swerve of Epicurus and Lucretius. "The probability of finding an electron or any other particle at one point or another," Rovelli explains, "can be imagined as a diffuse cloud, denser where the probability of seeing the particle is stronger."[97] This essential probability of fluctuations constitutes an irreducible indeterminacy of existence.

Rovelli says that the three basic conclusions of the revolution in quantum physics are "granularity, indeterminacy, and relationality."[98] Electrons are granular, because there are only certain specific orbits or regions that they can occupy. They are indeterminate, because there is only a probability of finding an election at a given time and place. Finally, they are relational, because they only exist when they interact with something else. This is the most radical conclusion of quantum mechanics. Reality is *relational*. Things do not exist in separation. Electrons come into existence when they interact with other particles. They "materialize in a place when they collide with something else."[99] Despite many attempts to get rid of this strange situation by suggesting that quantum mechanics is only an *epistemological* phenomenon due to the limits of our knowledge, time and time again experimentation has confirmed that it is a feature of *ontological* reality itself.

Temperature is a measure of the movement of atomic particles, and this grounds our understanding of energy and entropy in the nineteenth century. But thermodynamics is based on movement and what Deleuze calls the "movement-image" in his *Cinema* books. With the shift to subatomic particles, relativity, and quantum physics, there is a displacement of the movement image of matter and an opening to what Deleuze calls a "time-image." The time-image concerns how we are able to think about quantum physics in relation to time and to energy, which is extremely complex and counterintuitive. A time-image presents time more directly, but the delinking from movement makes it appear more static. This is not the right understanding, however. With contemporary cinema, as in the films of Resnais and Godard, Deleuze says that the image is taken out of the continuous stream of images and presented directly. In this case, what counts in the "interstice between two images: a spacing that means that each image is plucked from the void and falls back into it."[100] This interstice or spacing refers to the granularity that Rovelli emphasizes in terms of quantum physics, the lack of a continuous organic whole in nature. The key insight for Deleuze is what it call for in terms of cinema and philosophy, which is an operation. He says that "given one image, another image has to be chosen which will induce an interstice between the two. This is not an operation of association, but of differentiation, as mathematicians say, or of disappearance, as physicists say: given one potential, another one has to be chosen, not any whatever, but in such a way that a difference of potential is established between the two, which will be productive of a third or of something new."[101] The image is what physicists call a bit of "spacetime," and the time-image refers to the *process* of delinking and relinking these bits. Something akin to what Deleuze analyzes in cinema happens in nature, although the "choice" is much more indeterminate. Energy is what makes this occur, and the directionality of this process, which is not linear but goes in the direction of the reduction of gradient differentials, which Deleuze here calls difference potentials.

I think that Rovelli is correct to highlight the granularity, indeterminacy, and relationality of the picture that quantum physics presents us. We just need to not lose sight of the energy. These phenomena take place in the context of a field. Quantum field theory affirms that subatomic particles are the quanta of a field, and fields are granular, in that they interact in ways that produce or emit particles. Furthermore, quantum phenomena do not solely apply to subatomic particles and fields; they scale up, even though their appearance is more classical when they do. In her book *Meeting the Universe Halfway*, Karen Barad helps us understand and elaborate some of the most important aspects of quantum physics, including quantum field theory. She explains that,

> whereas classical mechanics and geometrical optics are (nowadays understood to be) approximation schemes that are useful under some circumstances, quantum mechanics and physical optics are understood to be formalisms that represent the full theory and can account for phenomena at all length scales. Significantly, quantum mechanics is not a theory that applies only to small objects; rather, quantum mechanics is thought to be the correct theory of nature that applies at all scales. As far as we know, the universe is not broken up into two separate domains (i.e., the microscopic and the macroscopic) identified with different length scales with different sets of physical laws for each.[102]

Barad offers a reinterpretation of Niels Bohr that counters how he is sometimes downplayed in comparison to Werner Heisenberg and Erwin Schrödinger. In doing so, she revisits the famous double-slit experiment, where a stream of electrons is directed one by one at a barrier with two openings, with a screen behind it to record the location at which the electrons strike the screen. The issue here is how the experiment presumes a number of discrete electrons, but the resulting pattern is an interference pattern, which is the result of wavelike behavior. "Unlike the behavior of water waves, which go through both slits at once, the electrons are sent through one at a time. Does an *individual* electron 'interfere' with itself? Does a *single* electron somehow go through both slits at once? How can this be?"[103] Is an electron a wave or a particle?

Bohr relies on a variation of this experiment to formulate his notion of complementarity. He conducts a thought experiment that suggests that if a device could measure which path the electron takes—which slit it goes through—then the interference pattern would disappear because the result would look like the electrons are simply particles. This is part of a theoretical dispute about the nature of quantum phenomena with Einstein, who wanted to contain the implications that his work on light quanta opened up. Bohr claims that for subatomic quantum particles, "wave and particle behaviors are exhibited under *complementary*—that is, *mutually exclusive*—circumstances."[104] Bohr is the originator of the so-called Copenhagen interpretation of quantum mechanics, which is the idea that the strange behavior of these particles is not due to our inability to observe or measure them correctly, but somehow intrinsic to the phenomena themselves.

Barad argues that complementarity depends on the experiment and, more important, the apparatus. If the electron double-slit experiment could be conducted with a measurement that determines which path each electron passes through, then the result is a classical one that makes it look like the electron is a particle. But when the experiment is conducted as it usually is, without determining which slit each electron passes through, the electrons demonstrate the interference pattern that is common to wave interaction and superposition. She cites later experiments of M. O. Scully and colleagues in the late 1980s and early 1990s that are able to determine which path the electron takes, and these experiments show that Bohr was correct. Wave particle complementarity exists, and this complementarity is an ontological notion. "What is the result? Despite the lack of disturbance [that was the counterargument of Einstein and others, that the striking of the screen "disturbs" the experiment and creates the appearance of interference] the experimenters nonetheless confirm the existence of which-path-interference complementarity."[105] Complementarity is not the result of an epistemic uncertainty; it is the result of an ontological indeterminacy.

Many nontechnical readers of quantum physics cite the famous Heisenberg "uncertainty principle," which states that the measurement of a particle's location cannot be fixed if we want to specify its momentum, or vice versa. This uncertainty exists across a tiny range, which is measured in terms of Planck's constant, h. This uncertainty is often seen as an epistemological uncertainty due to the limitations of our measuring devices. But Bohr argued that our lack of knowledge is ontological, based on a fundamental indeterminacy. Barad says that "Bohr understands entanglements in ontological terms (what are entangled are the "components" of phenomena. For Bohr, phenomena—entanglements of objects and agencies of observation—constitute physical reality; phenomena (not independent objects) are the objective referent of measure properties. *Complementarity is an ontic (not merely and epistemic) principle.*"[106] Phenomena are entangled, and their intra-actions can be teased out by interacting (and intra-acting) with them by means of an apparatus.

In an article called "Quantum Entanglements and Hauntological Relations of Inheritance: Dis/continuities, SpaceTime Enfoldings, and Justice-to-Come," Barad revisits some of the quantum material from *Meeting the Universe Halfway*, including her understanding of Bohrian indeterminacy. She also reflects on how quantum superposition indicates a state of quantum entanglement. The most famous example of this superposed state is Schrödinger's hypothesis about a cat whose life or death is determined by the state of decay of an atom. If the atom decays, it releases a gas that kills the cat. The classical presumption is that the atom is either in a state of decay or not, and therefore the cat is either alive or dead. The quantum suggestion is that somehow the cat is in a strange intermediate state, neither alive nor dead, or else both alive and dead at the same time.

Barad clarifies this situation. She argues that

> a *quantum superposition* is a nonclassical relation among different possibilities. In this case, the superposition of "alive" and "dead" entails the

following: it is not the case that the cat is either alive or dead and that we simply do not know which; nor that the cat is both alive and dead simultaneously (this possibility is logically excluded since "alive" and "dead" are understood to be mutually exclusive states); nor that the cat is partly alive and partly dead (presumably "dead" and "alive" are understood to be all or nothing states of affair); nor that the cat is in a definitive state of being not alive and not dead (in which case it presumably wouldn't qualify as a (once) living being). Quantum superpositions radically undo classical notions of identity and being (which ground the various incorrect interpretative options just considered). Quantum superpositions (at least on Bohr's account) tell us that being/becoming is an indeterminate matter: there simply *is not a determinate fact of the matter* concerning the cat's state of being alive or dead. It is a ghostly matter! But the really spooky issue is what happens to a quantum superposition when a measurement is made and we find the cat definitively alive or dead, one or the other.[107]

Quantum superposition means that phenomena are entangled in such a spooky way that there is no simple either/or.

Superposition is related to entanglement, which is the entanglement of particles and states in a nonclassical way. These states have to be measured, which makes the entanglement of a live and dead cat decohere into a classical situation where the cat is either dead or alive. Furthermore, this situation of quantum entanglement suggests nonlocality, which Einstein derisively called "spooky action at a distance." Given two entangled states or particles, say two electrons whose spin is correlated, then measuring one of the electrons gives the spin of the other one, no matter how far apart they are. And the result of this measurement appears to take place *faster than the speed of light*. This understanding of entanglement is the result of Bell's theorem, which John Bell proposed in the 1964 as a way of answering a thought challenge that Einstein proposed along with Boris Podolsky and Nathan Rosen known as the EPR paradox. Alain Aspect and others carried out experiments in the early 1980s that confirmed Bell's theory and the predictions of quantum mechanics against Einstein's criticisms.

According to Barad, "*Quantum entanglements* are generalised quantum superpositions, more than one, no more than one, impossible to count. They are far more ghostly than the colloquial sense of 'entanglement' suggests. *Quantum entanglements* are not the intertwining of two (or more) states/entities/events, but a calling into question of the very nature of two-ness, and ultimately of one-ness as well."[108] This is a materialism of a sort, but a very strange kind of materialism, that Barad calls a hauntological materialism. Our entangled intra-actions as large slow beings repeat in a different way the relations among subatomic particles. These entanglements haunt us like ghosts.

There is an ongoing materialization of matter, and an ongoing dynamic production of space and time, as the framework within which phenomena interact and intra-act. The apparatus names the agential cut that gives us the appearance of disparate phenomena, but we are still haunted, affected, and effected by the entangled superposition these phenomena remain, at least virtually. Responsibility involves "facing the ghosts, in their materiality, and acknowledging injustice without the empty promise of complete repair."[109] Quantum phenomena are intrinsically spooky, and they haunt us no less than larger-scale phenomena.

According to Barad, in quantum field theory, "there is a radical deconstruction of identity and of the equation of matter with essence in ways that transcend even the profound un/doings of (nonrelativistic) quantum mechanics."[110] In quantum field theory, a particle is the expression of the entire field at a specific point, a quantum. Conversely, the field is the expansion or generalization of the particle. For example, the photon is the quantum of an electromagnetic field. The particle and the field are two complementary ways of understanding the same phenomenon. Furthermore, the particle and the field are entangled with a void. Particles do not exist within a void; they are constitutively entangled with the void. The void is not a simple vacuum; it is "a living, breathing indeterminacy of non/being."[111] The vacuum is full of virtual particles.

What is a virtual particle? When quantum physicists explore the ways that particles act, they discover that these particles give rise to virtual particles, particles that appear to jump into existence and then just as quickly jump back out of it. There is a sort of perversity intrinsic to these fundamental subatomic particles. Here is a quote from Richard Feynman about electrons: "Instead of going directly from one point to another, the electron goes along for a while and suddenly emits a photon; then (horrors!) it absorbs its own photon. Perhaps there's something 'immoral' about that, but the electron does it!"[112] This is a "quantum leap" because the electron does not move classically from one atomic eigen shell orbit to another. It "winks" out of existence, releases a photon, and winks back into existence in a new atomic eigen shell.

Barad claims that *"virtual particles are quantized indeterminacies-in-action."*[113] These particles exhibit a propensity to touch and therefore self-touch every other possible particle as part of their paradoxical perversity. In order to handle the queer infinities produced by virtual particles and their interactions, physicists have to renormalize these infinities in practice. But that does not eliminate the strangeness of these virtual particles, it merely allows us to deal with them.

Barad is an important contemporary philosopher and quantum physicist, and her work requires enormous effort to comprehend. Her engagement with quantum physics should be combined—or superposed—with the work of Deleuze, whose thinking on differentiation and repetition is crucial for grappling with these complex physical phenomena.[114] Subjectivism, linguisticism, and certain forms of contructivism in philosophy cannot be maintained, while appeals to realism and materialism are naive if considered in terms of reductionist models of mechanical materialism. This is the important lesson of twentieth-century physics, including relativity theory, quantum mechanics, nonequilibrium thermodynamics, chaos theory, and complexity, or what Murray Gell-Mann calls "chaoplexity."

As energy gets assimilated into quantum physics, time is relativized in terms of space-time, heat is dislodged from the center of thermodynamics, and entropy recedes as a measure of the flow of energy composing an arrow of time. One reason entropy is less significant in twentieth-century dynamics is that it is much harder to measure entropy in nonlinear and nonequilibrium systems, as noted previously. Another is the fact that entropy in the twentieth century is probabilistic rather than deterministic. Finally, entropy gets associated with the newer science of information.

Just as theoretical physicists are struggling to articulate quantum gravity, there is a deep confusion about time in relation to entropy and energy. For many particle physicists, time does not exist, because it breaks down at the tiniest levels. Furthermore, many of the equations of quantum physics are time-symmetrical, which means that they run the same way forward as backward. Einstein felt that time as we experience it is an illusion, and many contemporary physicists agree, relegating time as we know it to a complex configuration space. Rovelli, for instance, says that "time plays no role at the fundamental level of physics."[115]

At the same time, Rovelli along with other physicists like Lee Smolin and Roger Penrose are convinced that some version of thermodynamics is crucial to understanding the evolution of the universe, especially the thermodynamics of black holes. Entropy allows us to distinguish past from future, but we are still not sure how fundamental entropy is, because it appears to be an emergent statistical property. And entropy is increasingly associated with information.

The problem with information is that it loses the essential connection between entropy and energy. Rovelli reduces everything in the universe to covariant quantum fields that are entangled within covariant spacetime. He then appeals to information theory, in the context of John Wheeler's phrase "It from bit," to argue that everything is information.[116] Information is a physical quality that refers to connections among particles, fields, and systems, not just a subjective understanding of reality. For Rovelli, entropy measures the loss of information because the relevant information of a system is finite, and it is always possible to obtain new information about a system, but it comes with a cost. He says that in "quantum mechanics, when we interact with a system, we don't only learn something; we also 'cancel' a part of the relevant information about the system."[117] Here entropy is negatively correlated with information.

But there is a problem, because that's not how Claude Shannon defines entropy. For Shannon, entropy *is* the information itself, not the lack of it. James Gleick says that Shannon, building on Alan Turing's work, defined information in terms of bits and developed a formula similar to Boltzmann's equation because it is also logarithmic law. Shannon established that "information is entropy."[118] Later, Charles Bennett developed the thermodynamics of computation and applied it to quantum mechanics. According to Gleick, Bennett found that "heat dissipation occurs only when information is erased."[119] This is the reversal that leads to understanding information the way that Rovelli explains it, as a physical relation where entropy is the erasure of information as heat. In quantum physics, the smallest bit is a qubit, and physicists understand a qubit as "a *superposition* of states; a combination of probability amplitudes."[120]

There are a number of ways to define and characterize information. According to Luciano Floridi, information can be viewed from three perspectives: "information *as* reality," information *about* reality," and "information *for* reality," as in a program, algorithm, or recipe.[121] Rovelli, Bennett, and other theoretical physicists view information in terms of reality itself, which is the first option listed by Floridi. I agree with this ontological understanding of information, but I think there is still some confusion about what information is, and I think that describing quantum phenomena in terms of information loses sight of the energy, which gets internalized into physical processes.

So is information entropy or is information the opposite of entropy? We need to view information in terms of gradients too; information maximizes the gradient differential between the amount of data and its compression into a useful algorithm. In some ways, this approach combines the first perspective, information *as* reality, with the third, information *for* reality. Information is both in and for reality. And entropy is the way that information flows, which is energetic for things and for us. Energy, information, and entropy all work based on a reduction of gradient differentials, which is the phenomenon that links them.

In the early 1800s, William Rowan Hamilton developed a geometric feature to better understand optics. He proposed a function, the Hamiltonian function H, "which related the 'positions' *and* the 'speeds' for all the particles [of light rays] together *at one time*."[122] Hamilton was a mathematical genius, but his function did not prove very useful for optics during his lifetime. Hamilton built on the work of Joseph-Louis Lagrange, who transformed an everyday three-dimensional space into an n-dimensional configuration space. This configuration space is then transformed by Rowan Hamilton into a $2n$-dimensional phase space. This is important, because it allows mathematicians and physicists to incorporate more coordinates and more degrees of freedom into their representations of the world. But what is truly amazing is that Hamilton found a way to transform his system "from one state of phase space to the next—and so on, through time."[123] For this reason, the Hamiltonian function became *the* most important function for quantum mechanics, and it was included in Schrödinger's famous wave equation, Ψ. H is the Hamiltonian function, and it is the crucial mathematical function for physics, and *it is energy*: "it has dimensions of energy," both kinetic and potential.[124] Even though what we understand as time is not linear or classical, Rovelli explains that "the Hamiltonian is the generator of time evolution" due to its function on a phase space.[125]

How is the Hamiltonian both the energy *and* the time? In one of his *Lectures on Physics*, Richard Feynman discusses the Lorentz transformation, which consists of another set of mathematical transformation—in this case primarily of mass—that are necessary for Einsteinian relativity. Feynman explains that the Lorentz "transformation gives three space parts that are like ordinary momentum components, and a fourth component, the time part, which is the *energy*."[126] Energy and time are connected, and entropy measures the statistical tendency for systems to dissipate toward equilibrium. Information, including the connections or interactions of a system and our information about it, which is also an interaction, is a measure of entropy and a way to describe its opposite. Energy tends toward gradient dissolution, but energy flow through a system organizes a system. If it is a somewhat stable system, energy flow constitutes a cycle.

According to Morowitz, there is an irreversible thermodynamic direction from a source to a sink in any system, because we cannot consider a system in total isolation from its environment. The energy flux orders an intermediate system, and that does not violate the second law of thermodynamics, because there exists an intermediate system between the energy source and the energy sink. "The flow of energy from a source to a sink will always lead to an entropy increase in the source-sink system."[127] But the intermediate system may see a decrease in entropy for a period of time. Every system tends toward equilibrium, increase of entropy, and dissolution. But the flow of energy organizes a system and leads to a cycle where the increase of entropy is temporarily suspended, although that situation demands a continuous flow of energy to sustain itself. The key here is time, because it is the time in the intermediate zone, between the source and the sink, that allows for organization.

Every system tends toward dissipation and dissolution. But energy is always conserved, at least in terms of mass-energy. What this means is that we like to talk about things like energy, entropy, information, time, and space in abstract terms, but these phenomena are all interrelated, and they are interrelated in terms of the dynamic flow of energy across gradients. What we call time, space, entropy, and information are emergent phenomena. Energy works, and as it works it dissipates as useful energy. Entropy is an extensive quality, as Deleuze and Coopersmith point out. But the intensive quality refers to what happens in this intermediate region, before the equations and scales are canceled out. Overall, nature has a tendency to go from the hot to the cool, and this dissipation of heat increases entropy and usually what we call disorder. But during the complex, interactive, interstitial part of any system, something is going on that is able to borrow against the canceling out of differences. This borrowing is expressed as a measure of time and energy. The time is the time it takes for energy to circulate through a system, and the quantity and quality of useful energy as well as the organization of the system helps to shape this temporal frame.

If we think about Feynman diagrams of subatomic particles in physics or Barad's discussion of quantum field theory, there is the possibility for virtual particles to wink into existence for a short period of time as a result of the intra-activity of a system. At the end of the day, the particles and their interactions have to balance out, and the Feynman diagram shows the result of the activity, but there is this intermediate region where strange and wonderful things can happen. The conditioning of things happening with virtual particles and queer inter- and intra-actions is given by energy as time. Time is an effect of energy, of the flow of energy as well as its conservation and its dissipation. Nothing works without energy transformation, and energy works on the basis of the establishment and then the reduction of gradients. But energy itself is never exhausted by these interactions and intra-actions. There is always something more, some element of energy that is conserved so as to be available for other actions, other transformations, and other changes. One of the most significant of these changes is life.

2

VITAL MATTERS

Bioenergetics and Life

DIFFERENCE, IDENTITY, AND CHANGE

Life is change. Many ancient Greek philosophers, including Parmenides, Plato, and Aristotle, believed that change involves corruption and degradation, and so they searched for and valorized that which does not change. To live is to be exposed to the inevitability of death and its final transformation. Death is an undesirable outcome for most, so there is something suspect about life in many forms of philosophy and theology, which consist of attempts to deny life in order to escape death. Living involves appropriating flows of energy, which both sustain life and, in terms of entropy, lead us inexorably toward death.

This chapter focuses on biology and organic life and considers how life is tied not only to biological form but also to change. Energy is what allows life to exist and to change, although it must be harnessed and transformed. Energy is always dynamic; it is never static. Energy is conserved as such, but it is always changing. Living things are a special kind of system, because the form that they take is metastable, which means that they are able to slow down the dissipation of entropy and maintain their form for a while. To do this, they require continual sources of energy, and they need to use these resources incredibly efficiently. Life involves feedback mechanisms that operate to conserve as much energy as possible for the maintenance of the organism, and this also involves something that we can call awareness. Living organisms possess a quality of existence that is different from nonliving things, but perhaps not so different as to transcend physical inorganic processes.

Many philosophers turned from important questions of biology and life that were raised by the theory of evolution in the nineteenth century to questions of language and social existence in the twentieth century. We need to acknowledge how some of the philosophies of organism were implicated in and influenced by social Darwinism, positivist scientism, and the excesses of vitalism in nineteenth- and early twentieth-century philosophies. During the mid-twentieth century, however, many European philosophers became engaged more explicitly with the social sciences than the natural sciences. Recently this situation has changed once again, as more philosophers in this century have come to reflect on the issues and conclusions of the biological sciences in addition to physics, chemistry, and mathematics.

Deleuze's philosophy, discussed in chapter 1, is an exception to this stereotypical avoidance of the natural sciences and mathematics, but many readers in English-speaking contexts struggle to understand the ways in which he draws upon these technical discourses. More recent French philosophers such as Alain Badiou and Quentin Meillassoux have championed mathematics and the ideas of set theory as important for philosophical reflection. Another contemporary French philosopher is Catherine Malabou, who has emerged as an important philosopher of biology and the brain sciences. Malabou's thought is crucial here because she expresses her philosophy of plasticity and change in complex biological terms.

Malabou is a philosopher of change, which is why I am directly engaging her work here. Poststructuralism emerges as a critique of structuralism in the wake of Deleuze, Jacques Derrida, and Michel Foucault. A major theme of what is called poststructuralism is its focus on the concept of difference. Difference is liberated from the strictures of sameness and identity. The poststructuralist affirmation of difference over against identity continues to inform many critical discussions about theory, politics, and philosophy. Malabou's philosophy, however, helps us to see how both difference and identity are grounded in *change*, and how change is an expression of material plasticity that refuses to oppose human sociality to biology. Change is in many way a better concept with which to grapple with the difficult theoretical and practical-political issues of identity and difference, and it is grounded in our physical biology, which is not simply determinist, but *plastic*.

According to Malabou, we need to think about plasticity, which derives from the Greek verb *plassein*, in at least three distinct ways: first, as the ability to give or shape form, as in an artwork of sculpture; second, as the capacity to receive form, to be formed, which is also part of this sculptural process; and third, there is a destructive or explosive element of plasticity, the auto-annihilation of form itself, which is indicated by the use of the word *plastics* (in French *plastique*) to designate an explosive substance. As she points out in her first book, *The Future of Hegel*, "plastic on its own is an explosive material with a nitroglycerine and nitrocellulose base that can set off violent detonations."[1] Plasticity in its threefold form is the concept that is most explicitly associated with Malabou's philosophy.

After her work on Hegel, Malabou turns to focus more explicitly on the brain. She considers the significance of neuroplasticity in contemporary brain studies, and she writes *What Should We Do with Our Brain?* as a way to pivot and directly engage with the philosophical and political significance of this neurobiological work. Neuroplasticity has to do with the differentiation and transdifferentiation of cells, including adult stem cells. She says that most adult stem cells are multipotent, and they "specialize, in order to produce all the types of cells in their tissue of origin that normally die." But some adult stem cells, like skin stem cells, are pluripotent; they "can transform themselves into different types of cells," which means that they "transdifferentiate," or literally "change their difference."[2]

Malabou critiques the ideological deployment of neuroscientific concepts in workplace networks of horizontal connectivity and the association of plasticity with the flexibility that characterizes twenty-first century neoliberal capitalism. She argues, instead, for a conception of plasticity that is closer to resilience, where resilient "reconfigurations and . . . becoming[s] are made up of rupture and resistance."[3] Malabou claims that "to exist is to be able to change difference while respecting the difference of change: the difference between continuous change, without limits, without negativity, and a formative change that tells an effective story and proceeds by ruptures, conflicts, dilemmas."[4] Our brains are not telling us to obey; they are also telling us to resist—to change, to become different.

Plasticity is about change; it is the way that change manifests itself dialectically. We cannot fully understand what Malabou means by plasticity unless we see how plasticity is all about change. As the editors of a recent collection on Malabou's work assert, "Malabou seeks to philosophically recover form by grasping it as always already in restless motion. She is foremost a philosopher of change."[5] And change concerns not only philosophy and dialectics, politics and social change, but also biology and neurology. Malabou affirms a biological materialism that she also associates with new materialism. In *Plasticity at the Dusk of Writing*, she claims that "it is my opinion therefore that we should certainly be engaging deconstruction in a *new materialism*."[6]

As already discussed in the introduction, new materialism is a nonreductionist materialism of complexity and process that is influenced by the philosophies of Whitehead, Merleau-Ponty, and Deleuze. Existence is already in process, and these dynamic processes drive systems to a state of chaotic complexity that is not at equilibrium, as discussed in chapter 1. Materialism is not about the smallest building blocks of nature, whether atoms or quarks or strings, but the energetic transformation of reality by means of physical, chemical, biological, psychological, and social interactions. As Jane Bennett explains, attention to the intrinsic "vitality of matter" counters "the image of dead or thoroughly instrumentalized matter [that] feeds human hubris and our earth-destroying fantasies of conquest and consumption."[7] Matter is not dead or static; it is intrinsically dynamic and transformational.

Malabou is more influenced by Hegel, Heidegger, and Derrida than Whitehead, Merleau-Pointy, and Deleuze, but she advocates a biological new materialism that has important resonances with these better-known conceptions of new materialism. For Malabou, material form is more significant than the flows of matter-energy, but we should not view them oppositionally, because form is the result of energy transformation, which is itself transformed. Because Malabou takes the perspective of biology, energy is understood as intrinsic to biological form, whereas, from the perspective of physics, energy is what generates form out of what appears to be nothing.

According to Malabou, "energetic explosion is the idea of nature," which is the third form of plasticity, the explosive annihilation of form.[8] But form is energetic and explosive only because it contains and manifests energy, which also gives rise to form. Here are two parallel ways to frame and think about nature, physically and biologically. It's not a question of choosing energy over form or vice versa, but of seeing where and how they intersect and interact.

What is the nature of being, Malabou asks? Change. Being changes, it transforms, and metamorphosizes itself, both the Being of being that Heidegger famously thinks about and the beings that transform themselves. Change is the transformation of form, or what she calls the transdifferentiation of form. According to Malabou, in her book *The Heidegger Change*, we should think about "metaphysics as a 'form' that changes from epoch to epoch by being re-formed . . . a *passage* or *transition* to another form."[9]

When we consider Heideggerian Being, we usually assume that the Being of beings doesn't change, even if beings do. But the good news here is that "the good old beings of metaphysics are no more." Malabou declares that "*there is an exchange between being and beings that is not an incarceration of the ontological difference, but its liberation.*"[10] This liberation concerns change as the transformation of form, the exchange of Being and being in a seemingly impossible exchange that is radical, real, and revolutionary. Change is exchange, and this exchange is not static but dynamic. What allows for exchange is what we call energy, which is the physical cause of transformation.

Malabou reads an economics of exchange at the heart of Heidegger's thought, to which we will return in chapter 3. She claims that "a proximity between Heidegger and Marx indeed exists, and it doubtlessly lies in the possibility of the ontological and economic coinciding within the definition of exchange, of exchange and mutability, of the metamorphosible and displaceable character of value, and of the impossibility of transgressing all this plasticity."[11] In this context that is economic, biological, and ontological at the same time, every modification of Dasein (the *there* of Being, or the being who asks the question of Being) is intrinsically revolutionary. She says that the genius of Heidegger consists "in having inscribed the possibility of revolution not in a future event to come but in the fact (so modest, slight, and tiny) of *being-there, of still being there after the accomplishment that was never accomplished.*"[12] Every slight change is the manifestation of transgressive power because it affects the being of change itself, *form*, which is the change of Being itself.

Being is plastic because it changes form. It is also metamorphic, it changes Being itself, because Being itself is change or exchange. There is an exchange of being that transforms existence in every being-there, every Dasein. "Existence itself surpasses metaphysics," writes Malabou, and *"we started a revolution without at all realizing we were."*[13] What we call nature or being is itself revolutionary, and we need to attend to what the nature of being is, which is change. For Malabou, it's about changing difference and seeing how difference and identity are both formed out of change.

In *What Should We Do with Our Brain?*, Malabou says that our brains are telling us to resist the tedium of our neoliberal existence: "What we are lacking is *life*, which is to say: *resistance*. Resistance is what we want."[14] In a new materialism there is no dualism between brain and body. Our bodies are telling us to resist, revolt, insurrect—change. Change the difference that we are. Stasis is not the idea of nature; "energetic explosion is the idea of nature," including the auto-destruction of form, which is the lesson of destructive plasticity.[15] Malabou says that life is about resistance and resilience, not flexibility, because change is not adaptation to this or that condition of global capitalism, it is the ability to change conditions, to blow up. If we are too flexible, "if we didn't explode at each transition, if we didn't destroy ourselves a bit, we could not live. Identity resists its own occurrence to the very extent that it forms it."[16] The formation of identity is not simply the play of differences, but the resistance of plasticity that creates it. Identity and difference are grounded in change.

We often think that human culture is an exception to natural processes, but this is a false dichotomy. In an essay on Darwin, Malabou points out the plasticity of the process of natural selection, and argues that we need to think social selection in more plastic terms. Darwinian variability attests to the existence of biological plasticity, which "designates the quasi-infinite possibility of changes of structure authorized by the living structure itself; in other words, the structural law of changing structure."[17] Appropriating Gilles Deleuze's interpretation of Nietzsche's eternal return, Malabou argues that selection is a "process of repetition" that "produces its own criteria as it operates" to select for differences rather than similarities.[18] This is a form of social selection that better accords with Darwinian natural selection. For Malabou, both social and natural selection meet at the level of epigenetic plasticity, a place where the genetic envelope and epigenetic variability coincide. Here the lessons of neural plasticity help "articulate the two types of selection and present a coherent theory regarding a certain continuity between nature and society."[19]

Malabou is just one of many contemporary philosophers who are attending more closely to the natural sciences, bringing these insights to bear on discourses of deconstruction, language, and political power. One of the most contested sites of philosophical, political, and biological theory is how our cultural ideas and practices of gender are interconnected with biological concepts of sex. In *Changing Difference: The Feminine and the Question of Philosophy*, Malabou directly reflects on these complex issues of gender and sexuality from the standpoint of her identity as a woman philosopher and her perspective of plasticity. She argues that "to construct one's identity is a process that can only be a development of an original biological malleability, a first transformability. If sex were not plastic, there would be no gender."[20] In an essay on "The Meaning of the 'Feminine,'" Malabou develops her own thought in relation to that of Luce Irigaray and Judith Butler. She cautiously endorses Irigaray's notion of the feminine as "the fold of the lips to one another, a withdrawal that is so easy to force open, to breach, to deflower, but which at the same time also marks the territory of the inviolable."[21] There is a sense in which the feminine for Malabou consists in the inviolable; "without the feminine, the inviolable cannot be thought."

Due to its essential fragility, the idea of the feminine as the inviolable exists within a context of its actual violability. She says that "no doubt woman will never become impenetrable, inviolable. That's why it is necessary to imagine the possibility of woman starting from the structural impossibility she experiences of not being violated, in herself and outside, everywhere."[22] But this situation leads Malabou to a problem, because to name the inviolable as the feminine "we run the risk of fixing this fragility, assigning it a residence and making a fetish out of it." At the same time, "if we resist it, we refuse to embody the inviolable and it becomes anything at all under the pretext of referring to anyone."[23] To name the inviolable as the feminine is to "interrupt a void in difference," whereas to refuse to name the inviolable is "to refuse to interrupt a void in difference." Both stances are equally justified and equally problematic. The specification of feminine difference risks fetishizing it, while the generalization of the inviolable beyond the feminine risks diffusing and emptying it within the context of patriarchal masculinity.

Malabou complicates the already complicated relationship between the feminine and woman. She says that the terms of this relation need to be displaced, and she refers to her analysis of the exchange between Being and beings in *The Heidegger Change*. "Being and being change from one into the other," she writes, "that's the plasticity of difference."[24] Being—here the feminine, and beings—in this case women—"exchange modes of being." This substitutability exceeds metaphysics, because both Being and beings change in their exchange. If "substitutability is the meaning of Being," then "transvestitism comes with difference."[25] Being is not incarnated in embodied beings, but bodies manifest Being as change even as they change Being by exchanging it.

In her work, Malabou opens up the question of the feminine to the transformation of Being and the change in difference that female beings make. This is a kind of transvestitism because the woman does not remain unchanged. She refers to a point in her Heidegger book where she and her translator, Peter Skafish, decided that the word *essence* in Heidegger's philosophy is a kind of *"going-in-drag."*[26] If gender is a *genos*, a genre or an essence, and essence is always going-in-drag, then that suggests a kind of transvestitism of Being and beings, a clothing across the heart of existence. Malabou concludes that "while the feminine or woman (we can use the terms interchangeably now) remains one of the unavoidable modes of ontological change, they themselves become passing, metabolic points of identity, which like others show the passing at the heart of gender."[27] Tracing the feminine leads us to a passing that is inscribed at the heart of gender.

There is no question that Malabou is a woman philosopher, that she *passes* for a woman philosopher, but it is not entirely clear what either of these signifiers means. She says that "if I'm a philosopher it is at the price of a tremendous violence, the violence that philosophy constantly does to me and the violence I inflict on it in return."[28] Philosophy is figured as masculine here, as the object of a "fierce quarrel" whose outcome is "ever more uncertain and unexpected," which produces "an absolute solitude."[29] Woman's liberation is essentially tied to the liberation of all of us, in our shared and unshareable absolute solitude, even those of us who do not pass as women. If Being were not change, there would be no possibility for liberation, and this gets directly at the heart of the entanglement of cultural conceptions of gender *and* the biological categories of sex. Malabou is a philosopher of change, and she advocates a biological new materialism that recognizes the plasticity of life and its potential for liberation. I am engaging with Malabou's philosophy of change to see how she confronts more typical continental philosophies (Hegel, Heidegger, Irigaray, Foucault, and Derrida) with biological developments of neuroplasticity and epigenesis as a way to reflect more deeply on life.

WHAT IS LIFE?

In 1926, Erwin Schrödinger published a paper in the *Annalen der Physick*, the same journal that published Einstein's famous papers in 1905. This paper presents the famous wave equation of quantum mechanics and demonstrates that it gives the correct eigen values for a hydrogen atom, establishing its legitimacy. Physicists are still not sure how to interpret the underlying reality behind this wave equation, but his paper revolutionized quantum physics and placed it on a solid mathematical basis. Schrödinger followed this paper up with three more papers that further refined and applied this equation.

Later, in 1944, Schrödinger published a set of lectures as a book, called *What Is Life?*, that applies some of the insights of physics to the questions of biology. He analyzes life as a fully material process and focuses attention on the structure of the chromosome. Schrödinger posits an important molecule that he called an "aperiodic crystal" at the core of the chromosome. This aperiodic crystal contrasts with the more typical periodic crystals studied by physicists, and it contributed to the breakthrough by James Watson and Francis Crick in 1953 that established modern genetics. Watson and Crick discovered the double helix structure of DNA, and this molecule becomes the "code-script" for the replication of life in all its forms.[30]

In addition to this influential suggestion, Schrödinger also discusses the problem of entropy for life. Eventually, all life dissolves, but its metabolism allows it to persist for a period of time by feeding off of what Schrödinger calls "negative entropy." The use of the phrase *negative entropy* is misleading, because as I noted in chapter 1, negative entropy does not exist. Schrödinger was actually discussing free energy, which "is the quantity of energy available that organisms can put to work."[31] Living organisms are open systems that feed off the energy that is available in the environment, and this energy exists in the form of gradients that can be reduced to produce free energy for the organism. Life is not an exception to the laws of thermodynamics, but a singular instance of an open nonequilibrium system that makes use of thermal and other gradients. Life constitutes *change*, which will should be understood in terms of Malabou's biological materialism.

There is a fundamental connection between living and non-living systems, and energy works across this boundary to organize both kinds of systems. According to Eric D. Schneider and Dorion Sagan, whose work was discussed in the previous chapter, "life is neither a thing apart from matter, nor merely 'living matter,' but an informational and energetic process at Earth's surface."[32] The evolutionary development of living organisms is not an exception to material thermodynamic processes, but an extraordinary instantiation of them. Thermodynamics, energy flow, and entropy are absolutely crucial to everything in the world, not just the tendency of an adiabatic system to move toward equilibrium, or the workings of a heat engine, or even the dissipation of a black hole. Life is not reducible to simple deterministic processes, because physical processes are already complex, dynamic, and nonreductive. Life is an incredible example of a metastable system, but it cannot be explained or understood without the ongoing flow of energy through the living system.

Bioenergetics is the name for thinking about biology and living systems in terms of the flow of energy. Biology meets physics along the gradients of chemical reactions. In his groundbreaking book *Energy Flow in Biology*, Harold J. Morowitz begins with the thermodynamics of complex nonequilibrium systems and shows how "*the flow of energy through a system acts to organize that system.*"[33] Morowitz says that living systems make use of a small number of basic, ubiquitous elements and pathways to construct and maintain living organisms. Water is the basic molecule, and then "the major atomic components in the covalently bonded portions of all functioning biological systems are carbon, nitrogen, oxygen, phosphorus, and sulfur."[34] All life involves the partial reduction of carbon compounds, and again there are a small number of "ubiquitous biochemical compounds" that are used to metabolize cellular systems. Morowitz concludes that "over 90% of the cellular material can be accounted for in less than 50 compounds and polymers of these compounds."[35]

In a steady state, the flow of energy leads to a cycle. Most of the statistics that are sometimes cited concerning the improbability of the origin of life out of nonlife ignore the flow of energy. Without a continuous flow of energy, there is no way that proteins, carbohydrates, lipids, nucleic, and amino acids can form themselves into a cell. Genetic replication of cells encoded in RNA and DNA are vital, but genetics alone cannot create or reproduce life. Genes store and produce information that controls transcription processes, but information cannot exist in a vacuum. Genetics is still crucial, but it is no less important than metabolism if we really want to understand life. In addition to Morowitz, whose book was published in 1968, a significant scholar of bioenergetics is Nick Lane, a biochemist who published *The Vital Question* in 2015. According to Lane, "energy is central to evolution, and . . . we can only understand the properties of life if we bring energy into the equation."[36] Energy is at the heart of life, and it is the ability to regulate the flow of energy that allows life to exist.

Our planet, where life began, is an open, complex nonequilibrium system that is transformed by the emergence and coexistence of life, which James Lovelock and Lynn Margulis have controversially named Gaia. In thermodynamic terms, Earth is a heat engine with a source, the Sun, and a sink, which is outer space. The solar radiation generated by nuclear reactions of the Sun floods the Earth, which is "suspended in the immense gradient between a 5,800 K Sun and the 2.7 K temperature of outer space."[37] Given a steady state of solar energy flow, Earth captures this high-energy quanta as light and then radiates much of it out to space as low-quanta heat. The flow of energy organizes the system, producing an atmosphere and chemical composition that allows for the production of life. Earth is a rocky planet that lies in the "Goldilocks" region of our solar system, neither too hot to form liquid water and organic molecules nor too cold to do so.

Too much radiation does not enable life as we know it to exist; and too little will never allow life to emerge. During the early formation of Earth, it was constantly showered by meteorites, including an enormous collision with another planet, Tethys, that produced our Moon. What is called the Hadeon era in geology lasted from 4.6 to about 4 billion years ago. After about 4 billion years ago, Earth cooled to a point where cellular life could exist, and the oldest traces of life coincide with the oldest rocks on the planet, somewhere around 3.8 billion years ago. So given the right material conditions, life emerged when it could.

Actually, life probably originated deep under the oceans near hydrothermal vents, rather than as organisms with direct access to solar radiation. The discovery of extremophiles that live in dark submarine hot springs called "black smokers" lends support for this theory. These "organisms living on the sulfide-oxygen gradient, rather than getting energy from light or food, took it from an ancient chemical gradient."[38] The hydrothermal vents supply a continuous flow of water and heat that provides a source of energy for the formation of organic compounds out of and on inorganic minerals. A vent "can be envisioned as a giant continuous reaction chamber."[39] A number of biochemists have speculated about this possibility, although it has not been proven.

Nick Lane argues that these black smokers, while they offer an environment that contains rare forms of life, are not really conducive to the origination of life because they are too hot, too unstable, and do not possess enough carbon monoxide to create organic life. He suggests, instead, that life emerges in alkaline vents that provide a better chemical environment. Basically, "the formation of organic matter from H_2 and CO_2 is thermodynamically favoured under alkaline hydrothermal conditions, so long as oxygen is excluded."[40] Lane argues that an alkaline vent creates a gradient of protein reduction potential (pH) between more alkaline and more acidic water that allows for the reduction of CO_2 to CH_2O. This situation requires a structure of iron sulfide minerals "in the thin inorganic dividing walls of microporous vents [to] conduct electrons."[41] CH_2O, formaldehyde, is the chemical "formula" for life. Carbon dioxide must be partially reduced to create formaldehyde, but not completely reduced to methane, CH_4. This is a tricky situation and requires just the right conditions of water, energy flow, pH gradients, and minerals to work, which Lane speculates occurs for the first time at hydrothermal alkaline vents. All living cells use redox chemistry as a source of free energy. This redox chemistry is based on the existence and reduction of kinetic barriers. "Life exploits these kinetic barriers, and in so doing increases entropy faster than would otherwise happen."[42] Life accelerates the production of entropy by utilizing the flow of energy across gradients to produce chemical reactions.

The basic form of life is a cell. A cell is an open system, but it has to be partially closed off from the surrounding environment or it cannot function as a separate thing. Lane lists the six basic properties shared by all cells:

(i) a continuous supply of reactive carbon for synthesizing new organics
(ii) a supply of free energy to drive metabolic biochemistry—the formation of new proteins, DNA, and so on;
(iii) catalysts to speed up and channel these metabolic reactions;
(iv) excretion of waste, to pay the debt to the second law of thermodynamics and drive chemical reactions in the correct direction;
(v) compartmentalization—a cell-like structure that separates the inside from the outside;
(vi) hereditary material—RNA, DNA or an equivalent, to specify the detailed form and function.[43]

The first thing that is necessary to construct a cell is (v), a membrane. The cell membrane must solid enough to enclose an area inside it that is protected from the external environment, but not so porous that it cannot allow materials to enter and leave the cell. A cell membrane is composed of a lipid, because oil and water do not mix. The thin layer of oil must constitute a barrier that both allows and arrests the flow of water and other materials through the system. This process allows for the chemical reactions and reductions that gives us an organic entity to take place.

The membrane barrier allows for gradient production and reduction. According to Lane, "when oily molecules nestle down together, and electrically charged proteins dissolve in water, energy is released: that is a physical stable, low-energy, 'comfortable' state of matter." Energy is released as heat, which is the movement of molecules that increases overall entropy when oil and water separate. Entropy increases overall relative to the system, because "an ordered oily membrane around a cell is a *higher* entropy state than a random mixture of immiscible [meaning a liquid that does not form a homogeneous mixture when added together] molecules, even though it *looks* more ordered."[44] Entropy always tends to increase, but sometimes this process can be reversed temporarily in the intermediate zone between source and sink, with the cost of increasing the entropy overall in terms of its dissipation into the environment. That is what we call order or organization, when the specific reduction of select gradients given a continuous flow of energy organizes itself to maximize this process, delaying its own dissolution for a temporary period of time.

Cells respire by oxidation and they excrete both degraded/reduced waste materials and heat. Cells derive energy by making use of redox gradients. *Redox* means "reduction and oxidation," and it refers to the type of chemical reaction that sustains organic life. Respiration "is simply the transfer of one or more electrons from a donor to a receptor."[45] This transfer of electrons, usually from a hydrogen atom, oxidizes a substance, because it reduces oxygen, O_2. Ultimately, electrons are passed along a chain of carriers, ending up with oxygen. With each transfer, energy is released as heat, increasing entropy. As Lane explains, "all chemistry ultimately increases the heat of the surroundings and lowers the energy of the system itself; the reaction of iron and food with oxygen does that particularly well, releasing a large amount of energy (as in a fire). So respiration is a kind of burning, but with a huge difference. The difference is that during the transfer "respiration *conserves* some of the energy released from that reaction in the form of ATP."[46] This conservation is a slight delay, and this is what generates what we call life.

What is ATP? Adenosine triphosphate, ATP, is the molecule that generates energy for a cell. As Morowitz states, "the flow of energy in the biosphere is accompanied by the formation and hydrolysis of phosphate bonds, usually those of adenosine triphosphate."[47] The molecule ATP is continuously recycled through the cell and the body to produce ADP (adenosine diphosphate) and inorganic phosphate (PO_4^{-3}). This process switches a protein from one stable state to another and then uses the energy that is released from the reaction of food with oxygen to produce more ATP.[48] This process occurs over and over, using ATP to produce energy and then energy to produce more ATP. It is a cycle.

Respiration sets up an electric current, channeling the electrons from food to oxygen. Every time an electron is passed along, it releases protons that can be passed across a membrane. This membrane is not the cellular membrane, but a membrane that is set up inside the cell. In multicellular organisms, called eurkaryotes, this work is done by mitochondria. Mitochondria set up protein complexes where electrons are passed down a chain, and with each step protons are pumped across a membrane. The mitochondria are "the thermodynamic epicentre" of the cell, and they generate energy for the organism by pushing protons across an internal membrane.[49] According to Lane, an ordinary human being contains forty trillion cells, which in turn contain at least a quadrillion mitochondria. The job of these mitochondria is to pump protons, and "together they pump more than 10^{21} of them—nearly as many as there are stars in the universe—*every second*."[50] Pumping protons across a membrane generates energy because it concentrates the protons to create a difference in electrical charge between the protons inside and outside the membrane. This electrical charge is then used to synthesize ATP, which is then consumed by cells as energy. The electrical potential of the concentrated protons that are generated with every transfer and reduction of electrons toward oxygen becomes the motive power that produces ATP.

The production of ATP occurs inside a rotary motor, "in which the flow of protons turns a crank shaft, which in turn rotates a catalytic head. These mechanical forces drive the synthesis of ATP. The protein works like a hydroelectric turbine, whereby protons, pent up in a reservoir behind the barrier of the membrane, flood through the turbine like water cascading downhill, turning the rotating motor."[51] We all contain heat engines within the heart of our cells! This is why the laws of thermodynamics are so important, even though they are so often misunderstood. The basic principles of heat engines discovered by Sadi Carnot work in terms of organic cellular life. However, no organism is a closed system, because it must constantly ward off equilibrium by taking in food and giving off waste and heat. Entropy explains how living systems function too, although we have to take into account the insights of nonequilibrium thermodynamics, including Prigogine's dissipative structures. Morowitz argues that life takes place along the contact point where biochemistry, ecology, and thermodynamics intersect, and the order that we see in living systems is a thermodynamic measure: "in a thermodynamic system the only meaningful measure of order is related to some measure of how far the system is from equilibrium."[52]

Life makes use of chemical pathways that have been established in inorganic processes, and these are preserved in organic metabolism. According to Lynn Margulis, "because certain carbon-chemical metabolic pathways are absolutely necessary for all metabolism, the earliest ones that underlie the cellular phenomenon of self-maintenance were present from the beginning."[53] The most important pathway involves the synthase of ATP.

Respiration is primary, even though most of us are aware of photosynthesis as a primary way to convert solar energy to carbohydrates. In fact, respiration comes first, and photosynthesis is a form of respiration that also uses an electron chain, proton gradients, and ATP synthase. In this case, bacteria developed a pigment called chlorophyll that absorbs the photons and excites an electron, "sending it off down a chain of redox centres to an acceptor, in this case carbon dioxide itself."[54] Photosynthesis taps into the energy of the sun, which is a huge breakthrough for life, but it makes use of a similar process to that originally developed underwater to generate energy and sustain life.

The first living organisms were single-celled prokaryotes, usually called bacteria. Recently we have discovered that another kind of single-celled order exists, which is called archaea. We do not know exactly how archaea, bacteria, and organisms called eukaryotes are related, but it appears that archaea and bacteria evolved first, either from a common ancestor or in two distinct origins of living matter. For nearly two billion years, life remained confined to a single cell. In fact, Nick Lane argues that the transition from prokaryotes to eukaryotes was more unlikely than the formation of life in the first place.

Eukaryotes are defined as organisms that contain a nucleus, and they appeared on Earth between 2.1 and 1.6 billion years ago. They originally began as single-celled organisms, but their greater size and internal nucleus allowed the later development of multicellular organisms. The emergence of eukaryotes from prokaryotes is usually viewed as a gradual process, but it may be that is was a singular event. According to Margulis, "a sulfur- and heat-loving kind of bacterium, called a fermenting 'archaebacterium' (or 'thermocidophil'), merged with a swimming bacterium. Together the two components of the integrated merger became the nucleocytoplasm, the basic substance of the ancestors of animal, plant, and fungal cells."[55] This "archaebacterium" that Margulis refers to is now considered an archaeon, although she herself resisted this new order of prokaryote because she viewed the evolution of a bacterial cell from an archaebacterial cell in more linear terms. What she calls a "fermenting archaebacterium" does not really exist, because these are later organisms that produce energy through fermentation, which was invented *after* respiration.

Nick Lane claims that "the consensus view today is that the entire group [of archaebacterial, or "archezoa"] is a mirage—every single eukaryote that has ever been examined either has, or once had, mitochondria."[56] The symbiogenetic merger probably happened once, and the result of this merger created the eukaryotes, with a nucleus and internal organelles, the most important of which are the mitochondria. In 1998, Biller Martin and Markos Müller introduced the "hydrogen hypothesis," according to which the prokaryote ancestor of mitochondria was a hydrogen waste-producing hydrogenosome. This bacterium, which is called an anaerobic eubacterium or α-proteobacterium, had a hydrogen metabolism rather than an oxygen metabolism. Because it gave off hydrogen, it was attractive to methanogens, which require hydrogen to live and were threatened by the increase in oxygen in the environment.[57] Lane explains this process in his book *Power, Sex, and Suicide: Mitochondria and the Meaning of Life*. The α-proteobacterium belongs to the bacteria order and may have been something like the parasite *Rickettsia*, whereas the methanogen belonged to the order archaea. As the α-proteobacterium and the methanogen became more and mutually dependent in an oxygen-rich environment, eventually the methanogen grew large enough to swallow the α-proteobacterium.

This is a just-so story, which may or may not have actually happened, or happened in this way, but it seems that something extraordinary and unlikely did occur, and Lane declares that "the evolution of the eukaryotic cell was fundamentally a chance event, and happened but once on earth."[58] This chance event is a swerve, a change that changed everything because it allowed for life to grow bigger and more complex. In an oxygenated world, organisms that feed off hydrogen like the methanogens are pushed to the limits of survival, and they engage in desperate acts of symbiosis with other organisms, including the α-proteobacterium that gives off hydrogen. The specific interactions between these two kinds of cells probably happened millions of times, but if Lane is right it only worked once to create a successful and surviving eukaryote.

As the methanogen embraced and began to swallow the α-proteobacterium, the α-proteobacterium gradually lost its surface to absorb food and was threatened with starvation. Since it was by that point tightly bound to the methanogen, it was not possible to leave. So the alternative was to move inside the methanogen, which it did. "The methanogen could then use its own surface to absorb all the food needed, and the two could continue their cozy arrangement."[59] This sounds great, but there are still problems, which are solved by the sharing of genes, or lateral gene transfer. Bacteria and archaea can swap genes easily and quickly, because they do not require the sexual cell fusion that occurs in meiosis. The point is that the new organism acquired two sets of genes it could deploy, and this symbiotic interaction allowed it to work.

In addition to gene swapping, the new organism needed a tap, "an ATP pump which it could plug into the membrane of its α-proteobacterial guest to drain off its ATP."[60] The α-proteobacteria evolved into mitochondria, and the new nucleated cell gained a power supply to fuel its growth. We do not know if this is what actually happened, and biologists are still unclear on the specific separation of eukaryotes from archaea, partly due to the discovery in 2015 of Lokiarcheota, a new phylum of archaea that could serve as an intermediate link between archaea and eukaryotes. An intermediate link that contains elements of both archaea and eukaryotes would probably invalidate the hydrogen hypothesis. The point is not whether this specific explanation is correct; it is the fact that the generation of a eukaryotic cell was an extraordinary accomplishment, perhaps as extraordinary and unlikely as the creation of life itself. And the endosymbiotic merger of two different kinds of prokaryote is what made this possible in morphological and energetic terms.

The existence of mitochondria inside a cell internalizes energy generation, allowing the cell to dispense with an external cell wall. The lack of a cell wall means that the cell membrane can perform other tasks, like movement, signaling, and swallowing other cells. "Most importantly of all," Lane writes, "internalization releases the eukaryotic cell from the geometric constraints that oppress bacteria. Eukaryotes are on average 10,000 to 100,000 times the volume of bacteria, but as they become larger, their respiratory efficiency doesn't slope off the same way."[61] The eukaryotic cells can grow much larger and still maintain energy efficiency simply by increasing the surface area of mitochondrial membranes within the cell. Since energy efficiency does not decrease, there is an advantage to having a larger size. "As animals become larger, their metabolic rate falls, giving them a lower cost of living," according to Lane.[62] Living systems are special systems, but they are still thermodynamic systems, driven by energetic and entropic demands. Life is a pause, a slight delay in the process of dissipation and dissolution toward equilibrium.

THE POSTSTRUCTURE OF EVOLUTIONARY THEORY

Once a living organism exists, we can talk about the development of life in evolutionary terms. Evolution is the name that describes Darwin's theory of natural selection, proposed to explain how species change. After his famous voyage on the HMS *Beagle* in the 1830s, Darwin developed his radical theory of evolution, but he was reluctant to publish it until forced to by the similar work of Alfred Russell Wallace. Darwin published his masterwork, *On the Origin of Species*, in 1859, but he waited until 1871 in *The Descent of Man* to publish his understanding of how evolution works on human beings. Darwin's work is revolutionary, but he shrank from publicly endorsing the implications of his ideas.

The key to the evolution of species involves the process of natural selection. Natural selection works due to random variations, and variations or mutations that allow an organism to better survive are then "selected." Some Darwinians use the phrase *survival of the fittest*, but this is problematic because fitness is always relevant to the environment, not some transcendent or objective standard. Darwin states that the "preservation of favourable variations and the rejection of injurious variations I call Natural Selection. Variations neither useful nor injurious would not be affected by natural selection, and would be left a fluctuating element, as perhaps we see in the species called polymorphic."[63]

Stephen Jay Gould explains that evolution is a mixture of chance and necessity, and what made Darwin so controversial was his argument that evolution has no purpose. "Darwin maintained that evolution has no direction," Gould writes, "it does not lead inevitably to higher things."[64] Darwin maintained a consistent philosophy of materialism, even though he was cautious about advertising it too explicitly. In his book *Marx's Ecology*, mentioned in the introduction, John Bellamy Foster argues that Marx is a new materialist, based on his understanding and application of Epicurus and Lucretius. Foster also claims that Darwin's work shares this new materialist perspective, and it is true that Marx admired Darwin a great deal, and they exchanged letters.

According to Foster, Darwin is a perfect counterpoint to Marx because they both shared a materialist perspective that is not determinist. Both Darwin and Marx rejected teleology, and just as Marx criticized religion as the opium of the masses, Darwin's theory of natural selection was directed against the teleology of natural theology. For most scientists who embraced a form of natural theology, nature was fixed into essential forms. "For Darwin, in contrast," explains Foster, "all species were mutable, and there were in fact no firm divisions—species designations were heuristically useful but inherently arbitrary and changing."[65] Marx and Engels were both strongly impacted by Darwin's work, while they criticized his crude English style of writing. For Marx, Darwin's theory of human evolution, which remained implicit until *The Descent of Man*, led him "to form a definite hypothesis on the relation of human labor to human evolution."[66] Foster traces the thread of materialist evolutionary biology into the twentieth century, culminating in the work of Richard Lewontin, Richard Lewis, and Stephen Jay Gould. Even if these thinkers were more obviously influenced by Darwin, their debt to Marx and a complex Marxist materialism is clear.

Gould is a significant reader and promoter of Darwin, and his work on evolutionary theory needs to be appreciated and in some cases updated. Gould provides his synthesis of evolution in his massive book *The Structure of Evolutionary Theory*, published in 2002, the year of his death. Gould's work is incredibly important in terms of large-scale understandings of biology as a historical science and what it means to be a natural biologist. In his book, he argues for a hierarchical theory of selection in terms of six basic levels. Each of these levels is "banded together in a rising series of increasingly greater inclusion, one within the next."[67] The six levels that Gould posits are genes, cells, organisms, demes, species, and clades.

The term *hierarchy* in biology consists of an inclusion principle, not the assertion that a higher level is more valuable than another, which is how the word is more commonly understood. A deme is a subdivision of closely related organisms of the same species, and a clade is a branch, or a group of organisms believed to have evolved from a common ancestor. The key is that at every level it is the individual that is important for evolutionary change, not the group. It's not that individuals are more important, it's that evolutionary change takes place in terms of the individual element as a focal unit, whether the individual is a gene, a cell, an organism, a deme, a species, or a clade.

Gould's most famous contribution to evolutionary biology is the theory that he advanced in 1972 with Niles Eldridge on "punctuated equilibrium." Darwin presumed that change happened slowly and gradually in geological time, but the fossil record appears much more irregular, with bursts of new activity followed by long periods of stasis. Gould argues that "the theory of punctuated equilibrium attempts to explain the macroevolutionary role of species and speciation as expressed in geological time."[68] This theory does not argue for any specific time frame for all changes, but only the evolution of species in geological timeframes. Gould mentions that punctual changes occur in other sciences, including "René Thom's catastrophe theory, Ilya Prigogine's bifurcations, several aspects of Benoit Mandelbrot's fractal geometry, and the chief themes behind a suite of useful ideas united under such notions as chaos theory, non-linear dynamics, and complexity theory."[69] Gould specifically discusses Per Bak's "sandpile" model of self-organized criticality, where the dropping of grains of sand onto a metastable sandpile can accumulate for long periods of time without any significant change in the pile, until suddenly a single grain of sand can cause a cascading avalanche.

Gould then notes that Thomas Ray's Tierra program, a computer simulation of artificial life, suggests evolutionary patterns that conform to the predictions of punctuated equilibrium. "Ray found 'a pattern which could be described as periods of stasis punctuated by periods of rapid evolutionary change, which appears to parallel the pattern of punctuated equilibrium described by Eldredge and Gould.'"[70] Life is not a gradual transition. We need to reinterpret change in biological terms as "a rare and rapid event experienced by systems only when their previous stabilities have been stretched beyond any capacity for equilibrial return, and when they must therefore undertake a rapid excursion to a new position of stability under changed conditions."[71] Of course, life does not and cannot exist at equilibrium, but only in a metastable state near equilibrium that is sustained by flows of matter and energy. This metastability persists until it cannot any more, and then it either breaks down or finds another gradient on which to live.

A punctuational change that occurs when a system reaches a point of bifurcation or criticality is also called a singularity. A singularity can be described using poststructuralist language as an event, which Gould also uses in the quote in the previous paragraph. Gould details the structure of evolutionary theory in his final work, but we require no less than a poststructural theory of evolution, building on Gould's insights along with others. He does not specifically discuss energy or energy flow in biological evolution, but he gives us an overview of evolutionary change that affirms its essentially contingent nature.

Gould gives us tools for a poststructural evolutionary theory, even if he does not present his theory in these specific terms. New materialism is based on a nondeterministic understanding of material processes that incorporates and affirms chance. The problem with most understandings of chance is that chance is seen as totalizing, which eliminates chance. Chance only exists as a stochastic description of stable and partially predictable laws. *Law* is probably too strong a term, but it is the word scientists use to refer to spontaneous tendencies in nature. Certain regularities exist, and chance plays a vital role in selecting which alternative will be adopted. There is a history to nature as well, because the past affects the present, and nature appears to contain some kind of "memory," or hysteresis. Chance is not a stand-alone quality; it is an element that plays between rigid order and sheer randomness. Chance is what Lucretius calls the swerve, and this swerve animates the materialisms of Marx, Darwin, Althusser, and Deleuze, among others.

In his book, Gould adopts a law of history from Nietzsche's *Genealogy of Morals*. According to Gould, "Nietzsche labels the need to distinguish historical origin from current utility as 'the major point of historical method.'"[72] Gould applies this method to biological history and claims that we should not confuse the current utility of something with its evolutionary origin. This "disengagement of current utility from historical origin establishes the ground of contingency and unpredictability in history."[73] New forms, features, and organs evolve, but later they may be put to different uses than the situation that originally brought them into existence.

According to Gould, we should not only talk about biological adaptations, we should also consider what he calls "exaptations." Exaptation refers to the "principle of quirky functional shift" whereby a thing that arises for a certain reason in a certain context may come to serve a quite different function later in a very different context.[74] Exaptation is the ground of contingency, because we cannot predict what uses will be made of any given material. Adaptations are crafted for a specific function, but exaptations are features that are co-opted later for a different purpose.[75] Exaptations are effects whereby useful functions are crafted from things that have a "nonadaptive ancestral status."[76] Basically, there are many things that take place in evolution that are simply nonadaptive; they do not help the organism survive, but they also do not hinder it, and they are retained in future generations, where a current use is then found.

Gould's most famous architectural example of an exaptation is a spandrel. In an essay on "The Spandrels of San Marco," he and Richard Lewontin explained that spandrels are "spaces left over" when a cathedral dome, like that of the Cathedral of San Marco in Venice, is built. Under the dome, in the four corners around the center, are four tapering triangular spaces that are each formed by the space left over between the dome and the pair of adjacent arches that meet at right angles at the sides. These four spaces are called *pendentives*, and they derive from previous architectural decisions and how buildings like this cathedral are structured. In each of the four left-over spaces, there is a mosaic of one of the four evangelists. Gould explains that nobody could argue that the spaces were created for the sake of displaying the evangelists. Rather, "the spandrels originated as a nonadaptive side consequence of a prior architectural decision."[77] It is ironic that many scientists now believe that religion is itself a spandrel, a phenomenon that emerges as an exaptation in evolutionary terms, not a thing that has any inherent evolutionary purpose. Of course, some scientists believe that religion is antiadaptive, although if that were truly the case it would not have survived for so long.

The twentieth-century theory of evolution is called the modern synthesis, or sometimes neo-Darwinism. This synthesis combines Darwin's theory of natural selection with Gregor Mendel's work on genes as the unit of selection. The main contributors to this synthesis were J. B. S. Haldane, R. A. Fisher, and Theodosius Dobzhansky, although it was Julian Huxley who gave it the name *modern synthesis* in a book published in 1942. This synthesis was an extraordinary achievement, but, as it became established in the middle part of the twentieth century, "this consensus hardened into orthodoxy, often accompanied by strong and largely rhetorical dismissal of dissenting views."[78] To Gould's credit, he consistently championed Darwin's fundamental insights while being willing to challenge neo-Darwinian orthodoxy.

One biologist whose work was dismissed by neo-Darwinianism and is now being reevaluated is that of Margulis. Gould fails to mention or cite her in his book, because she was marginalized for so long, but he does acknowledge the tremendous role that bacteria play in our understanding of life. Gould reproduces Carl Woese's designation of three multicellular kingdoms, Bacteria, Archaea, and Eukarya, which I mentioned above in relation to Lane (although Margulis resisted accepting the new kingdom of Archaea). Gould points out that single-celled organisms represent an underappreciated situation of complexity, due to our overvaluing of larger creatures. He says that bacteria and other prokaryotes reached a saturation point of development, and that left very little room for further development, except in the direction of larger forms of life. Gould targets the defenders of evolutionary progress who view the development of evolution over time as an increase in value and complexity of lifeforms. He says "we must reconceive the history of life as expansion and contraction of a full range of taxa under constraints of systems and environments, rather than the flux of central tendencies, valued extremes, or salient features."[79] The invention of a eukaryote was likely a very lucky random event, if Lane is correct, and Gould claims that if we reran the history of Earth again with the same starting conditions we would not arrive at the same results. Chance and fluctuation are intrinsic to all material and biological processes.

Gould states that the "modal position of complexity" has not shifted from bacteria to mammals or humans, but rather we still persist in an "age of bacteria." These organisms, which technically include the Archaea, have been, are, and will likely remain "the dominant creatures on earth by any standard evolutionary criterion of biochemical diversity."[80] Bacteria, or single-celled prokaryotes, also called protists, compose the overwhelming majority of life, but because they are so small we do not know as much about them. In addition, because they reproduce asexually, these single-celled protists are much less clearly differentiated into definable species.

Gould claims that when we turn from multicellular sexually reproducing species to "asexually reproducing unicells [such] as planktonic forams, designated 'species' cannot be construed as proper Darwinian individuals, and therefore cannot be primary causal agents (or interactors) in evolutionary trends."[81] A species works as an agent of Darwinian evolution given multicellular sexually reproducing organisms, but it does not work quite so clearly with single-celled organisms that are asexual. Here, Gould explains, we need to shift from the species to the *clone* as the primary evolutionary individual. Cloning occurs in nature when organisms reproduce asexually, producing genetically identical individuals by binary fission, or, in eukaryotic cells, mitosis.

All prokaryotes reproduce asexually, whereas some eukaryotes do, although most multicellular organisms include at least a certain amount of sexual reproduction. Lane argues that both sexual reproduction and the death of multicellular organisms, as we understand it, are interrelated. They stem equally from the original event of endosymbiosis, where one kind of protist partially consumed another, and this symbiotic merger generated the first eukaryote. Because each organism contributed genetic material, and, because the smaller protist evolved into the mitochondria, the symbiosis and the tension between these two sources of genetic material contributed to the development of sexual reproduction.

Sexual reproduction is much slower than asexual reproduction, but it is a good way to help eliminate damaged genes. Genes that become damaged by mutation or radiation are eliminated or masked. In a similar way, programmed cell death, called apoptosis, is a way to eliminate damaged cells in the body of a larger organism, making room for a new cell to replace it. According to Lane, "seen from the point of view of the 'higher' organism, sex repairs damaged cells and apoptosis repairs damaged bodies."[82] The mitochondria are responsible for apoptosis, which in a human being causes around ten billion cells to die every day. All the apoptotic proteins we know of are bacterial in origin, whereas archaea do not possess them. It was a bacterium that was swallowed by an archaeon to produce the first eukaryote, and the bacterium then became the mitochondria. The mitochondria generate energy for the cell and the organism, as we have seen, and they also bring the death machinery along with them into eukaryotic and multicellular organisms.

The desire for sexual fusion on the part of a cell is a sign of damage; it is a desperate cry for help that usually issues in death. Sex and death are fundamentally related at the deepest biological level. The desire for sex wells "up as a burst of free radicals from the mitochondria," and it is "also a redox signal." Because the signal for sex is a confession of damage, "there must have been a strong selection pressure to transmute a redox signal for sex into a signal for death."[83] We know that there are more than two sexes, but there is a natural tendency to verge toward two sexes in multicellular organisms. The reason for this, Lane says, is the merger of mitochondria with nuclear DNA. There needs to be a close match between the genes from the nucleus and the mitochondria, and that is much easier if only one parent contributes mitochondrial DNA. "To ensure the match is as perfect as it can be in each generation," Lane writes, "it is necessary to test a *single set* of mitochondrial genes against a *single set* of nuclear genes. This explains why the mitochondria need to come from just one parent," because it limits the danger of mismatches.[84]

Bacteria and archaea reproduce asexually, and much more quickly. The drawback is that genetic mutations or variations that are injurious to the organism are much harder to weed out. Prokaryotes do not recombine their genes in a sexual fusion; they clone themselves by cell fission, meiosis. The way that prokaryotic cells differentiate themselves genetically is by lateral gene transfer. Bacteria transfer genes laterally or horizontally, rather than vertically in the descent of a new generation. This lateral gene transfer means that single-celled organisms can swap genes much more easily and freely than multicellular organisms can. According to Margulis, "bacterial sex is always one-sided. Genes and only genes can may pass into the recipient cell from anywhere: the water, a virus, or a donor dead or alive."[85] We could say that bacteria are more promiscuous, except that they do not need sex to reproduce.

Asexual bacterial and archaeal reproduction means that we have to reevaluate how we understand evolution. The modern synthesis of neo-Darwinism focuses on the gene as the locus of heredity, but it also favors sex and eukaryote sexual reproduction in its emphasis on the exchange of DNA in recombinant fusion and transmission to descendants. Margulis may overemphasize the challenge to Darwinian evolution of our newer understandings of bacterial gene-swapping and endosymbiotic merging, but she stresses (and Gould acknowledges) that we have to at least broaden our focus. Bacteria are not clearly divided into species. The symbiogenesis of endosymbiotic mergers create new forms of life and allows life to evolve in ways that are not simply captured in conventional neo-Darwinian terms. Margulis asserts a diverse set of endosymbiotic mergers, while Lane attends to the singularity of the primary formation of a eukaryote out of an incredibly unlikely merger, but both indicate that things change in ways that are much different from orderly progression or descent.

According to Margulis, "symbiogenesis is far more splendid than sex as a generator of evolutionary novelty."[86] She suggests that "new species arise from symbiotic mergers among members of old ones," although she recognizes that this contention remains controversial in biological terms.[87] Endosymbiosis is well established, but its role in evolution of new species is unclear. Bacteria have become symbionts with other forms of life, allowing us to do extraordinary things. Mitochondria are the result of a bacterial symbiosis that drives eukaryotic and multicellular organisms. Plants make use of the bacteria that make up the cyanobacteria, the most prevalent form of life for almost two billion years, in the form of chloroplasts. These chloroplasts allow algal and plant cells to convert sunlight into usable energy by photosynthesis.[88]

Margulis notes that "bacteria are exemplary genetic engineers: splicers and dicers and mergers of genomes par excellence. We people just borrow their native skills."[89] Natural selection works at the level of prokaryotes, but not exactly the same way as in organisms that reproduce sexually. We need to be careful about how we overinterpret bacteria and archaea from the perspective of multicellular organisms like ourselves. They are not less evolved, even if they began earlier; in many ways they are more evolved than we are, and they will probably survive our extinction. Furthermore, we also have to be careful about equating natural selection simply with survival.

Even though Gould focuses on individual units of evolutionary selection, he does not mean to promote a careless individualism of self-propagating forms. He says that Darwin affirmed the idea of a "blending inheritance" from both parents, which means that "faithful replication is not—and never was—the defining characteristic (or even a necessary property) of a unit of selection. The reason that replication is not the purpose of selection is because "units of selection are evolutionary individuals that interact with the environment and plurify as a causal result."[90] This plurification is the goal, not replication. And plurification is also the purpose of bacterial selection, although this is not done sexually. Cloning is not simple replication either, because of the possibility of lateral gene transfers. *Change is what is desired, at the heart of biological selection.*

Gould says that we should understand the units of selection not as replicators but as *interactors*.[91] Individuals as units of selection are interacting agents, or more precisely what Karen Barad would call intra-acting agents, that inter- and intra-act with their environment and each other, as well as promiscuously with other species including many kinds of bacteria. Success of these interactions is measured in reproductive terms, but we should not overlook the primary impulse to plurification. Life is an abundance, an incredible expression of *exuberance*, to put it in Bruce Bagemihl's terms, given his extraordinary book on animal homosexuality.[92] Darwin's observations and conclusions have opened up a world for us, and we have mostly succeeded in narrowing it down. Like Marx, Darwin affirmed the role of chance in evolution, and Gould is right to emphasize this element. Life is neither strict determinism nor total randomness; chance is the swerve, the indeterminacy amid interacting patterns, the chance for change that gives us a chance.

GENETICS AND EPIGENETICS

The modern synthesis of evolutionary theory is only possible via the merging of natural selection with genetics, with the gene as the unit of selection. The problem with genetics, however, despite the extraordinary accomplishments of molecular biology in the twentieth century, is the reductionist and determinist perspective on the gene. Before he became one of the "Four Horsemen" of contemporary atheism (along with Sam Harris, Christopher Hitchens, and Daniel Dennett), Richard Dawkins was celebrated as the courageous promoter of the selfish gene. According to Dawkins, "the fundamental unit of selection, and therefore self-interest, is not the species, nor the group, nor even, strictly, the individual. It is the gene, the unit of heredity."[93] The gene is a selfish replicator, but it is also blind.

In his follow-up book, *The Extended Phenotype*, Dawkins argues that we should consider all the effects of a gene on its environment, both inside and outside the organism. This extension amplifies the ability of genes to affect organisms and species, but it continues to restrict the unit of selection to the gene. And the gene is a simple replicator. As we have seen, Gould argues against this simplistic notion of replication. The goal of a "unit of selection is not unitary persistence (faithful replication).... The 'goal' of a unit of selection is concentration by plurifaction—that is, the differential passage of 'youness' into the next generation, an increase in relative representation of your heritable attributes."[94] The gene-based approach to evolution that Dawkins champions represents an uncompromising Darwinian fundamentalism, according to Gould.

Genes are units of replication, but they are not agents of selection. Dawkins and others who insist on an exclusively gene-based approach to evolution confuse bookkeeping with causality. Gould argues that "the causality of selection resides in interaction, not in replication."[95] Interaction takes place at multiple levels, and genes simply record the results of what occurs so that they can be passed along to later generations. Genes in themselves do not cause anything; they are units of storage of information and replication that are necessary for inheritance to happen. The overwhelming focus on genetics in evolutionary biology in the twentieth century is a result of an oversimplified reductionism and determinism. Although Gould does not talk specifically about the role of energy in biological evolution, his overview of evolutionary processes that work at multiple levels offers a much richer picture of how evolution happens than that of Dawkins.

If Dawkins is correct about selfish genes, then there is no point of having all the noncoding DNA that exists in our genomes. So-called junk DNA refers to noncoding DNA, or DNA that does not encode protein sequences. Most of the human genome consists of noncoding DNA, and it appears that the more complex an organism is the higher the percentage of noncoding DNA. According to Nessa Carey, only about 2 percent of our human genome codes for protein, and "the numbers of genes, or the sizes of these genes, don't scale for complexity. The only feature of a genome that really seems to get bigger as organisms get more complicated is the section that *doesn't* code for proteins."[96] There are many arguments about the usefulness of this noncoding DNA, and many speculations about its current and future utility, but if natural selection was purely genetic in Dawkins's terms, it would seem far from parsimonious for humans and other organisms to retain all of this noncoding DNA. Gould claims that these noncoding sequences "are nonadaptive spandrels with great exaptation to utility," but what if there are other possibilities?[97]

Gould fails to discuss epigenetics in his book, but epigenetics has become an important if somewhat contested topic in contemporary biology. According to Carey, "epigenetics can be defined as the set of modifications to our genetic material that changes the ways genes are switched on and off, but which don't alter the genes themselves."[98] Genetics concerns the sequences of DNA and RNA in a cell, and these are passed along to offspring during conception, but epigenetic changes concern how genes are activated or not. Epigenetic modifications exist beside or on top of the genetic code, which is why they carry the prefix *epi*, which means at, on, over, above, or beyond. Something is going on in addition to genetics that affects how the organism exists, even when the underlying DNA is unchanged.

In 1957, Conrad Waddington presented an image to explain what he called the epigenetic landscape. Basically, it is a curved space with a ball, and the idea is that the ball will roll down a hill to rest at its lowest point. The journey from a hill to a trough in the epigenetic landscape represents the development of cells from the highest point of a zygote, which is the fusion of one egg cell and one sperm cell as a result of conception. The single-celled zygote is totipotent, which means that it "has the potential to form every cell in the body, including the placenta."[99] As cell differentiation proceeds, it becomes fixed into a specific kind of cell, which represents the trough in Waddington's epigenetic landscape.

As cells develop into an organism, they lose their potency. Embryonic stem cells are not totipotent, because they cannot form a placenta, but they are considered to be pluripotent, because they can form just about any other cell. The pluripotency of embryonic stem cells is what makes them so valuable for researchers and doctors, because they can be stimulated to grow many different kinds of cells. Carey says that "differentiated cells are epigenetically modified in specific ways, at a molecular level," which is why they cease to become other kinds of cells. Scientists have developed ways to reprogram differentiated cells to become pluripotent cells. In these cases, "the differentiation-specific epigenetic signature must be removed so that the nucleus becomes more like that of a newly fertilized zygote."[100]

Epigenetic modification involves changing whether a gene is expressed, whether it is switched on or off. The activation of genes transforms the cell and leads to changes in the organism. One of the main kinds of epigenetic modification is DNA methylation. Methylation involves adding a methyl group onto a DNA strand, and this creates an epigenetic mark. The mark of the added methyl group is "stuck" onto the DNA "but doesn't actually alter the underlying genetic sequence." The methylation of DNA by adding a methyl group is a small change that "has profound effects on how genes are expressed, and ultimately on cellular, tissue and whole-body functions."[101] Ordinarily, the more methylation that occurs in a DNA strand, the less transcription that strand does, which means that DNA methylation switches genes off.

The other main kind of epigenetic modification is called acetylation, which involves modification of histones. Histones are a family of proteins that are positively charged, allowing negatively charged DNA strands to coil around them so they can fit within the nucleus and form chromosomes. Acetylation modifies histone proteins in cells, and this activity increases the expression of genes. So, in basic terms, acetylation turns genes on, while methylation switches them off. But the processes are not nearly so simple. Carey says that "gene expression is much more subtle than genes being on or off. Gene expression is rarely an on-off toggle switch; it's much more like the volume dial on a traditional radio."[102] Furthermore, there are many other histone modifications besides acetylation, and some of these increase the expression of genes, while other modifications depress it.

Genetic and epigenetic processes interact and work together in a cell to regulate the expression of genes. DNA methylation is a fairly stable epigenetic change that tends to remain in place once activated. Histone modifications, however, "are much more plastic than this. A specific modification can be put on a histone at a particular gene, removed and then later put back on again."[103] Why is this so important? Partly because it indicates the importance of the environment for an organism at the molecular level. Environmental changes stimulate the production of hormones that then generate epigenetic modifications. Hormones change the epigenetic pattern of specific genes. They do not change the sequence of the underlying gene, but they do change how the gene gets expressed. And these epigenetic changes may be inherited.

This is where epigenetics gets controversial, because we do not know exactly whether or how epigenetic changes get passed along to offspring. There are really interesting phenomena that provide evidence of "transgenerational inheritance," but it is not certain that this is due to epigenetic factors. However, if a mechanism "transmitted an environmentally-induced epigenetic modification from an individual to their offspring, we would have a mechanism for a sort of Lamarckian inheritance. An epigenetic (as opposed to genetic) change would be passed down from parent to child."[104] Towards the end of World War II, there was a severe cold spell and famine that stuck hardest in the Netherlands, and this is called the Dutch Hunger Winter. Many pregnant women were malnourished and passed along the effects to their offspring. The timing of malnourishment during the pregnancy affected the birth and subsequent weights of the children. A woman who was malnourished during the first trimester gave birth to a normal birth-weight baby, while a woman who was malnourished in her third trimester gave birth to a baby who was underweight. This connection is not controversial in any way. But researchers have followed the effects of this malnourishment on the *children's children*, that is, the grandchildren of the original pregnant women during the Dutch Hunger Winter.

Women whose mothers were malnourished during their first trimester gave birth to babies who were heavier than average, while women whose mothers were malnourished during their third trimester gave birth to babies with normal birth weight.[105] Something was transmitted from mother to child and daughter to grandchild that is not simply genetic. This inheritance may be a result of specifically epigenetic changes, but that is not conclusive. There is good reason to consider, however, that epigenetic modifications can be passed on to offspring in a quasi-Lamarckian manner.

Another important example that appears even more clearly epigenetic occurs in agouti mice. The agouti gene determines hair color in mice, and when it is switched on the hair is yellow, whereas when it is switched off as a result of DNA methylation the hair is black. Emma Whitelaw bred female agouti mice and discovered that the expression of the methylated gene affects the coat color of their offspring. These are genetically identical female mice, so the color is not the result of genetic variation or inheritance. Carey concludes that "the result from these experiments showed that an epigenetically-mediated effect (the DNA methylation-dependent coat pattern) in an animal was transmitted to its offspring."[106] Again, we have to be careful how far we extend this epigenetic effect, but it seems that it is real.

Energy, chemicals, hormones, and material protein processes transform the expression of genes. We know that genes mutate, but epigenetics concerns a more radical change that opens up a wider context of evolutionary agency. We need to think about evolution in a more complex way. In their book *Evolution in Four Dimensions*, Eva Jablonka and Marion J.

Lamb discuss genetic, epigenetic, behavioral, and symbolic processes of evolution. They acknowledge the tentativeness of some of the research on epigenetic inheritance, but affirm that "cells can transmit information to daughter cells through non-DNA (epigenetic) inheritance." This means that there is more to heredity than genes: "epigenetic, behavioral, and symbolic inheritance also provide variation on which natural selection can act."[107] The explication of distinct levels of evolutionary change is what biologists call hierarchy, which we also saw in Gould, and it is important to keep in mind that hierarchy does not have the same meaning in biology that it does in philosophy. In terms of philosophy, it might be good to think in terms of what Deleuze and Guattari call plateaus in *A Thousand Plateaus*, because a plateau is a distinct level that emerges from and interacts with other levels.

According to Jablonka and Lamb, "evolution can occur through the epigenetic dimension of heredity even if nothing is happening in the genetic dimension."[108] Further, they emphasize that epigenetic variation takes place much more quickly than genetic variation, so adaptation through selection of epigenetic variation can be much faster than adaptation in genetic terms. We need to modify our understanding of genetic evolution to account for the real possibility of epigenetic effects that take place over a shorter period of time compared to slow genetic variations. Jablonka and Lamb speculate that epigenetics may contribute to speciation, the evolution of new species. Generally, new species evolve when populations are isolation from each other, and, when they are separate, their populations change to such an extent that interbreeding is no longer possible if they were to meet up again. "It is usually assumed that the changes are genetic," they assert, "but we believe that they may often be epigenetic."[109] Epigenetic changes can affect the formation of viable hybrid embryos that results in a new species being created.

Behavioral and symbolic evolution is less striking, and much of their discussion follows from their claims about epigenetic evolution, but it is interesting to see how it proceeds. Behavioral inheritance systems function based on the transmission and acquisition of information. This information can be transmitted through imprinting or learning, but it is also transmitted via physical substances like the placenta, breast milk, and even in some cases feces. Jablonka and Lamb suggest that "information transmitted through observational learning is not essentially different from any other types of inheritance. All provide heritable variations which, through selective retention or elimination, may lead to evolutionary change."[110] Symbolic variation concerns cultural evolution, and many biologists and philosophers have speculated about the differences and continuity between natural and cultural evolution. For humans, language seems to be the key development that enables cultural evolution by means of symbolic variation.

Jablonka and Lamb argue that language has evolved through genes *and* cultural linguistic practices, and the point is not to reduce one to the other but to become more aware of how they interact. They claim that hypotheses of memes, introduced by Richard Dawkins in *The Selfish Gene*, or modules, as proposed in evolutionary psychology, are not sufficient to explain cultural evolution: "What is missing from both memetics and evolutionary psychology is development."[111] The focus on historical development allows Jablonka and Lamb to take into account the other elements of cultural evolution. It is not just the fidelity of transmission but the ability to fit into an existing society that decides what practices are continued. They claim that "what matters is not the fidelity of transmission, but the *functional adequacy* of any change in a cultural element. Usually a changed element must continue to play a role similar to that of the original one, and remain integrated with other aspects of the culture."[112] Recall that Gould stresses the importance of interactors over replicators in evolutionary transformation. According to Jablonka and Lamb, the four dimensions of evolution all *interact* in complex ways.

Jablonka and Lamb admit that the hard evidence for epigenetic inheritance systems is sparse, but they affirm their belief that these systems function in inheritance in Lamarckian ways. Furthermore, as have just seen, "genetic and epigenetic changes interact (such as increased methylation) leading to genetic changes (such as mutations in genes coding for chromatin proteins) leading to further epigenetic changes."[113] Evolution concerns how and why organisms change in a physical and biological way. These changes incorporate genetic mutations, but also epigenetic variations, behavioral transmission of information, and symbolic cultural development that all interact in complex ways.

How do we think about epigenetics in philosophical terms? In her philosophy, Malabou connects epigenetics to epigenesis. As we have already seen, Malabou understands change in terms of a plasticity that comprehends its functions as biological form. She claims that "plasticity is situated between two extremes: on the one side the sensible image of taking form (sculpture or plastic objects), and on the other side that of the annihilation of all form (explosion)."[114] Initially, Malabou focuses her work on the brain mainly on neuroplasticity, but more recently she has taken up the findings of epigenetics and epigenetic transformation.

In *Before Tomorrow*, Malabou offers a very complex interpretation of Kant. She rethinks Kant's notion of epigenesis as a way of responding to contemporary philosophical attempts to eliminate the transcendental from philosophy. Since Kant is associated with transcendentalism in philosophy, he is the object of critique by many recent philosophers, including Quentin Meillassoux. In *After Finitude*, Meillassoux argues that most post-Kantian philosophy is haunted by correlationism. Correlation means that any object that is known must be correlated with a knowing subject. Kant deduces the categories and conditions that determine knowledge of an object, but this produces a vicious circle whereby we cannot know anything about an object without knowing how it conforms to our processes of knowing. Part of the promise of newer philosophies of speculative realism and object-oriented ontology is that it frees us from the tyranny of subjectivism that is established by Kant.

In their opposition to correlationism, Meillassoux and others want to relinquish the transcendental. The transcendental concerns the conditions of possibility for knowing an object, whereas Meillassoux and other want to consider what it means to think from an object itself. For example, Meillassoux discusses what he calls the "arche-fossil" to name something anterior to every form of human relation to the world. This arche-fossil refers to "materials indicating the existence of an ancestral reality or event; one that is anterior to terrestrial life."[115] The point is not the trivial fact that things existed before conscious human beings evolved, but the epistemological complication that we have to think something anterior to any possible correlation. This situation of the arche-fossil complicates correlationism and challenges philosophical transcendentalism. Meillassoux tries to escape correlationism by affirming an absolute necessity of contingency that he grounds in mathematical set theory based on the work of Georg Cantor and Alain Badiou.[116]

Malabou accepts Meillassoux's challenge to the transcendental, but she then returns to Kant to reconfigure the transcendental in epigenetic terms. She focuses on Kant's use of the term *epigenesis* in the *Critique of Pure Reason*, where Kant affirms that the "*a priori* agreement between the categories and experience opens what amounts to 'as it were a system of the *epigenesis* of *pure* reason.'"[117] Kant uses the term *epigenesis* to describe the formation of the categories as a way to avoid the biological theory of preformationism, which suggests that the categories develop from a pre-given seed. Kant affirms an a priori element of epigenesis rather than simply an a posteriori one, and that is where Malabou intervenes. She wants to bring together Kantian epigenesis with contemporary epigenetics.

Malabou draws on contemporary findings in epigenetics that involve both cellular differentiation and evolutionary inheritance. She claims that "epigenetic mechanisms structure the self-differentiation of the living being."[118] Epigenetic expression involves a kind of interpretation of the genetic code, and Malabou provocatively suggests that the phenotypical event is an epigenetic version of the genetic program, citing the work of Jablonka and Lamb. In this way, epigenetics indicates "the opening of a hermeneutic dimension in the heart of the biological."[119] Most biologists and philosophers would consider epigenetics to be an a posteriori phenomenon, but Malabou wants to think epigenetics in a priori terms, which is paradoxical.

According to Malabou, Kant cannot resolve the contradictions of his usage of the term *epigenesis* in the *Critique of Pure Reason*, so she turns to the *Critique of Judgment*. In the Third Critique, Kant draws an analogy between the purposiveness of nature and the design of an artist. We tend to view this analogy simplistically as the attribution to design in nature in a teleological way that Darwin later destroyed, but Malabou suggests a much more complex reading. She argues that what animates the *Critique of Judgment*, and implicitly the *Critique of Pure Reason*, is the idea of *life*. Life is the outside that transforms the entire system of critique, the epigenesis of reason. That is, the transcendental evolves in time as it interacts with the living. Malabou says that "*the resolution of this heterogeneity between the transcendental and life is exactly that which, along with the categories and the objective reference, is also subject to epigenesis.*"[120] There is an epigenetic structure to our categories of thinking that evolve in their encounter with life, which leads to new expressions and manifestations of existence.

The transcendental is not outside of life; life is outside the transcendental in a way that draws it out of itself and *changes* it. Life is contingent, and thought is dependent on life, and they are not grounded in mathematical set theory in the way that Meillassoux suggests. What Kant calls the epigenesis of pure reason manifests epigenetically, in a way that allows Malabou to combine Kant with Darwin along the lines indicated by the *Critique of Judgment*, which she reads back into the *Critique of Pure Reason*. She argues for the validity of the transcendental as a way of taking into account the stability of a system as it undergoes transformation. "Ultimately," Malabou concludes, "my argument is that in Kantian philosophy, *the transcendental is that which ensures both the stability and the transformability of the whole.*"[121] The transcendental functions not as a static foundation, but "as a *passage* and *conductor* between invariance and modification."[122]

The transcendental understood as epigenesis is situated between the categories that make sense of experience and the ideas that Kant insists that we require to make sense of our own thinking. Epigenesis provides a new understanding of time, because it does not consist of a simple genesis, but a complex process of temporalization that brings together the natural and the ontological. Evolution names this process of epigenesis and epigenetic metamorphosis. According to Malabou, "the unique temporality of epigenesis places it 'above' or 'at the surface' of genesis and is instead the temporality of a synthetic continuum within which all the parts are presented together in a movement of growth whereby the whole is formed through self-differentiation."[123] Evolution gives us a way to think about time in epigenetic terms, beyond the modern Darwinian synthesis of genetics. Malabou reads Kant's Third Critique back into the First Critique and then forward into Darwin, as well as into contemporary epigenetics, to fashion a novel account of rationality that is in constant touch with the living.

WHAT MAKES US THINK?

In *Before Tomorrow*, Malabou affirms a neural Darwinism that brings Darwinian evolutionary biology into contemporary neurobiology. Malabou understands neurology in epigenetic terms. She claims that neural Darwinism is based on "the epigenesis of neural networks by selective stabilization of synapses."[124] Neuroepigenetics is still somewhat contested and controversial, mainly because we do not know exactly how DNA methylation works in neurons, or, more specifically, decreased DNA methylation.[125] Malabou wagers that tomorrow we will understand more deeply the epigenetic mechanisms of the brain, while before tomorrow, today, we need to think more adequately about the process of *epigenesis* in philosophical terms.

Why do we have a brain? Brains evolved due to the need to process the movement of animals. When organisms acquire the capacity to move—swim, walk, or fly—then the movement of these organisms demands a more complex bundle of nerve fibers that coalesces into a brain. This brain then becomes bigger and more complex. When animals can move around, they need to sense and signal in more intentional and multifaceted ways. They need to process and coordinate their own movements with those of others.

Animals evolved not only to eat plants, but to hunt and eat other animals. The brain as such seems to have emerged as a result of what is called the Cambrian explosion, the incredible proliferation of most types of living beings around five hundred million years ago. We do not know exactly what caused this explosion, but it seems to have involved the scaling up of multicellular life into larger and larger forms, as well as the escalation of a predator-prey arms race involving armor and teeth.

The first clumps of neurons that later develop into brain structures appear in flattened worms around six hundred million years ago, during the Ediacaran period. The Ediacaran preceded the Cambrian, and it was a much more peaceful geological era, without apparent predation. It was during the Ediacaran that processes of sensing and signaling emerged, both between and then within multicellular organisms. In most animals, the chemical interactions between cells that sense and signal "become the basis for a *nervous system*, small or large. And in some of these animals, a mass of such cells concentrated together, sparking a chemo-electrical storm of repurposed signaling, become a brain."[126] Neural structures evolve to process movement, but the brain as we know is a result of the Cambrian era. Peter Godfrey-Smith explains that "in the Cambrian, animals became part of each other's lives in a new way, especially through predation."[127] As animal behavior became more directed, it required the investment in complex internal processing, including an eye to see prey and avoid predation.

Brains as we know them evolve in animals as a way to process the complex representations of movement to allow for more efficient predation and avoidance. Predation drives evolutionary change along with environmental transformations. Life embarks on a high-stakes venture into larger and larger organisms. The largest are usually herbivores, but there are always large carnivores too, and the interaction between and among these species accelerates the process. We probably have a brain so that we can detect the movements of predators—and prey. As brains develop, they also take on and allow for more complex social roles within species.

The brain is incredibly important, but we need to be careful about simply equating the brain with awareness, intentionality, cognition, and consciousness. This equation is what Alfred North Whitehead calls the "fallacy of misplaced concreteness." Another danger with our emphasis on the brain as an organ involves the assumption of teleology—that nature evolves towards larger and more complex brains—and superiority—that animals like us with big brains are somehow better than other organisms. At the same time, we cannot ignore the fact that there is no awareness without a material basis; there is no consciousness that can exist without a physical body.

According to Margulis, bacteria invented consciousness. She claims that "the effects we recognize as sensitivity to light, sense of touch, hearing, smell and indeed our senses in general evolved from a property called 'bacterial consciousness.'"[128] The cells of the brain and nerve cells contain long, skinny tubules called neurotubules. Margulis thinks that these skinny tubules composed of nine pairs of tubes wrapped around a middle pair originated in swimming bacteria that were then acquired as symbionts by eukaryotic cells.[129] These specific tubular forms became nerve cells and neurons. Just as bacteria developed the process of photosynthesis that was then incorporated into plants, what we call brains originated in bacterial innovations, even if it is a stretch to call it consciousness at this level.

The development of a brain requires massive amounts of energy. According to Godfrey-Smith, "Neurons cost a great deal of energy to run and maintain. Creating their electrical spasms is like the continual charging and discharging of a battery, hundreds of times each second."[130] A large brain demands much more energy to fuel. In his book *Catching Fire*, Richard Wrangham claims that cooking food with fire allows humans to extract much more energy from it without having to digest it as fully, which shifts physiological resources from the digestive system to the brain. He says that there is a correlation between a large brains and small guts, and a small gut depends on a high-quality diet. He cites the work of Leslie Aiello and Peter Wheeler, who realized that "brains are exceptionally greedy for glucose—in other words, energy." Our brain makes up about 2.5 percent of our body weight, but uses 20 percent of our basic metabolism.[131]

To have a large brain, we have to have the ability to fuel it, and the only way to deliver extra energy to the brain is to offset it by a reduction of energy elsewhere. In primates, "the size of most organs is closely predicted by body weight because of inescapable physiological rules."[132] Humans are able to reduce the size of their gut and devote extra energy to their brains because they consume a higher-quality diet. This diet comes from the ability to cook food and break it down, making it easier to digest.

We know that our guts are incredibly important, and there is a vital connection between our gut and our brain. Our guts contain some four to six hundred neurons, leading to the term *gut brain*. The brain as nervous system is extended throughout the body, not neatly located within the skull. Furthermore, books like *I Contain Multitudes* demonstrate the significance of microbial bacteria within our bodies, most importantly our gut. We are not simply ourselves, because who we are is composed of multiple symbiotic species, as Margulis contends. Ed Yong argues that "every individual is more like an archipelago—a *chain* of islands"—than a distinct self or continent.[133] Our microbes shape our bodies; they shape all animal bodies, and this is a symbiotic process. Scientists have discovered that specific microbes induce animal development into adult maturity, like the microbe *V. fischeri* that transforms "the surface of a squid into a landscape that attracts more of its kind and deters competitors."[134] Evolution is also a negotiation among species, a kind of coevolution that fosters a deeper understanding and appreciation of coexistence.[135] An entire ecosystem unfolds within us as well as around us. Epigenetics is one of the ways that development and evolution works, and not only for *us*.

Malabou draws on the work of Jean-Pierre Changeux, Antonio Damasio, Joseph LeDoux, and other important neuroscientists to fashion her philosophy of neuroplasticity, most explicitly in *What Should We Do with Our Brain?* According to Changeux, learning involves "epigenetic selection" that "acts on preformed synaptic substrates. To learn is to stabilize preestablished synaptic combinations, and to *eliminate* the surplus."[136] Epigenetic selection involves filtering out too many potential combinations and too much potential information. Stabilizing a brain involves paring down the synaptic connections.

LeDoux argues that our synapses make us who we are. "Synaptic connections hold the self together most of the time," he concludes in *The Synaptic Self*.[137] Brains exhibit parallel processing rather than serial processing, which means that many different functions can be performed at the same time. The results of this parallel processing can then be reintegrated and, more important, *changed* as a result of the plasticity of the brain. This parallel plasticity marks human brains as extraordinary things. Our brain is bigger relative to our size compared to most other animals, and it has been reorganized as it has evolved and changed. Each of the major functions of the brain has evolved somewhat separately, but they have been integrated together. LeDoux says that this synchrony integrates plasticity across regions. Parallel systems are integrated in convergence zones that exhibit parallel plasticity.[138] These convergence zones exhibit self-assembly, or self-organization. Convergence first "takes place within systems before it takes place between systems."[139] The self consists of implicit and explicit aspects that overlap, but not completely. We are our brains, but not in a simple deterministic way, because our brains are plastic.

In *What Should We Do with Our Brain?*, as already discussed at the beginning of this chapter, Malabou engages with the findings of neuroplasticity and argues that we have to be careful not to allow them to conform to the ideology of contemporary capitalism. The plasticity of the brain is not a total malleability or flexibility. The findings of neurobiology can easily accord with the aspects of labor and corporate capitalism that focus on being flexible and accommodating to whatever economic situation occurs. Malabou calls this "*neuronal ideology*": we have shifted from the brain as a homunculus, and a top-down command center, but then the temptation is to see it as a distributed network that efficiently responds to whatever situation is imposed.[140] Malabou emphasizes the breaks, the gaps, and the resistance of synaptic plasticity, rather than the connections and convergences that LeDoux and Changeux highlight. She agrees with them that we are our synapses, but these should not be viewed solely in terms of connection. Plasticity involves resistance and resilience;

if we were totally flexible, "if we didn't destroy ourselves a bit, we could not live. Identity resists its own occurrence to the very extent that it forms it."[141] We are tempted to think about the synaptic plasticity of our brain in terms of homeostatic equilibrium, but it would be better to think about it as the ability to change the system, as "self-generation."

Malabou criticizes recent European philosophy for ignoring the biological and brain sciences, although the main exception here is the work of Deleuze. In his later work, including *What Is Philosophy?* and his two books on cinema, Deleuze does philosophize explicitly about the brain. He and Guattari claim that "it is the brain that thinks and not man—the latter being only a cerebral crystallization."[142] Here we should recall their distinction between the organs of the body and the body without organs from *A Thousand Plateaus*. Insofar as we think of the brain solely as an organ, no matter how important and complex, we miss what Deleuze and Guattari are saying about the brain. And I think that we also miss the significance of Malabou's philosophy too. The brain is plastic and the brain is synaptic, but it's not just the physical organ that is being discussed. The brain is extended; it is a body without organs insofar as it is a thing that thinks. The brain should not be opposed to the body. The brain is an extended material phenomenon, and it requires energy to fuel it. The brain involves a *metabolism*, because it is energy that creates form and allows for change. Brain is a physical manifestation and cause of thinking, but it cannot be reduced to the literal organ that rests within the skull because it refers to any and all neurological processes.

There is a profound epistemological confusion here. But it is not merely epistemological; it is also ontological. Once we are thinking in conscious language, which is necessary to read this sentence, we are tempted to think at least one of two things: either language is a transparent medium, through which we can designate objects, or language is its own phenomenon, divorced from ontological reality. Neither of these alternatives is true. Consciousness and language conceal as much as they reveal about reality, but that does not mean that ontological reality disappears. When we talk about the brain, we usually mean the organ within us that allows us to think. The brain is not the mind, but it gives rise to it. The problem becomes when we want to specify the brain precisely not only in our experimentation but in our language, because there is a paradoxical self-reference that is unavoidable. We usually cannot perceive our brains as objects, but most of us do not doubt that if our skull was opened up we would be able to see it. Well, not literally, but perhaps with the assistance of technology. My point is that we do not necessarily know what we talk about when we talk about the brain, not because we don't know what a brain is, and not only because we don't know what a brain can do, but because we cannot precisely demarcate what is thinking from what is not from the standpoint of our thinking.

Deleuze and Guattari say that "we will speak about the brain as Cézanne spoke of the landscape: man absent from, but completely within the brain."[143] This claim is literally nonsensical, but it gets at something important. They are attempting to shift how we conceive the brain, so that we can transform how we think about what it means to do philosophy. Is the human completely within the brain? Of course not, but that's not the point, as the reference to Paul Cézanne implies. Cézanne tries to do the impossible; he wants to paint the landscape without any humanity, but also to include the human being completely within the landscape. And to the extent he succeeded, he is considered a great artist and painter. How is a brain like a landscape or a horizon?

The brain is extended across the biosphere. Richard Dawkins is guilty of an overemphasis on genes as the agent of change, but his book *The Extended Phenotype* helps show how the phenotype of the organism extends into and affects the environment. I don't accept the neat division Dawkins makes between the genotype and the phenotype, but I do think it is helpful to think about the extended brain in the context of what he calls the extended phenotype. A main example would be the dam building of a beaver. The beaver's phenotype expresses the behavior of dam building, which affects the landscape. Does a beaver know that it is changing the nature of the river? Yes and no, or maybe that question does not make sense, depending on how we understand and define knowledge in this context. But it does have an effect, it does make a change.

We need to think about the brain more deeply and more broadly, beyond any simple application of neurological discoveries. We need to attend to such results, but that does not mean that we are limited by them. We want to think about the brain as an organ, and this is not wrong, but it is a limited perspective. In his books on cinema, as noted in chapter 1, Deleuze contrasts what he calls the movement-image with the time-image. I think that we usually conceive the brain from the perspective of movement. The brain is what makes us move, and it is the swift movement of neurological signals across channels and cells and synaptic gaps that generates thinking and action. We think because of the movement of electrical and chemical signals. But the brain is also a time-image. Deleuze takes from Henri Bergson the idea that we normally reduce time to space and spatial movement. Time is viewed as a kind of current or stream, something that flows from one point to another. But the time-image as it emerges in modern cinema gives us another view of time. And this time-image teaches us something deep and profound about what makes us think.

Peter Godfrey-Smith is a philosopher of biology who studies cephalopods. He argues that consciousness emerges as a result of the subjective experience of animals with nervous systems. Two pathways develop that are not symmetrical: one is the sense-to-motor, and the other is motor-to-sense. According to his hypothesis, "nervous systems originated twice," one as a response to light, which it uses "to control bodily rhythms and regulate hormones. Another nervous system evolves to control movement, initially just the movement of the mouth."[144] Eventually these two systems merge within the same organism to form a kind of loop. The first system, the sense-to-motor, is the more fundamental and more sensitive, but the other system of motor-to-sense is also incredibly important. Godfrey-Smith claims that the entanglement of the two systems within an animal produces a workspace that generates a white noise that later becomes what we call consciousness.[145]

On this view, consciousness is not restricted to the higher-order reflection of which humans are capable. The white noise produced by the interaction of these two loops becomes a workspace where thought or inner speech can take place. He takes an important term from the brain sciences to explain this process, that is, an *efference copy*. An efference copy is a mechanism that allows an organism to account for its own bodily movements as it acts. An efference mechanism lets you recognize something that moves in your environment without being distracted by the movement of your own eyes. Godfrey-Smith explains that "with an efference copy mechanism, as you decide to act, sending a 'command' of some sort to your muscles, you also send a faint *image* of the same command (a 'copy' of it, in a rough sense of the term) to that part of the brain that deals with visual input."[146] An efference copy is a kind of image that makes an internal subjective mark, which makes the phenomenon of memory possible. Memory is a kind of communication between a past and a present, or present and future self. An efference copy is not a literal representation but a way for the body to register the effects of its own movements as it moves.

I think that when Deleuze talks about images in his works on cinema, he is not simply referring to a literal representation. He is tracking the technical establishment of something like an efference copy in the history of film, a way to account for and work beyond the sensory-motor link between image and movement. This is another kind of image, a time-image that would not be reduced to movement, but directs action in a way similar to how Godfrey-Smith articulates the "motor-to-sense" pathway that loops into the "sense-to-motor" path. The second path is less obvious, and it is underdeveloped in relation to the first path, but it is what allows for anything to be or become thought. Deleuze is concerned in *Cinema 2* with how cinema can become thought, how it becomes a brain.

Something forces us to think, something that comes from outside us but affects us inside us. The shock forces us out of complacency and suggests to us that we are not yet thinking. This is a technical development, but our entire understanding of neurology is mediated by technical apparatuses. Something about the invention and distribution of modern cinema shocks us into thinking anew about how we think, and this reveals something about how our brain already works. The image is what Deleuze calls the time-image, and it is similar to what Godfrey-Smith calls an efference copy.

Deleuze argues that there is a convergence between how we think about cinema and how we think about the brain, because both show us how we think and also how we are not yet truly thinking. There is a similarity to the loop that Deleuze describes in noological cinema and the loop that Godfrey-Smith presents in brain evolution. Classically, we conceive of the brain as the intersection where integration of different sensations and association of similar phenomena coincide. But according to Deleuze, "scientific knowledge of the brain has evolved, and carried out a general rearrangement."[147] The organic processes of integration and differentiation give way to a more absolute disjunction of inside and outside that do not fit together. This provides "a topological cerebral space" that gives us "the co-presence of an inside deeper than any internal medium, and an outside more distant than any external medium."[148] At the same time, our assumptions about conceptual association run up against "cuts in the continuous network of the brain," microfissures that operate as mechanisms to send and receive messages of association.

According to Deleuze, the brain is an acentered system, because it is comprised of the two asymmetrical neural systems of motor-to-sense (sensation or integration) and sense-to-motor (action or association). And it is the loop that is constituted that forms the topological cerebral workspace where thought occurs. The time-image lies at the heart of the loop where sensation and action cross paths and purposes, underlying both of them. Memory for Deleuze is "no longer the faculty of having recollections; it is the membrane which, in the most varied ways . . . makes sheets of past and layers of reality correspond."[149] Memory is now understood as a membrane, a screen, or a fold that records the messages we send to ourselves from the absolute outside to the deepest inside and back. What makes us think? Bacteria, fungi, worms, cephalopods, primates, patterns, a web, a tree, an enemy, a lover, a book, a film, a cloud.

COGNITIVE CONSTRAINTS

Most of our thinking is unconscious; it takes place before or beyond the level of consciousness. Freud distinguished strongly between what he called preconscious and conscious processes, on the one hand, and unconscious ones, on the other: unconscious processes distinguished for Freud by their resistance to consciousness, which indicates some mechanism of repression. Whereas most scientists today reject Freud's model of thinking, they often affirm a "new" unconscious where many physical and mental processes occur outside the realm of consciousness, and if these processes do enter consciousness, they are not simply represented as they naturally are, but are distorted and reshaped in terms of consciousness.

According to N. Katherine Hayles, we need to pay more attention to nonconscious cognition. Nonconscious cognition works between basic material processes and higher-level conscious processes that constitute more intentional modes of awareness. Cognition is a better concept than information, because cognition includes and incorporates context. "Cognition," she writes, "*is a process that interprets information within contexts that connect it to a meaning.*[150] Nonconscious cognition allows Hayles to mediate between organic processes of thought and more technical ones, like computational processes and artificial intelligence. She extends the range of cognition beyond a narrow anthropocentric humanism toward other forms of life and nonlife. Here we can consider nonconscious cognitive assemblages that "function as *systems*, with well-defined interfaces and communication circuits between sensors, actuators, processor, storage media, and distribution networks, and which include human, biological, technical, and material components."[151]

Hayles helps us develop resources to expand our cognitive ecology to include animals, plants, and complex technical systems. We cannot simply ignore the fact that humanity and other forms of life are embedded in and intertwined with technology and technical objects. Bernard Stiegler's work on *Time and Technics* demonstrates the inextricability of human being with technical processes. In his later work, Stiegler emphasizes a broadly pharmacological perspective of technology, where technology is both the disease and the cure, the poison and the gift, at the same time.[152] To put it in terms of this book: all change comes with a cost, because there is no free lunch.

Hayles minimizes the significance of conscious awareness in favor of these technical and organic processes of nonconscious cognition. I broadly endorse her project and her work, and she does raise an important question about levels in her critique of new materialism. According to Hayles, "the framework of nonconscious cognition offers a useful corrective to new materialist theories and claims." New materialists make interesting observations and contributions, but they often confuse distinct levels and processes. Sometimes new materialism is so strongly influenced by Deleuze that it is more invested in applying his concepts and language than with actually describing reality in any useful way. Hayles also makes use of Deleuzean terms, but she is worried about the conflation of levels in new materialism.

For most new materialists, "the issue of level-specific dynamics gets short shrift in their discourses, as does the empirical fact that these levels are characterized by different modes of organization."[153] Yes, this is absolutely true, and it addresses the problem of hierarchy in biology, which means this differentiation of levels and contexts. Many theorists who are not trained in the technical sciences view hierarchy in moral terms as a value judgment for the levels that are generally represented as "higher." So there is some confusion, and most English-language scholars of theory lack the competence in scientific discourses and contexts that Hayles possesses. It is incredibly difficult not to overgeneralize, and to address issues and problems of interdisciplinary importance, as this book does, opens one up to all sorts of criticisms of confusion and oversimplification.

What we call energy works at multiple levels and in various ways, but it is impossible to call it energy if there is no consistency or continuity. To highlight the role of energy in physical, biological, political, economic, and even religious terms is to risk one-sidedness and the seduction of monocausality, to reduce everything to the role of energy. However, it is sometimes necessary to overemphasize something to draw attention to it.

Furthermore, the problem with distinguishing levels is that there appears to be no neat and clean separation between the levels that are so designated. Hayles appeals to empirical fact, and she is right to do so, but the epistemological issue is that certain assumptions must be made to group certain processes in terms of one level and other processes in terms of a different one. So to distinguish nonconscious cognition from material processes that do not cognize as well as conscious modes of awareness is extremely helpful, and her book shows us how and why. But the representation of this model as a pyramid creates the impression that these processes can be not only neatly separated but also arranged in an order with consciousness at the top.

We are conscious beings and we presume that our consciousness is the pinnacle of thought. We know that there are many things we do not know, but we often expect that we could potentially know anything and everything. We know that there are these levels, and we often assume that we know how to clearly tell the difference between one level and another. The stacking of levels hierarchically institutes a teleology whether explicit or implicit, because there is always something at the top, which is usually associated with the human being or sometimes God. The other danger of the emphasis on nonconscious cognition is that it threatens to swallow everything that is important about the other two levels, because conscious awareness is more of an add-on, and material processes themselves are simplified to the point that they cannot think. So I want to resonate with Hayles's thought, and her critique, but I also want to struggle with and against it.

It is extremely difficult to emphasize life as a phenomenon without overemphasizing and valorizing it, or under-emphasizing it to the point of failing to do justice to the significance of the living organism. Of course, there is no such thing as a living organism as such; only specific organisms that cognize, act, and reproduce in particular ways. We cannot avoid some type of generalization, at least in language. I don't think that Hayles's critique invalidates new materialism, but new materialists should engage with and learn from her work.

For me, thermodynamics understood in broad terms helps to understand the formation and persistence of structures and systems, including organic and inorganic ones. Thermodynamics is nonlinear and nonequilibrium, as discussed in chapter 1, although these terms are also easily misused and misunderstood. Thermodynamics must be understood in terms of energy, although it is not clear what happens to energy in the twentieth century as it is replaced as a fundamental scientific term by information. Energy is not just heat, and heat is less fundamental as the ground and name of what is called thermodynamics. Other gradients are equally significant.

Life is a (thermo-) dynamic process. Here it is it useful to distinguish different levels of thermodynamic process, to try to understand what makes living organisms so unique. I am not trying to reduce life to inorganic thermodynamics, but rather to expand our understanding of material dynamics to incorporate living processes as well as nonliving ones, including technical ones. According to Terrence Deacon, if we want to understand the phenomenon of life, we need to focus on thermodynamics and how it works on three different levels.

In his book *Incomplete Nature*, Deacon argues that consciousness is an absential cause, which means that it makes a difference precisely by not being a thing. Part of this difference involves the insight that consciousness is an ongoing process, and part of it involves thinking about life and mind as a constraint rather than something that is superadded onto inorganic material processes. When we consider thermodynamics, most people who are only casually acquainted with it think of the first level that Deacon explains, which he calls homeodynamics. Homeodynamics means a system that is relatively isolated and close to equilibrium. When such a system is perturbed, it quickly moves back to a stable, equilibrial state.

Some systems, however, exhibit what Deacon calls morphodynamic behavior. These states are what I called nonequilibrium thermodynamic systems in chapter 1. In the case of morphodynamics, which are mostly inorganic, entropy is maximized by adding another gradient to the process. That is, there are multiple gradients, and the system can increase overall entropy by constraining flow through it along one gradient while another or others help channel this flow. Morphodynamic processes constitute dissipative systems because these "processes maximize energy flow—that is, the dissipation of constraints—but as fast as entropy increase diffuses the introduced distributional asymmetry, external perturbation reestablishes it. The result is a constant throughput of energy and a constant rate of energy production."[154]

Morphodynamic systems are dissipative systems, and Deacon cites Prigogine, Swenson, and Schneider (each of whom I have discussed in chapter 1) in his analysis of these systems. They are not homeodynamic, because the maximization of entropy along multiple gradients produces forms that last as long as the energy flows through the system. Constraints are key, because without constraints the system would collapse into homeostasis. And the "redistribution of constraint into other dimensions of difference provides more ways for constraints to be eliminated as well," which is what entropy means.[155] These morphodynamic systems are emergent, in terms of the physics of complexity. But they are not autoproductive or self-directed.

Deacon says that life is fundamentally different, because life is goal-oriented or teleological. Living organisms constitute their own purpose and function to sustain their own forms as well as reproduce them. Living organisms develop teleological processes of self-repair and self-replication. These two functions combine in a way that constitutes another constraint, but a fundamentally different kind of constraint. According to Deacon, the third level of thermodynamics is teleodynamics, which are the self-directed, goal-oriented processes that characterize life and consciousness. He does simply not equate teleodynamic systems with life, but he says that living things are the only things we know that exhibit such teleodynamic processes. He tries to construct a stripped-down model of a teleodynamic system that he calls an autogen. An autogen is the basic form of teleodynamism, and it is possibly the simplest form of life, although Deacon does not go so far as to assert this with any certainty.

In autogenesis, the two functions of self-repair and self-reproduction are combined; they interact and *constrain* each other, forcing energy to become more concentrated and entropy to become more focused. Here the key notion is not energy as such, which is too broad for Deacon, but work. Work is the way that energy gets ratcheted together and productively deployed for the autogen. Each of these dynamic processes are overlaid onto the other, but their interaction in the way of producing and reproducing constraints makes an important difference. Life is a material process, but it is one where morphodynamic and teleodynamic processes occur and interact so as to perpetuate the form that is produced. Morphodynamic processes maximize entropy to generate forms, but this speeds up the dissipative process. Teleodynamic processes act as constraints in a different way, to slow the dissipation down. They cannot stop it, and entropy has to increase, but there is a delay that is exploited for life and later for mind.

The constraints that differentiate morphodynamic systems and maximize entropy production here become complementary and in a way undermine the maximization of entropy production. The "progression toward optimal entropy production rate is also toward a state where dynamical change ceases. Regularity is built up, only to be frozen by closure."[156] This temporary freezing allows the processes to be controlled and directed in the direction of self-assembly, self-maintenance, and self-repair. This same constraint allows for self-replication, which works against the processes of self-regulation, but in a way that perpetuates the species, not the individual organism. It is a trade-off, and this interaction generates what we call natural selection, and for Deacon natural selection is an emergent law that develops out of teleodynamic autogenesis.

Work is for someone or something, and living organisms are purposeful; they exist for themselves and for their offspring. Work occurs by the ratcheting together of dynamic constraints, such that energy flow goes one way, which works against the maximization of energy and wards off dissipation. The ratchet effect "conserves constraint at the cost of stopping entropy generation prematurely," which is "the secret to life's tendency to preserve information about past adaptive organization."[157] A ratchet occurs when one gear is aligned with another mechanism so that the assembly can only rotate one way. This means that if the assembly is subjected to random forces or perturbations, the ones that work against the directionality of the gear are resisted, while those that go in the preferred direction turn the gear. Deacon calls this a *negentropy ratchet*, but I think it is better to avoid the term *negentropy*, since technically there is no such thing. What is accomplished is a kind of deferral of the dissipation of entropy, and this is only temporary, because no organism or species can live forever. Every ratchet or gear breaks down.

In his book, Deacon pays much less attention to the emergence of consciousness from life, but he argues that this must also be the result of teleodynamic processes of constraint. So the most important difference, or level, for Deacon is between the inorganic dissipative processes and the organic teleological ones. Again, the differentiation into levels is important and helpful heuristically and technically, but epistemologically it perpetuates a certain naivete. What difference makes a difference depends on a reference frame or a point of view. We tend to overemphasize the goal-directed teleological processes over the seemingly automatic or less purposeful ones, because we prefer our own framework and our own being and our own consciousness and our own language. We need this distinction of levels, but we should be careful not to reify them. I think that what Deacon calls teleodynamic processes are a special kind of morphodynamic process, while what he calls work is a special case of energy transformation and direction. We cannot prevent dissipation and entropy maximization, only temporarily slow it down. Eventually we cannot stave off dissolution, but we can delay it for a while.

In *Before Tomorrow*, which I discussed earlier, Malabou returns to Kant to reconfigure the transcendental in biological terms. She says that her argument is "that in Kantian philosophy, *the transcendental is that which ensures both the stability and the transformability of the whole*" in biological terms.[158] The transcendental is not an additional object or phenomenon; it is a *constraint*. In Deacon's book, this constraint functions teleodynamically and works as an "absential cause." I am less invested in the strong distinction that both Deacon and Malabou make between living and nonliving processes; I am more intrigued by the possibility that what we call the transcendental is really an absent cause, because it functions as a constraint, not a thing.

We fall into confusion and error when we take the transcendental for something, but the simple elimination of what is called the transcendental is impossible, because of how it *works*. The transcendental refers to the absent cause, the fundamental constraint that makes life something and at another level makes thinking possible. These complex processes cannot be explained or understood in additive terms, as if we take a material inorganic object and then *add* life onto it. Then we have a living thing and we *add* consciousness. No, they are both the result of dynamic constraints that delay the dissipation of form and the maximization of entropy for a little while. Life is something less than nonlife, because it amplifies *its own* constraints to pause the dissolution that brings it into existence.

We can explain life, mind, and consciousness in material terms. We may not be able to exhaustively explain or reproduce life from nonlife, but that does not mean that it is something nonmaterial. Life emerges out of the constraints of thermodynamics. The progress of evolution in generating more complex forms of life is also a result of a deferral and delay. According to Gould, what really characterizes the difference of human beings in relation to other species is neoteny. The theory of that delay the dissipation of form and the maximization of entropy for a litt evolution as recapitulation emerged in the nineteenth century, with its slogan coined by Ernst Haeckel: "ontogeny recapitulates phylogeny." But this is false, because in fact any "advance" is due to a retardation, a slowing down. "Neotenic characters are *retarded* since juvenile features of ancestors are delayed to appear in adult stages of descendants."[159] Humans have a longer gestation and are born prematurely compared to other animals, including other primates, and take much longer to develop. Adulthood is postponed, which gives more time for *learning*. But life in general is also a kind of retardation that postpones the dissipation of energy and the dissolution of structure. What we call the transcendental in philosophy refers to the condition that works to constrain, ratchet, and channel energy in directional terms. This accounts for all kinds of dynamic self-organized systems, including living ones, conscious ones, and complex social systems.

Life is not the only form of change, but it does constitute an important difference. As Jeffrey W. Robbins put it, in the context of Malabou's philosophy, all differences are "real, biological, and material," but this "need not imply that we are stuck in or with these differences, captive to this history, with an endless perpetuation of the same. Because just as change comes before difference, change never stops. It is without beginning or end, a metabolic ontology that just might be the basis of a new and different liberationist thinking."[160] Materiality is dynamic plasticity, and this means that, while we must recognize distinct levels, we cannot cordon them off from each other, as existence exhibits a form of self-similarity.

Life is not an exception to the second law of thermodynamics; it is a consequence of it. One of the most intriguing fields of study in the twenty-first century is quantum thermodynamics. As I discussed at the end of chapter 1, quantum physics can be correlated with thermodynamics in important and compelling ways. An experiment conducted by Tiago Batalhão and his colleagues confirms that thermodynamic processes are irreversible in a quantum system. They measured entropy change caused by an oscillating magnetic field applied to Carbon-13 atoms. When perturbed, their spins did not return to equilibrium; they remained out of equilibrium. According to an article published in 2015, "The measurements of the spins indicated that entropy was increasing in the isolated system, showing that the quantum thermodynamic process was irreversible."[161] The entanglement of quantum particles occurs in a thermodynamic manner; it has a history.

A physics professor at MIT, Jeremy England, has developed a mathematical formula that he claims can explain the emergence of life. According to a story in *Quanta Magazine*, "The formula, based on established physics, indicates that when a group of atoms is driven by an external source of energy (like the sun or chemical fuel) and surrounded by a heat bath (like the ocean or atmosphere), it will often gradually restructure itself in order to dissipate increasingly more energy."[162] This is what Schneider and others call nonequilibrium thermodynamics and what Deacon calls morphodynamics. The point is that entropy always increases, but in open systems this increase can accomplish the formation of complex structures, including living ones. At the lowest level of atomic phenomena, there is a way to capture and direct the flow of energy that occurs spontaneously.

As physicists Chris Jarzynski and Gavin Crooks showed in the late 1990s, "the entropy produced by a thermodynamic process, such as the cooling of a cup of coffee, corresponds to a simple ratio: the probability that the atoms will undergo that process divided by their probability of undergoing the reverse process (that is, spontaneously interacting in such a way that the coffee warms up). As entropy production increases, so does this ratio: A system's behavior becomes more and more 'irreversible.'"[163] Take a random system based on probability: any given change is random, but the multiplication of changes take on an irreversibility or directionality. This means that these dynamic systems are already teleodynamic in Deacon's terms, because they naturally acquire constraints. There is something in nature that constrains the way that processes work, and we call this entropy. Entropy is often correlated with the information we possess about a system, but it should be more correctly understood as the result of interacting constraints that scale from the smallest to the largest levels. As systems evolve over time, they increase their irreversibility, which means both their entropy *and* their complexity, so long as they are subjected to flows of energy.

The *Quanta* article "A New Physics Theory of Life" states that "particles tend to dissipate more energy when they resonate with a driving force, or move in the direction it is pushing them, and they are more likely to move in that direction than any other at any given moment."[164] This directionality is what Deacon is trying to get at in his discussion, but the mechanism of teleodynamic processes, with its interlocking constraints and ratcheting effect, *already takes place already at the level of physics and even quantum thermodynamic processes*. England's work is still being evaluated, but it is an intriguing hypothesis. The self-replication and self-maintenance that characterizes life is a special kind of dissipation that occurs along already established lines of energy dissipation and entropy production. Life is a special kind of inorganic system that makes use of thermodynamics to increase entropy dissipation and delay entropic dissolution.

As Elizabeth Grosz puts it in her book *Becoming Undone*, life is vital because "it cleaves to materiality, because all of life has a common interest both in mimicking and harnessing materiality, and in seeking those sites of material indetermination which it can exploit to 'invent' new forms and new practices, to evolve and become other."[165] Life redoubles or enfolds material processes themselves, and this repetition is a repetition of difference that participates in and prolongs the ongoing change occurring through energy transformation. Life extends before and beyond living organisms, and bioenergetics, quantum thermodynamics, and nonequilibrium processes help us better understand what it means to live. "We need to reconceptualize the real as forces, energies, impacts that preexist and function both before and beyond, as well as within, representation," Grosz claims.[166]

Biological natural selection is one kind of change, and it is incredibly important, but it is not the only one. As humans become more sedentary and form more complex societies, a kind of social or cultural selection takes place on top of biological natural selection. It takes place at a much faster speed, even as natural selection has speeded up over the time-scales of geological eras. The acceleration of the rate of change is also a result of entropy, including the ratcheting effect that Deacon identifies. While the locking in of a process gives more efficiency, unfortunately it can also cut off alternative avenues for change.

Human technological civilization is the result of the exploitation of energy gradients in more and more effective and efficient ways; however, we are reaching planetary limits. What we call human culture, society, and civilization concerns the exploitation and management of vital natural resources, including energy, for the purpose of work. The production of excess available energy allows for the sedimentation and stratification of people in place, along with the domestication of plants and animals to supplement our labor. We create an economy that never ceases to be an ecology that serves to organize and maintain these systems of production and exchange. The interaction of political economy and political ecology in human society is the focus of the next chapter.

3

POLITICAL ECONOMY AND POLITICAL ECOLOGY

Energy, General Economy, and Exchange

LEARNING HOW TO DIE

In 399 BCE, in Athens, the death of Socrates serves to define the birth of Western philosophy. Plato, the devoted student of Socrates, writes the story, most explicitly in his dialogue *Phaedo*. According to Plato, philosophy is the profession of training to die. The philosopher strives to "live in a state as close as possible to death" and should welcome it when it arrives.[1] Plato has Socrates argue that the body lives and dies, decays and perishes, but there is another part of the person that does not perish.

The soul is immortal, it cannot die. "If what is un-dying is also imperishable," declares Socrates, "it is impossible that at the approach of death soul should cease to be."[2] Philosophy is the care of the soul, which must survive the death of the body. At the end of the dialogue, the last words of Socrates are recorded as: "Crito, we ought to offer a cock to Asclepius. See to it, and don't forget."[3] Asclepius is the Greek god of healing, and the call of Socrates to sacrifice a cock to Asclepius means that he is celebrating the fact that he is being healed of life.

Much of philosophy and religion, indeed much of human civilization, involves the search for what is undying. However, in the contemporary world the idea of an eternal soul is less credible than in previous eras, at least for educated intellectuals. What if death is the perishing of everything? Then the significance of life is this very mortality, what Heidegger calls "being-toward-death." For the Heidegger of *Being and Time*, it is the individual Dasein who confronts death in a relation of authentic responsibility. This individualism characterizes modern existentialism. However, in the Anthropocene we are confronted with death on a much larger scale, including the real possibility of human extinction.

According to the *Encyclopedia of Earth*,

> The Anthropocene defines Earth's most recent geologic time period (Anthropocene) as being human-influenced, or anthropogenic, based on overwhelming global evidence that atmospheric, geologic, hydrologic, biospheric and other earth system processes are now altered by humans. The word combines the root "anthropo," meaning "human" with the root "-cene," the standard suffix for "epoch" in geologic time. The Anthropocene is distinguished as a new period either after or within the Holocene, the current epoch, which began approximately 10,000 years ago (about 8000 B.C.) with the end of the last glacial period.[4]

The name *Anthropocene* was coined by Paul Crutzen in 2000, and it has become more and more accepted as a viable term for a new geological era. The International Commission on Stratigraphy (ICS) established an "Anthropocene working group" in 2009 to consider whether the new epoch should be officially recognized in geological terms, and this discussion is ongoing as of 2020.

Even if scientists eventually agree on the existence of the Anthropocene, they still disagree on when it began. They are arguing over a "golden spike" in stratigraphic terms, where rock formations show an abrupt discontinuity in the geological record of Earth's surface. The most commonly proposed beginnings are the Industrial Revolution in the early 1800s, or the nuclear age and the Great Acceleration that began in the 1940s or around 1950, although some scholars and environmentalists claim that it should be placed early as the dawn of human civilization, about six thousand year ago, or around 1492, as a result of the encounter between Europeans and the American hemisphere.[5]

Whenever it begins, the Anthropocene would succeed the Holocene era, which we are still living in according to the ICS. The Holocene started around twelve thousand years ago, after the end of the last major glacial period, and it has been marked by an extraordinarily stable climate that contributed to the emergence of human agriculture and civilization. This stable climate is currently unraveling because of the effects of human beings and their technological impact on the planet.

According to Roy Scranton, the Anthropocene marks the most explicitly philosophical era of humanity, because philosophy traditionally means learning how to die. He says that "the rub now is that we have to learn to die not as individuals, but as a civilization."[6] Our greatest challenge now is not technical but philosophical: we have to comprehend the fact that our "civilization is already dead."[7] Why is our civilization dead? Because it is unsustainable. Our civilization is based on growth, and an ecological perspective means that there are real physical limits to growth. This planet has a finite amount of natural resources available to humans, including fresh water, fossil fuels, arable land, and rare earth minerals. It is impossible to have indefinite growth given a finite resource base. The global population is approximately 7.5 billion and rising, and if we wanted each human being to live at same the material level as the average American, we would need the material resources of about five planets. We only have one. We are in an overshoot situation. As Scranton explains, "everybody already knows" what's going on. "The problem is that the problem is too big," and it is impossible to change.[8]

We are living in the middle of what Elizabeth Kolbert calls the "sixth extinction," the sixth mass extinction event in the history of our planet.[9] According to the Center for Biological Diversity, "scientists estimate we're now losing species at up to 1,000 times the background rate, with literally dozens going extinct every day."[10] The difference between this mass extinction event and previous ones is that most of these extinctions are caused by human activities. The sheer scope of mass death and species extinction is staggering. We are the death-doers and, at the same time, as Scranton says, "We are the dead. They have become us." The dead are a part of us, even as we anticipate the death of our selves, our civilization, and even our species.[11]

How did we get here? According to Scranton, "the key is energy: energy production and social energetics." Human civilization is structured around labor, domestication of fire, animals and plants, and the exploitation of energy sources like water, wind, coal, gas, oil, and nuclear fission. We have had three major revolutions in "the political structures of energy production in the past 200,000 years: the Agricultural Revolution, the

Industrial Revolution, and the Great Acceleration."[12] Each of these revolutions harnesses a new source of fuel and new technologies that provides excess energy for an increasingly complex human society. The problem with energy exploitation is entropy; the tendency for usable work to decline and deteriorate over time.

Our unimaginable growth and material wealth comes at a cost, which is ecological. One way to situate our planetary condition of being-unto-death is to think about ecological practice as a form of hospice.[13] We are providing terminal care for end-of-life individuals, species, and ecosystems as the planet shifts into a new environment. This ecological situation spells the collapse of our current economic system. One of the sharpest debates around environmentalism and ecology concerns the question of capitalism. The question is to what extent capitalism is specifically responsible for the climate crisis as opposed to the activities of human being more broadly.

Here we could consider those scholars and scientists who think about the Anthropocene in the context of the first revolution Scranton points out: the development of agriculture and the dawn of human civilization. This periodization assigns blame more widely to human societies as such, at least once we became settled and sedentary and set up cities, states, and empires. The other side, which is more influenced by Marx, assigns specific cause and blame to the rise of industrial capitalism. This is sometimes called the Capitalocene, even though that is a very awkward word.

Jason W. Moore argues that Capitalocene does not refer to capitalism simply as a political and economic system, but rather "the Capitalocene signifies capitalism as a way of organizing nature—as a multispecies, situated, capitalist world-ecology."[14] Part of the problem here is that capitalism has always been a way of organizing nature, not just human social and economic relations. So there is no such thing as capitalism that is not part of what Moore calls the Capitalocene. The word *Anthropocene* seems to have caught on in a way that the word *Capitalocene* is unlikely to do. Beyond the nomenclature, however, it raises an important issue that is critical to how we understand and grapple with our precarious situation on the planet.

One proposed date for the start of the Anthropocene is with the Industrial Revolution. The Industrial Revolution in the early 1800s marks the deployment of the steam engine as well as the transition from an economy based on animal power, water, and wind to a fossil fuel economy. The Industrial Revolution begins in Great Britain and is fueled by coal, whereas the shift to oil takes place later in the nineteenth century along with the invention of the internal combustion engine. The transition to the extraction and burning of enormous amounts of stored energy in the form of oil, coal, and gas signifies what Marx calls a "metabolic rift" in the history of the planet, as noted in the introduction. Furthermore, the invention of the steam engine eventually leads to the development of thermodynamics and energy science, as we saw in chapter 1.

As human societies have become more complex, they become more and more specialized, stratified, and hierarchical. The elites are the ones who take responsibility and power over decisions that affect the whole society, and eventually the entire planet. The rift that European capitalism opens up is the most significant and irreversible rift to have been generated between humanity and nature, but that does not mean there have not been others. Metabolism works by means of rifts, that is, by setting up gradients and maintaining them so that the energy available can be maximized.

In some ways, it is an academic question of whether capitalism is to blame for our present ecological crisis, or whether it is human nature to occupy whatever niche is possible and to overshoot and desperately search for other environments when they are full. It's not an either/or question. We need to understand the historical and the current conditions that shape our social, political, economic, and ecological reality, but it is not really helpful to isolate any one cause, even if that one cause—capitalism—is the clear and present danger right now.

According to Naomi Klein, our current situation is one of irreducible conflict: "our economic system and our planetary system are now at war."[15] Whatever we call our current economic system—capitalism, savage or disaster capitalism, neoliberalism, neocolonialism—is less important than recognizing the nature and stakes of the conflict. Klein calls for "a massive mobilization larger than any in history. We need a Marshall Plan for the Earth."[16] This is absolutely necessary, even if there is no realistic way to conceive of such a plan happening. Or succeeding.

What is unique about our current situation, Klein says, is that it is not our activists and revolutionaries who are the most urgent voices right now. It is the science itself and the scientists who are grappling with it that are calling for humans to revolt against our current economic and political system. In her article "How Science Is Telling Us to Revolt," she says that there are "a small but increasingly influential group of scientists whose research into the destabilization of natural systems—particularly the climate system—is leading them to similarly transformative, even revolutionary, conclusions."[17]

Insofar as we are alive, we have to hope that what we do makes a difference. We want to argue that there is still time, even if there is not, and we need to give people reasons to resist, revolt, rise up, and dismantle capitalism to make possible a newly sustainable relationship with the planet. This is not impossible, but as Klein argues, *"This Changes Everything."* Everything must change. And it will, but will it be soon enough? Or will it be too late? And perhaps things will change for the worse—or even the worst. We do not and cannot know the future; we can only see how things appear to be playing out, and for the climate things do not seem to be going well unless we simply deny what is happening.

I trying to think in new ways about energy. New ways and new energies might be transformative, at least in the short run. Or they might not. And entropy might be the end, but it also might be the beginning, if not of us as us, at least of something else. In this chapter I draw together some strands of energy and entropy that were developed in chapter 1 to reframe our understandings of political economy and political ecology. To do this, we need to follow Georges Bataille and shift our perspective from a particular to a *general* economy. And, while we keep in mind issues of energy and entropy, we need to focus specifically on the concept of *exchange*.

ENERGY, ECONOMICS, AND FOSSIL-FUELED CAPITALISM

European economics emerges at a certain time and place in the context of colonialism and mercantilism. The early 1600s witness the formation of the first conglomerate joint stock companies in the form of the British East India Company and the Dutch East India Company, as well as the first major stock exchange in Amsterdam in the early 1600s. The classical discourse of economics is called political economy because it combines the disciplines of politics and economics, where emergent nation-states manage their land, their labor, their trade, and attempt to maximize their financial wealth. This economic discipline is not just domestic but occurs in the context of European colonialism, where the management of the affairs of a nation incorporates overseas territories. The word *economics* comes from the Greek *oikomenos*, which is the management of the *oikos*, the household, even if the household is generalized to a whole community, city, or nation. In the eighteenth century, the term *political economy* was used to refer specifically to how the statesman or political ruler "could best manage the affairs of the state so that the wants of the citizen could be met."[18]

Our modern word economics comes into existence when the economy is seen as a separate institution from other elements of a society. Political economy originates when it is possible to view politics and economics as distinct, though relatable, spheres. Classical economics and political economy are fundamentally based on the idea of a quasi-independent, self-regulating market.[19] In the context of political economy, the economy and the market must still be overseen by the nation-state for the harmony and wealth of the entire nation. These European nation-states compete with each other in economic, colonial, and military terms, with Great Britain becoming the most powerful nation and empire in the world in the nineteenth century.

Classical political economists include François Quesnay, Adam Smith, Robert Malthus, David Ricardo, Jean-Baptiste Say, and Karl Marx. They theorize the newly emerging markets and the role and nature of the economy as a distinct realm of human activity in the eighteenth and nineteenth centuries. Toward the end of the nineteenth century, political economy gives way to the contemporary discipline of economics as such, based on mathematical modeling of these self-regulating markets. Neoclassical economics in the twentieth century views the economy and the market as more distinct and separate from the political decisions of nation-states, although, of course, they are still subject to their policies. The key point, however, is the assumption that the economy should be managed by technical experts rather than wielded primarily by politicians.

Neoclassical economics dominates the economic thinking of the twentieth century, although it works mainly by means of abstractions. It abstracts the market from the rest of society and imagines that markets function smoothly and efficiently on their own terms to maximize wealth for the nation or people as a whole. Although classical economics retained marks of the connections of markets to nations, politics, peoples, and the context of colonial possessions, neoclassical economics strives to eliminate as many of these factors as possible. Wealth is measured solely in financial terms, and general growth is presupposed as a given, largely based on creative technological innovations. External costs, including the effects on the environment, are discarded. Economics loses sight of the world in which it is situated, which includes social, material, and ecological contexts. Ironically, modern economics is based on a conception of energy, but it loses sight of this connection during the transition from classical to neoclassical economics. Ideas about energy and work saturate the Industrial Revolution, but we should not view energy in narrow terms, because it incorporates all of our social and natural relations on the planet.

In his book *Fossil Capital*, Andreas Malm shows how the invention of the steam engine and the transition of Great Britain and then other parts of the world to a machine-based fossil fuel economy was a complex transformation, driven by a number of diverse factors. First of all, we can locate the origin of the fossil economy in Britain. Malm states that "Britain accounted for 80 percent of global emissions of CO_2 from fossil fuel combustion in 1825 and 62 percent in 1850."[20] Malm traces the development of the fossil economy, and the transition from water to coal as a natural resource, in the context of labor relations in the nineteenth century. He claims that the steam engine was not obviously more efficient and productive; it more importantly made it easier for capitalists to maximize control of labor. We cannot just focus on the natural and physical side of the process. We must consider how the fossil fuel economy is also "a materialization of social relations."[21] Human labor is the point of contact between the natural and the social.

Economic power is not simply about the power of physical energy; it is the way that human labor is organized to produce and distribute goods and products for profit. Capitalism emerges in the context of European colonialism and the seizing of "natural" resources from indigenous and non-European peoples. These human societies and their resources as viewed simply as natural resources to be exploited. Labor is stolen not only from the urban proletariat in Europe but from the natives in the colonies through enslavement, impoverishment, economic exploitation, and theft.

In the 1800s, as a result of the Industrial Revolution, the science of energy emerges in the form of classical thermodynamics. Thermodynamics, as already discussed in chapter 1, arises from the development of steam engines and the attempt to make them work as productively and efficiently as possible. In *The Birth of Energy*, Cara New Daggett shows how energy gets essentially correlated with work in the nineteenth century, and this is both an economic and a political process. "Energy does not travel across history, a unit free of context," she writes, "but rather arose at the moment when a handful of deep historical things collided: fossil fuels, steam engines, global capitalism, human terraforming, the slave trade, climate systems, empires."[22]

This constellation of political and economic phenomena produces the science of energy in the form of thermodynamics, which is not a value-free form of knowledge. The scientific concept of energy that arose in nineteenth-century thermodynamics is tied to these historical events, and energy as such is not a timeless unit free of context. However, that does not mean no other frameworks and means in which to think about and conceptualize energy exist. Daggett herself claims that "a genealogy of energy suggests that there are other ways of knowing and living energy, and that energy and work can be decoupled."[23] In chapter 1, I contextualized a philosophical and scientific understanding of energy that relativizes the centrality of thermodynamics and therefore the goal of productive *work*.

In *Fossil Capital*, Malm is working against the assumption that energy resources are adopted and utilized primarily from the standpoint of scarcity. It's not that the steam engine was necessarily more productive than the waterwheel, at least in the early 1800s. There was no shortage of water available to fuel textile and other industries. He argues that "steam had the prime advantage of overcoming the barriers to procurement not of energy, but of *labour*. The engine was a superior medium of extracting surplus wealth from the working class, because, unlike the waterwheel, it could be put up practically anywhere."[24] Water could not be picked up and moved anywhere where there is no water, which gave workers some control over their labor in terms of a water-based economy. The earliest cotton mills in Britain were built around sources of water, but during the development of the Industrial Revolution these waterwheels were replaced by steam engines, with the resulting development of factories, which could be built anywhere.

Malm, along with Daggett, complicates the traditional story of how new energy sources and transitions occur. They are not simply due to physical scarcity, but involve larger economic issues. Once the Industrial Revolution was complete, and the coal-powered steam engine instantiated the fossil economy, workers found new ways to resist. Timothy Mitchell argues that the transition from coal to oil is also connected to capitalist desires to control and limit the power of labor. In *Carbon Democracy*, Mitchell explains that with coal, "great volumes of energy flowed along narrow, purpose-built channels" that could be disrupted by workers. In fact, coal miners "played a leading role in contesting work regimes and the private powers of employers in the labour activism and political mobilization of the 1880s and onward."[25] Oil pipelines required a smaller workforce that could be more easily controlled.

Oil proved more powerful than coal, but it also required both a mechanism—the internal combustion engine—and a financial economy that was largely put in place toward the end of World War II. The problem at the beginning of the oil economy was not scarcity, but rather the opposite. In the 1860s, John D. Rockefeller built a monopoly based on the refinement and transportation of oil in the form of Standard Oil. Once oil was discovered in large wells outside the United States (and USSR), oil companies "collaborated to divide the world's resources between themselves, and to limit production to maintain prices."[26] There is a complex chaotic link between energy, economy, politics, and the organization of society around all of these issues, but energy remains at the center.

Energy is not simply the reduction to natural resources but also is exhibited in the control, production, limiting, pricing, and destruction of these resources. Energy in a broadened sense runs like a red thread through the history of human technological civilization, including the fossil economy of the past two centuries. Even if scarcity was not the primary factor in the adoption of these key fossil fuels, there remains the situation of a certain phenomenon of scarcity on a global scale at the present. Mitchell says that "the ecosystem appears to be approaching two limits simultaneously: an end to the easy availability of fossil fuel . . . and the loss of the ability to regulate global temperatures within the range that allowed human sociality itself to develop."[27] These two factors are interlinked and cannot simply be separated.

The excess surplus of human, animal, and material resources provides the *capital* to produce human societies. This energy gradient was intensified following the tragic encounter of Europe and the Americas, because the European nation-states were able to steal land, money, raw materials, and wealth to fuel the rise of the modern world system. The enormous surplus that entered Spain, and later the Netherlands, England, and France, propelled these nations to the role of masters of the world stage, a new era of exploitation and domination. A profound need for human labor created by the destruction of indigenous American populations led to the African slave trade, and this excess labor then generated the ability to create and establish mercantilism and capitalism.[28]

The current question, however, is whether we now exist finally in a situation of scarcity and limits even amid continued concentrations of enormous wealth. Scarcity is a relative term, because it does not mean that we are literally running out of these resources, but they are becoming more expensive to extract. This difficulty challenges the presumption of constant growth that is a requirement for capitalism to work in its present form. In a fossil economy, oil succeeds coal to propel human civilization to incredible material heights, despite the intrinsic inequality of the economic process. As Antti Salminen and Tere Vadén write, "the age of oil has been the unrecognized twin of the triumph of capitalism and globalization."[29] We cannot understand ourselves without understanding and reflecting on how pervasive this fossil economy is in everything we do. Refined hydrocarbons not only fuel our vehicles, but form all of our plastics, and lubricate the tiny parts necessary for computers, televisions, and smart phones. "The existence of fossil fuels as a natural, human-independent endowment," they write, "is essential for the spiritual, social, and experiential/phenomenological nature of industrial civilization and its machinery."[30] Fossil fuels have provided humans by far the cheapest energy surplus we have ever had, and we are using it up.

The existence of what is sometimes called peak oil does not mean that we will run out of oil or any other fossil fuel. It means that there is a limit to how much oil we can extract and produce and distribute at a certain financial and energy cost on a global scale. As Mitchell says, we are at or near the end of the easy availability of fossil fuel, which is why natural gas fracking, tar sands oil, shale oil, and offshore drilling for oil becomes profitable. These less conventional forms of fossil fuel are warding off the effects of peak oil, but they are themselves possible only for a limited time. At the moment, however, we remain locked into a fossil fuel economy. We are thus using up what Thom Hartmann calls "the last hours of ancient sunlight," because fossil fuels are nonrenewable by any measure of human time scales.[31]

It is important to note that while Malm and Mitchell focus on the impact of and on human labor in their studies of coal and oil respectively, they both see the vital role of energy across human and nonhuman thresholds. As Malm asserts, "*all* economic activities are ultimately a matter of energy conversion ... objects in the world can only be transformed, transferred, treated in whatever way by means of energy."[32] Mitchell takes this one step further. He points out that an abstract entity called "the economy" did not exist until the 1930s and 1940s.[33] "The economy" occurs because of the triumph of neoclassical economics, which destroyed the "political economy" of classical economics.

A major result of neoclassical economics was to obscure these fundamental links between energy, environment, and economy. Of course, the real intrudes into the twentieth century in powerful ways, even if these shocks are reduced or elided in neoclassical economic theories. For example, it was in some respects John Maynard Keynes who "saved" capitalism during the Great Depression by developing mechanisms to manage and control the economy that checked the destructive impact of unregulated markets. According to Philip Mirowski, what Keynes did was propose a new value substance, national income, to replace vague theories of general production in the 1930s and 1940s.[34] The idea of national income encourages nations to intervene into economic systems by invoking the more traditional methods of political economy, even if the financial tools are much more sophisticated. Keynesianism is then appropriated into the emerging consensus of neoclassical economics, even though Keynes himself is later marginalized and dismissed as utopian.

In *Capital in the Twenty-First Century*, Thomas Picketty explains that it was the tremendous shocks of the twentieth century, including two world wars and the Great Depression, that reduced capital and income inequality in most leading nations.[35] These devastating wars were a result of imperialism and social revolutions, which destroyed and redistributed wealth on a global scale and also shifted power from a declining Great Britain and a rising Germany to the USA and USSR. Ironically, it is this creative destruction that allows for the generation of unbelievable wealth and power after the Second World War. The Great Acceleration, from about 1945–1970, was made possible in the wake of the destruction of capital in war and depression by developing new financial mechanisms to harness the enormous energy of oil to fuel an unprecedented economic expansion along lines laid out in Bretton Woods, New Hampshire, in 1944.

Recently, the inequality of wealth and income has returned to levels at or near those at the end of the nineteenth century. For the United States, for example, "from 1977–2007, we find that the richest 10 percent appropriated three-quarters of the growth. The richest 1 percent alone absorbed nearly 60 percent of the total increase of US national income in this period. Hence for the bottom 60%, the rate of income growth was less than 0.5 percent per year."[36] Although the rise of socialist revolutions and devastating wars redistributed wealth during the twentieth century, this process goes into reverse in the 1970s and concentrates wealth over the last few decades.

During the Great Acceleration, the world saw unprecedented levels of increasing production, based on the widespread utilization of an almost unbelievable source of energy in the form of hydrocarbon petroleum. The so-called Green Revolution in the 1960s was actually the application of petroleum products and methods to agriculture, which produced unsurpassed yields. But beginning in the early 1970s, real productive growth began to slow in per capita terms, and the dreams of utopia in First World nations as well as the hopes for development in Third World countries—not to mention the drive for communist revolution in the Second—all ground slowly to a halt.

The early 1970s constitutes a key time period in the transition to disaster capitalism or neoliberalism. According to David Harvey, "the liberation of money creation from its money-commodity restraints in the early 1970s happened at a time when profitability prospects in productive activities were particularly low and when capital began to experience the impact of an inflexion point in the trajectory of exponential growth."[37] This inflexion point in the trajectory of exponential growth is the first impact of a physical limit on post–World War II capitalism. As profitability begins to decline, surplus money was lent out to developing countries in the form of government debt, generating a Third World debt crisis that rages through the 1980s. Another response to this inflexion point was the development of new asset markets, including speculation on the financial system itself in the form of derivatives—futures, swaps, and collateralized debt obligations.

It is in the early 1970s that, for the first time in global terms, human societies start to come up against physical ecological limits as a planet. In 1970, domestic oil production peaked in the lower forty-eight United States, not counting Alaska. In 1971, President Nixon was forced to abandon the Bretton Woods accord that established the post–World War II economic framework with a dollar that was pegged to $35 for an ounce of gold. After this gold standard disappeared, the U.S. currency became a fiat currency. Soon afterward, the OPEC oil embargo, which was a response to the U.S. support of Israel in the Yom Kippur War of 1973, shocked the American economy. As a result, the United States reaffirmed its special alliance with Saudi Arabia, and the Saudis pledged to ramp up supply to fuel the U.S. economy and to sell oil in dollars. In the early 1970s, the financial economy essentially delinked from the real economy, which is why the stock market continued to grow tremendously over the next four decades while inflation increased dramatically and real wages stagnated. The early 1970s also saw the emergence of a global ecological movement, including the famous Club of Rome's book *The Limits to Growth*, published in 1972.

This shift toward a new form of capitalism called neoliberalism coincides with the abandonment of Lyndon Johnson's ambitious War on Poverty as well as the intensification of U.S. military engagement in Vietnam, the murders of Martin Luther King Jr. and Robert F. Kennedy, the 1968 insurrections in France and Mexico, the betrayal of the Chinese Cultural Revolution, and the rise of what Naomi Klein calls "disaster capitalism."[38] Capitalism is based on indefinite growth, but surging population levels, industrialization of remaining rural areas across the globe, and overutilization of finite natural resources have combined to make it impossible to grow anymore in overall terms. We are running up against real limits. If corporate capitalism cannot grow in absolute terms, then the only way that it can grow is in relative terms. That is why the rich are getting richer, and the poor poorer. This is happening both within the United States and other countries and between rich and poor countries. It's a physical process, and we need to come to terms with it if we want our thinking and our actions to be efficacious.

Global economic growth is coming to an end, even as global emissions continue to increase due to previous growth. The only people who are acquiring wealth today are the capitalist corporate elite. It's not simply that corporate capitalists want to crush the poor and steal their money, although that desire is partly intrinsic to the system; it's also that they have no choice if they want to survive. Capitalism has mutated into a more savage form, even as it presents a more seductive facade, because it is consuming its own means of production in a desperate attempt to stave off collapse. At the same time, most of our contemporary economic theories ignore their ecological situatedness and simply externalize environmental costs. The economy is struggling to grow, which demands energy inputs, but we are struggling to generate more of these inputs, which are getting scarcer and more expensive. That's why we never fully recovered from the global recession of 2008 and will not completely emerge from the economic devastation wrought by the COVID-19 pandemic in 2020. And that's also why the United States has to spend so much money on its military, which is essentially a police force for global oil and gas pipelines, to ensure that this country, which has less than 5 percent of the world's population, continues to consume nearly a quarter of the world's energy.[39]

In his book *Planet of Slums*, Mike Davis charts the rise of slums as urban populations exceed rural populations, which is the intensification and culmination of the rift Marx noted between town and country. In the first decade of the twenty-first century, "for the first time the urban population ... outnumber[s] the rural."[40] Future population growth during the rest of the century will be in urban cities, which are increasingly overpopulated, vulnerable, and consist of slums. The most recent cause of this massive population shift is the Green Revolution of the 1960s, which applied fossil fueled industrial machines to develop mass agriculture, devastating farmers and rural peoples who were left without means to subsist. These developments were supported by "policies of agricultural deregulation and financial discipline enforced by the IMF and World Bank [that] continued to generate an exodus of surplus rural labor to urban slums even as cities ceased to be job machines."[41]

We are exceeding the carrying capacity of the Earth for human beings, especially in terms of our urban industrial and postindustrial way of life. What we call contemporary capitalism or neoliberalism is reaching real limits to growth. We are straining to grow, and any growth is largely due to the impoverishing and "pauperization" of others, largely including people who are poor, weak, nonwhite, and women.[42] We desperately need to dismantle the capitalist machine, but it is in the process of shredding itself apart. The problem is that this process is happening too slowly to stop the processes of extinction, environmental devastation, and global warming, and the corporate financial and political elites are invested in sticking with this doomed system to the end rather than adopting something else.

As Samir Amin states, "the system commonly termed 'neoliberalism,' which in fact is the system of financialized, globalized, and generalized monopoly capitalism, is imploding before our eyes. This system, plainly unable to overcome its own contradictions, cannot avoid plunging forward in its mad race."[43] Amin does not focus specifically on the ecological contradictions of contemporary capitalism, but the implosion that he describes is happening largely due to these ecological factors, including resource depletion, extinction of species, and global warming. We cannot separate the economic processes of modern and contemporary capitalism from its entanglement with and sustainment by energy, including fossil fuels.

ENERGY, UTILITY, AND ENTROPY IN ECONOMICS

Energy and economics have always been closely linked, although much of neoclassical economics tries to render this connection invisible. Mirowski traces the parallel development of physics and economics in the nineteenth century in his book *More Heat Than Light*. He shows how physical ideas about energy inform economics, but also how many economists fail to fully comprehend the nature of energy in physical terms and what it means for their theories. Basically, a unified concept of energy emerges in the physics and thermodynamics toward the end of the nineteenth century. The ontology of energy is understood in terms of a field. A physical field is "a spatial distribution of energy that varies with time."[44] Here energy is understood as a real thing, and according to the first law of thermodynamics it is always generally conserved. Fields are how we conceive and measure energy as potential or kinetic. The problem with this understanding of energy, Mirowski explains, is that with the increasingly complex and abstract mathematics used to describe these fields and their interactions, along with the emergence of relativity and quantum mechanics, the unified concept of energy begins to unravel.

First, the Lagrangian (named after Joseph-Louis Lagrange) and Hamiltonian (named after William Rowan Hamilton) mathematical techniques that were developed in physical and mechanical terms become more and more formalized. Energy "became more a mathematical concept and less an intuitive one" due to the development and application of these powerful techniques.[45] Instead of a material force that can be quantified mathematically, energy becomes an abstract representation of these mathematical operations. Furthermore, the mathematics themselves become so much more complex that they do not simply refer to what they seemed to refer to in their original deployments by Lagrange and Hamilton. A Hamiltonian, for example, is a mathematical formalism that is used to measure the energy of an integrable system, including a quantum mechanical one, as noted in chapter 1.

The problem is the amount of abstraction needed to transform a real system into one that is subject to such mathematical solutions. For Mirowski, this means that energy becomes less of an ontological substance and more of a hypothetical presupposition. In addition, the emergence of special relativity theory qualifies the conservation of energy because it correlates energy with mass. Here, as in Einstein's famous equation $E=mc^2$, it is the mass and the energy together that are conserved, because they are convertible in terms of the speed of light. With the appearance of quantum physics, it becomes even less apparent that energy is anything at all, as it becomes dispersed into so many probability wave/particle amplitudes. I argue that energy does not simply disappear, but many of the scientists and economists absorb energy into abstract mathematical formulations, including the concept of information.

Classical dynamics is based on finding solutions to systems that are presupposed to be integrable. That is, an integrable system can be solved using Hamiltonian equations. These systems are also assumed to be symmetric; that is, they are symmetrical in time rather than asymmetrical. Nonlinear dynamics demonstrates that integrable systems are a small and artificial subset of actual systems, and eventually chaos and complexity theories do away with the dream of establishing perfectly integrable systems that are conserved or symmetrical in time. These developments suggest newer conceptions of energy in terms of nonequilibrium thermodynamics, but they completely undermine the ontology of the unified concept of energy as it appears in the late nineteenth century.

As Mirowski sums up, "the spread of field formalisms, the elaboration of Hamiltonians, the rise of statistical mechanics . . . and chaos theory were tearing the energy concept in three or four different directions, and nobody felt inclined to pick up the shreds and knit them together again."[46] Why is this understanding of physics important for economics? Because the transition from political economy and classical economics to neoclassical economics takes place at the same time and in many of the same contexts as the physics. More specifically, neoclassical economics takes shape around the nineteenth century concept of energy as understood in physics.

The counterpoint to the concept of energy in neoclassical economics is utility. Utility is a measure of satisfaction or value, one that measures the usefulness of economic goods similarly to the way that energy measures the work that can be accomplished in any system. If utility is analogous to energy, then the phrase that indicates entropy would be *marginal utility*. That is, as consumption of goods increases, there occurs a decrease of utility. This is the law of diminishing returns, which was formulated in terms of the conservation laws of physics. Overall utility is conserved, whereas there is a necessary diminishment in marginal utility.

The transition to neoclassical economics is often described as a marginal revolution. Mirowski asserts that the fundamental break in economic theory in the 1870s and 1880s is not simply a new conception of utility, understood in terms of marginal utility, but is the result of "the successful penetration of mathematical discourse into economic theory."[47] These mathematical theories are drawn from physics, although Mirowski points out that most economists did not accurately understand the physics and mathematics that they drew upon. Economists base their discipline on physical understandings of energy, but these are being mathematically treated in such a way as to dissipate energy as a real thing.

The difference between twentieth-century physics and twentieth-century economics, Mirowski claims, is that physicists understood that energy was becoming an abstraction with the adoption of formalized mathematical models, even as they were clinging to the idea of an integrable system. Economists, on the other hand, still maintained that they were modeling and measuring something real. One way to describe both physics and economics during the twentieth century is to say that they were caught up in symbolic mathematical representations, whereas the end of the century and the beginning of the twenty-first brings about a return of the real in more explicitly ecological terms.

In 1971, around the critical period of transition I have delineated, Nicolas Georgescu-Roegen published *The Entropy Law and the Economic Process*. This book explicitly reconnects economics back up with thermodynamics and pushes economic thinking beyond the abstractions of neoclassicism. For Georgescu-Roegen, any and all economic theory must grapple with the law of entropy, which means that the amount of usable free energy for work must decline over time. He explains that "in the universe there is a *continuous* and *irrevocable* qualitative degradation of free into bound energy."[48] The irrevocability of this process in economic terms sets up a fundamental limit to growth. Due to the entropy law, we cannot avoid scarcity in material terms because we cannot keep recycling and reusing the same materials.

Georgescu-Roegen addresses the confusion that has occurred by the conflation of entropy of thermodynamic systems with theories of information, where information is coded as a sort of negative entropy. Describing entropy as correlating to the amount of information is what obscures economists and others from the true meaning of the entropy law. "The entropic phenomenon of a piece of coal burning irrevocably into ashes," he writes, "is neither a flow of probability from a lower to a higher value, nor an increase in the onlooker's ignorance, nor man's illusion of temporal succession."[49] The entropy law provides us the reality of temporal change, which also gives us "the feeling of the entropy flow."[50]

Furthermore, the entropy law is not deterministic; it tells us the general direction of a "the entropic process of an isolated system," but it does not tell us when we are in a closed system or precisely what will happen within it. As I explained in chapter 1, it is the entropy law itself in the form of gradient reduction that makes possible *the emergence of novelty by combination*. The statistical interactions of elements within a directional process produce novelty because they cannot be precisely predicted.

Here we are back to the idea of energy and entropy more as physical processes than as mathematical formalisms. Mirowski is right to say that the concept of energy gets diffused in the twentieth century, but I think that the way in which it returns in the latter part of this century is significant, despite the incredible complexity of our mathematical tools.

Georgescu-Roegen is one of the few economists of the twentieth century who is attentive to the implications of the thermodynamics of nonlinear chaotic systems.

Economists measure stocks of goods, and they also measure flows. Economists want to measure the flow of stocks through intervals of time. The problem is that the complexity of the statistical graphs and equations implies that the stocks, which are quantifiable, and the flows, which are not, are interchangeable. We attempt to quantify the flows by reducing them to measurements of the passage of time, but Georgescu-Roegen points out that this assumption of the symmetry of time ignores the entropy law. He says that "time always flows, but never exists as a stock."[51] Time cannot be reduced to a measurable stock, or presupposed as a uniform measure, because there is always a process of entropy over time so that what we are measuring necessarily changes.

The entropy law is not only the basis of what we call economics. Georgescu-Roegen asserts that "the relationship between the economic process that the Entropy Law is only an aspect of a more general fact, namely, that this law is the basis of the *economy* of life at all levels."[52] Entropy is what provides and conditions a general economy. He concludes that "in actuality only locomotion is qualityless and ahistorical; everything else is Change, in the fullest sense of the world."[53]

The entropy law is how we measure and understand *change*. Change involves the binding and using up of free energy, and this is an irrevocable process. At the same time, this very binding also produces "the emergence of novelty by combination." Combination takes place by and through the flow of energy. Energy flows across time and distance, conserving itself in a certain sense and generating more and more entropy in another as gradients are established and reduced. In a closed system, entropy can only increase to the point of equilibrium, but in an open system the lessons of nonequilibrium thermodynamics show how novelty emerges through organization. Energy flow through a system organizes a system, as Morowitz claims. This same energy flow through a system uses up the free energy of a system by binding it and removing it from use. And this is the same law and the same energy flow and the same system that generates the most incredible differences in kind, including organic, psychic, social, and technical systems.

WHAT IS MONEY?

I am arguing that there is a broader energy economy that is the basis of all human and animal interactions, because we need energy to live. Energetic processes and transactions govern the rise of complex human societies when people discover how to domesticate fire, animals, and plants, as well as control the flow of water. This is the energy economy, which is fundamental, and it is ultimately based on what we call physical and chemical thermodynamic processes.

At a certain point in time, energy gets represented and mediated by money. In a money economy we have a much more complex situation, because money constitutes a kind of exchange that supersedes and *ratchets* together (in Terrance Deacon's term) with the energy economy. The energy economy grounds the money economy, but it does so in a nonlinear way because of the nature of how money works. Money itself represents a claim, the drawing of a debt or a promise to pay. This monetary economy overlays the energy economy and makes it work in powerful if unequal ways.

In *The Entropy Law and the Economic Process*, Georgescu-Roegen argues against the notion that money measures economic entropy. More specifically, he criticizes the idea that there is a simple relationship between economic value and low entropy, which is quantified in money. Money is an attempt to quantify value, but it cannot be simply equated to entropy in Georgescu-Roegen's terms. If we only measure life in terms of input and output flows, the general equivalence of these flows means that the value of life is reduced to zero. Instead, we should see that "the true 'produce' of the economic process is not a material *flow*, but a psychic *flux*—the enjoyment of life by every member of the population."[54]

This enjoyment is the true value of life, which cannot be fixed, quantified, or measured in terms of money, even though this value is always caught up in a general economy of exchange. For Marx, the true source of value is labor time, which is commodified in the product of labor. This commodity is then calculated in terms of an exchange value, which is money. Money captures the value of an exchange of commodities. The value of the commodity is constituted by labor time, but it is a qualitatively different form of labor time compared to the living labor time that generates the product. The labor time represented by exchange value is not the same as the labor time that produces the commodity, because "it is not labour time as labour time, but materialized labour time; labour time not in the form of motion, but of rest; not in the form of process, but of result."[55] There is an original, living labor that is then quantified in the labor time of exchange value. This distinction is similar to the modern idea proposed by Leibniz of energy as *vis viva*, a living force as opposed to a dead one. Money is simply an operation that lets us calculate and track this exchange value.

In the *Grundrisse*, Marx explains that *"money provides the possibility of an absolute division of labour"* because of this very commodification.[56] The generation of exchange value by virtue of producing a commodity that can be exchanged provides the foundation of what later becomes capitalism. The notation Marx uses here is C-M-C, where C stands for commodity and M stands for money. Even if this equation is closer to the original labor time, it is already a distortion of it. In terms of how we usually think about entropy, the price of a commodity tends to an equilibrium where the supply and demand curves meet. But the economy is not a closed system since it is always based on the flows of labor time and the circulation of capital as speculation.

Marx shows how capitalism reverses the process of C-M-C, into M-C-M, where money becomes the origin and the outcome of the production of commodities. However, the original formulation, C-M-C, already reifies the living labor time that produces the product by commodifying it and making it into an object that can then be exchanged. Capitalism simply turns this process around, allowing money to preserve and allow capital as the exchange rate to circulate. As Marx says, "only with *capital* is exchange value posited as exchange value in such a way that it preserves itself in circulation."[57] Capitalism circulates the original commodification that is produced by labor time in the exchange value.

In the *Grundrisse*, and later in his volumes on *Capital*, Marx is attempting to pull apart the elements that constitute capitalism so as to provide tools to undo it. In many ways, what he posits as the original living labor time does not exist without already being caught up in exchange. But it is crucial to be able to see it, because it allows us to comprehend what capital is and does in terms of capitalism. Capitalism is parasitic on this essential living labor time that is always already caught up in exchange and exchange value.

We think that money is something real because it represents value, or else we imagine that money is an arbitrary abstraction that does not mean anything except what people have decided it means. Money is a form of energy in economic terms, although it does not represent energy as a substance. Energy flows, and money circulates as capital. These flows are entropic flows, but they also generate what Georgescu-Roegen calls "the emergence of novelty by combination." There is no such thing as living labor time apart from the circulation of money as a medium of exchange.

Money expresses a social relation of credit and debt, as Geoffrey Ingham points out. He says that "money is a 'claim' or 'credit' that is constituted by social relations that *exist independently of the production and exchange of commodities*."[58] This means that Marx is wrong to think that money originates as the price that designates the exchange value of commodities as the product of labor. But Marx is not wrong about how money circulates as capital in and through commodities. We imagine that money comes about as a medium of exchange to replace an original barter economy that exchanges goods directly, but there was never such an economy. David Graeber explains that virtual money in the form of credit comes first, then coinage and the possibility of bartering. "Barter," he writes, "appears to be largely a kind of accidental byproduct of the use of coinage or paper money."[59] The original equation is not C-M-C, but M-C-M. The earliest states or empires created what Ingham calls "monetary spaces that encompassed and integrated social groups whose interaction was embedded in particular social ties or specific economic interests."[60] Money was already a form of asymmetrical exchange between creditors and debtors from the beginning of human civilization.

Money is created by taking on a debt, which is a promise to pay or repay an obligation. According to Ingham, "it is the *existence of a debt that gives the money value*."[61] And a debt, Graeber says, is "just a perversion of a promise. It is a promise corrupted by both math and violence."[62] In his book *Debt: The First 5,000 Years*, Graeber argues that the original economic relation is a kind of communism, where social relations are understood and enacted as a form of sharing of resources in common. This is a "baseline communism" that exists among the smallest social units that takes the form of sharing.[63] Later, as social relations become more complex, a logic of exchange emerges. Exchange is all about equivalence, "a back-and-forth process involving two sides in which each side gives as good as it gets."⁶⁴ Finally, hierarchies develop based on the practice of exchange that work to sustain inequality and postpone equivalence. Exchange for Graeber is characterized by reciprocity, whereas hierarchy works "by a logic of precedent."⁶⁵

The problem with Graeber's account is the same as the problem with Marx's—he posits an original form of communism that underlies all subsequent economic relations. In fact, all three of these forms of interaction—communism, exchange, and hierarchy—emerge and exist at the same time. It's only possible to distinguish them in structural terms and then to posit them retroactively in temporal terms. His study is incredibly valuable as a means to describe how debt works perversely and violently, but it is utopian and unrealistic to imagine that there actually was a world of communist sharing without exchange or hierarchy. What Ingham calls money and what Graeber calls virtual money is the original economic relation, and it occurs as a relation of credit and debt, which is already a system of asymmetrical exchange. Asymmetrical exchange is subject to what Georgescu-Roegen calls the entropy law, and this law extends beyond what we call the economy to incorporate physical and psychic processes.

There is another relatively obscure book published in the early 1970s that gets at the heart of what we mean by economy, money, and exchange here. In *Living Currency*, Pierre Klossowski contrasts the utopian fantasies of Charles Fourier with the controversial and perverse writings of the Marquis de Sade. He asks the question: "How can a voluptuous emotion be reduced to a commodified object and thereby become, in our era of excessive industrialization, a factor in the economy?"⁶⁶ The focus here is on the Industrial Revolution and the rise of industrial capitalism, which is also the subject of Malm's book. The Industrial Revolution is a kind of repetition of difference (Deleuze) of previous human social transformations. It is singular and unique, and it opens a new and anthropogenic era, but it is not thereby completely unrelated to earlier transformations.

Klossowski starts with the idea of a voluptuous emotion, which gives value to life. Our lives have meaning insofar as we are capable of experiencing voluptuous pleasure. Everyone has the ability to experience voluptuous pleasure and voluptuous emotions, which means that this capacity is freely given to everyone. What is freely given has no price. Klossowski affirms that Sade is closer to the truth of human reality, because we are driven by our perversions. We may desire the utopia of Fourier, but we are constrained by the perverse economy that Sade elaborates. The Industrial Revolution represents the triumph of the instinct to reproduce over the immediate desire to experience voluptuous emotion. Humans want to both survive and reproduce themselves and their forms of life at the same time that they want to experience and express voluptuous emotion, which is more ephemeral.

The affirmation of the individual comes at a cost involving the attempt to put a price on what has no price. The perversity of human society causes us to want to value voluptuous emotion not because it is freely available to everyone but precisely insofar as are able to create a situation of scarcity and price. Klossowski says that "in our world of industrial fabrication, what appeals to people is not what seems naturally free of charge, but rather the price that is put on what is naturally free of charge."[67] The utopian desire is to experience this naturally free-of-charge element of human existence separate from any economy; this is the fantasy of keeping something intrinsically free-of-charge actually free from charge. But *unfortunately this is impossible.* The modern economy is not just about the production of consumer goods; it is also the production and reproduction of voluptuous pleasure in terms of a monetary economy. We separate the experience of something that everyone has the ability to experience without any restriction or price from its actual experience. We are only really able to value something if it appears unavailable to everyone. It has to have a price to be an experience of value.

Klossowski is analyzing the formation of the modern psychic economy—at least for Europeans—at the moment that the capitalist economy is being developed. He says that we separate the means of experiencing voluptuous emotion, which is available only for a price, from the capacity of experiencing it, which is available to everyone. In this way, "the emotion ceases to be indifferent and gains in value."[68] This perversion of our instinct to experience voluptuous emotion characterizes modern human being, and it represents "the victory of the instinct to reproduce" over the experience of the emotion itself.[69] We are forced to choose between our immediate pleasure, which sacrifices our sense of an individual self, and the self-affirmation of this unitary self, which occurs only with the cost of giving up our ability to experience pleasure.

This forced choice is a perversion of our natural instinct to experience and express emotion, and it is fabricated in and by industrial capitalism. This perversion in turn shapes our own sense of who and what we are in terms of our desires, not simply our ability to buy and consume goods. Our very basic desires are driven to find equivalent exchanges in the form of fabricated objects. The fabricated object is also an object of desire, and it must be correlated with a psychic exchange, not merely a monetary one. Or rather, what we call money is both the "actual" price *and* the psychic exchange, the need to impose a price onto the free experience of voluptuous emotion. Even though Klossowski asserts an original baseline form of voluptuous emotion prior to its being caught up in an economy of exchange, this is no more possible than the natural states that Marx and Graeber assume. The perversity that Klossowski recognizes is fundamental, because our emotions are always already caught up in a kind of equivalency and exchange if they are to be of any sort of value.

What money means in a broader sense is this basic situation of equivalency and exchange. We cannot eliminate money without getting rid of human nature. According to Klossowski, "money establishes a link between the closed world of anomalies and the world of institutional norms." Money is the equivalent of wealth, but it retains its value precisely by destroying that wealth. Money, "even as it represents and guarantees what exists, now becomes a sign of *what does not exist*.[70] What does this mean? For Klossowski, our basic impulses and images constitute phantasms, or fleeting images of desire. Money works the way that it does because it is entangled with our deepest phantasms. Money is "the freedom to choose or refuse one good from among all existing goods," and "this ability to choose or refuse diminishes the value of what exists in favour of what does not exist."[71] The nature of money indicates the possibility of transgressing what exists in the name of something that does not exist.

Again, this is a fundamental condition of what it means to be human, whatever specific form that takes. The utopian dreams of Fourier and others are symptoms of this ability to transgress what exists in favor of what does not but could exist. The problem is that Fourier and others want to extricate this very possibility from money, from any and all economy, and that is impossible. Sade provides Klossowski the understanding of how our perverse desire economizes any and all emotion.

A living person is already a commodity, and the ultimate end of what Klossowski analyzes in his short but powerful book is a kind of "living currency." Klossowski imagines an economy in which workers are paid in living currency, that is, in the form of people. The value of these people would be incalculable in terms of the living labor required to earn them. They would constitute an "object of sensation," or a universal psychic state that could be convertible into currency. The industrial worker and the contemporary celebrity are examples of this attempt to quantitatively derive a value of and for human emotion. "As 'living currency,'" he writes, "the industrial slave has value both as a sign of wealth and as wealth itself."[72]

For Klossowski, the actual slave would not constitute living currency, because the slave is denied their dignity in a modern slave economy, even if they retain value as a source of voluptuous pleasure. The dignity and value of a worker lies in the ability to be experienced solely as money, as a kind of commodity and living currency, but this situation requires a certain amount of freedom that the slave never possesses, and a freedom that is being removed from more and more workers in a postindustrial economy.

In his book, Klossowski develops the parameters of what Jacques Lacan calls "surplus jouissance," in his seminar 17 on *The Other Side of Psychoanalysis*, and what Jean-François Lyotard later calls a "libidinal economy."[73] The point is that an emotion or passion that is originally seen as uncountable and unquantifiable becomes countable and quantified, and this transformation leads us to a new experience of humanity and a new experience of money. In neoclassical economics, money is characterized primarily in terms of utility, but Klossowski and others stress the ways in which economics works precisely in terms of *disutility*.

Klossowski cites Keynes concerning "the disutility of labour," which "would indicate the ability to thwart a 'need,' even if only thorough 'a desire to do nothing.'" He says that disutility "measures the difference between the *intelligibility* in the act of fabricating objects suitable for use and the originally *unintelligible* character of the 'phantasmatic' constraint."[74] Money works not simply by means of utility but more profoundly as a form of disutility. Money makes it possible to destroy a present situation in favor of a not-yet-existing possibility. This circulation remains a kind of exchange, but it involves the phantasmatic nature of human impulses, as well as the general physical situation of energy transformations and nonlinear thermodynamics as suggested by Georgescu-Roegen.

THE GIFT

The disutility that Klossowski points to signifies the *asymmetrical* nature of exchange. Money, like energy, is all about exchange. We need to consider a much wider general economy, and here Georges Bataille's work is crucial. What Bataille calls a general economy includes both the energy economy and the money economy. It also opens onto an ecology, because it takes the environment into account. In his three volumes of *The Accursed Share*, Bataille is completely opposed to the idea of utility, which means to all forms of neoclassical economics. In order to appreciate what Bataille has accomplished in *The Accursed Share*, we need to situate his work in terms of change and exchange.

In the preface to volume 1, Bataille says that his intention with the book is "to make clear the notion of a 'general economy,' in which the 'expenditure' (the 'consumption') of wealth, rather than production, was the primary object."[75] The expenditure of wealth as a surplus energy is a form of consumption, but consumption is also a kind of exchange. And these are nonequilibrium thermodynamic processes that require entropy or, in economic terms, disutility. To frame Bataille's crucial contribution, I will first consider the Kojin Karatani's treatment of social and economic formations as modes of exchange. Then, with Karatani's work as context, I will engage directly with Bataille's work in *The Accursed Share*.

In *The Structure of World History*, Karatani analyzes political economy and shifts from a more standard focus on modes of production to emphasize modes of exchange. He begins by noting the trinity of Capital, Nation, and State as it occurs in Hegel and Marx. Karatani says that capital, nation, and state are each "grounded in its own distinct set of principles, but here they are joined together in a mutually supplementary manner" such that "the whole system will fail if one of the three are missing."[76] Capital, nation, and state function and interact in complex ways, but they are more correctly understood in terms of modes of exchange rather than modes of production. Karatani says that "if we posit that economic base equals mode of production, we are unable to explain precapitalist societies. Worse, we remain unable to understand even capitalist economies."[77] If we solely focus on modes of production, we risk relegating nonmodern and noncapitalist societies to a place anterior to and outside of real human history.

Karatani sketches four broad types of exchange: A, which is based on the reciprocity of the gift, is found primarily in clan societies; B is the exchange based on plunder and redistribution and comes about with the formation of states and empires; C is commodity exchange, which comes to the fore in modern capitalism; finally, D is a sort of unknown X that stands for a utopian vision of what a return to A might look like in the wake of capitalism.[78] He argues that although these modes of exchange develop historically, the ones that are replaced do not disappear but continue to exist in different and sometimes muted forms. Today, he equates mode of exchange A (reciprocity) with the nation, B (domination) with the state, and C (commodity) with capital.

The form of exchange that Karatani calls D is an unknown X that does not actually exist but must be posited and presupposed to make sense of the others. D is utopian in the way that communism is for Marx and Graeber. D cannot simply be equated with democracy, but the letter D can be correlated with a potentially more democratic form of political economy. Democracy here is not the form of representative democracy that is implicated in liberal and neoliberal capitalism, but D invokes the spectral form of a radical democracy that calls into question every status quo. Here D is a democracy *to come*, to use Derrida's formulation. According to Derrida, thinking about democracy as an event that breaks into the present in an unforeseeable way means "an extension of the democratic beyond nation-state sovereignty."[79]

It's not that commodity exchange C will simply give way to D in a linear developmental fashion, but that D haunts C and B in their present form as the return to reciprocity or A. In his historical analysis of these four modes of exchange, Karatani associates D with the existence of universal religion, although he stresses that D does not have to take a religious form. The point is that while religion is always complicit in the other modes of exchange, it also takes the form of their critique: "universal religions emerged as mode of exchange D—as a criticism of modes of exchange B and C, which were the dominant modes of world empires."[80] Religion is not the necessary form of mode of exchange D, but it takes this form during much of world history. Under modern capitalism, the invocation of mode of exchange D as a return of the reciprocity that characterizes clan society is expressed with the term *socialism*. Again, socialism here is a sign of democracy at least as a utopian hope.

Karatani is right to shift the focus of political economy from production to exchange, and his typology is both heuristic and instructive. It's not that any of these four forms ever exist independently, but we can see how various modes interact in different situations with one or more coming to the fore. Along with Graeber and others, we see more of an emphasis on preagricultural human societies, and this is also important as we envision new possibilities. At the same time, Karatani, like Graeber, posits this society A based on reciprocity based on a subtractive projection. Any society would have to include all four elements, including this openness to a future form of society that D represents.

For example, as soon as we have ancient empires, we have a system of money. As soon as there is money, there is commodity exchange. We cannot restrict C to modern capitalism: C and B emerge together and are woven together. Karatani cites Karl Polanyi's argument that it is the emergence of a "self-regulating market" that characterizes modern capitalism.[81] This involves the simultaneous commodification of labor and of land, which takes place at the end of the eighteenth century. Land and labor are converted into stock, and these stocks are traded in markets, which is a new form of commodification. Commodities, however, exist as soon as there is a monetary economy, which occurs with the creation of writing as a form of accounting in ancient Sumer. Commodities are in fact *created* by a money economy.

The establishment of a money economy is tied to the rise of ancient states and empires. These forms of exchange replace a previous kind of reciprocity, but they do not eliminate it. A gift economy is never symmetrical or equal. It is the fiction of a monetary economy that makes things appear equal. Reciprocity is asymmetrical, which means that it is also shaped by broadly understood thermodynamic and entropic relations. To invoke a renewal of something like A, a mode of exchange based on reciprocity, we have to better understand how reciprocity functions as a mode of exchange prior to the emergence of a monetary economy and ancient states and then how it interacts with B and with C.

Karatani associates D with religion, with socialism, and with democracy. It is a repetition of the original gift economy, A, in a new form. As a way to open up D as a possibility for contemporary human beings, we need to follow Karatani's shift from production to exchange, and read Bataille's analysis of consumption in light of this conception of exchange. In many ways, the key to Bataille's thought is his understanding of nonliterate societies practicing the reciprocity that Karatani calls the form of exchange A. This reciprocity is based on gift giving rather than physical money as a medium of exchange. In Karatani's form of exchange A, reciprocity is nonreciprocal in equivalent terms. It's asymmetrical and essentially involves a using up.

Both Bataille and Karatani are profoundly influenced by Marcel Mauss's famous essay on *The Gift: The Form and Reason for Exchange in Ancient Societies*. This study inaugurates a sea change in how anthropologists understand indigenous nonliterate peoples. The analysis of the gift, and specifically the potlatch of the Native Americans of the Pacific Northwest, shifts our comprehension from an economy based on currency to the possibility of an economy based on reciprocity. The gift economy is seen as preceding and prefiguring the later monetary economy, offering ways to think outside our contemporary capitalist economy that is ruled by money in the form of credit and debt, as Graeber points out.

Bataille follows Mauss in focusing on the potlatch practiced by the "Indians of the American Northwest," whose exchanges consist of "a regular sequence of gifts." He contrasts potlatch to bartering, which Graeber shows is not at the basis of human economic interactions. Potlatch is "a means of circulating wealth, but it excludes bargaining."[82] The chief or powerful figure offers riches to a rival "for the purpose of humiliating, challenging, and obligating him. The recipient has to erase the humiliation and take up the challenge; he must satisfy the *obligation* that was contracted by accepting."[83] Bataille argues that the practice of potlatch as an elementary form of gift giving is asymmetrical and obligating. He also claims that potlatch shows that the essence of economic activity is not acquisition but rather "the dissipation of useful wealth."[84] The acceptance of the gift obligates the recipient to pay back the wealth *with interest* in the form of a future potlatch. This is already a virtual form of money because it's a system of credit based on a form of exchange.

Bataille argues that it is impossible to understand the phenomenon of potlatch without the perspective of a general economy. We require a general understanding of exchange, an economy of exchange common to all humans and set in the context of the terrestrial earth. Sometimes this gift economy that characterizes potlatch and other practices of so-called pre-civilized societies is seen as the primary form of original human economy. This is somewhat misleading, as Karatani distinguishes between nomadic bands of humans who did not live in fixed settlements and later sedentary peoples, including agriculturalists and hunter-gatherers. For Karatani, the fundamental change in human society comes about with "the adoption of fixed settlements, which preceded the appearance of agriculture."[85]

Karatani claims that the nomadic bands of hunter-gatherers were composed of interactions that were much more equal than later groupings. Band societies pool their resources because "they are unable to store up the spoils of their activities."[86] This is the ground zero of later forms of communist nostalgia. Inequality appears along with the establishment of fixed settlements, because they allow the storing up of products. According to Karatani, once humans become sedentary, inequality becomes unavoidable, but it is essential to analyze the reciprocal form of exchange that characterizes clan societies. The clan society appears before the emergence of the state, and the state exacerbates these inequalities in the form of social and economic classes.

Why do humans adopt fixed settlements? Due to climate change. After the end of the Ice Age, the planet warmed up, and this meant that "temperate areas of the midlatitudes saw increasing forestation and a concomitant disappearance of large-game animal stocks."[87] The seasonal variation of temperatures in a warming world affected human foraging, and so the humans who had the opportunity turned to fishing. Fishing requires tools and equipment that cannot be moved around, so it led to more sedentary settlements along the coasts and at the mouths of rivers.

Fixed settlements created stockpiles, which in turn generated inequality and war. Karatani says that this sets in motion the process that led to the establishment of the state. However, "clan society was formed so as to prevent this" by forcing and reinforcing the pooling of resources as reciprocity in the form of "the obligations of the gift."[88] The formation of clan society as a bulwark against the state (or the empire) is why it is so significant for Karatani. Might it be possible to recover some of these elements of reciprocity to avoid the worst ravages of empire states?

The equality of nomadic bands of humans is a bit of a projection—a kind of degree zero state of human society that contrasts with later developments. This is impossible to reproduce, but we can look at the emergence of clan societies that practice exchange based on gift giving and reciprocity so long as we understand that they are not inherently or essentially equal. Karatani says that "through the reciprocity of the gift, the community leaves behind the 'state of nature' in its relation with another community, producing instead the condition of peace."[89] This is an unstable and precarious peace, because it is always has the danger of setting off a vendetta of revenge and counter-revenge, as well as gift and counter-gift. The state then abolishes both the gift and the vendetta by taking on itself the responsibility for judging crime and inflicting violence, along with distributing goods.

The reciprocity of exchange in the form of gift giving is unequal and asymmetrical, but it does establish a kind of peace that is different from that of the state. "The reciprocity of the gift," Karatani claims, "establishes a federation among multiple communities—a kind of world system."[90] This is the form of world system that he would like to return to, in the form of a federation of states set within the context of a United Nations that would possess something like genuine sovereignty.

What about the form of commodity exchange, C? According to Karatani, we have to be careful not to simply associate C with contemporary capitalism, even though capitalism takes C to an extreme form. In fact, "commodity exchange exists only with the support of the community and the state," and in fact both the community or clan society that practices gift giving and the state that possesses sovereign power and mints or prints money *require* commodity exchange.[91] The power of money that distinguishes mode of exchange C involves the creation of markets explicitly set up to foster this form of commodity exchange, whether real or virtual. What is the difference between commodity exchange and gift giving? The reciprocity of mode of exchange A requires a kind of commodity exchange based on the power of the gift, because there is always already a kind of equivalence set up to measure the status and wealth of the gift and the obligation it confers on the recipient. The difference, however, is that in commodity exchange "one specific commodity—gold, for example—possesses the power of being exchangeable for all other commodities. We call this money."[92] Money concentrates the process of exchange by filtering it through one (supposedly) universal medium of exchange.

Karatani wants to emphasize the difference between commodity exchange in the form of money from reciprocal exchange in the form of the gift. At the same time, he is forced to acknowledge the resemblances between the two. My argument is that the reciprocal exchange of gift giving is already a kind of virtual money, even if that is not actualized in the form of currency. Why? Because money is essentially the creation of a debt, one that produces the distinction between a creditor and a debtor. Money already exists in a virtual form in the obligation established by the gift. I think we need such a broad and abstract definition of money to account for the arrangements of human society and their various forms of inequality based on their modes of exchange. Once you have exchange, you have something like money, even if you do not have literal currency.

I don't want to trivialize Karatani's distinction and his emphasis on mode of exchange A. I just think he goes too far in trying to separate reciprocal exchange from the exchange of money in the form of a commodity. The clan society based on reciprocity already has inequality and commodities, even if they are regulated differently. This society may not possess literal currency, but it does trade in *living currency*. Why? Because, as anthropologists have pointed out, women are the first form of commodity exchange.

In his discussion of early human societies Bataille conflates the nomadic bands of humans that Karatani distinguishes from later clan societies based on reciprocity. In volume 2 of *The Accursed Share*, which treats the subject of human eroticism, Bataille relies on Claude Lévi-Strauss to understand human culture as defined by the incest taboo. Bataille overemphasizes the separation of human beings from nonhuman animals, because he associates eroticism, anguish, intimacy, and sacrifice solely with human consciousness and relegates animal consciousness to a realm of total unawareness. For Bataille and Lévi-Strauss, what distinguishes human beings from animals is the rejection of incest. However, as Karatani understands, the role of the incest taboo and the practice of exogamy is more fundamentally linked to the clan societies that result from fixed human settlement.

Bataille agrees with Lévi-Strauss that the original form of exchange is that of women for the sake of exogamous marriage. The exchange of women is the basis of the gift economy. The exchange of women between different groups or clans brings about the incest taboo, because the need to affirm marriage with women from other groups requires prohibiting marriage between members within the clan. Karatani agrees that "the incest taboo cannot be separated from the obligations of the gift," which is prohibited in the context of the establishment of exogamy.[93]

Bataille affirms the material and economic utility of this exchange of women, but he argues that there is an erotic connection as well, which ties into his understanding of general economy. Bataille says that "on the one hand, the exchange, or rather the giving of women brings into play the interest of the one who gives—who gives only on condition of a return gift. On the other hand, it is a function of his generosity."[94] The gift economy captures the essence of a general economy because it contains both an exorbitant generosity and a calculated interest at one and the same time. Both are at work in the potlatch ceremony: "potlatch is at once a surpassing of calculation and the height of calculation."[95]

The difference between women as objects of exchange and later human slaves as well as material objects is that women possess an *erotic* quality that infuses the gift. The gift is at the heart of an economics of calculation and utility while it simultaneously exceeds all calculation and utility. Bataille says that "the principle of the *gift*, which propels the movement of general activity, is at the basis of sexual activity."[96] The gift represents and instantiates both the particular economy and the general one. And because of its erotic nature, it "propels the movement of general activity" for human beings.

We should not confuse Bataille's speculative (and heterosexist) historical account with his logic here. In many ways, all of these anthropological accounts of early human activities and their development are what E. E. Evans-Pritchard calls "clever guesswork."[97] Bataille's assumption, following Lévi-Strauss, that clan societies are the original human societies, has been disproved by later scholarship, as Karatani demonstrates. According to Karatani, the transition from nomadic band society to sedentary clan society created problems with regard to the status of women.

Once hunting becomes more ritualized and symbolic, "the necessary production was increasingly carried out by women," although "this change led not to an elevation but to a lowering in the status of women."[98]

Karatani argues that the shift from nomadic to sedentary society lowered the status of women, although the practice of reciprocity helped to check this inequality, rather than accentuate it. It was really the start of agricultural civilization and the establishment of the state that brought about the permanent existence of patriarchy and the decisive decline in the status of women. The clan exchange economy was a mode of transition from one fundamental way of being in the world, as small nomadic hunting and gathering bands, to another, which is the massive sedentary society of the state with its militarized and monetized economy. At the same time, this pause is absolutely significant for Karatani, because he thinks that we can draw on some of the strategies these clan societies practiced to help us resist the predations of the contemporary state empire and its infusion by corporate capital.

According to Karatani, "the clan community is structured through reciprocal exogamy, which also leads to the establishment of a higher-order community (tribe or tribal confederation) that links together various clans."[99] The reciprocity inaugurated by the gift allows the creation of kinship-based societies that are based on social bonds rather than blood ties. Karatani wants to recover and *generalize* a society based on reciprocal exchange, which he calls A, in the form of a new socialist society, which he calls D, because that is the only way out of the hell that is the current combination of B—state and imperial society—and C—a society based on the bonds of money as capital that serves the state-form and generates wealth at the expense of people, animals, and, increasingly, the entire earth.

Bataille conflates these two early modes of social practice—the band society and the clan society—in his analysis. He assumes that the gift economy and its reciprocity lie at the origin of human society, and this is wrong. He also assumes a more absolute break between the social world of humans and the natural world of animals that is common in twentieth century continental philosophy, but also does not hold up in light of more recent research. I am not endorsing his specific history, but rather following his more general logic in setting up a general economy based on exchange, which involves both a material utility and an exuberant-erotic display of surplus energy. The identification of women as the original objects of exchange in the gift economy in some ways prefigures what Klossowski later imagines as "living currency." Women are the original form of currency that gets replaced by other people, domestic animals, tools, crops, and then coins in the form of money.

BATAILLE AND A GENERAL ENERGY ECONOMY

In volume 1 of the *The Accursed Share*, Bataille develops his idea of a general economy. A general economy is an energy economy, because it depends on "the circulation of energy upon the Earth."[100] The systems of human economic production and consumption are set within a wider framework because they are only possible due to the movements of energy around the world. According to Bataille, we profoundly disregard the material basis of life and so we err in how we understand human economic processes. We think that we work on the basis of utility and set up systems to organize and distribute the results of these systems in the most efficient way possible, but that is false. We use material resources for immediate ends, but we fail to understand the ultimate goal of our activities, because we mistake the immediate ends for final ends.

We think that human activities are structured around utilitarian goals, but our "activity in fact pursues the useless and infinite fulfillment of the universe."[101] Economics is based on the idea of scarcity, which determines our immediate constraints and ends, but a general economy is instead based on an excess of energy. Life is possible due to an excess of energy. The ultimate source of life's development is solar energy. Bataille says "the origin and essence of our wealth are given in the radiation of the sun, which dispenses energy—wealth—without any return."[102] Even though life probably originated in deep undersea vents, or smokers, most of the energy of and for life on earth is supplied by the sun. This solar radiation gives us a "superabundance of energy on the surface of the globe."[103]

The constant flow of energy from the sun to the earth is largely wasted, but its superabundance makes possible an economy of life. If this excess did not exist, there would be no evolution. Life spreads across the planet and fills every available niche, then doubles upon itself in its development.

The flow of energy around the globe makes life possible, and the living organism generally receives more energy than it needs to maintain itself. Since energy cannot be easily stored or long saved, it has to be used. Energy must be used up, and consumed, even if that is wasteful from the standpoint of utility.

Bataille says that if a system can no longer grow, based on the available energy, "it must be spent, willingly or not, gloriously or catastrophically."[104] Bataille understands that there is always a limit to growth, and he knows that the excess has to be spent or consumed. Everything is based on the flow of energy, including economics and human civilization. Energy transformations make possible human life and labor and social interactions and organizations. The excess energy of the sun, wind, water, and the compressed energy stored in fossil fuels enable our incredible technical civilization in material terms. This excess energy contributes to the unbelievable growth that we have seen over the past couple centuries, but it is also being spent and consumed. Our excess energy is entropic; it is being used up.

Energy flow is excessive; it is always being wasted. In order not to end, life has to find new ways to use this energy, or to use it up. According to Bataille, "its extreme exuberance pours out in a movement always bordering on explosion."[105] The pressure of and on life is this excessive energy, this superabundance that demands to be put to use. We want to calculate the utility of our actions, but they are essentially driven by this exuberance. "It is no doubt possible to *use* it for growth" up to a certain point, acknowledges Bataille. However, once we reach a limit to growth, "what is to be done with the seething energy that remains?" We have to find a way to consume it, or else it consumes us.

In *The Accursed Share*, Bataille imagines a state of even distribution of life that exists in a state of equilibrium. He argues that a "pressure everywhere equal to itself would result in a state of rest, in a general substitution of heat loss for reproduction. But real pressure has different results."[106] There is no general equilibrium at the level of life, and there is not any actual equilibrium in real physical systems either. Bataille is mainly talking about organic life, but his analysis applies broadly to physics and thermodynamics in a nonlinear nonequilibrium state, as we have seen.

Ultimately, Bataille claims, "there is generally no growth but only a luxurious squandering of energy in every form! The history of life on earth is mainly the effect of a wild exuberance."[107] Growth is only possible under very specific and local conditions. The general situation of life and of nature is that of exuberance based on the superabundance of energy. The particular situation of scarcity is radically opposed to the general perspective that is "based on the exuberance of living matter as a whole."[108]

Energy cannot ever fully be used, although it has to be useful in order to work. We mistake this utility and this usefulness for the reality of existence, when in fact it is the opposite. All of our systems are dissipative, as Prigogine and other theorists of nonequilibrium thermodynamics point out. Bataille is not a physicist, and he prioritizes biological realities, but he nevertheless grasps some of the basic principles at work. He says that "a surplus must be dissipated through deficit operations: The final dissipation cannot fail to carry out the movement that animates terrestrial energy."[109] Economics as a discipline usually deals with isolated closed systems, just as in equilibrium thermodynamics. Bataille blows this open with his conception of a general economy. He says that there is exists on the earth "a play of energy that no particular end limits"; it is this play or energy that generates life, growth, wealth, excess, and surplus.[110] Energy transformation never stops; it can be partially stored and measured but never completely fixed. Energy is how we measure change. Change is what is real about reality. Change is always interaction and relation; *change is always exchange.*

Consumption is absolutely opposed to any and all utility, even though we have to reckon with utility in particular economies. Consumption is the using and using up of excess energies, which is a basic law of life and existence. Consumption here incorporates at least two activities: first, consumption is the making use of "free" energies that exist due to the circulation of energy around the world as well as all across the universe; second, consumption contributes to entropy, because there is always a remainder or an excess that cannot be completely consumed. The term *consumption* is somewhat counterintuitive because of its association with what comes to be known as an economy of consumption, which replaces the economy of production. Here goods and services are consumed by consumers, and this is a consumerism that distinguishes wealthy nations and peoples under the reign of neoliberalism.

For Bataille, consumption has nothing to do with contemporary consumerism, which remains tied to a principle of utility. We need to follow

Karatani and avoid thinking about economy primarily in terms of either production or consumption. The economy in general has to do with exchange. Bataille shifts our thinking about economics from a framework of scarcity to one of excess and surplus. This is correct, but we should not lose sight of the role and function of entropy, even if he does not use this word. Bataille talks about the sacrificial consumption that allows separate beings to communicate in a form of intimacy. He says that "sacrifice is heat, in which the intimacy of those who make up the system of common works is rediscovered."[111] Heat is the waste or entropic result of the process of consumption, as well as the fuel for the process itself. Entropy and energy are conjoined in a complex, albeit confusing, way.

Consumption is characterized as an "expenditure without return." This expenditure is always an exchange, even though a necessary component of the exchange is its dissipative element. The "without return" refers to this entropic aspect of every exchange, which Bataille contrasts with the utility that governs the work that is produced. Nothing returns in itself or as itself, as Deleuze argues in *Difference and Repetition*. Repetition is always difference, and the principle of Nietzsche's eternal return is that only what is different returns.[112] The identical never returns. The expenditure is the process of repetition, and the "without return" is the always different that returns as a result of a selection.

Every exchange is asymmetrical; it is not just between two people or organisms or systems, but it includes the wider environment. That is why every economy is also an ecology. The general economy is an ecology, as we are being forced to confront. In his book *Bataille's Peak*, Allan Stoekl explains that Bataille's thought is incredibly relevant in this century because of the rediscovery of the critical role of energy in economics, nature, and life. Stoekl says that Bataille is unique "among twentieth-century thinkers in that he put energy at the forefront of his thinking of society: we are energy, our very being consists of the expenditure of quantities of energy."[113]

All our human and social activities involve the acquisition as well as the squandering of various forms of energy. These two—acquisition and exploitation of energy, as well as the using up and inevitable heat loss of energy—are part of the same process of energy. We think that energy and entropy are two different things, but they are actually two sides of the same coin. Bataille's energy incorporates both useful productive energy that works as well as entropic, useless energy. He often emphasizes the latter given how it ruins the former. There is always an excess of energy that cannot be used, that can only be used up and consumed. But there is always *more*. Energy is both an "infinite *force* and profoundly limited *resource*," and we need to comprehend both at the same time.[114]

The movement of energy "cannot accumulate limitlessly in the productive forces" of our economic activities; "eventually, like a river to a sea, it is bound to escape us and is lost to us," due to the entropic directionality of energy.[115] The excessive nature of surplus energy works to bring us to the point of "catastrophic destructions."[116] Since we always reach the point where we cannot continue to use this energy that builds up, we either have to destroy this excess or it will destroy us. That is what is happening with the excess of energy unleashed by modern capitalism. Its excess is destroying us and our planet, and it will thoroughly consume us unless we find some way to destroy it.

It is perhaps too easy to read Bataille as someone who celebrates the glorious excesses of capitalisms with its squandering of resources and destruction of the planet. Stoekl points out the flaws in this approach to Bataille: "there is a profound difference between expenditure as a feature of [what Heidegger calls] the standing reserve and expenditure as it appears as a function of intimate ritual." In the first case, the expenditure serves the maintenance of the sovereign self, whereas the second leads to the ruin of the self in "loss, dread, eroticism, death."[117] This death of the self is not the same as the literal destruction of the planet, but contains the seeds of a "postsustainable" world.

Postsustainability understands the inevitability of loss and the impossibility of equilibrium in nature or in human society. Even though we are using up our available resources of energy that has fueled the last two centuries of human growth, this does not mean that energy is being used up. Our world is postsustainable, because we cannot simply manage or sustain our energy usage and consumption on an Anthropocenic planet. At the same time, "the rapid decline of inert energy reserves is thus, paradoxically, a world full of expendable energy."[118] We will need to find ways to indulge in excessive practices of giving and reciprocity with the planet and with each other, even as these processes lead us to our doom.

Bataille's insights into energy and its connection with a general economy "requires the overturning of economic principles" as well as "the overturning of the ethics that grounds them."[119] We need to completely overturn our understandings of economy and ethics to do justice to energetics and entropy in nonequilibrium terms. We need to rethink everything if we want to survive in a postsustainable world. As Stoekl writes:

> If there is to be a postsustainable world, it will open itself as the aftereffect of gleaning: of the charged object, the charged body, the collision of past and future in and through death. It is a realm where there is a convergence of responsible recycling, defiant ritual, the sacrificial destruction of use and meaning, and social commitment beyond the narrow desires of the self. Community is an aftereffect of such postsustainable generosity.[120]

Postsustainable community cannot be merely human community; we are embedded in too many entanglements with other nonhuman organisms to survive alone. We must rethink what it means to be in community and take on the task of making kin beyond any form of familial kinship. This is what Donna Haraway advocates in *Staying with the Trouble*. She says that "the task is to make kin in lives of inventive connection as a practice of learning to live and die well with each other in a thick present."[121] Rather than an Anthropocene or even a Capitalocene, Haraway suggests that we are living in the Chthulucene, a name that indicates a thick presence for earth-beings. Chthulucene names "a kind of timeplace for learning to stay with the trouble of living and dying in response-ability on a damaged earth."[122] And I think her description of the Chthulucene resonates with Stoekl's understanding of postsustainability.

CHANGE AND EXCHANGE

Change is not just change; it is always already exchange. I discussed Malabou's philosophy in some detail in chapter 2, but I think we need to revisit her argument that change is always exchange here in connection to Bataille, Karatani, and political ecology. In her book *The Heidegger Change*, Malabou says that change as exchange designates barter, "the exchange of one object for another," as well as "a name for the place where economic negotiations are carried out, such as *le marché des changes*."[123] Although Malabou is engaged in a dense philosophical intervention into Heidegger's thought, it is helpful to situate her discussion of exchange in the context of my interpretation of Bataille.

Malabou suggests, in her interpretation of Heidegger, that Being itself is (ex)change. In his *Contributions to Philosophy*, Heidegger discusses what he calls the first beginning, which is the appropriation of being by the ancient Greeks. The exhaustion of this beginning in our contemporary world calls for a new beginning and an other way to receive and respond to the call of Being. Malabou, however, questions this priority. She claims that *"there is thus not or no longer a first (ex)change properly speaking. Change comes about by being put into play, meaning as soon as being is given."*[124] Being withdraws and conceals itself as it presents itself in and as particular beings. This is the way Heidegger defines truth, as *aletheia*, which means an uncovering or unconcealing of the Being of being. The uncovering of Being in beings also hides the essential nature of Being itself. According to Malabou, however, *"the thinking of originary withdrawal does not dismiss the idea of an originary (ex)change but instead economizes it differently."*[125] Here is an original economy of being, which is change.

Being gives itself in and as beings. This is what Heidegger calls the *Ereignis*, which is sometimes translated as "event of appropriation" and sometimes as "en-owning." The appropriating event of Being calls or claims the thinker-poet of Being, or Dasein, the "there" of Being, who is able to ask the question of Being. Being gives itself in its appropriating event, and Heidegger makes use of the German phrase *"es gibt"* as "it gives" which is normally translated as "there is." The gift of Being sets up a gift economy, an understanding that is also indebted to Mauss's anthropological work. Malabou argues that this giving of Being in an appropriating event "is a structure of substitution, a giving of change at the origin that metamorphoses giving itself by transforming the originary understanding of it. It is impossible to think what giving change might mean without changing the gift."[126] Malabou thinks Heideggerian Being as change, and this change is an exchange, a gift exchange and a reciprocal economy of the gift. Reciprocity is not equality, but an interaction, or "interchange."

At the heart of Being itself lies this notion of exchange. Exchange is the essence of Being. "My proposal is that *Ereignis*," Malabou writes, "must be envisaged as an *interchange* in which the elements that circulate or 'play' stop seeking to exercise mastery *on* each other and being value *for* each other."[127] *Being is interchange*, which means that there is an exchange of Being and beings, without the former being the primary, originary, and privileged form of the other. What Malabou does with her reading of Heidegger is posit *a general economy of being* that complements Bataille's general economy in *The Accursed Share*. The metaphysical perspective of Heidegger does not supersede the historical-anthropological approach of Mauss, Bataille, and Karatani. The metaphysical and the material-historical here are (ex)changed for each other. We cannot simply have one without the other. This crossing constitutes an economy, what makes an economy, which is meaning, value and utility, exuberance and consumption, giving and using up.

Malabou calls this "*absolute exchangeability of the originary gift*" of being an economy of the "favor."[128] The withdrawal of the privilege of Being favors the being it gives (to). Being does not master and lord it over beings, which must be sacrificed for Being; rather Being sacrifices itself and withdraws in order to favor the beings it exchanges for. "The 'favor' marks the coming of an exchange without privilege," Malabou says, "in which no instance, rightly, receives *favorable treatment*" because every being can be exchanged not only for another being but also for Being itself.[129]

Malabou does not call the fundamental exchange of being energy, but that is really what it is. In most of her work, she privileges form, particularly the plasticity of biological form, and this is absolutely novel and crucial for understanding what is happening in the world. However, she neglects the "form" of energy, of energy transformation, including the (ex)change of energy (Being) for form (as in, beings). Energy *favors* the creation of forms, including organic ones, under specific circumstances, as I have tried to show. For Bataille, the general economy of the Earth is characterized by the flows of energy across the planet. Every economy is an energy economy. If there is an economy of being, would it not have to be energy? Of course, Malabou could say that I privilege energy over form, but that is precisely the *interchange* that I am trying to get at, which is not a way of simply substituting Energy for Being as if it were something, some entity that controls and directs our lives. Her general economy of (ex)change of being is how I understand energy. Being is energy transformation, which means energy (ex)change. The material site of energy exchange is form, which is plastic and metamorphic. Malabou says that when Heidegger is talking about the *Ereignis* and the *Gestell* (the enframing of things in a technological society) he is really thinking about "the *metabolic unity* of *holding together* that is not a rigid framing but a changing bond and supple relation. *A plastic, phenomenal crossing of things*."[130] This metabolic "holding together" is energy, which is also "a plastic, phenomenal crossing of things." Energy is not some immaterial force disconnected from material form. Energy takes form in and as change, as exchange. Energy withholds itself as energy in the form of matter, but it does not exempt itself from change, because energy is change. And change is always exchange.

The (ex)change of energy constitutes an economy. In human history, this is a political economy, whereas in the context of our planet it forms an ecological economy. That is the nexus I am trying to comprehend in this chapter. Every general economy is exchanged for a particular economy, and vice versa, if we follow Malabou's logic. We cannot simply leave behind the particular economies in which we exist and participate for an abstract general economy. At the same time, every particular economy participates in a general economy by means of (ex)change. The gift is both the historical form of a particular clan society's economy at a particular point in time, as Karatani shows, and it signifies the general economy of reciprocity. Reciprocity is always exchange, but it is never equivalent. Nothing occurs in a state of equilibrium. Energy flow never takes place at equilibrium, and neither does what we call thermodynamics, or organic life. Economy is nonequilibrium, and so is ecology, as well as human history and politics. We need to trace and track and follow these exchanges.

Malabou addresses the interchange of metaphysics and history toward the end of her Heidegger book. She argues that the question of Heidegger "cannot be divorced from a critique of capitalism," which tries to fix exchange and occlude change.[131] Metaphysics tends to think about abstract concepts like being, justice, and beauty without history, whereas historical analysis often neglects its basic metaphysical presuppositions about the nature of reality. Our attempt to reflect on political economy and political ecology in terms of a general economy of energy cannot be divorced from a critique of capitalism.

Malabou asserts that "a proximity between Heidegger and Marx indeed exists, and it doubtlessly lies in the possibility of the ontological and the economic coinciding in the definition of exchange, of exchange and mutability, of the metamorphisable and displaceable character of value, and of the impossibility of transgressing all this plasticity."[132] She retrieves or develops an improbable notion of revolution in Heidegger based on the idea of change. The historical nature of being reveals the absence of revolution, the absence of genuine, substantial change, because all we can see is more of the same. At the same time, for Malabou being is change, and revolution constitutes the idea and possibility of real change.

Revolutionary change for Malabou is suggested not in a future event that would exchange this world for another utopian world, but in the fracture that constitutes every being, including us. We are Dasein, being-there, and we are marked by the fracture of an exchange, which is the difference between two regimes of (ex)change: the capitalist one and the noncapitalist one. This fracture, or rift, is the very essence of revolution. "*The mark of revolution is the fracture constituting us*," she concludes.[133] The crossing of the line between the capitalist and the non- or alter-capitalist regime is what makes revolution.

The economic law of being is exchange, which is the possibility for Heidegger of crossing from the first beginning to the other beginning, but for Malabou it is more precisely the crossing of the line from the capitalist world of value to *an other world of (ex)change*. The end of History as a project of modernist linear progress is both an obstacle to and an opportunity for revolutionary change. In order to posit and to think the existence of the other noncapitalist, regime, *we have to have already crossed over the line*.

Even if this is entirely too conceptual, metaphysical, hypothetical, and abstract, we need to take into account the real possibility for change beyond our world of capitalism and its values. Malabou claims that "form can cross the line, becoming precisely the other of the idea—a non-ideal form that is at once both the condition and the result of change. Form can cross the line . . . and the line becomes form, creative minds *giving form* to the line; the form of a life that is from here out revolutionized, reversed, and opened in the middle: a market of (ex)changes, an agora, a negotiating table between two exchanges, *a space of responsibility*."[134] These are the spaces that Bataille and Karatani, Mitchell and Malm, Georgescu-Roegen and Klossowski, Haraway, and Latour, as well as so many other anthropological and revolutionary thinkers, have opened up and given form.

The revolutionary nature of the gift is its ability to open up precisely this exchange and challenge the seemingly unassailable logic of capitalism. We know that capitalism cannot work, but we still cling to it and worship it with our labor and our love. We also have to work for change, for true revolutionary change, to give form to *an other world* (but not another world, say, for example, Mars or some sort of planetary escape). This demand for change, heard all around us, forces us back into the particular phenomenon of the gift economy, to offer resources for resistance to neoliberal capitalism and possibilities for a human society beyond capitalism. This is most clearly seen in clan societies, but these clan societies are not simply relics of the past, as I will show in the next chapter.

A NEW POLITICS OF NATURE

The world is changing all around us, whether we call it the Anthropocene or something else. The planet is in the middle of an exchange of one climate for other. All our politics and our economies and our energies and our forms will have to confront this fact, or we will die. We will die anyway, but what else can we do? We would like to name the catastrophe and resist the barbarism now and future. Isabelle Stengers calls for an intervention into our ways of living that would respond to "the intrusion of Gaia," and the ensuing "global climatic disorder," even if it is too late to prevent it.[135]

We need to resist capitalism, but we also need to resist our own instincts to turn to quick fixes and modes of salvation from our desperate situation. We need a new political ecology and economy—a new politics of nature. Nature here cannot simply mean what it once did, referring to the opposite of human culture and cultural production. Nature is part of everything because we are also nature; nature is nothing because there is nothing that is not natural.

Michel Serres combines natural and human modes of knowing and understanding and expresses these in powerful and sometimes poetic ways. In *The Natural Contract*, published in French in 1990, he explicitly argues for a new natural contract with the planet that would supersede the notion of a political and social contract among humans. Human culture "abhors the world," but now "earth, waters, and climate, the mute world, the voiceless things once placed as a décor surrounding the usual spectacles, all those things that never interested anyone, from now on have thrust themselves brutally and without warning into our schemes and maneuvers."[136] Human history is a history of war and violence that pits kin or clan groups of people against each other and against the world as a whole. The only possibility for peace is the idea of revising the original social contract and signing a new natural contract with the world. We have the idea of perpetual peace, but we do not know how to bring it into existence, because we remain tied to the interests of separate groups, cultures, and nations. According to Serres, "we must decide on peace among ourselves to protect the world, and peace with the world to protect ourselves."[137]

This peace appears improbable, if not impossible. Humans have not abated their wars against nature, or each other, and climate change has spurred conflicts and violence anew. We cannot change, even as we know we must. How can we learn to live with the Earth? Bruno Latour is strongly influenced by Serres, although he jettisons the language of nature and the opposition between nature and culture that Serres appears to retain. In his work, Latour articulates the philosophical epistemology that Serres finds so wanting in his studies of philosophy.

In *We Have Never Been Modern* and later works, Latour argues that Western modernity installs a false separation between the realm of human politics and the realm of nonhuman nature. This split induces a schizophrenic divide between the scientists who investigate natural laws and politicians who prescribe laws for human societies. In *Politics of Nature*, Latour states that most of the contemporary discourse on political ecology "merely rehashes the modern Constitution of a *two-house* politics in which one house is called politics, and the other, under the name of nature, renders the first one powerless."[138] Politics happens at the social level, between and among us speaking humans, whereas nature is mute, subjected to our gaze and our use. The only way to have a genuine political ecology is to eliminate this split.

Our human agential world is usually seen as the sole site of ethics and value, because such values are denied to nonhuman objects. For Latour, "political ecology does not speak about nature" because nature refuses the possibility of political ecology.[139] Ecological movements have been constrained by their commitment to a false conception of nature that they wish to protect. This commitment and this conception perpetuates the split that Latour is trying to help us overcome. So long as we see nature as something that lacks agency and moral value, we cannot value and affirm it. We can only exploit it as a natural resource for our use. This concept of nature makes political ecology impossible because it aborts the very idea of politics from the start.

We need to let go of the idea of a separate realm of nature so that we can help fashion a "collective"—one that addresses the "progressive composition of the common world."[140] The problem with the idea of nature is that it suggests a mute entity rather than a collective of agencies. There is no clear separation of natural and social collectives; they all take place in a common world, which is rife with agency and animation. In *Facing Gaia*, Latour brings up the example of two struggles over the flow of the Mississippi River: one is the struggle between the river and the Army Corps of Engineers who attempt to control it and the other is a struggle between the Mississippi River itself and another smaller river, the Atchafalaya. The small river lies below the Mississippi River and tries to capture the waters of its massive neighbor. The Army Corps of Engineers works to prevent this exchange, because its success would flood a huge region of the Mississippi delta.[141]

Climate change is accelerating this battle, which the Atchafalaya is winning. In June 2019, the Morganza spillway was opened for the third time in sixty-five years, flooding massive parts of the delta to relieve some of the high waters of the Mississippi River. In response, humans whose homes and land have been flooded are calling for the Trump administration to "Finish the Pumps," a reference to a proposed plan that is eighty years old called the Yazoo Pumps. Every politician in Mississippi has to support "finishing" or, actually in fact, building these pumps, which would cost hundreds of millions of dollars to construct and destroy tens of thousands of acres of vital wetlands that would be drained in the process.[142] In late 2020, the Trump administration green-lit this project, but a year later, in 2021, the EPA overturned this decision and shut down this massive flood control project.

This is a complex conflict among multiple political agents, including people, organizations, rivers and wetlands. The rivers are not simply objects that are subjected to the whims of humans; they act in a variety of ways that compete against each other and against some of our agential activities. In our modern world, we have worked to deny the agency and animation of the natural world, and this deanimation is both false and dangerous. Latour says that "animation is the essential phenomenon; and deanimation is the superficial, auxiliary, polemical, and often defensive phenomenon."[143] Nature is always already animated in various important ways, including political ones. We need to escape the opposition between nature and culture and instead see a multiplicity of animated existents operating in ways that compose and decompose worlds.[144]

These animated agents are constantly undergoing *metamorphoses*. "The actors," Latour writes, "with their multiple forms and capacities, never stop exchanging their properties."[145] Instead of a world of human subjects who subdue and control inanimate nature, we must see the world as a complex multiplicity of agents who are constantly changing and exchanging. Nature and culture are always exchanging themselves, in and for each other, in continual metamorphosis. The retention of any significance between the two blinds us to what is happening in the world today.

In *Down to Earth*, Latour argues that the only way we can make sense of what is going on politically over the last few decades is to understand how the ongoing deregulation of global capitalism, the explosion of inequalities, and the amplification of migrations around the world are all connected to climate change. He argues that "it is as though a significant segment of the ruling classes . . . had concluded that the earth no longer had room enough for them and for everyone else."[146] The denial of climate change by the elites who know better constitutes the incredible nonsense that characterizes our political discourse.

Globalization is losing its appeal as these inequalities and catastrophes mount. There is no land that could support this globalization, because Earth does not possess sufficient resources to maintain the growth that capitalism requires. Political discourse has become more and more detached from reality, and Latour argues that the only way to comprehend this is to understand that the ruling elites have decided to "*stop pretending, even in their dreams, to share the earth with the rest of the world.*"[147] The traditional oppositions between liberal and conservative, right and left, global and local, have completely broken down. "Everything has to be mapped out anew, with new costs."[148]

Latour offers a schema to visualize his analysis and to help us understand what is at stake. He argues that the elites are supporting an "Out-of-This-World" mentality that pushes people to fantasize about other worlds or nonearthly realities. In contrast, Latour offers another attractor, a "Terrestrial" attractor that would work to bring politics, society, and human activities *down to the real earth*. He posits the terrestrial as a "*new political actor.*"[149] A terrestrial return to earth opposes the out-of-this-world scenario that our ruling elites are promoting, with varying degrees of success. This terrestrial attractor also avoids the oppositions between right and left (as well as local and global) that so many people continue to get hung up on.

Globalized capitalist modernity has failed, but so have contemporary environmental and ecological movements. Ecology has failed to stem the tide of capitalist accumulation and destruction. We cannot enact effective change if we fail to understand the stakes of what is happening. And, if we do, there is always the danger of nihilism and despair. However, Latour offers at least a blueprint for how to conceptualize a new political orientation that would be explicitly terrestrial and force us to confront the realities of life on an unstable planet, as well as provide resources to resist the elites who have decided that we do not deserve to inhabit it anymore.

Latour argues that we need to shift our analyses of what is happening in the world from "a *system of production* to an analysis focused on a *system of engendering.*"[150] This shift is similar to Karatani's shift of historical analysis from a system of production to a system of exchange. Because exchange is always metamorphosis, and therefore change, as Malabou points out, a system of exchange is also a system of engendering new dynamics and new relations. Latour argues that the system of production emphasizes the freedom and centrality of human beings, as well as a mechanistic development to describe how human beings operate upon the world. Conversely, a system of engendering would emphasize human dependency on other processes, where humanity itself is a distributed effect of other agencies and activities. Finally, the development that takes place in the world would be a kind of genesis rather than a deterministic mechanism.Genesis is another name for metamorphosis, but it is not creation out of nothing, ex nihilo. Nothing is generated out of nothing. Systems and organisms are not self-generating and self-regulating; they are heterogenetic. They develop along gradients of energy exchange. Energy is (ex)change. Everything has to be mapped out anew.

In his Gifford Lectures, published as *Facing Gaia*, Latour notes that the novelist William Golding suggested the name Gaia to James Lovelock as a way to capture the notion of a complex adaptive system that is metastable, such as Earth's atmosphere. According to Latour, Gaia is not simply the name of a god or goddess. In ancient Greek, Hesiod says that Gaia is one of the basic elemental forces that emerges from Chaos, the other being Eros. Gaia is a dark chthonic power that has deep affinities with what Haraway calls the Chthulucene. For Latour, Gaia is a fitting name, but not a proper name of Earth. Gaia is a secular name or figure for what we are used to calling Nature. He claims that Gaia is "composed of agents that are neither *deanimated* nor *overanimated*." As important, Gaia is not a closed system: "it is made up of agents that are not *prematurely unified* in a single active totality."[151] Gaia is not an entity but a name for a complex process of terrestrial genesis and generation.

Latour calls us to face up to Gaia, to come to terms with the intrinsic animacy of existence and the specific terrestrial location of earth-bound entities. Gaia points us beyond the stupid and dangerous oppositions between nature and culture, human and nonhuman. Gaia helps us confront our situation on this planet in a serious way. Latour says that "Gaia is *an injunction to rematerialize our belonging to the world*."[152] New materialisms are not new; they are efforts at rematerialization, or renewable materialisms, which is another way to think about history. History cannot be divided into natural and cultural, human histories. In *Facing Gaia*, Latour cites Serres and his idea of a natural contract. In his book, *Biogea*, Serres develops a similar logic to that of Latour, although Serres does not use the name Gaia. For Serres, Biogea is the preferred name for the terrestrial processes of change and exchange they both invoke. The Earth under the guise of Biogea intrudes into human history, and henceforth we need to learn to think like the Earth, change such that "my body thinks like the Earth."[153]

Serres develops a language to think like and with the Earth, and he calls this a peace treaty as well as a natural contract. Language is about coding and decoding, but we are not the only beings who use language; "we are not the only ones to write and read, to code, to decipher the codes of others, to get decoded by others, to understand, mutate, invent, communicate, exchange signals, process information, encounter one another."[154] This common language is shared with all things in the world, creating the potential for something like peace. We need to learn to read the codes attached to things, to understand and interpret these codes and codings that constitute a universal language if we want to survive.

This universal language is not just a scientific and mathematical language. It is also a poetic language that Serres forges with and through Biogea, using its energy and its movements to code and recode terrestrial existence. Serres calls the energy that flows through everything in the world a kind of joy, even if he does not specifically use the word *energy*. The eruption in and of a world is an explosion of joy, whether the universe, the creation of a star, a planet, life, or an ecosystem. "So, dense, intense, explosive," he exclaims, "joy came, from the left, from the right, in high waves, at ground level, in cataracts and rushing tides, like a tsunami."[155] This joy is the surplus energy that Bataille names in *The Accursed Share*. This joy is "the matter from which the Biogea is made."[156] The joy that Serres associates with Biogea is energy; it is also spirit, to which I turn in the next chapter with the aid of specific non-Western traditions.

4

OF SPIRIT IN AMERINDIAN, VODOU, AND CHINESE TRADITIONS

YOU MUST CHANGE YOUR PERSPECTIVE

To better comprehend spirit in nondual terms, in this chapter I shift our conceptions of spirit and nature from the dominant Eurocentric perspective in the direction of certain forms of animism in the context of indigenous and so-called syncretistic traditions. Here I turn explicitly to some non-Western traditions, including Amerindian (specifically Amazonian and Haudenosaunee) worldviews, the complex phenomenon that is Haitian Vodou, and neo-Confucian *qi* philosophy. As Mark Rifkin explains, "the practices, knowledges, and forms of collective identification often characterized as *tradition* can be understood as distinct ways of being in time." These traditions "emerge from material processes of reckoning with an environment and are open to change," even as they maintain metastable processes to slow down energy dissipation in the form of entropy.[1]

We can think about energy in physical and material terms. One of the problems of many religions and metaphysical systems is the dualist opposition between spirit and matter, at least in terms of how it is expressed. From the perspective of new materialism and nonequilibrium thermodynamics, energy is fully material, but in such a way that it produces "spiritual" effects. If we think about energy as spirit, this can risk sounding like some sort of New Age mysticism or neovitalism. But the ways of thinking about energy that I've developed in this book show a perspective on energy from which something like spirit can be extrapolated. In Chinese philosophy, for instance, the notion of *qi* 氣, which is usually translated as energy, sometimes as psychophysical energy, evades the dualism of matter and spirit, because qi is fully material, but it can become spiritual under specific circumstances. I will discuss qi more fully at the conclusion of this chapter.

According to two of our most important contemporary philosophers, Barad and Latour, we need to think about physical matter less in terms of inanimate stuff and more in terms of agents or agentialism—what they call agential realism. Agents are one form of spirit, and in many nonmodern cultures these spirits have been criticized as irredeemably anthropomorphic, because they are considered as persons with humanlike minds and wills. However, I argue that this is not necessarily the case, and things are much more complex from the perspective of Latour, Barad, and others.

The world "is" an irreducible multiplicity; whatever exists naturally or objectively cannot be reduced or compressed into a unity except in terms of how our language and conceptuality organizes it socially, subtracting from the infinite potentiality of its appearance. As Deleuze explains in *Difference and Repetition*, we compare difference to difference, in the form of two or more series, and the interstices take shape as the new difference that is produced. This is similar to how Barad explains a diffraction pattern in *Meeting the Universe Halfway*, and in this chapter I am setting up a diffraction pattern or effects series between and among the minor tradition of neo-Confucian qi philosophy, the complex assemblage of Vodou practices that constitutes a time-image, and the multinaturalist perspectivism of Amerindian spirituality.

Amerindians are an example of what Karatani calls clan societies in his book *The Structure of World History*, as discussed in the previous chapter. For Karatani, these clan societies represent the mode of exchange he labels A, which is based on reciprocity. Clan societies practice a form of reciprocity focused around the gift, which he calls mode of exchange A, and this form of society differs from earlier hunter-gatherer forms of social operation. The reciprocity that takes place in clan societies provides Karatani the basis for his argument that we need new modes of social and economic exchange, that he calls D. D lies beyond the modes of exchange B (the state or empire form of exchange based on centralization and expansion) and C (the economic mode of exchange based on equivalence of a monetary currency). D is therefore a renewal or return to A in a different form, or a repetition of difference across a long historical gradient. According to Karatani, this fourth type of exchange, D, is first inaugurated with the appearance of universal religion and philosophy around the sixth century BCE.

He ties the birth of philosophy in Ionia, a Greek colony in Asia Minor, to the emergence of universal religion in Jewish Babylon, as well as the profound changes that were occurring around the same time in India and China. Karatani claims that figures like the Hebrew prophets (Isaiah, Jeremiah, Ezekiel, and in a retroactive sense Moses), as well as Ionian thinkers, Chinese sages, and Indian reformers, characterize what he calls "exemplary prophets," a concept that is necessary to comprehend "the emergence of mode of exchange D into human history."[2]

Fast forward to the early twenty-first century, where Karatani is advocating the adoption of mode of exchange D over those of B (the nationalist state) and C (the system of imperial global capitalism). This mode of exchange is also a kind of religion or a quasi-religious mode of exchange. That is, D accomplishes a *spiritual* exchange. My contention is that attending to the clan practices of reciprocity organized around the gift provides insight into a new materialist political ecology that is at the same time a form of spirituality. This spirituality is not nostalgia for some illusory harmony but rather the effect of specific forms of social exchange. And these societies are not relics of the past; they are potential harbingers of our future.

The spirituality of these societies appears irreducibly anthropomorphic, which is why they have often been relegated to a historical past. In his anthropological work, however, Eduardo Viveiros de Castro gives us better ways to understand the anthropomorphism of these Amerindian clans, which he studies (largely in Brazil) in agential terms. The anthropomorphism of Amerindians and other indigenous peoples constitutes what Viveiros de Castro calls a *relational multinaturalism* that contrasts with more familiar multiculturalisms.

One example of a critical perspective on European multiculturalism is Peter Sloterdijk, a German philosopher who is the author of *Critique of Cynical Reason* as well as a massive trilogy, *Spheres*. Sloterdijk illuminates much of what is going on in our world today in terms of spiritual practices, although he does so in an explicitly cynical way. This cynicism is appropriate to the phenomena he analyzes in our postindustrial culture, but, instead of absolutizing this approach, I want to use it as a foil for looking at indigenous and other non-European traditions. Here I turn Sloterdijk's perspective inside out, using the thought of Viveiros de Castro.

In *You Must Change Your Life*, Sloterdijk argues that there is no such thing as "religion"; no religions actually exist. Instead, there exist "spiritual regimens" of a collective or individual nature.[3] In a contemporary technological (first) world, we participate in spiritual regimes of transformation to make us better people. Sometimes this takes the form of what we normally think of when we think of a religion, but more often in secular terms it looks like a practice of self-improvement, success, health, and/or fitness.

All these practices are ascetic, because we engage in practices of self-denial for some physical, moral, financial, or spiritual benefit. Many of our ascetic practices are less obviously or explicitly spiritual and more somatic, focused on competitive sports. Here the emphasis is upon vitality, which is "understood both somatically and mentally, [and] is itself the medium that contains a gradient between more and less."[4] God as the externally intended object of spirituality is less important than the intrinsic form of the person who practices these regimes. *Vitality* is one word for energy, at least in popular language and understanding; it conveys a certain vulgar understanding that Sloterdijk critiques. We are concerned with energy because we are concerned with vitality, because our technical society is so focused on these spiritual regimes of self-improvement. And this energy animates our machines, our bodies, our psyches, and our new age mysticisms.

Sloterdijk cynically unmasks our pretensions in a postmodern, postindustrial world, and he does so with clarity, discernment, and wit. He demonstrates how empty so many of our lives are, and how they are driven by a quasi-spiritual ascetic quest to continuously improve. He uses the metaphor of the tightrope walker that Nietzsche employs in *Thus Spoke Zarathustra*. Even if there is no ground beneath us and no fixed destination, the activity of walking the rope suspended above an abyss gives our lives a sense of meaning. Education is about training, to learn the steps to walk across the rope. "Walking on the rope means gathering all that has been in the present," Sloterdijk explains. "Only then can the imperative, 'You must change your life!' be transformed into daily sequences of exercises."[5] This imperative is a line from a poem by Rilke, which gives the title of the book by Sloterdijk: *You Must Change Your Life*. Life is a training ground for these spiritual, psychological, and athletic regimens to be enacted.

There is something deeply nihilistic about how Sloterdijk exposes the triviality of our existence, and how he argues that this imperative for change ironically locks us into a repetition of sameness. The change Sloterdijk refers to is the change that we mock when we see someone naively trying to "change the world." Barack Obama ran for president of the U.S. in 2008 touting "Change We Can Believe In," and then simply resumed neoliberalism as usual in economic and political terms, and this neoliberalism has been largely restored by Joe Biden in 2021 after the Trump interregnum. Isn't there something trivial, simplistic, and empty about change? And isn't energy understood as vitality also empty and vague? Certainly many contemporary incantations of both of these words ring hollow.

Sloterdijk cites Pierre Hadot's saying that "all education is conversion," where conversion involves this very form of change that has become secularized and universalized in our world today.[6] Conversion today involves an exchange of trainers in a pathetic pantomime of Bataille's and Malabou's ideas of exchange, which were discussed in chapter 3. We trade one trainer, teacher, guru, hero, inspiration, coach, or boss for another. The ultimate authority of this imperative to change for Sloterdijk is "the global crisis, which, as everyone has been noticing for some time, has begun to send out its apostles. Its authority is real because it is based on something unimaginable of which it is the harbinger: the global catastrophe."[7] The unimaginable global catastrophe is often global warming, the climate change that augurs a disastrous transformation of our planet, rendering it uninhabitable for human life. But it can also take the form of nuclear war or a global pandemic like COVID-19. In the meantime, as we anticipate the unimaginable apocalyptic catastrophe, we need to make the best of it and ourselves with recourse to these spiritual regimens.

Why is this detour through Sloterdijk relevant? Because he points out something truly important about our discourse, and he draws upon as well as mocks our current mode of understanding. We think that we are something or someone. We are forms, bodies, natures, or beings who must change ourselves. We must change our minds, our views, our perspectives so that we can do what needs to be done, which is change the world. And this is wrong. And we all know that it is absolutely useless, but we continue to say and do it because we cannot imagine doing anything else. We have inherited a society based on narcissistic desire for personal happiness and improvement that reinforces capitalist production and consumption. My argument is that we need to reimagine energy so that we can change our lives, but we know that's also ideological nonsense. Our spiritual practices are so degraded and embedded in neoliberal capitalism that we cannot extricate them, so we say "change" as a mantra and hold our breath and hope for the miracle that never occurs.

We need to turn this whole scenario inside out. We need to think about spirits and spiritual practices differently, less superficially, and certainly less separate from matter and nature. We need to turn toward the very example that Karatani lifts up for us to emulate, the clan society that inaugurates mode of exchange A that then opens us up to the possibility of mode of exchange D.

The most common way to characterize contemporary postmodernism is in terms of cultural perspectivism and relativism. We know that there is one nature out there, but we can only access it through our language, our cultural habits, and our conscious minds that shape it into something for us to know and use. Everyone's reality is their own subjective reality; there is a posited objective reality, but we cannot know it because we can only know our own. This is a quasi-Kantian argument, adapted to the cultural and linguistic turns that characterize contemporary multiculturalism. There is nature, but nature, or objective reality, is a thing in itself, a noumenal reality that we cannot know. All we have is our own phenomenal reality, which is how the world and its characteristics appear to us. We each possess our individual subjective and collective social perspective on the world in which we live and act.

Attention to these particular or local narratives both obscures and reinforces the partially hidden global narrative that it presumes. This is the tension that Dipesh Chakrabarty identifies in his influential book *Provincializing Europe* when he contrasts the universal history of capital—History 1, with all of the particular social and cultural histories that sustain, modify, reinforce, and interrupt it, which he names History 2.[8]

So long as we embrace this subjective social perspectivism, whether we oppose or assert it in relation to a universal natural or human history, we perpetuate the same problem, which is the problem of neoliberal capitalism. Neoliberal capitalism is dividing and destroying us, giving us the promise of change while deferring and denying it in practice.

This is why Fredric Jameson's expression, attributed to an unnamed other and repeated by Slavoj Žižek, that it is easier to imagine the end of the world than an alternative to capitalism, is so insightful and pervasive.[9] *We need to turn this scenario inside out* if we want to envision an actual future society for human beings that is not capitalist. And this is a spiritual work, a work of religion, in Karatani's terms. Instead of a social perspectivism that posits an objective natural world, we need a natural perspectivism that generates an objective social reality.

THE ENDS OF THE WORLD: AMERINDIAN PERSPECTIVISM AS MULTINATURALISM

This perspectivism is an indigenous and Amerindian perspectivism, according to Viveiros de Castro. And my argument is that this natural perspectivism allows us to glimpse something like what Karatani invokes when we talks about mode of exchange D. Furthermore, this is the link where nature and spirit intersect and entangle, constituting a spiritual (new) materialism, which is a vital repetition of these indigenous material and spiritual traditions. The place of spirit is what we have called nature, but it is confused and confusing to talk about native traditions, cultures, or religions if we assume that nature and spirit mean the same thing that they do for Western Europeans. According to this multinaturalism, nature is an irreducible perspectival multiplicity, whereas social human reality is more solid and substantial and unified.

In *The Relative Native*, Viveiros de Castro argues that "the problem for indigenous perspectivism is not therefore one of discovering the common referent (say, the planet Venus) to two different representations (say, 'Morning Star' and 'Evening Star.')." Rather, it is a question "of making explicit the equivocation implied in imagining that when the jaguar says 'manioc beer' he is referring to the same thing as us (i.e., a tasty, nutritious and heady brew)." That is, indigenous perspectivism combines a constant and consistent epistemology with a variable ontology, "a single meaning and multiple referents."[10] Here is what is the same is the social meaning, not the external nature. Nature is multiple and open to multiple perspectives, while what is shared is the social reality of human (and potentially other) beings.

In Western epistemology, one can contrast a social constructionist perspectivism with a more objective positivist representation of reality. This perspectivism is associated with Leibniz, Nietzsche, Foucault, and Deleuze, among others. Viveiros de Castro affirms perspectivism and notes that "virtually all peoples of the New World share a conception of the world as composed of a multiplicity of points of view."[11] The problem, however, is that this perspectivism is usually imagined as a multiplicity of social perspectives that opens onto one unified nature. This social perspectivism generates the shallow multiculturalism that liberals affirm and Sloterdijk scorns. It founds the various spiritual regimens that underlie postmodern narcissism: *"You* Must Change *Your* Life" because the world is malleable and subject to your perspective and your practice.

Instead of a social perspectivism and subsequent multiculturalism, however, Viveiros de Castro advocates a multinaturalism based on his work with Amazonian Amerindians. Where contemporary multicultural relativism "supposes a diversity of subjective and partial representations, each striving to grasp an external and unified nature," Amerindian thought does the opposite. Here the unity is a proposed phenomenological or representational unity that constitutes human culture, and this is applied to a "radically objective diversity."[12] We need to *exchange* our social multicultural perspectivism for a more multinatural perspectivism.

There is something that is universal at the level of humanity, but it should be understood differently from modern anthropocentric humanism. Viveiros de Castro contrasts the Amerindian viewpoint on humanity with that of Marx. For Marx, the human "produces universally," which means that humanity is the universal animal in a sense. But when Marx says that "humans can 'be' any animal," he is saying that "we have more being than any other species." The Amerindian understanding is an inversion of this contention. When Amerindians "say that 'any' animal can be human," they claim "that there is more being to an animal than meets the eye."[13] From our and every being's shared cultural perspective, there is something that characterizes a being that is understood in terms of humanity, but it acts on a radically diverse and differentiated nature.

Viveiros de Castro argues that "Amazonian multinaturalism affirms not so much a variety of natures as the naturalness of variation—variation *as* nature."[14] This is also the perspective of evolution I emphasized in chapter 2. Change is at the heart of reality, not as subjective voluntarism but rather as nature itself, insofar as there is such a thing. Change names this variation as nature, and that turns the more well-known cultural perspectivism inside out. And change is always exchange, as we saw in chapter 3.

In this multinatural situation, "'culture' is a reflexive perspective of the subject," whereas "'nature' is the viewpoint which the subject takes of the other body," as Viveiros de Castro puts it. Here *"nature is the form of the other as body."*[15] The other being is encountered in the form of an external body, and that consists of its "nature," which is always multiple, relational, and variable. We have to begin with "culture" because that is how we make sense, but this culture is what is shared, not our "nature." This twist is what characterizes Amerindian thought, and it is much more subtle and significant than we likely assume. Multinaturalism generates what we call animism, which characterizes clan societies.

Euromodern intellectuals often think that animism is the invalid attribution of an invisible force or spirit to something in the natural world that is intrinsically inanimate. However, Viveiros de Castro and Déborah Danowski claim that animism proceeds from a proto-world multiverse that is essentially anthropomorphic because humanity is the universal substance that animates it—"the active principle at the origin of the proliferation of living forms in a rich, plural world."[16] In the Amerindian world, humans come first and the rest of creation proceeds from them. Nature is generated out of primordial human culture. This is less naive than it sounds, because it posits a nonhuman humanity that "animates" the production of forms in the world, which are differentiated as "nature."

In Amerindian cosmology, "every existing being in the cosmos thus sees itself as human, but does not see other species in the same way."[17] The only way to see oneself as an animating principle is as a human or, more generally, as a person. This animating principle is a differentiating and individuating process that generates others in the form of bodies, which is what Viveiros de Castro calls nature. In the beginning, everything was human in a sense, and various forms including the beings considered *homo sapiens* were differentiated out of this primordial humanity. Here the human is "placed as *empirically anterior* in relation to the world," which means that the world is *subtracted* from the original unification or correlation with the human.[18]

What Amerindians designate as human is an animating agential process that produces natural reality in material forms. This primordial animating principle is what we call *spirit*, and I want to associate this understanding of spirit with the vision of energy articulated in chapter 1. From the perspective of contemporary physics, energy is impersonal and non-anthropomorphic, and it is incredible to attribute human or personal qualities to energy. One strategy is we intellectuals can adopt is to bracket some of the anthropomorphic baggage that comes along with thinking about indigenous animisms and focus on what this animating principle does, which is virtually the same thing that energy does. More profoundly than that, however, we need to better understand what this anthropomorphism is and what it does, which is agential in nature.

In *The Relative Nature*, Viveiros de Castro argues that the form of the gift exchange characterizes clan societies. This practice of gift exchange, what Karatani calls A, leads these societies to view this form of exchange as an exchange of *persons*, which is both an economic and a voluptuous exchange. Furthermore, Viveiros de Castro argues that "gift exchange, kinship, and animism are merely different names for the same personification process: the economic, political, and religious faces of a single generalized symbolic economy, as it were."[19]

Reading Viveiros de Castro in relation to Bataille and to Karatani helps us better understand what he is doing and why it is so important. Since it is persons who are fundamentally the objects of exchange in a reciprocal economy, these societies fundamentally envision objects as persons. At the same time, if Being is (ex)change, as Malabou argues, then we cannot simply cordon off human persons from the rest of existence. There is something genuinely personal about every being insofar as it matters.

I am appealing not just to Viveiros de Castro's poststructural anthropology but also contemporary philosophers like Latour and Barad to suggest that what is important is seeing these and all objects as agents. We normally describe indigenous spirituality as animist, but it is better characterized as agential. Agentialism is a principle of multinaturalism, and it opens onto a differentiated multiverse of bodies. Material bodies are not the opposite of spirits; they embody this "spiritual" potential in their individuation.

Many writers both indigenous and nonindigenous have noted the significance of something like energy to describe animated indigenous worldviews. Viveiros de Castro cautions against the careless use of the word *energy* to describe notions that are present in indigenous societies, such as spirit or *mana*: "I do not like it because it does no more than provide difficult native concepts with an equally mysterious gloss." In fact, he claims that the way that we use the word *energy* in modern terms is actually a *mana* concept. Energy is "the mana-concept of our physically minded modern tradition: the old 'matter/spirit' opposition gave way to 'matter/energy,' with 'energy' doing pretty much the same job as the old 'spirit.'"[20] In this book, I am attempting to diversify something called energy in agential and new materialist terms and differentially relate them to native or Amerindian conceptions, which is hopefully not as mystifying as Viveiros de Castro warns.

He later distinguishes potential from actual energy closer to the way in which contemporary physicists do, and he applies the notion of *potential* energy to mana. Spirit as energy could be better understood "in the sense of potential, that is, positional and differential energy." This potential energy is then contrasted with "formal energy, energy which is 'contained' in bodily form, due to the difference in 'position or condition'—in affect—of each type of body relative to other bodily forms."[21] This distinction does not follow the traditional Aristotelian opposition between potential and actual energy, and it draws nearer to how contemporary science and philosophers of science are thinking about energy.

In this respect, *energy as such is the universal potentiating principle* that Amazonians think in terms of an anthropomorphic humanity, *and* it is the differentiated form of energy that is contained in material bodies and beings. Viveiros de Castro argues perspectivism can be understood as a "radical polytheism" that is "applied to a universe which recognizes no *ontological* dualism between body and soul, created universe and creator spirit."[22] Such a radical polytheism converges with the pantheism advocated by Mary-Jane Rubenstein in her book *Pantheologies*, and I will return to this notion of pantheology as a form of radical theology in chapter 5.[23]

In their book *The Ends of the World*, Déborah Danowski and Viveiros de Castro recount the situation of the Earth in the present Anthropocenic moment where we teeter on the edge of global warming, which represents the global catastrophe that Sloterdijk mocks. This represents "the sudden collision of Humans with the Earth" that "contributes decisively to crumbling the foundational distinction of the modern *episteme*—the one between the cosmological and the anthropological orders, separated since 'forever.'"[24] We can no longer separate our human history from Earth's natural history, although this distinction is what founded Euro-modernity.

Danowski and Viveiros de Castro invoke Latour's name of Terrans, people who understand that we live in and of the Earth, who are in a state of war against the modern and contemporary Humans who imagine that they can transcend and control it. For Latour, the Terrans cut across the Humans geographically, epistemologically, and technologically. But Latour does not explicitly embrace nonmodern indigenous peoples or their worldviews, despite the significance they have for our current situation. Danowski and Viveiros de Castro charge that Latour does not seem to appreciate the extent to which the people for whom he writes are the ones who inhabit the Capitalist Core, the ones who "are highly dependent on a monumental consumption (or rather, waste) of energy" and who will have to scale down our ways of living.[25] At the same time, they cite a note added to Latour's online version of *Inquiry Into Modes of Existence* that acknowledges the "special relationship between the aboriginals' 'Neo-lithic' technology and the future unmaking of the modernization front" that Latour calls for.[26] They suggest that Latour acknowledges the resemblance between Terrans and indigenous peoples, but does not go far enough to appreciate how close and how vital this connection is. We need, according to Danowski and Viveiros de Castro, a *"slowing down*, a *diseconomy* no longer mesmerized by the hallucination of continuous growth, a *cultural insurrection* . . . against the zombification of the citizen-consumer."[27]

Part of the problem is the linear view of time that moderns have inherited, which assigns the "native" peoples to a technological past, which then forecloses them from a viable future. This perspective of time is secular, progressive, and modern, and it is deeply problematic. We need to challenge this understanding of time and the understanding of technology that it implies. Technology is not simply new, modern, and good or new, modern, and bad. We need to appreciate how deeply *technological* so-called indigenous peoples are. And here precisely is where we have something to learn from Amerindians, who have something "to teach us about the end of the world."[28]

First of all, the end of the world already happened. It occurred on October 12, 1492, and it is still happening today all around us. "The genocide of the Amerindian people," Danowski and Viveiros de Castro write, "was the beginning of the modern world for Europe."[29] Without the despoiled wealth drawn from the Americas, Europe never would have become the center of world power. We are learning more and more about the Americas that existed and in many ways thrived prior to the advent of Columbus, including the massive population of Amerindian people. According to Henry F. Dobyns, the New World was comprised of approximately 100 million people in 1491, which is higher than Europe at the time.[30] If we want to comprehend the anticipated end of the world, we should look to this tragic encounter for lessons.

According to Danowski and Viveiros de Castro, Amerindian thought and practice has much to teach "us" about the end of the world, especially one that is facing the end of a period of unprecedented growth due to the limits of natural global resources. They submit that the indigenous peoples have a better claim to the name—coined by Latour—of Terrans than European or other modern peoples. The Amerindians who survived the Columbian apocalypse were "fully entitled Terrans from the New World" who "reciprocally found themselves as *humans without world*," forced to adapt and create new ones.[31]

We are witnessing the results of the modernization process that began in 1492 and is still playing itself out across the world in a fractal way. Danowski and Viveiros de Castro claim that "it is as if the end of the world were a truly *fractal* event, indefinitely reproduced at different scales, from ethnocidal wars in parts of Africa to the systematic assassination of indigenous leaders and environmental activists in the Amazon, from the purchase of vast portions of poor countries by hyperindustrial powers to the squatting and deforestation of indigenous land by mining and agribusiness."[32] It's not that indigenous people are the only Terrans, but the indigenous people are here the model of what Latour and others are calling Terrans, as opposed to the Humans who are rapaciously consuming and destroying the planet.

To embrace this reality is to uproot the modern vision and view of the world. And this perspective of indigeneity is also a better way to understand spirit. So long as indigenous means backward in contrast to modern as progressive and oriented to the future, we misunderstand the entire point of this discussion. Danowski and Viveiros de Castro advocate a *becoming-indigenous*, where the indigenous are a figure of what, in *Cinema 2*, Deleuze calls "the people who are missing." Amerindian peoples, "with their comparatively modest populations, their relatively simple technologies that are nonetheless open to high-intensity syncretic assemblages, are a 'figuration of the future' . . . *not a remnant of the past.*"[33]

INDIGENOUS SPIRITS—THE HAUDENOSAUNEE CALL TO CONSCIOUSNESS

When we think about indigenous traditions, we often think about a people of the past who practiced premodern ways of life. These earlier technologies may be celebrated or deplored, but they are viewed as irreparably replaced by modern technologies and ways of life. The situation we are facing now is that modernity has failed, inasmuch as it has brought about ecological devastation and global catastrophe, so we have to question the assumptions of linear time and progress that underlie our assumptions about modern and indigenous peoples. One of the wrong assumptions about indigenous societies is that they lived or live in some sort of harmony with nature. This is Rousseau's idea of the "noble savage," the Amerindian who lives in a state of nature prior to the fundamental break that produces human culture as something that lies outside or beyond nature. This break may be viewed alternatively as fortuitous or disastrous, but it is seen as irrevocable, and that is what leads to the production of the moderns, the people who have inherited or taken over the world. And this process leads to the irrelevance and ultimately to the extinction of the nonmodern peoples.

The work of Viveiros de Castro and others helps us resist these presumptions. Robin Wall Kimmerer, a botanist and member of the Citizen Potawatomi Nation, argues that all of us immigrants—and we as a species are all immigrants at some point to every land except for Africa—need to become indigenous. She explains that "becoming indigenous to a place means living as if your children's future mattered, to take care of the land as if our lives, both material and spiritual, depended on it."[34] Which it does. If the Amerindians and others who are in the process of becoming indigenous or becoming Terrans are a "figuration of our future," then what else has to change?

Certainly our understanding of spirit has to change. Spirit needs to be de-Hegelianized, ripped out of a framework of teleological development. According to a scholar of indigenous religion, Mary L. Keller, "Not only do Indigenous traditions provide overwhelming evidence that spirits are of ultimate significance to the community, but even more importantly is the consistent Indigenous orientation toward the created world as itself spirited with an energetic force that has the ambivalent power to heal and harm."[35] A created world "spirited with energetic force" can be appropriated for a superficial Westernized New Age spirituality, to the scorn of intellectuals like Sloterdijk, but it also resonates with some of the most cutting-edge work being done in contemporary philosophy and the theoretical sciences. If we really want to comprehend energy, we have to view it in physical, material terms, but just as much in agential and in spiritual terms.

The spirituality of energy or the energy of spirit does not replace or deny all the historical, political, and economic aspects of energy. In fact, the problems with popular understandings of indigenous traditions lies in seeing these cultures as somehow outside of history, stripped of their historical context, including that of the fraught encounter with Western colonialism. It is, rather, the ongoing situation of coloniality that shapes our comprehension of these traditions and their values, as Aníbal Quijano and Walter Mignolo have argued in their influential work. Euromodern civilization is founded on and by a "colonial matrix of power" derived from Christian theology and fueled by subsequent secular philosophy and sciences of racial classification and control.[36] "Many Western institutions are in fact colonial institutions of Western culture," shaped and set into non-European contexts to control and discipline the natives according to the dictates of this colonial matrix of power.[37]

In so many ways we remain in the grip of these colonial epistemologies, especially since colonialism and capitalism are not opposites, but develop in concert in complementary ways. Mignolo argues that decolonial thinking allows us to wrest free from this colonial matrix and open up genuine "decolonial options—a vision of life and society that requires decolonial subjects, decolonial knowledges, and decolonial institutions."[38] Viveiros de Castro's anthropological work offers a significant decolonial option that helps us to think beyond a colonial matrix of power.

The popular imagination often views the American hemisphere prior to 1492 as loosely populated by scattered bands of Native Americans who engage in a hunter-gatherer lifestyle with some supplemental farming. The main exceptions of course are the empires of Mesoamerica and Peru, the great Aztec and Inca empires that were quickly conquered by Spanish soldiers, horses, and weapons. This virgin land is then inhabited by Europeans who know how to make it productive. This generic picture is a myth, and it is almost completely false.

For example, in Amazonia, researchers in the 1990s were studying *terra preta do Índio*, a rich fertile soil. They realized that this soil does not occur naturally, but was produced by Amerindians using a complicated process of "slash-and-char" agriculture, beginning around 360 BCE.[39] Native Americans did not live in a state of nature, but rather in a dynamic interaction with the land and its resources. It was actually the depopulation of the American Hemisphere that created a superabundant natural landscape, teeming with flora and fauna Europeans could exploit. As Charles Mann explains: "Until Columbus, Indians were a keystone species in most of the hemisphere. Annually burning undergrowth, clearing and replanting forests, building canals and raising fields, hunting bison and netting salmon, growing maize, manioc, and the Eastern Agricultural Complex, Native Americans had been managing their environment for thousands of years."[40] When the Native American populations were subjected to genocide, the natural world rebounded, reaching a peak of carbon sequestration in 1610, one of the dates proposed for the start of the Anthropocene. The forests that greeted European in the seventeenth century were not natural and enduring, but instead the result of "violent change and demographic collapse."[41]

Despite the apocalyptic destruction of the world, beginning in 1492, many of these indigenous peoples have survived, and in many cases thrived, often under brutal and oppressive circumstances. One example is the Haudenosaunee people, a confederacy composed of six (originally five) Amerindian nations. In English the Haudenosaunee are called the Iroquois, a people originally from around Montreal who settled in Southern Canada and upstate New York. We don't know exactly when it began, but, according to oral tradition, a Peacekeeper, Deganawidah, founded this league centuries before European contact as a response to a situation of prevalent warfare.[42] The constitution of this league of nations is known as the Great Law of Peace, which encapsulates Deganawidah's teachings.

A few elements of this Haudenosaunee constitution are noteworthy, including the designation of women as heads of each of the clans that make up the nations. The males attended to matters of war, but "the female-led councils set the agenda of the League."[43] Furthermore, the political laws of the League were explicitly implemented as a check on any one person, clan, group or nation taking authoritarian rule. The emphases on personal liberty and social equality by the Haudenosaunee served to inspire the English colonists in their revolt against the tyranny of Great Britain. There has been controversy about how much the Haudenosaunee league influenced the formation of the government of the United States of America, but it is clear that it served as an inspiration to Benjamin Franklin and others.[44] The Haudenosaunee were a fully functioning federation, and it was "the Haudenosaunee constitution, called the Great Law of Peace, that inspired essential elements of the US Constitution."[45]

Mann, the author of *1491*, states that he surveyed seven "anthropologists, archaeologists, and historians whether they would rather have been a typical citizen of Europe or the Haudenosaunee in 1491." They were wary of anachronistic value judgments about the past, but "every one of the seven chose the Indians."[46] This unanimity is telling, and it indicates the extent to which Europe should not be seen as more civilized and advanced in social, political, ethical or cultural terms before the Columbian disaster. The Haudenosaunee remain today, not as a figuration of the past but just as importantly a call to a future. This is not to elevate this particular people above other indigenous peoples, but simply to point out a continuity and vitality of a specific Amerindian tradition.

In 1977, a delegation of over 250 indigenous people from over 60 native nations and 15 American countries attended a conference in Geneva at the United Nations held on "Discrimination Against Indigenous Populations in the Americas." This meeting was a watershed moment in the political recognition of indigenous peoples around the world and led to the UN designating an International Decade of Indigenous Peoples (1995–2004), establishing a permanent forum at the United Nations.[47] A dozen or so Haudenosaunees participated in the delegation, including José Barreiro, editor of the newspaper *Akwasanee Notes*, which published stories about the proceedings, later collected and published as a book called *Basic Call to Consciousness*.

The Haudenosaunee address to the UN was given by a man named Segwalise, and it was called "Spiritualism: The Highest Form of Political Consciousness." According to this speech, spiritual consciousness is the highest form of politics for the Haudenosaunee. This viewpoint asserts: "We believe that all living beings are spiritual beings. Spirits can be expressed as energy forms manifested in matter."[48] From the standpoint of this book, what we call spirits or spiritual beings are manifestations of energy in material form, as is all matter. What makes them spiritual is what Segwalise calls consciousness. Not merely a physical awareness, but a moral consciousness attuned to the resonance and value of beings in their interaction, intra-action, and interconnection.

Everything in the universe possesses real material existence as a concentrated metastable form of energy transformation. The designation of something as spiritual means that it has value to and for other beings, including people. The consciousness of this material-energetic-spiritual universe is "manifest to man at the Creation, the Creation that supports life."[49] Here is what Viveiros de Castro is calling Amerindian anthropomorphism, whereby human beings are the original form of beings, the pure potential from whom all other beings are separated off, including actually existing human beings. The Creation is not a literal event; it contains and consolidates the spiritual awareness of the vitality of these material beings. The Creation is multinatural, because it produces irreducibly multiple worlds from the stability of this projected social anthropomorphic perspective.

Indigenous perspectives are crucial because they show how these peoples are not living fossils to be celebrated or deplored. Indigenous

Amerindians like the Haudenosaunee comprehend better than most Westerners what is happening and what is at stake in the world in planetary ecological and spiritual terms. It's not just the struggle of the natives to survive in a modern world. As Segwalise explains, "the way known as 'Western civilization' is on a death path, and its culture has no viable answers." We keep striving to find more efficient ways to exploit, grow, and destroy the inhabitability of our planet. "The air is foul, the waters poisoned, the trees dying, the animals are disappearing. We think even the systems of weather are changing," Segwalise proclaims in 1977. The call to consciousness is a political and spiritual call to wake up that has mostly gone unheeded over the last forty-plus years. Ultimately, he asserts, "when the last of our Natural Way of Life is gone, all hope for human survival will be gone with it. And our Way of Life is fast disappearing, a victim of the destructive processes."[50] It's not just native ways of life that are disappearing; it's everyone's.

In another document presented at the conference, "Our Strategy for Survival," the Haudenosaunee point out that "the roots of a future world that promises misery, poverty, starvation, and chaos lie in the processes that control and destroy the locally specific cultures of the peoples of the world." This process is named as an ongoing colonialism, which is the process "by which Indigenous cultures are subverted and ultimately destroyed in the interests of the worldwide market economy."[51] Colonialism is at the heart of the world crisis that is engulfing us, and we do not understand our present existence without comprehending that. Colonialism is not in the past; colonialism and capitalism are two sides of the same coin. The Haudenosaunee are calling for the development of new "liberation technologies" that are not wedded to the colonial matrix of power. These technologies must be able to be "implemented by a specific people in a specific locality and free those people from dependency on multinational corporations and the governments that multinational corporations control."[52] These are vital political, economic, and material concerns upon which the survival of our species may depend.

I am not claiming that indigenous or Amerindian peoples are the salvation of the moderns who are destroying the world. I am following Karatani, Viveiros de Castro, Danowski, and Mann in arguing that we need to learn from these indigenous clan societies that exist in a complex relationship of reciprocity with other people, nonhuman animals, plants, and objects. In fact, all these phenomena are what Latour calls actants or agents; they possess a capacity for interacting with and in the world. They are more precisely what Barad calls intra-active; they are not separate or separable from the rest of existence except in hypothetical terms, because there is no such thing as an entirely closed system.

Many indigenous societies consider the "spirits" that inhabit and act upon their world as "persons," and this is an anthropomorphic designation. We can resist this specific anthropomorphism and yet retain the idea of complex systems as agents, actants, or even spirits, since they manifest and distribute energy across gradients. The point is that, whether they are persons or processes, spirits or forces, these agents effect change. They can be described alternatively in material-scientific or spiritual-moral terms, but the challenge is to resist this either-or.

TELL MY HORSE: ANTHROPOMORPHIC SPIRITS IN HAITIAN VODOU

As Danowski and Viveiros de Castro remind us, the end of the world took place on October 12, 1492. Christopher Columbus, a Genoan sailing under the flag of Spain, landed on the island that was called Ayiti by the native Tainos, and by the Spanish Española (Hispaniola). This European encounter with a "New World" marks the profound shift to what is later called modernity. The natives were enslaved to make the land profitable and productive, but they were quickly devastated by disease and the brutal conditions and practically wiped out. The Europeans then imported people purchased as slaves from West Africa to work the plantations, and it was this continuous supply of human beings from Africa that enriched Europe with the enormous production of the American colonies. Colonialism, slavery, and racism, as well as the displacement and destruction of indigenous peoples, represents the messy underside of liberal modernity, and this provides the *capital* that sparked the Industrial Revolution.

France acquired the Western half of Hispaniola from Spain in 1697 and called their new colony Saint-Domingue. This colony became the most profitable in the world in the eighteenth century. The profit came from the enormous success of its sugar and coffee plantations, but it was achieved at a terrible cost. African slaves were treated with horrible cruelty, and the death rate was extremely high: "on average, half of the slaves who arrived from Africa died within a few years."[53] In August 1791, however, in the wake of the French Revolution of 1789, a huge slave insurrection broke out that culminated in the independence of Haiti in 1804. This was the only fully successful slave revolution in the New World, although it was won at an enormous cost, including the killing of whites, the enfranchisement of a mulatto elite, and the ostracism and impoverishment of the new country. Haiti only established diplomatic relations with France in 1825 by agreeing to pay 150 million francs as compensation for the loss of its slaves. The United States, horrified by the success of the Haitian Revolution and its implications for U.S. slaves, refused to recognize Haiti as an independent nation until 1861. However, it was the defeat of the French army by Haitian rebels that led Napoleon to abandon his New World possession and sell the Louisiana Territory to the nascent U.S. in 1804.

One way to characterize modernity is to say that it depersonalizes non-human powers, viewing personal gods and spirits as forces. Indigenous peoples usually personalize these forces, and upon contact with these peoples most European intellectuals relegated these spiritual views to pre-civilized savages. For many contemporary secular humans, the idea of a personal agent who interacts with humans seems incredible.

For example, during a Haitian Vodou service, a *lwa* such as Papa Legba may enter and take over the consciousness of a Hougan (male priest) or a Mambo (priestess), who becomes the horse ridden by the lwa. These lwa (in Haitian Kreyòl; sometimes written as loa) are spirits who originated primarily from the Fon and Dahomey peoples in West Africa (now the country of Benin), but they also include lwa from other African peoples such as the Yoruba and Kongo who were brought to the New World, as well as native Taino spirits and ancestors. These spirits are named and personalized, and then further identified with Roman Catholic saints because they were colonized by Catholic Christian Europeans.

We may well sympathize with the desperate plight of the Haitian people, and perhaps we are charmed at a distance by the colorful and powerful rituals of Vodou, but westernized scholars are unlikely to accept these lwa literally as spirits, even if they want to take the phenomenology of such practices seriously. However, the perspective of this book has argued that it is not so simple. As we are criticizing the presuppositions and prejudices of modernity, we are also seeing how the dismissal of indigenous gods and spirits is premature. Latour has traced the effects of the modern separation of nature as an object of specialized scientific study from the world of human society that consists of agents who possess intentionality and moral value. And it is this separation that is coming undone in our contemporary postmodern world.

We can no longer maintain a consistent distinction between humans and nonhumans, because what is important is "the exchange of forms of action through the transactions between agencies of multiple origins and forms at the core of the metamorphic zone," as Latour puts it.[54] Personification is an operation that multiplies worlds, including our own. We may not wish to simply deem forces or energies "persons," but this animation or agentialism is present in a way that destabilizes the divisions between human peoples and nonhuman things. These nonhuman things are not inert things, but possess their own agency, sometimes in terms of themselves as *objects* and other times in connection with other objects as processes or complex systems.[55]

Vodou is a rich tradition, and it is not restricted to Haiti, although it originated there. Haiti has often been described as 70 percent Catholic, 30 percent Protestant, and 100 percent Vodou. Haiti itself is an incredibly significant nation, because it represents the only completely successful slave revolt in the modern world and was both influenced by and had an impact, in turn, upon the French Revolution in Europe. The 1791 insurrection staged by the slaves against the French colonists of the island of Saint-Domingue was touched off by a secret ceremony, held at Bois-Caïman in the north of the island, that was conducted by a Vodou priest named Boukman, which culminated in "drinking the blood of a black pig sacrificed before" the conspirators.[56]. Eventually this revolt led to a full-scale revolution against France and its white colonists, even as it radicalized the French Revolution itself.

The role of Vodou in Haiti's political insurrection and later history is complex and multifaceted, as is the very definition and identity of Vodou itself. Vodou is often presented in world religions textbooks and courses as a "syncretistic religion," but this implies that it is a simple mixture or blending of indigenous, African, and Roman Catholic elements, which ignores the complexity of the evolution of Vodou from Dahomey and Kongo in Africa and how it adopted and integrated Taino elements in

Hispaniola and then was forced to hide beneath a Catholic Christian veneer in order to survive.

So-called indigenous religions are distinguished from world religions by the fact that they work to maintain cosmic balance or harmony, whereas world religions are usually more progressive and linear and work toward transformation of the world in material and spiritual terms. At the same time, the classification of religion into world religions serves to marginalize indigenous traditions that are seen as older and more primitive, as well as newer, more complex forms that are denigrated as syncretistic. The privilege of world religions over against the others also serves to continue to privilege Christianity in subtle or not so subtle ways.[57] Haitian Vodou is characterized by a concern for cosmic balance in an ambivalent universe, but it is a mistake to suggest that it is primitive compared to more modern religious traditions. According to Patrick Bellegarde-Smith, "Vodou is a coherent and comprehensive belief system and world view in which every person and every thing is sacred and must be treated accordingly."[58] In fact, Vodou can be better characterized primarily in terms of religious and social practice, that of serving the lwa or spirit, and only indirectly and implicitly in terms of a belief system.

In Haitian Vodou, there is a supreme God called Bondye, and after Bondye there are usually considered to be twenty-one "Nations," of which the main ones are the Rada, Petro, and Gede nations. The Rada are mostly from an area of West Africa called Arada that created the kingdom of Dahomey. Arada "was remembered among Haiti's former slaves as the people who had come *nan Ginen* or 'from Ginen/Guinea.'"[59] These Rada lwa are seen as calmer and and more peaceful in contrast to the Petro lwa. The Rada lwa are generally acknowledged first in any Vodou service, which consists of dancing and music in which the lwa may take possession of a priest or any other member participating in the ritual. This possession of the person's consciousness by the lwa completely wipes out any awareness of the person possessed until the lwa departs. The person "becomes the horse" for the lwa to ride and interact with other people. The Rada lwa are followed by the Petro and then the Gede lwa. The most important Rada lwa is Papa Legba, who represents the crossroads, and this lwa opens the door to the spirit realm.

The Petro lwa are more hot or intense spirits. They represent the lwa who emerge with the formation of the Haitian people in their quest for independence and their continuous struggle for survival. Many of these Petro lwa have similar names to the Rada lwa, but they are considered to be more aggressive and dangerous. Finally, the Gede lwa are the spirits of the dead, led by the lwa Baron Samedi, who personifies death. Each specific house may be dedicated to different Rada and/or Petro lwa, although any and all recognize the Gede spirits. Although the majority of lwa originate from Africa, some are adopted from native Taino spirits, or Zemi. As Mambo Chita Tann explains, "the Taino of Ayiiti drew images of the zemi, either in chalk or various plant powders, on their sacred rocks or even on their own bodies, to be invoked in a ceremony."[60] This is the origin of the *veve*, which are ritual diagrams or drawings representing various lwa.

Haitian Vodou is not a religion that is focused on beliefs, and it has no authorities other than the houngans and mambos who are called to initiate the ceremonies and are explicitly dedicated to the lwa. Vodou is a more democratic practice, although it has often had to be practiced in secret because of the French colonists and representatives of the Catholic Church who attempted to suppress it. Vodou is a complex tradition that is intrinsically entangled with Haiti and its history and people in Haiti and elsewhere. These lwa are fascinating examples of personalized spirits who engage with people in transactional ways.

Anthony Pinn, a scholar of African American traditions who focuses on those that exist outside traditional forms of Protestant Christianity, explains that "for practitioners, the structure and expense of service to the *lwa* is essential because it provides for the basic spiritual and physical needs of life; the energy necessary to maintain 'balance' is available through communication with and attention to cosmic forces."[61] These lwa are anthropomorphized energy forces that cannot be ignored, but they can be tapped into and used for good or ill.

The crucial factor here is not the supernatural pantheon of lwa, or even their division into Rada, Petro, and Gede lwa. The issue is the notion that there is no free lunch: every transaction—moral, physical, and spiritual—has a cost. We cannot set up a human society with a political economy that is completely divorced from the natural world. Eventually there will be a reckoning. Mambo Chita Tann sums up the fundamental lesson of Haitian Vodou as "Nothing in the universe is free."[62] What we could call

"Vodou economics" is an economics of scarcity, reflecting the true conditions of existence, rather than the fantasy of infinite growth or globalization at no cost.

Another Native American example is the Meso-American view of the world as an "eating landscape" in which humans both consume and are consumed in an environment of scarcity.[63] Each of these traditions exemplify the clan society of reciprocity that is oriented around the gift, as Karatani explains. And we have to understand that the gift is not free, because you cannot get something for nothing. Energy is not free; it is a complex transaction and transformation, but it makes possible everything that occurs, including forms, life, consciousness, people, society, spirits, religion, and philosophy.

In a provocative account, Susan Buck-Morss argues that Hegel's famous master and slave dialectic is derived from the Haitian slave revolt. There is circumstantial evidence that Hegel was following the Haitian Revolution in newspaper reports while he was in Jena in 1803–1805, which was when the master-slave dialectic was first developed, before its publication in the *Phenomenology of Spirit* in 1807. Buck-Morss suggests that "Hegel knew—knew about real slaves revolting successfully against real masters, and he elaborated his dialectic of lordship and bondage deliberately within this contemporary context."[64] Although this argument remains somewhat speculative, here is another place where Haiti has profoundly influenced the modern world, and its religion is at the core of this identity.

Although it is intriguing to associate Haiti with Hegel's master-slave dialectic, I also want to affirm a more speculative connection to Derrida and Deleuze. The modern age is the age of Enlightenment, science, colonialism, Black and other skin-color based forms of racism, and slavery, as well as an era of revolts and revolutions. We forget history by relegating Haiti and its revolution to the margins rather than seeing it at the center. And we misunderstand Vodou if we treat it simply as a fascinating magical practice subject to anthropological or popular curiosity.

The North African–French Jewish philosopher Jacques Derrida has theorized a "democracy to-come," a democratic justice that would subvert all (liberal) democracies. In his book *Rogues*, Derrida explains that democracy is not a past or present idea, but rather an invocation, because there is "no idea of democracy. And so, in the final analysis, no democratic ideal."[65] Democracy is radicalized by assigning it to an impossible future, a future to come, that is, not a future which is simply an extension of the present, but the shadow of an unforeseen event.

"Democracy in Haiti will be an Africanizing process," according to the Haitian scholar Patrick Bellegarde-Smith, asserting the African core of Haitian identity.[66] I want to understand the resonance of this provocative statement not in terms of racial or geographical essence but in terms of a general democratizing of democracy. Radical democracy is not the same liberal democracy, but a refashioning of democracy anew, as Derrida understands it. This is an attempt to think democracy beyond liberalism and colonialism, and essentially beyond capitalism. Haiti's former president, the liberation theologian Jean-Baptiste Aristide, claims that "our concept and practice of democracy must make a giant leap forward. We must democratize democracy."[67] Democracy is not based upon a present arrangement or explicit state of affairs, but is predicated on justice and freedom, which are technically incalculable and exceed any and all determinate horizons.

According to Derrida, there is always and necessarily a religious element inscribed in this invocation, even though Derrida is ambivalent about religion in its present forms. As he puts it in his famous essay, "Force of Law," there is a mystical foundation to the establishment of every authority, which paradoxically keeps it from being an absolute foundation.[68] Derrida relates the opening of a democracy to come to Martin Heidegger's claim that "only a god can save us," suggesting that we must think the god in that phrase beyond our monotheistic conceptions of a sovereign God. "A god," Derrida states, is "neither the One God nor gods, neither the One God of the Bible nor the God or gods of the philosophers and of ontotheology."[69] Of this god who could save us, Heidegger says that "I am not convinced that it is democracy," but Derrida stresses the hesitation and the uncertainty in that phrase, suggesting that perhaps it does concern democracy after all, just not in its liberal and technocratic form.[70]

But what if the god that Heidegger calls for and that Derrida invokes in the name of democracy is a lwa? What if democracy here involves serving the lwa, becoming the horse to assist in serving the people, even if Derrida never thought about it in these terms? Just as with the Haudenosaunee, we need to comprehend indigenous and more composite spiritual traditions less in terms of their technological distance from

Euro-modernity and more in terms of how they help reshape how to think about our contemporary world.

And finally, what if the lwa is not merely an anthropomorphized person or a physical energy force but also contributes to the production of a time-image in Deleuze's terms? In *Cinema 2: The Time-Image*, Deleuze analyzes the history of cinema in the twentieth century and shows where the traditional understanding of time based on movement breaks down. Deleuze perceives a crisis in the movement image that occurs around World War II. As Paola Marrati writes, "the twentieth century begins only after the war. It is the rise of Fascism, Nazism, Stalinism and World War II that destroys the faith of history."[71] In Italian neorealism and French New Wave cinema in particular, Deleuze glimpses the postwar posing of a new problem that arises at the level of thought: time is no longer subordinated to movement, but movement can be seen as an effect of time.

This new form of image is a time-image, and the time-image is the revolutionary concept of Deleuze's later philosophy. It is not just cinema that reaches a state of crisis; it is philosophy itself, especially a philosophy and even a politics that is based on movement. Philosophy and politics based on movement implies an organic conception of the Whole and of History, which disappears in the collapse of the movement-image. Describing a scene from a film by Yasujiro Ozu, Deleuze explains that it presents a direct time-image, which "is time, time itself, 'a little time in its pure state.'"[72] The breakdown of the movement-image allows time to surface directly as a pure image.

In *Cinema 2*, Deleuze is interested in building a brain, as we saw in chapter 2. Building a brain involves producing an event as a time-image, a pure image of time that cuts entities away from their automatic sensory-motor linkages and reconstitutes them in another series or another order. The time-image proper "concerns the series of time, which brings together the before and after in a becoming, instead of separating them; its paradox is to introduce an enduring interval in the moment itself." The time-image "shatter[s] the empirical continuation of time, the chronological succession, the separation of the before and the after."[73] It is the interval or interstice that *gives* time its character and dynamism as thought.

With the interstice as the time-image, "the question is no longer that or association or attraction of images. What counts is on the contrary the *interstice* between two images: a spacing which means that each image is plucked from the void and falls back into it."[74] Deleuze says that the process works as follows: "Given one image, another image has to be chosen which will induce an interstice between the two. This is not an operation of association, but of differentiation, as mathematicians say, or of disappearance, as physicists say: given one potential, another one has to be chosen, not any whatsoever, but in such a way that a difference of potential is established between the two, which will be productive of a third or of something new."[75] This choosing of images so as to induce an interstice is what it means to think and what it means to construct a brain.

The interstice is what links the images, creating a time-image and therefore a brain, but the brain is produced. It is the difference in potential that generates the intensity to close that gap, and the process of collapsing the interstice produces the third. Because time is the interstice, the gap is never fully closed; it is repeated differently, with a new interstice. As Deleuze says, the time-image is not ordinal but serial: it is a series of images and the interstitial cuts between them, which produces the time-image as event. The cinematic event occurs through "the method of BETWEEN, 'between two images,' which does away with all cinema of the One." The whole is not the "One-Being" but "the constitutive between-two of images."[76]

The interstice is the cinematic cut, but the cut does not take place along preestablished lines of movement or action; the cut as interstice both cuts and relinks images in a novel way. The series of cuts constitutes a brain, "a topological cerebral space" populated by "micro-fissures which were not simply voids to be crossed, but random mechanisms introducing themselves at each moment between the sending and receiving of an association message."[77] Our understanding of the synaptic brain where the interstitial gaps constitute the lived brain itself provides Deleuze with evidence for his theorization of cinema and philosophical thought. He pulls the interstice out from the series it links together and offers it to us as a pure time-image; it operates as "the equivalent of an irrational cut, which determines the non-commensurable relations between images."[78]

As the interstices develop synaptically, the brain expands by means of these cuts and relinkages, becoming a screen. "If the cut no longer forms part of either of the two series of images which it determines," Deleuze repeats, then "there are only relinkages on either side." If the cuts and relinkages continue to grow and expand, they absorb the images and it becomes a screen, "a new brain which would be at once the screen, the film stock and the camera, each time membrane of the outside and the inside."[79] We produce images directly by means of the time-image, rather than indirectly by reference to movement. Building a brain does not simply take place against an organic template of the representational Whole to which the brain would refer, and it does not exist simply to relay thoughts along an inscribed circuit to produce prescribed commands of action. The interstitial time-image is a new form of subjectivity that replaces the nineteenth-century view of History in a grand sense, because this teleological or progressive history is no longer believable in our world today.

What if the images of indigenous peoples and their spiritual forms are not just energies but also new time-images, because of how they displace our chronological assumption of linear time, and offer new ways to constitute a brain for our species, provoking a new nomos of the Earth? Here the Vodou service is a cinematic event, where the mambo or houngan is the director, or auteur, to frame it in terms of *Cinema 2*. The energies of the lwa descend upon the people, transforming them into something else, at least for the duration of the service. Then the question becomes, do they change as a result of their becoming a horse? Even if their consciousness is not explicitly altered, there must be a transformation at the level of the unconscious whereby the Vodou participant becomes different as a result of being possessed by the lwa.

The veve is the representative drawing of the lwa, which is sketched on the floor by the priest with a cornmeal and ash powder.[80] These drawings most likely originated with the indigenous Taino people where they represented spirits called zemi, and they were later incorporated into Vodou. This drawing or symbol serves as a beacon to draw the lwa to the event, because they are obliged to descend to the place their veves exist. The veve represents a time-image in a Deleuzean sense, but not literally. Its function in signaling to and attracting the lwa or energy-spirit to the ceremony is what is important, as well as its linkages with other veves and other lwas in the context of the performance.

The lwa along with its veve, its drawing, constitutes a time-image insofar as it concentrates virtual potentiality and actual power in a precarious and unstable form. This form then links to other forms, other lwa and other practices, constituting a signifying process based not on representation and movement but pure time. So long as Vodou is understood as representing another realm of spiritual forces, one that communicates with and acts within this one, it is not a time-image. But if the forces of Vodou are seen as themselves links with which to refashion the world and our belief in it, then perhaps these elements of Vodou compose a time-image.

Here is another connection to the people who are missing that Deleuze invokes toward the end of *Cinema 2*. This is the promise of Third World cinema, but perhaps we need to think this cinematically, beyond a literal movie screen? He argues: "if there were a modern political cinema, it would be on this basis: the people no longer exist, or not yet . . . *the people are missing*."[81] If the people are missing, then they need to be filmed, they need to be invented, and that is the task of contemporary cinema, which Deleuze associates with Third World or minority cinema. He says that "there is the consciousness that "there were no people, but always several peoples, an infinity of peoples, who remained to be united, or should not be united, in order for the problem to change."[82] The people who are missing are the indigenous, the Terrans, the minorities, the wretched of the earth, the nonmoderns who are becoming united in and by the Anthropocene, and who must come to be seen in order for the problem to change. From a technological perspective, Vodou is not literally a form of cinema, of course. But Vodou is intrinsically cinematic, in a Deleuzean sense, insofar as it constitutes a time-image.

We need to experiment with new practices of spirit. These experimentations produce what Deleuze (along with Guattari) call assemblages. In *A Thousand Plateaus*, an assemblage (in French, *agencement*) is an arrangement where the whole is constituted by the connections between and among various heterogeneous parts. These connections compose a more fluid constellation rather than a fixed structure. There are elements of improvisation and contingency in the creation of an assemblage. A Vodou ceremony is an example of such an assemblage, with the intersections of priests, lwa, veves, peristil (the main ceremonial room within a Vodou temple), altar, offerings, and participants. The descent of the lwa during the ceremony generate new permutations of material and spiritual reality.

These improvisational practices make connections among heterogeneous cultures, religions, and forms. They open up new ways to experience and understand reality. Haitian religion and Haitian democracy have much to teach us about what it means to live and to think in a shrinking world marked by limits on the exploitation of natural resources. The Haitian people have found ways to live and survive under brutal, desperate, oppressive, and tragic circumstances. The Flood (*Fanmi Lavalas*) endures despite the exile of Aristide, the devastating earthquake and the neoliberal response of 2010, and, most recently, the assignation of Jovenal Moise in 2021.

According to Neil Roberts, we should think about freedom less in terms of rights and more in terms of the experience of marronage. Maroons are people who fled from slavery and formed societies apart from the unjust social order they escaped. This practice occurred throughout the Americas, including in the United States, but notably in Haiti, Jamaica, and other Caribbean locations. The success of the Haitian Revolution inspired Afro-Caribbean writers in the twentieth century to develop "an idea of a creolized, Afro-Caribbean political imaginary, fusing together the poeticist and historicist dimensions of modern and contemporary political theory in the now rich Caribbean intellectual tradition."[83] This tradition includes Aimé Cesairé, C. L. R. James, Édouard Glissant, Sylvia Wynter, and Michel-Rolphe Trouillot.

These acts of flight away from slavery toward freedom constitute a new assemblage of society that is more fluid, unsettled, and dynamic compared to how most European discourses define and apply the concept of freedom. Such liberating movements of escape perform what Deleuze and Guattari call "lines of flight" in *A Thousand Plateaus*. According to Roberts, "marronage is a multidimensional, constant act of flight that involves what I ascertain to be four interrelated pillars: distance, movement, property, and purpose."[84] Each of these pillars undergoes changes during the movement of marronage. Although Roberts analyzes marronage primarily in terms of movement, I think that what Deleuze calls the time-image is relevant for how we think about marronage in Afro-Caribbean contexts, including Vodou. The time-element consists in specifically understanding how these elements are interlinked in their interstitial cuts and how they generate a new form of thought, a brain by which marronage can not only act but also think on its own terms. In Haiti, and other places inspired by this particular assemblage, Vodou can be seen as a time-image, whereas other Afro-Caribbean religions like Santería, Palo, or Candomblé may play this role in different contexts.

QI AS DYNAMIC ENERGY TRANSFORMATION IN NEO-CONFUCIAN PHILOSOPHY

Finally, as the third of these non-Western traditions of spirit, I consider energy in terms of the Chinese concept of qi 氣. If everything in nature is dynamic and animated, then it is also energetic. Energy is not just a Western concept of scientific measurement, but from a different perspective it is the spirit of an Asian worldview. Qi is often translated as energy, although it is variously named psychophysical energy, material force, and vital power. From the perspective of Chinese philosophy, qi is material in the same way that energy is from the standpoint of nonlinear thermodynamics in contemporary physics. At the same time, qi is also spiritual, or rather it can become spiritual in certain cases and under certain conditions.

In Chinese philosophy, qi is not simply matter that is divorced from spirit, but it is at once material and spiritual. Spirit is a refinement or purification of material qi, but it is not a different kind of thing. As the contemporary philosopher Du Weiming explains, "the continuous presence in Chinese philosophy of the idea of ch'i [qi] as a way of conceptualizing the basic structure and function of the cosmos . . . signifies a conscious refusal to abandon a mode of thought that synthesizes spirit and matter as an undifferentiated whole."[85] What we call spirit and what we call matter are not dualistically opposed, but occur together in energy, which is a dynamic process or ongoing event of creation. We can distinguish between physical thermodynamic energy, biological metabolic energy, human psychic emotional energy, and spiritual or religious energy, but these are all repetitions of difference based on transformations of intensive energy.

During the Song dynasty in China (960–1279), there was a resurgence of Confucianism over against the religious influence of Chinese Buddhism. Part of this was a nativist rejection of Buddhism as a foreign religion, but there was also a flowering of Chinese philosophy that became known as neo-Confucianism. Even while it criticizes Buddhism and Daoism, neo-Confucian philosophy assimilates Daoist and Buddhist concepts into a naturalized metaphysics that is asserted as Confucian.

For many scholars, the quintessential representative of neo-Confucianism is Zhu Xi (1130–1200). Zhu Xi develops a contrast between qi and *li* 理, where li is translated as "principle," although a better word would be "pattern," as argued by Eiho Baba and other contemporary scholars of Zhu Xi.[86] This contrast is often viewed by non-Chinese philosophers in quasi-Aristotelian terms, where li as form is prior to and superior to qi, which is simply the material manifestation of li. I cannot say whether this is the correct interpretation of Zhu Xi's philosophy, which is complex and important. However, the predominant focus on Zhu Xi as representative of neo-Confucianism obscures the earlier work of Zhang Zai (1020–1077).

Zhu Xi's philosophy appears to subordinate qi as the actualization of myriad material things to the idea of li as an underlying eternal principle. In this traditional account of Chinese philosophy, Zhang Zai is an earlier instance of neo-Confucian philosophy who is surpassed by Zhu Xi. In most accounts of Chinese philosophy, Zhang's thought is downplayed in favor of Zhu Xi as well as Zhang's direct philosophical successors, the Cheng brothers: Cheng Hao and Cheng Yi.

In distinction from Zhu Xi, Zhang does not privilege the term *li* as a concept as the Chengs and Zhu Xi do, but instead proposes a philosophy and cosmology based primarily on qi, which is a kind of material energy. I want to understand qi in Zhang's philosophy and later neo-Confucian thinkers more fundamentally in terms of energy, rather than material substance, and this perspective is consistent with a post-Einsteinian cosmology. Energy is not a thing, but a process.

Song neo-Confucianism is incredibly complex in philosophical and political terms, and this results from the need for an official imperial philosophy of Confucianism to combat and appropriate elements of Daoism and Buddhism. As Ira Kasoff explains, much of the intellectual activity in eleventh-century China "can be seen as an attempt to establish an orthodoxy, an ideology for the new socio-political elite."[87] A lot of the political-philosophical factionalism of this period was a response to the reforms of Wang An-shih beginning in 1069. Wang, an adviser to the emperor Shenzong, promoted what are called New Policies to curb government expenditures and strengthen the military. He was forced to resign after a famine in 1074, after which his policies were the subject of much dispute between reformers who wanted to continue his policies and conservatives who wanted to abandon them. Wang was not a philosopher (although he was a poet), but his attempts at reform stimulated many of the intellectuals who were associated with Song neo-Confucianism, including Zhou Dunyi and Zhang Zai.

Eventually, and partly in response to the later Mongol invasions, neo-Confucianism (called *daoxue*) was established as the dominant ideology, but Zhang Zai's "philosophy came to be viewed through the distorting lens of the Ch'eng [Cheng] school's interpretation, and has not received the attention it deserves."[88] The Cheng brothers, Cheng Hao and Cheng Yi, were nephews of Zhang Zai, and the traditional understanding of neo-Confucianism claims that the Chengs corrected Zhang Zai's philosophy by subordinating qi to li, a concept that Zhang did not sufficiently emphasize. Furthermore, it was claimed that Zhang later acknowledged his error as a result of the Chengs' critique. Eventually the Chengs' corrected philosophy was fully elaborated by Zhu Xi.

Zhang's complex understanding of qi was incorporated by Zhu Xi into neo-Confucian daoxue philosophy, but it was seen as too material and too anarchic on its own, so it had to be distinguished from and in some ways subordinated to li. However, this supposed recantation by Zhang Zai is almost certainly fabricated to justify the success of Zhu Xi's philosophy.[89] Zhang's philosophy is based primarily on qi, and he sees li more as an effect of qi rather than the manifestation of it.

His major text is the *Zhengmeng*, which is usually translated as "Correcting Ignorance." Zhang begins with the Great Harmony or Great Unity of everything, *datong*, which he identifies with the *dao*. Everything that exists is a process, and understanding these processes allows us to comprehend *the nature of reality and change*. Change is the nature of reality. Zhang uses the notion of qi to comprehend and explain change. The laws of thermodynamics and the scientific understandings of energy also all relate to the concept of change, as we saw in chapter 1.

Where does energy come from? The second paragraph of the *Zhengmeng* posits the Great Void, *taixu* 太虛, as the source of everything, which is characterized in terms of qi. The Great Void "is the original substance of material force."⁹⁰ The myriad things are generated and destroyed out of the integration and disintegration of qi from taixu, in an ongoing and infinite process of change. There are multiple ways to interpret these difficult and subtle Chinese texts, and it is important to see how the neo-Confucian philosophers both based and built upon earlier classical ones. In classical Chinese thought, qi originally refers to breath, and indicates a gaseous substance. "In certain ancient texts," Kasoff writes, qi "was used to describe an original undifferentiated state out of which heaven-and-earth emerged."⁹¹

This is close to the way that Zhang understands it, but at the same time, Kasoff says, "no previous thinker used the concept the way Chang [Zhang] did."⁹² Zhang claims that "as an entity, material force [qi] simply reverts to its original substance when it disintegrates and becomes formless. When it integrates and assumes form, it does not lose the essential principle (of Change)."⁹³ The Great Void is composed of qi, and qi integrates or assumes form to become the myriad things. These things then disintegrate or lose their form and return to the Great Void.

Zhang Zai places the Great Void at the origin of everything, in contrast to what other Chinese philosophers like Zhu Xi call the Great Ultimate, *taiji*. Taixu is a void or vacuity, a kind of emptiness, which sounds Buddhist, although Zhang is at pains to distinguish his Great Void from Buddhist emptiness. As Kasoff explains, Zhang Zai "explained the Great Void in a decidedly non-Buddhist, non-Taoist way as being Ch'i [qi], and as having, therefore, real physical existence."⁹⁴ Zhang appropriates a Buddhist or Daoist term and alters the meaning, whereas other neo-Confucian philosophers criticized Zhang for adopting such Buddhist terminology. The Great Void is the source of qi, and qi is then divided into the two polar concepts of yin and yang. Yang is the expanding force, and yin is the contracting force, but "yin and yang are complementary aspects of the one qi."⁹⁵

Because of his emphasis on qi, Zhang Zai has been called a materialist, a monist, and a monist-realist philosopher.⁹⁶ In his study of *Zhang Zai's Philosophy of Qi*, Jung-Yeup Kim argues that both materialism and monism are problematic ways to describe Zhang. Kim points out that recent scholarship on Zhang Zai concludes that his philosophy should not be understood as materialist and that his notion of qi "cannot be understood in a materialist way."⁹⁷ I agree, insofar as materialism is understood in terms of early modern Western mechanical materialism, but I think that new materialism, as presented and developed in this book, has important resonances with Zhang's work and with the broader neo-Confucian philosophy of qi that he inaugurates. Qi is not a singular, monistic substance, and neither is energy. Kim suggests that monism and materialism go together, because the substantialized, reductionist, materialist interpretation of qi reduces it to a monistic substance, a One that is then later differentiated into forms. According to Kim, Zhang's "philosophy of qi is best understood as an organic pluralism."[98] I agree that we should understand qi in essentially pluralistic ways, but that is not incompatible with new materialism, because physical reality is not primarily *substance*.

Zhang articulates his understanding of qi in terms of both vertical and horizontal development. Kim goes on to explain that "in his vertical development of qi Zhang Zai focuses on explaining the relationship between the vast emptiness (*taixu*) and the myriad things (*wanwu*) in terms of qi. In his horizontal development of qi he focuses on explaining the relationship between the myriad things (*wanwu*) in terms of qi."[99] The latter horizontal development of qi is the more practical aspect of Zhang's teachings, and it is this element that Kim emphasizes in his book. *Wu* is the multiplicity of things: this is a process as well as an event (*shi* 事). The process of the interaction of qi in terms of yin and yang "scatters and becomes the myriad entities" in a "unity of plurality." Ultimately, for Kim, "Zhang Zai's worldview presented in his horizontal development of qi can be understood as an ecology, that is, a worldview that emphasizes the vital interconnection amongst plurality."[100]

I want to consider what Kim calls the vertical and the horizontal processes together rather than separately, in terms of *immanence*. Immanence means that there is no important difference between what we consider horizontal and what we call vertical processes, because these are solely heuristic distinctions. The immanent development of qi as energy transformation accords with new materialist philosophy and the ideas of nonequilibrium thermodynamics that I am using in this book. Chinese philosophy is traditionally less dualistic than Western philosophy, but there is a subtle dualism that operates when we oppose the so-called vertical emergence of qi from the Great Void to the more horizontal interactions of qi among the myriad things. This opposition deconstructs, because we posit something like the Great Void as an origin to make sense of the energy transformations we can experience and measure.

According to Zhang, qi is the fundamental element of change. He says "that which is dispersed, differentiated, and capable of assuming form becomes material force (qi), and that which is pure, penetrating, and not capable of assuming form becomes spirit."[101] This distinction between qi and spirit appears to instantiate a duality, because qi refers to material form or force, whereas spirit is what is not capable of assuming form in a material way. The Chinese word for spirit is *shen* 神, and this word usually refers to a spirit or deity in the typical anthropomorphic sense. But Kasoff explains that when Zhang uses the term *shen* he does not simply mean spirit in the way we normally think about it, as an anthropomorphic deity. For Zhang, shen refers to what is inscrutable or unfathomable, in contrast to what is knowable and conceivable. The knowable and comprehensible elements of existence are explained by qi in the forms of yin and yang. But "that which is unfathomable in the yin and yang is what is meant by shen." Shen here is "the inscrutable, wondrous aspect of this process" of change.[102]

We usually describe what is knowable, and we do this by virtue of qi. However, there is always something inscrutable or unknowable that occurs in any change. Zhang uses the word *spirit* in a more philosophical way to indicate this unknowable element of what happens. This is the "spiritual" aspect of energy. We do now know where energy comes from, or where it goes, because thermodynamics works only if we presume that energy is conserved, which means that it cannot be created or destroyed. There is something deeply wondrous and inscrutable about this, and Zhang Zai's philosophy gives us a language that helps appreciate and express it, even though his conception of energy is very different from the modern scientific perspective.

That which takes material form is knowable as qi and that which does not take material form is also a kind of qi, material force as energy. The inscrutable aspect of *both* material form *and* material force is designated as *spirit*. What we call li is a pattern that emerges out of the dynamic nonlinear inter- and intra-actions of qi. By viewing qi as energy transformation in new materialist terms, I oppose idealist and vitalist understandings that denigrate and downgrade physical and material change, but I am not thereby eliminating spirit. Spirit needs to be redefined in more new materialist and energetic ways, and I think that Zhang helps us do this with his understanding of shen as that which is "inscrutable" in the process of change.

Qi refers to the process of change (*yi*) as that which actualizes the manifestations of reality by means of potency and creativity, multiplying resonance and relation: "the more diversity, the more relations; the more relations, the more resonations; and the more resonations, the more the capacity for resonance or the potency of nature can get expressed."[103] In the *Zhengmeng*, Zhang critiques the perspective of the ordinary person as well as the viewpoint of the Buddhist. Zhang presumes (incorrectly) that Buddhism is otherworldly and that it opposes the transcendent emptiness or void to worldly processes and things. By contrast, Zhang wants to understand and affirm the continuity between the Great Void and the myriad things, and also affirm the processes of change that create relations, resonances, and patterns between and among things. According to Kim, Zhang "articulates his position in terms of a continuous process of realizing the capacity for resonance hidden within this world manifest to us."[104]

The fact that qi emerges from the taixu in Zhang's philosophy is technically incompatible with the thermodynamic notion that energy cannot be created or destroyed, if taixu is literally thought of as a void. Zhang Zai says that everything that exists is qi, which emerges from the Great Void. Zhang identifies the Great Void with what Hyo Dong Lee calls "the One Psychophysical Energy (*yiqi*) in a state of utter stillness, purity, and translucent unity."[105] But energy is never in a state of utter stillness; it is always dynamic.

We should posit the taixu not as an actual origin but as an infinite multiplicity from which material processes of qi subtract. This is similar in some respects to how Viveiros de Castro understands Amerindian thought. Amazonian cultures posit an originary anthropomorphic person who contains all the potentialities that get subtracted in their manifestation. This origin is not literally a void or a person or a thing, but a presumption about how the differentiation of nature in its intrinsic multiplicity occurs.

I want to recover Zhang Zai's philosophy of qi without grounding it in the taixu as an original void. The Taixu to which Zhang refers is related to another term, *taiji*, which, as I have noted, is usually translated as Great Ultimate. This term originally appears in a commentary on the *Yijing* (the famous *Book of Changes*), and it becomes a philosophical term later in the work of Zhou Dunyi (1017–1073), who was a contemporary of Zhang Zhai.

In the *Xici* or "Appended Phrases of the *Yijing*," the two modes of yin and yang proceed from the taiji, the Great Ultimate. For Zhou Dunyi, the taiji is also understood as pure potentiality, or *wuji*.[106] *Ji* translates as limit, and *wu* is a negative or negation, so *wuji* literally means "unlimited." The taiji is wuji, for Zhou Dunyi. Instead of adopting either of these terms, Zhang Zai coins a new term, the taixu, or Great Void, to account for the unlimited quality of the taiji.

I think that *wuji* is probably a better term than *taixu* because it is less easy to substantialize. In some respects, it appears similar to what Anaxamander calls the *apeiron*, which also means "unlimited." Wuji as the "source" of qi is closer to how we conceptualize energy, as unlimited insofar as we have to posit its conservation in all interactions. This limitless qi indicates the immanent productivity and creativity of the universe.

Perhaps a better Chinese term than taiji or taixu, however, is *neng* 能. *Neng* in Chinese usually just means "can," as in "I can operate this machine." Sometimes, in more philosophical terms, *neng* is translated as subject, because it refers to the capacity of a human subject to operate on the world. In more general terms, however, neng refers to an infinite capacity or potentiality to do anything whatsoever.[107] Qi designates the material manifestation of the myriad things that exist. The world universe is made up of this qi-energy. Neng is the abstract background of infinite potential to change that qi manifests—the virtually infinite web from which qi emerges as matter/energy. It can be characterized as an irreducible multiplicity. The manifestation of neng as qi is a subtraction from this multiplicity and its emergence as a more definite potentiality (*shi* 势).

This kind of potentiality, shi, is a more concrete potential for how things change. Shi is closer to the idea of potential energy as measured in physics, and *shi neng* is the Chinese translation of potential energy 势能. From the point of view of neng in itself, neng is infinite or unlimited, which is practically how we have to think about energy in terms of the first law of thermodynamics. But from the point of view of potential and actual manifestations of matter-energy, neng is constantly changing. Neng is a more abstract way to name what Viveiros de Castro calls the infinite potentiality that is usually figured in anthropomorphic terms in Amerindian traditions.

Chinese philosophy does have a good conception of entropy, which is the focus of the second law. Thermodynamic entropy in Chinese is called shang 熵, which includes the symbol for fire and another that means "quotient." This word was coined by Hu Ganfu in 1923. In traditional Chinese philosophy, the fact that qi becomes less and less useful for us over time is less important than the idea of its intrinsic inexhaustibility. But I am arguing from a standpoint of nonequilibrium thermodynamics that entropy is not simply thermal and its increase does not necessarily lead to a state of disorder and heat death. So I think that qi can be amplified with an understanding of entropy in theoretical and practical terms.

Because Zhang's emphasis on qi was obscured by the later influence of the Cheng brothers and Zhu Xi, with their stress on the importance of li, we need to liberate his philosophy from theirs and understand it more on its own terms. We need to return to Zhang Zai, along with Zhou Dunyi, and trace this somewhat minor tradition of East Asian qi to its later expression in the materialist philosophy of Wang Fuzhi (1619–1692).[108] In the seventeenth century, Wang Fuzhi picks up on and elaborates this materialism of Zhang Zai when he says that "principle (li) depends on material force (qi)."[109] According to Wang, li is "not a principle that can be grasped. It is invisible.... Therefore the first time there is any principle is when it is seen in qi. After principles have been found, they of course appear to become tendencies. We see principle only in the necessary aspect of tendencies."[110] Principles can only be grasped as tendencies (shi) after the appearance of qi. They are invisible or practically nonexistent prior to the working of material energy. Physical laws or principles are tendencies because they express how things work and interact.

Wang also criticizes the abstract quality of Zhang's Great Void, insisting on the concreteness of particular things. In this way he helps us collapse what Kim Jung-Yeup calls the vertical dimension of Zhang's philosophy into the horizontal. Wang says that "few people are capable of saying that without a concrete thing there cannot be the Way, but it is certainly true."[111] Here the Great Void is not any sort of absolute origin, and as a term it is misleading, as Wang points out. We need something like this conception of an infinite multiplicity of potentiality, but we need to comprehend it in more "horizontal" or immanent terms, and the word *neng* perhaps offers a better way to express this.

Wang's philosophy coincides with a more empirical turn in Chinese philosophy, and this empiricism is a correction to abstract metaphysical speculation. Insofar as Wang is read in terms supplied by modern Western materialism, his empiricism appears limited, but a more energetic materialism allows us to read Zhang and Wang together in more productive ways. In his study of Wang Fuhzi, Nicholas S. Brasovan claims that Wang's thought is relevant for an ecological humanism that views physical reality as qi in new materialist terms. This new materialism "reconstructs and reconceives matter as vital, vibrant, self-structuring, energy." For Brasovan, both qi and new materialism "look to undercut the severances of substance dualism by redirecting our attention to the unified event/experience of persons-in-the-world" in their irreducible complexity.[112]

Qi as energy is always differentiated, not unified. The harmony comes after, and the patterned li that emerges is retrojected back to explain the nature of the process. Li possesses a virtuality that is always present, but it is only actualized after the fact of the manifestation of qi. Qi is how Zhang thinks about change. According to Peter Atkins, a physical chemist, thermodynamics "provides a foundation for understanding why *any* change occurs." It's not just steam engines, turbines, and chemical processes, but it also allows us to understand "those most exquisite consequences of chemical reaction, the acts of literary, artistic, and musical activity that enhance our culture."[113] And not just *ours*. So much of what we think of as the distinctive Chinese cultural, intellectual, and religious tradition traces back to the incredible significance of the *Book of Changes*, the *Yijing*.

The *Yijing* provides a pattern to analyze, interpret, discern, comprehend, and predict the events that occur, which are multiple manifestations of qi organized into the complementary modes of yin and yang. Yin and yang are not things, and they are not simply forces. They are expressions of qi that are derived from the taiji or wuji as it divides and interacts, and then these two modes in turn produce the four images and the eight trigrams, as the *Yijing* encapsulates. The *Yijing* is not simply a book of mystical divination, but, more important, a combinatorial that also contains traces of the early Chinese dynasty, the Zhou.[114] The *Yijing* is the *Book of Change(s)*, and it runs as a through line across Chinese intellectual history.

Zhang advocates a Great Harmony of the universe, and we need a new perception of harmony that is material and dynamic as well as spiritual and aesthetic. This New Harmony would refuse any simple opposition between East and West, even as it is capable of being infused with the knowledge and practices of indigeneity. A "harmonious" new materialism of energy transformation is spiritual, personal, natural, and cosmic at distinct levels of transformation that are neither reducible to nor exchangeable with each other. Focusing on energy also allows us to better understand, in practical terms, our material situation, which is one of depletion of finite energy reserves and other natural resources *for us*, as human population and industrial civilization strains the limits of the planet.

In this chapter, I have engaged with Amerindian, Vodou, and neo-Confucian ideas about energy and spirit from the perspectives of new materialism and nonequilibrium thermodynamics. I do not want to amalgamate these traditions together, even if my discussion gives that appearance due to the necessary brevity of their treatment. I do not want to collapse these contemporary philosophical and scientific ideas into the non-Western spiritual traditions. I also do not want to appropriate these traditions for the purposes of a contemporary Western discourse. Instead, I am reading them diffractively, setting up a pattern by superposing the three traditions onto each other and interpreting what resonates through them, which accords with nonequilibrium thermodynamics and new materialist philosophies.

Too many people are misled by the logic of either/or. Either one tradition—Eastern, Western, or indigenous—is better and superior to the other, and is privileged as a lens of interpretation and understanding, or, if this is denied, then the assumption is that they are saying the same thing. That is not the point of this chapter or of this book. I am trying to develop an understanding and articulation of energy that views these distinct peoples, practices, cultures, traditions, philosophies, and perspectives in terms of an infinite multiplicity that cannot be reduced to any sameness or oneness. Following the insights of Viveiros de Castro, I think that a multinaturalist perspectivism helps shifts the focus of our understanding. Here we can affirm the infinite multiplicity of the myriad natural things that make up our world(s), as well as try to account for the stabilizing social discourse that selects from this multiplicity to generate a coherent comprehension of it.

Today, the "objective" social reality that we inherit and inhabit is named as the Anthropocene, for better and for worse, even if this is also a fetish.[115] This fact is what increasingly shapes our lives and the possibilities for practicing them in meaningful ways. And it is not a question of the future, of what is coming, because anthropogenic climate change is already here, it is already taking place around us and affecting us in myriad ways. The non-Western and nonmodern perspectives I have engaged here offer better understandings and possibilities than the current social forms in which we are implicated, predominantly neoliberal capitalism. These other perspectives are the effect of other forms of social organization and practices of exchange, which are also constantly at work.

Centering this engagement of spirit around energy in new materialist and nonequilibrium thermodynamic terms helps us elucidate and appreciate new insights into these traditions, and they offer new ways for us to understand and imagine our own. We know that we have to change. Everything is changing, the world is changing, and often we want to find something eternal to hold onto. Everything is change, and energy is how things change. Spirit consists of our ability to understand and value what is inscrutable about this process. It's not about saving anything or anyone. Another way to talk about change, following Malabou, is to think about the destructive plasticity inherent in form. It's not about recouping or recovering this or that tradition, it's about blowing them up. Or rather seeing how they are always already explosive in their very nature, despite the efforts of capitalism to control and constrain them.

In chapter 5, I turn to another tradition, theology, which is often seen as the most traditional and unchanging discipline, whether apologetically linked to this or that faith tradition or nostalgically viewed as the "queen" of the sciences. Here I show how a nondogmatic radical theology offers a discourse to think about energy and divinity, because, if there is something like a god, it would also have to change. Or God would be Change. Radical theology is fundamentally about change, as Jeffrey W. Robbins explains in his book *Radical Theology: A Vision for Change*.[116] The point is not to interpret the world, as Marx asserts; it is to *change* it. To change is to change everything, including the logics by which we seek to make sense of it. What if what we call God is not a prime mover, a fixed universal essence, or a supreme being, but a way to designate change itself?

5

RADICAL THEOLOGY AND THE NATURE OF GOD

A RHIZOMATIC THEOLOGY

What happens to theology if we give up the idea of something that does not change? What if divinity is not that which does not change, but encompasses all that does change? Here the "science of divine things" is focused on energy transformation at the heart of reality, rather than an other world that exists in a different dimension. God is an effect of spirit, which is itself a complex form of energy transformation. The divine things are not the puppet masters of the universe, but the phenomena that help us best explain and make sense of what we experience in its inscrutable complexity.

When we abandon a theistic God and give up the Greek desire for immutability, we do not simply eliminate theology. We *radicalize* it along immanent lines. The Latin word *radix* means root, but we have to be careful here because the word *radical* has multiple connotations. It's not about going beneath the surface to get to the root of divine things, because this metaphorics of surface and depth is also problematic. A depth hidden beneath the surface is another version of a God who lies above or behind the reality that exists. We should think about radical theology in more rhizomatic ways, following Deleuze and Guattari.

In *A Thousand Plateaus*, Deleuze and Guattari introduce their conception of the rhizome, but what is less appreciated is that they characterize this idea in the context of a book. They state that a book is a machinic assemblage that composes an irreducible multiplicity. When we think about a book in more traditional terms, say a Bible, we resort to the idea of a root-book, following the model of a simplified tree. When we think about roots, we imagine a depth that grounds the structure above. But this is a distortion, because "nature doesn't work that way: in nature, roots are taproots with a more multiple, lateral, and circular system of representation."[1] Many readers presume that the rhizome would be the alternate model to this root-book; however, there is another model that represents the transition to the rhizome, which is a radicle-system.

Deleuze and Guattari contrast the figure of the root-book with a more modern "radicle-system." The radicle-system book is not yet rhizomatic, as we will see, but it represents an advance compared to the typical root-book. Here, "the principal root has been aborted, or its tip has been destroyed; and immediate, indefinite multiplicity of secondary roots grafts onto it and undergoes a flourishing development."[2] The modern book, which they associate with William S. Burroughs and James Joyce, is an essentially fragmented work presented as a total work. This totality is a dream that can only be presented in fragments, which is the dream of modernity. The radicle-system book suggests this chaosmos is opposed to the more traditional cosmos of the root-book, upon which it conducts "a strange mystification." The roots themselves are tangled and aborted, but something persists or can be evoked that indicates the totality of nature or the world.

In the first figure of the book, the world can be represented as a tree with a clear grounding in the earth. This is how many theologians treat the Bible, as a root-book that allows them to develop, follow, and prune the branches of a religious metaphysics. But in the modern world the root-book fragments and gives way to the radicle-system. The radicle-system book uses an indirect mode of representation to better show the whole, which can only be given and glimpsed radically, in terms of its multiple roots. These roots grow in a circular or cyclical fashion as opposed to the more linear roots of the root-book. This is why the major representative of radical theology and the death of God, Thomas J. J. Altizer, argues that *Finnegans Wake* is the ultimate theological text of our contemporary world. *Its fragmentary totality expresses the death of God in a positive and powerful way.*

However, Deleuze and Guattari are also critical of this second figure of the book, even if they privilege it in comparison to the first one. The problem with the radicle-system book is that it still attempts to represent the whole, even if it does so in a fragmentary way. The tradition of radical theology is a modern form of theology that embraces the radicle-system approach to the text; it engages texts and textuality to see how these necessarily fragmented radicles continue to show us the total God's-eye picture, even if God is dead and we cannot see the Whole. Radical theology is an improvement on traditional theistic theology, but it remains too rooted in its representational role and fails to liberate itself and us from the trappings of modern liberalism.

The transition to the rhizome is a change, or radicalization, of the second figure of the book. Here is the crucial insight, which Deleuze expresses in *Cinema 2* as well: "the multiple *must be made*," not by "adding a higher dimension" but by subtraction.[3] This is the "only way the one belongs to the multiple: always subtracted." We constitute the multiplicity by means of subtraction of the unique. This making of multiplicity by subtraction actually constitutes it, as odd as that sounds. Here writing takes place at n-1 dimensions. The multiplicity does not already exist, and it does not get represented by adding up fragmentary representations. We generate the multiple by paring away the excess that then retroactively constitutes it, the way that the brain takes shape by the elimination of neurons and their interconnections. This is also how Amerindians produce the multiplicity from which their society is subtracted, according to Viveiros de Castro.

This system of producing a multiplicity by subtraction is a rhizome. According to Deleuze and Guattari, "a rhizome as subterranean stem is absolutely different from root and radicles."[4] This subterranean stem is created by paring down and away a potential multiplicity that does not actually exist prior to its virtual elaboration in the very process of constituting a unique and singular form. The rhizome "itself assumes very diverse forms, from ramified surface directions to concretion into bulbs and tubers," as well as when animals like "rats swarm over each other."[5] We assume a rhizomatic perspective when we treat the multiple as a substantive multiplicity that "ceases to have any relation to the One as subject or object, natural or spiritual reality, image and world."[6]

This description is somewhat abstract, but I am trying to argue that whereas traditional theology is dominated by a simple representational perspective of root and tree, radical theology as it develops in the U.S. and UK constitutes the formation in theology of a radicle-system, but it remains tied to an image of the whole. Radical theology must become more rhizomatic, which I suggest it does when it becomes more explicitly a radical political theology in the work of Jeffrey W. Robbins, an apophatic panentheistic theology in the work of Catherine Keller, or the pluralist pantheism of Mary-Jane Rubenstein.

When we think about energy and about spirit, we should conceive them both as dynamic transformational processes operating on what Deleuze and Guattari call a plane of immanence. A plane of immanence is also a plane of consistency, which means that philosophical concepts do not require another dimension to give them sense and value. In *What Is Philosophy?*, they assert that "concepts are the multiple waves, rising and falling, but a plane of immanence is the single wave that rolls them up and unrolls them."[7] The plane of immanence gives us an image of thought, a conception of multiplicity that helps us organize our thinking and comprehend it immanently, that is, on the basis of its own plane or its own efficacy, rather than borrowing meaning from elsewhere. We make the multiple of radical theology by subtraction from traditional confessional theologies.

Transcendence for Deleuze and Guattari is less an invisible higher dimension than a refusal to allow thought to develop on its own terms, with its own sense and logic. We resort to transcendent explanations when we reach an impasse and do not know how to think. We throw up our hands and grasp for an other explanation that would assist us. I am trying to develop a conception of energy that allows it to function on its own plane, albeit with multiple thresholds of transformation, including matter, form, life, complex systems, society, mind, and even spirit. One reason that neo-Confucian qi is an important concept is that it can also take place in the context of a plane of immanence and help us recontextualize energy in immanent terms.

We need to rethink spirit and God in terms of immanence, and these multiple indigenous, Asian, and African traditions that were discussed in chapter 4 give us tools to do this. They amplify and extend philosophical ideas of new materialism in important ways, as well as show how new materialism is not necessarily new, but also renewable in relation to other spiritual traditions. This is a kind of effects series (Deleuze) or diffractive pattern (Barad) whereby these indigenous, Afro-Caribbean, and Chinese understandings of energy as spirit serve to open up alternative resonances from the stereotypical Western European tradition. In linking these insights to the tradition of radical theology, I am using them to help open up what passes for radical theology beyond itself. Radical theology is not simply a secular attempt to wrestle with the loss of transcendence in the form of Supreme Being; it is an effort to think otherwise in spiritual and material terms. Radical theology is Deleuzean in nature in its effort to affirm immanence in profoundly new and renewable materialist ways.

RADICAL THEOLOGY AND THE DEATH OF GOD

Radical theology as such emerges in the U.S. and the UK in the middle of the twentieth century. Radical theology is a way to name the controversial death of God theology associated with Thomas J. J. Altizer, William Hamilton, Gabriel Vahanian, Richard Rubenstein, and others. In hindsight, we can see the emergence of a wider variety of radical theologies coming out of liberal theology after the Second World War. These radical theologies can include forms of process theology as a radical new natural theology, indebted to the work of Alfred North Whitehead, Charles Hartshorne, and John B. Cobb Jr. They can also include many of the liberations theologies that emerge around the world, including Latin American liberation theologies with their insistence on God's option for the poor, as well as feminist, Black, and other minorities' radical development of theologies of liberation for oppressed and marginalized peoples. Sometimes the radical elements of these distinct forms of theological thinking (such as their scientific and/or political perspectives) are encased within more orthodox theological frameworks, and other times the radicality and changeability of theological thinking itself is foregrounded.

From the perspective of the twenty-first century, we can see more family resemblances as opposed to methodological, doctrinal, and/or practical differences among these nonconservative forms of theology. Today, radical theology has a new impetus and some new adherents, but how it is defined is less important than the "spirit" of radical theology that animates our thinking and our practice. Radical theology refuses the false choice of liberal versus conservative in theology and in politics; it makes no apology for any orthodoxy or traditionalism; and finally it sees through, and ideally past, the limits and aporias of liberalism, no matter how appealing or repelling.

Altizer's theology becomes well-known in the middle of the 1960s with his theological declaration that God is dead. In *The Gospel of Christian Atheism*, the death of God is a metaphysical and dialectical statement about the being of God. The transcendent father God incarnates in and as Jesus, and this divinity "dies" on the cross. The death of Christ attests not to the resurrection of Christ, but to the death of any transcendent otherworldly God. The resurrection for Altizer refers to the spiritual presence of Christ in the community of believers who carry on this powerful insight. The Church appropriates and domesticates the "good news" of the death of God, but it gets retained and reexpressed by the most visionary poets, writers, and philosophers in the history of the Western European tradition, including Dante, Cusa, Blake, Hegel, Nietzsche, and Joyce.

In many ways, the idea of the death of God in theology became a fad, and it inspired a best-selling 1966 *Time* magazine cover that read, in red letters on a black background, "Is God Dead?" Altizer became the center of many controversial debates, including an attempt to get him fired from his professional position at Emory University. He also put together a book on *Radical Theology and the Death of God*, coauthored with William Hamilton and published in 1966, that drew a great deal of attention to the new movement.[8] In addition to the aforementioned Altizer and Hamilton, other representatives of the death of God theology include Richard Rubenstein, Gabriel Vahanian, Harvey Cox, and Paul van Buren. Although many of these theologians were strongly influenced by Karl Barth's neo-orthodoxy, the main inspiration for radical theology was the cultural theology of Paul Tillich.

In the preface to *The Gospel of Christian Atheism*, Altizer argues that "among twentieth-century theologians, it was Tillich alone who made possible a way to a truly contemporary theology. While I have been forced to resist and oppose Tillich's theological conclusions, I do so with the conviction that they are not yet radical enough, and the memory of Tillich's words to me that the real Tillich is the radical Tillich."[9] Tillich's three-volume *Systematic Theology* is far less radical than the searching and honest books he wrote such as *The Courage to Be* and *The Dynamics of Faith*. And it was his collected essays on a *Theology of Culture* that inspired many radical theologians by showing how theology is a discourse that is entangled with other cultural discourses.[10]

In retrospect, for many observers, this movement is viewed as a consistent if marginal articulation of a theological conclusion that God is dead, or simply never existed, and in a secular world we need to move on. However, it is perhaps better to view what is called death of God theology as a radicalization of theology and an insistence on the questionability of theology and its relevance to the world today. The most important element of death of God theology is the repudiation of the orthodox God of transcendence in a way that does not succumb to a comfortable secularist atheism.

In many respects it was Langdon Gilkey, a student of Tillich, who consolidated the death of God as a theological movement in his oppositions to it. As an article by Michael Grimshaw explains, Gilkey "outlined his position as one of seeking the grounded, defensible reality of Christian faith in God in a secular age; this reality of God being opposed to God's death."[11] This responsible but apologetic Christian position was set out in articles published in the influential *Christian Century*, which formed the basis of his book *Naming the Whirlwind: The Renewal of God-Language*. Gilkey fleshed out and criticized death of God theology in order to highlight his own countertheological position, which was an apologetic liberal theology informed by Tillich, Barth, and Reinhold Niebuhr, as well as Friedrich Schleiermacher. Unfortunately, however, to simplify these theological works and perspectives under the heading of the "Death of God" was already to distort and dismiss the variety of radical theological concepts that were being expressed.

Of course, Tillich's work had far less influence on liberation theology as it developed in the 1960s and 1970s, including Roman Catholic liberation theology, Black liberation theology, and feminist liberation theology. His theology was seen as part of the dominant European theological tradition; however, it was viewed less explicitly as an obstacle to liberation compared to many other representatives of this tradition. In his book *The Cross and the Lynching Tree*, Black liberation theologian James Cone singles out Niebuhr as a problematic representative of white Christianity, and he barely mentions Tillich, but he does affirm the language of "the courage to be" in the struggle of Blacks for hope and salvation.[12] Tillich had a more explicit influence on Mary Daly's feminist theology, including

Beyond God the Father, which makes extensive use of Tillich's language and concepts. Daly ends up endorsing Tillich's affirmation of love, power, and justice as "The Most Holy and Whole Trinity," even though Tillich's analysis does not go far enough in its failure to consider the harm done by socialization into sex roles.[13]

In an insightful study of Daly, Christopher D. Rodkey demonstrates how Daly "pirated" many of Tillich's ideas as they informed her feminist analysis, even while she lamented that Tillich's systematic theology "is not radical enough" because of its emphasis on self-affirmation.[14] Daly saw Tillich's personal manifestations of sadomasochism as linked to this perverse self-affirmation. In a more complicated way, a later liberation theologian, Marcella Althaus-Reid, laments less Tillich's expressions of deviant sexuality than the need to keep it a secret. In *Indecent Theology*, she claims that "what is to be condemned regretted is not that Tillich was a sadomasochist, but the fact that he did not find 'the courage to be' out of the closet of his sexuality."[15] Tillich's misogynist treatment of women in his work and in his life should be condemned, but BDSM itself may be less an instance of masculine self-affirmation than a complex and negotiated sexual-political and religious space teeming with intensities and potentialities for care.[16]

Althaus-Reid's work is inspired by both European and Latin American sources. Liberation theology develops out of Marxist and socialist ideas and developments in Europe and throughout the world. In Latin America, liberation theology is tied to the liberation of the poor, mainly Catholic Christians, from oppressive regimes and a hierarchical Catholic Church. For Gustavo Gutiérrez, whose work is seen as foundational for Latin American liberation theology, the problem of poverty emerges as the central question for contemporary Christian theology. The central theme here is the "preferential option for the poor," affirmed by the conference of Catholic bishops at Médellin in Columbia in 1968. Liberation theology is a crucial form of radical theology, although in its early iterations its theological orthodoxy was often affirmed as a way to make it influential for practicing Christians.

In her work, Althaus-Reid affirms an *un*orthodox liberation of sexuality that is at the same time theological and political. Unfortunately, theological orthodoxies tend to uphold hierarchical and repressive sexual norms that serve political and economic interests. She explains that "it would be right to say that Liberation Theology belongs to an idealist theological market, because laws and offers and demands in this theology have been thought around certain faith presuppositions (which are unchallengeable as a given)."[17] To radicalize liberation theology is to make it less orthodox and more indecent, along the lines opened up by Althaus-Reid with the image of a woman buying lemons in Buenos Aires without wearing underwear.

In a more conventional theological perspective, the present evil of the world is overcome by the rightful power of the Kingdom of God, for which we live and struggle. In a more radical sense, the idea of the kingdom itself and God as sovereign power become suspect because they reinforce colonialism and patriarchy. "Heterosexuality is the ideology of patriarchalism," Althaus-Reid explains, "and also its true God, and Christianity reinforced this alliance of heterosexually constructed gods in continents such as Latin America."[18] We need a deeper and more radical, indecent theological sensibility informed by the critiques of coloniality and decoloniality of Quijano and Mignolo (referenced in chapter 4).

Liberation theology as it emerged in the 1960s radicalizes theology in political terms but not always in theological terms. More recent liberation theologians like Althaus-Reid and Ivan Petrella more explicitly radicalize liberation theology in important ways. Rather than a theological ethics of hope grounded in a more conventional Christian idealism, Miguel de la Torre calls "for a theology of desperation that leads to hopelessness" as more truthful to the experience of the ultra-poor and marginalized peoples in the world today.[19] This embrace of the reality of hopelessness for so many people discarded by Euromodern capitalism issues in the praxis of what de la Torre calls "an *ethics para joder.*"[20] *Joder* in Spanish means "fuck it," so this means practicing a hopeless but nonetheless liberatory praxis with and for the people who are screwed by the normal workings of our globalized world. We need to be liberated from neoliberal and neocolonial hope.

So a broader and more inclusive perspective on the development of radical theology affirms the continuity from Tillich to the death of God theologies, while incorporating nonorthodox strands of liberation theology as well as process theology, which I will discuss more fully in the next section. Process theology rejects the grounding of theology in an orthodox Christian framework and transforms the image of thought of theological thinking in light of new understandings of environmentalism and the natural sciences. Process theology builds on the process philosophy of Alfred North Whitehead, and it resists the subjective and linguistic constructivism that dominated much intellectual discourse in the late twentieth century.

There has been a renewal of interest in the tradition of radical theology in the twenty-first century, and much of this work has been done in terms of political theology. In the wake of the terrorist attacks of 9/11, and the ensuing wars against Afghanistan and Iraq, as well as the U.S. Patriot Act, many theologians took up more explicitly political themes. It was Robbins who criticized traditional radical theology for being insufficiently radical in political terms in his 2006 essay, "Terror and the Postmodern Tradition."[21] This critique and its elaboration of a more radical political theology involves the attempt to wed the continental discussions of political theology associated with philosophers such as Derrida, Giorgio Agamben, and others who have engaged with the work of Carl Schmitt, with the tradition of American radical theology.[22] By reading radical theology in terms of Schmitt, we can see how sovereignty operates in both political and theological spheres, and much of this work involves contesting both the theological sovereignty of God *and* the political sovereignty of the state.

In his introduction to the dialogue and debate that he staged between Slavoj Žižek and John Milbank, *The Monstrosity of Christ*, Creston Davis points toward a conclusion about religion in material and political terms: "humanity is material; thus the material world cannot be written off in favor of some kind of retreat into an ethereal transcendence. Thus accounts of human flourishing and resistance to capitalist nihilism must be thoroughly material."[23] Yes. From the classical materialist critiques of religion as otherwordly in Euromodernity, we have passed through the linguistic turn, the Great Depression, two devastating world wars, the subsequent Great Acceleration, a prolonged cold war, and the postcolonial/liberationist aspirations of peoples around the world—many of which were cut off by American/European imperialism and neoliberalism.

After far too many *posts* to number, we arrive at a new materialist appreciation and understanding of religion, one simultaneously less dismissive and more radical, which finds its expression most clearly in the emerging political theologies that are together rethinking the conceptual bases not only of God but democracy itself. The contemporary challenge for radical theology is to acknowledge and draw upon all (or at least some) of these resources, as well as others "outside" the tradition, without losing the material and political edge of radical theology itself, wherever and however it is done.

Radical theology is a form of theology that affirms immanence as opposed to transcendence. Many expressions of radical theology in the twentieth century were influenced more by existentialism, hermeneutics, linguistics, and the social sciences and were less engaged with the natural sciences. The main exception to this is process theology, which draws on the philosophical work of Whitehead to develop an explicit theology of nature. I want to reflect on the presumed subject matter of theology, the word *God*, in the context of Whitehead's process philosophy, then later process theology, to show how creative process theologies, in particular that of Catherine Keller, can also be viewed as forms of radical theology.

IMAGINING GOD OTHERWISE: PROCESS PANENTHEISM AND PANTHEISM AS RADICAL THEOLOGIES

Process theology objects to the elimination of nature and being from many forms of philosophy and theology in the twentieth century. In its most radical form, process theology affirms the inextricable interrelation of God and world. Process theology often uses the term pan*e*ntheism, where God and the world exist in a complex interdependent relationship without being collapsed into each other. The complete identification of God and world is called *pantheism*, from which *panentheism* is at pains to distinguish itself. Pantheism is often viewed as a substance monism where everything that exists is the same, and this one substance is identified as God. Pantheism, in philosophical terms, is often ascribed to the philosophy of Spinoza, because he argues in the *Ethics* that there is only one substance, and that substance should be understood as God, or Nature. We will see, however, with Mary-Jane Rubenstein, that there are much better ways to understand pantheism.

Today in our postmodern world, scholars and scientists are discovering that much of the world that appeared to be inert and impersonal is nonetheless animated by strange forces. And these mysterious powers complicate any simple description of reality as divided into separate objects and beings. As we saw in previous chapters, the natural world cannot be simply separated from the world of human activity, and the life of human beings cannot be separated from the workings of all sorts of animals, plants, bacteria, and inorganic forces. We cannot draw neat and clear lines between humans and other things, or between living and nonliving beings. In scientific terms, we need to think less about separate beings and more about complex adaptive systems. Systems can be used to describe living and nonliving systems. Systems are dynamic, in the sense that they change and evolve over time. But they are also resilient, because they have a certain structure that persists over time, and they are organized and sustained by flows of energy.

Some scholars talk about a new animism or even a new polytheism in our contemporary world. Instead of using the word *animism*, Latour and Barad use the term *agency*, as we have seen. An agent is a force for change, and it may be a river, a person, an ecosystem, or a galaxy. At an extreme level, quantum forces display a very strange agency, because they do not operate in ways that make sense to us in conventional terms. They appear to be divided into particles and waves, but they are actually both, at the same time. They can appear to be fixed at a certain location, but they can also be spread out along a tiny but significant distance. Quantum particles can be entangled in such a way that they appear to violate locality, which means that there cannot be any strange action at a distance. These particles can also be virtual and appear to simply wink in and out of existence. Barad argues, in *Meeting the Universe Halfway*, that quantum effects are not limited to the minuscule scale of subatomic particles, as we saw in chapter 1. These effects actually scale up to human and cosmic levels of existence in tiny but significant ways.

In his philosophy, Whitehead develops a new way to think about the world in light of the discoveries of quantum physics in the early twentieth century. Whitehead was also a leading mathematician who worked with his student Bertrand Russell on systematizing mathematical logic, in their *Principia Mathematica*. Later, Whitehead turned to broader scientific, philosophical, and religious studies. At the end of his book *Process and Reality*, Whitehead relates God and the world. For Whitehead, the world is in a state of constant becoming; nature is not static or predictable. Whitehead emphasizes creativity and novelty as ways to evaluate the situation of the world; the more novelty the better.

Whitehead wants to find a way to think about the world as a whole, and in doing so he comes up with a kind of differentiation in the idea of God. God is not simply one absolute being; God is defined by two distinct "natures." On the one hand, God is the source, or ground, of everything that exists, including the world. On the other hand, God is also the result of everything that happens in the world, so God changes as a result of the world's becoming. Whitehead calls the first idea of God the "primordial nature of God" and the second is the "consequent nature of God."

God is dipolar; however, there are not two Gods. There are two very different aspects and ways to think and talk about God. God is the source of everything, and God is the result of everything. In some ways the world exists between these two natures of God. But Whitehead does not say that God and world will be finally unified in some eschatological way.

God is less of a supreme being, or a person, and more of a way to think about the world. Whitehead needs the idea of God to comprehend the world the way that he does. We need the idea of God to think the world, but we also need to understand the world in order to understand what it means to think about God. They are essentially interrelated and intimately entangled. God is both one and many, and the world is also both one and many. According to Whitehead, "It is as true to say that God is one and the World many, as that the World is one and God many."[24] The primordial nature of God gives us an original unity out of which the world can emerge and develop. The consequent nature of God incorporates all the many processes and things that happen in the world and harmonizes them together in and as the divine experience. This is not a total unity, or a reunification, but a way to think about God as actual, that is, alive and in process.

The actualization of God means that there is purpose and goodness in the world, in its creative advance toward novelty. The world is not a meaningless process, but the processes that occur matter insofar as they are contributing to the development of what is called the consequent nature of God. God incorporates the harmonization of the world and its progression of creativity and rationality. This allows all the actions of the world to continue to exist in a certain way, even as they perish as specific, individual actions. Everything that happens makes up God, and God incorporates and harmonizes everything that happens. The world is constantly changing and becoming, but so is God, at least the consequent nature of God.

The philosopher of religion Charles Hartshorne was a student of Whitehead and a teacher of John C. Cobb, who then used and applied the thinking of Hartshorne and Whitehead to his Christian faith to come up with his process theology. His 1965 book *A Christian Natural Theology* is the most formative work on process theology. In this book, Cobb argues for a Christian natural theology based on the philosophy of Whitehead. What Cobb does in this book is introduce Whitehead's philosophy into theology, thereby developing process theology as a serious contender among contemporary theological positions.

Process theology is one of the few examples of theology in the second half of the twentieth century that seriously engages with science, nature, and the environment. In fact, Cobb also wrote the first single-authored book on environmental ethics from a theological perspective, *Is It Too Late?: A Theology of Ecology*, published in 1971. Process theology is a natural theology, because it takes the physical universe seriously in a way that most forms of orthodox theology do not.

In *A Christian Natural Theology*, Cobb asserts that God is best understood in personal terms. For Whitehead, God is clearly not a person, even though God is an actual occasion that persists through time. Cobb synthesizes the eternal and temporal natures of God into a personal God that serves to ground process theology. Cobb argues that we cannot truly assert the temporal nature of God without this conception of personhood. "Unless we speak of him as temporal," Cobb claims, "we cannot speak of him as a living person, for the living person is defined by a temporal relationship among actual occasions."[25] Here the assumption of Whitehead's process philosophy into theology is marked by the transformation of God from an impersonal process to a personal being.

I think that Cobb's retrieval of the notion of person as a way to comprehend divinity is problematic and, despite the significance of Cobb's theology, serves to endorse a more conventional and less radical theological perspective than that of Whitehead. Whitehead offers a "philosophy of organism." For Whitehead, the world is more like a living organism than an inanimate object, and his philosophy is one of the influences upon new materialism. A person is a very complex kind of organism, made up of multiple interconnecting processes that give rise to new forms of awareness. This is part of the progression of nature toward creativity and novelty, although it is not a simple linear process. For Whitehead, God is not a person. God is a permanent actual occasion because God retains the effects of all the other actual occasions. God makes the things that happen matter because they continue to exist in the idea of God. Cobb reshapes Whiteheadian philosophy into process theology by comprehending God in personal terms, but this image of God is more traditional in many ways, and it appears incredible to most nontheists.

Catherine Keller is a student of Cobb, and she is one of the most important process theologians as well as one of the most creative and significant religious thinkers of the twenty-first century. Her work is poetic, allusive, technical, and complex, but her theology is a rich resource for posttheistic reflection. Keller draws on the most cutting-edge theology and philosophy to fashion her work, and she does not eliminate the personal aspect of what she calls God, but she does relativize this personal element beyond Cobb's version of it. Furthermore, Keller's theology is deeply responsive to the urgency of our political, social, economic, and ecological situation on a precarious planet, and her work incorporates process, postmodern, and liberationist expressions in compelling ways. She opens up process theology to many other kinds of thinking, including continental philosophy, feminist and womanist theology, ecotheology, and mysticism. In this sense, she can be seen as a truly radical theologian, affirming an irreducible pluralism that retains an emphasis upon immanence.

In *Face of the Deep*, Keller takes up the beginning of the book of Genesis. She focuses on the first sentence of Genesis 1:1–2: "When in the beginning God created heaven and earth, the earth was without form and void; and darkness was on the face of the deep. And the spirit of God vibrated upon the face of the waters." Orthodox Christian theology argues that God created the world out of nothing, *ex nihilo*. But Keller focuses on the word *deep*, which in Hebrew is *tehom*, to criticize and reject this traditional understanding of creation. God did not create the world out of nothing by an act of will. This idea of creation out of nothing is a reflection of the omnipotent God of classical theism who snaps his fingers and magically brings something into existence.

By contrast, and relying on Jewish and Christian scholarship of the Bible, Keller shows how a better understanding of creation can be called *creatio ex profundis*, creation out a profound deep. The Deep is the unformed potential or chaos, the source and primary stuff of creation that God will call into a structured world or cosmos. Keller's tehomic theology is a theology of becoming out of and with the depths of creation. God works with the Deep, giving it form and purpose. She argues that her "theology of becoming flows not just between the waters of nihilism and pantheism (with which it mingles many currents), but also around the rock of classical theism."[26]

According to Keller, the convergence of mystical theology with Whitehead's philosophy produces what she calls an "apophatic panentheism." Apophaticism is a method of negation that is present in many forms of mystical theology. Apophatic language means that instead of using language that identifies something in positive terms, one uses language to describe what something is not. In apophatic theology, the emphasis is less on what God is than on what God is *not*. We cannot grasp God in straightforward positive terms, so we are forced to use negative language if we want to talk about God. An apophatic panentheism means that we do not know in positive terms exactly what we mean by each of the three words—God, world, or "in," when we use this term. We cannot simply fix the terms or the relations. There is something unknowable about God and about the world, and we confess that we cannot simply grasp it.

The *en* of panentheism does not mean "in" in the normal way. It does not mean that the world is *in* God in the way that soup is in a bowl. Neither one is a container, but both are somehow wrapped up in the other is such a way that neither can be completely disentangled. If we think about the All that is in God in a very literal way, that reproduces the logic of classical theism, where you have God and God exceeds the world, but somehow God contains the world and everything in the world is derivative of God. If one asserts the interconnection of God and world, however, it is all too easy to collapse the distinction, which becomes a simple pantheism where God and the world are identified. Pantheism should not be limited to this caricature, however, as Mary-Jane Rubenstein argues in her work.

The world is not static. It becomes, in God. God is not apart from the world. God changes with the world, in response to the world. The "in" is a kind of bottomless depth that forms a matrix where they relate. Both change and become in different ways, according to different rhythms. Panentheism here is less of a definition and more of a dance. In *Cloud of the Impossible*, Keller shifts her theological metaphor from the deep to a cloud. Here she develops the apophatic or negative theology that she opens up in *Face of the Deep*. Negative theology is a better way to think about God, because it refuses to be trapped within definite names. God here is not simply a God of possibility and actuality, one who makes things happen. Here God is connected with a cloud of *impossibility*. Impossibility does not mean something that literally cannot occur; it means that what God names should be thought beyond what we think of as possible.

The cloud is an abstract conceptual space where we can encounter the divine in a mystical experience, and it is also a physical piece of our fragile atmosphere. Keller opens up theology to other voices and other visions. She argues for a planetary entanglement where everything is somehow, however distantly, related to everything else. Both the world and God are incredibly complex, and they are interrelated in profound ways that cannot be completely spelled out. We need better names and metaphors for God if we are still going to use that word. Keller gives us two important names with the deep and the cloud. In this book, I am thinking about what we call God more in terms of energy, more specifically dynamic energy transformation, in a way that is also agential and relational because it generates "things." God is not a thing, a person, a noun, a source, or a static entity. *God* is a word we have inherited that often indicates the all of the universe. However, with Keller's panentheism there remains a tension between the all and God. The *en* is a slash, a cut, a relation, or a fold that displaces everything from itself, opening it up to an irreducible multiplicity. This is a radical multinaturalism in Viveiros de Castro's terms.

All our identities are indeterminate and unstable. We can never know and name exactly who or what we are. Keller asks: "Are we feminists or womanists or mujeristas; negroes or blacks or African Americans; homosexuals or lesbians/gays or queers. . . . We might speak of an apophasis, dynamic and on principle open-ended, determinately indeterminate, of human identities."[27] Our identities in the social and natural world are unstable, as is our relationship to what we call God. But God's identity is also unstable or in flux; God does not and cannot fix our identities. The more we try to sort everything out, the more cloudy things become. Panentheism is not about defining a proper relationship between the All and God; it is about recognizing and affirming the open-ended multiplicity of these relationships.

We need to propose solidarities of diverse peoples, cultures, and religious perspectives that can assist in transforming our relationship to the planet. The modern world we have inherited from Europe treated nonhuman nature as a resource, a deposit to be extracted and exploited for short-term human benefit. We have to get rid of such attitudes and practices if we want to have a world much longer. We need the inception of new forms of collective practices as well as new kinds of theological thinking. Keller's panentheism gives her the openness and the flexibility to incorporate these diverse approaches.

In another turn of the screw, pantheism collapses the All and God that panentheism is at pains to distinguish. For many thinkers, this collapse is a train wreck—it creates confusion and chaos, even panic. For others, particularly Rubenstein, pantheism represents an opportunity to embrace an even more radical immanence in theology. Her book *Pantheologies* opens up a crucial perspective to resituate radical theology amid its intrinsically pantheist implications.

Pantheism is distinct from panentheism because the *en* of *panentheism* preserves a difference between the All and God, while *pantheism* apparently collapses that difference. In much of Western thought, pantheism has functioned as a limit concept. That is, if we want to think about or have faith in a divinity, it needs to be related to the world, the all or everything. The problem with pantheism is that it involves the collapse of this God into everything else to the extent that there is nothing that is not God. And if everything is God, what is the point of saying that anything is God?

Pantheologies builds upon and partly presupposes the work that Rubenstein does in her previous book, *Worlds Without End*. In that book, she explores multiverse cosmologies in both historical and contemporary frameworks. At the end of *Pantheologies* she returns to some of these cosmological issues, explaining why and how Albert Einstein recoiled from the world that he helped to reveal with quantum physics. Quantum physics opens up multiple and endless worlds that cannot be easily constrained or reappropriated, although these worlds themselves proliferate in chaotic and confusing ways.

For Rubenstein, and I would argue for anyone who is invested in profoundly comples theoretical thinking, the question is how best to understand and articulate a perspective of multiplicity. Here she divides pantheism into monist and pluralist versions, pantheisms that stress unity versus those that emphasize multiplicity. Pantheism is a valuable and useful discourse, insofar as we can canalize it along these fecund lines of pluralism and multiplicity. How can we better think about the world as a pluralist multiplicity? For Rubenstein, recent "para-scientific" studies, "loosely assembled under the category of theories of immanence," include "ecofeminisms, 'new' materialisms, new animisms, animal studies, vegetal studies, assemblage and actor-network theories, speculative realism, complexity theory, and nonlinear science studies . . . [that] open the possibility of something like a pluralist pantheism—or, to metabolize the plurality, 'pantheologies.'"[28] These newer studies, which greatly inform this book as well, both emphasize immanence and contribute to a pluralist pantheism that affirms the irreducible multiplicity of the world.

Rubenstein discusses Lynn Margulis's theories of the symbiogenesis of bacteria, which I discussed in chapter 2, and she explains how Margulis affirms the name Gaia after its coining by James Lovelock. Margolis, however, understands Gaia differently from Lovelock. For Lovelock, Gaia is a name for the complex adaptive system of Earth as a whole, and he "was happy to call Gaia 'a single organism.'" For Margulis, on the contrary, Gaia is not a single organism; "the chimerical multitudes of Gaia compose not a monistic whole but interdetermined multiplicities" composed primarily of bacteria.[29] Although Lovelock and Margulis were largely ridiculed by the orthodox scientific communities that evaluated them, their ideas have remained relevant, especially in light of newer forms of systems theory, complexity theory, and the insistence of anthropogenic climate change.

Contemporary theorists like Bruno Latour, Isabelle Stengers, William Connolly, and Donna Haraway draw on the ideas of Margulis, Lovelock, and others to fashion contemporary accounts of ecological multiplicity. In *Facing Gaia*, Latour takes pains to emphasize that Gaia is not God; Gaia represents a means to think across all these disparate but connected processes in a way that does not unify them, along the lines envisioned by Margolis. Rubenstein claims, however, that Latour cannot steer clear of "deceptively theological waters." He consistently denies that Gaia is God to such an extent that it raises the question why he "enacts this multiplicitous outpouring to 'make sure Gaia is not God.' And yet in all of these over- and unsayings, Latour recapitulates a classic theological strategy—namely the 'negative' or 'apophatic' effort to call God by every name, thereby acknowledging and preserving God's transcendence in all of them."[30] Latour protests too much. Gaia is not exactly God, but Gaia contains theological residues, as it offers an increasingly useful place from which to situate our multiple perspectives on existence. For Rubenstein, Gaia is a pantheistic concept not because Gaia is an anthropomorphic goddess but because Gaia helps us to frame a pluralistic pantheology in immanent terms. If there exists an irreducible multiplicity, then there are not just multiple subjective perspectives on a world, but there are in fact multiple—endless—worlds.

Pluralist pantheology means that we share an orientation onto multiple worlds that are incommensurable and irreducible to one world. This natural-cosmological perspectivism argues that what we share is our all, the *pan* we have in common that both constitutes and unsettles us. If Pan (in Greek mythology, Pan is a hybrid of animality, humanity, and divinity) is what we have in common, it refers to so many uncountable and uncontainable gods, worlds, and monsters that we often want to resist, to deny, and to shrink back from. Rubenstein's insightful courage lies in exposing this irreducible pantheism at the heart of "our" thinking, our philosophy, our language, and our theology. Pantheology does not name "a" God; it is a shared name for the multiple gods that we cannot escape, either via atheism or theism. To signify is to signify gods, worlds, and monsters, necessarily, as well as animals, people, systems, processes, and energies. According to Rubenstein, we need to reconceive divinity as "immanent, self-exceeding, relational, changing, and multiply perspectival, to such an extent that the 'pantheism' in question would collide with a certain kind of polytheism."[31]

This polytheism is often used to name the spiritual worldview of the indigenous traditions, which was examined in chapter 4, and the work of Viveiros de Castro and Rubenstein helps us better conceptualize both indigenous spirituality and contemporary radical theology. Rubenstein cites Viveiros de Castro's multinaturalism and notes the Yoruba *orisha* and the "radical polytheism" of Amerindian cosmology in her affirmation of "such manifold, contradictory, and incalculable unfoldings" of "endless, particular loci of divinity." In all these multiple expressions of divinity, pantheology affirms a material "pancarnation," because there is no way to understand god/pan/Gaia as other than embodied in and as "the endlessly, stubbornly un-totalized run of all things."[32]

Rubenstein does not explicitly self-identify as a radical theologian, but I would like to affirm her work as a species of radical theology, in addition to the work of Catherine Keller, Jeffrey W. Robbins, John D. Caputo, Noëlle Vahanian, An Yountae, Karen Bray and others. In 2018 Palgrave Macmillan published a *Handbook of Radical Theology* edited by Christopher D. Rodkey and Jordan E. Miller, in a series devoted to the topic Radical Theologies and Philosophies. Rubenstein contributes an entry on "Science" to this handbook, in which she argues that "just as it is the task of radical theology to uncover the human processes that make the gods, then, it would be the task of a radical theology of science to unravel the tangle of human, mechanical, bacterial, technological, ideological, and elemental processes that act together to *make* any particular truth: a production Latour calls a *factish*."[33] Rubenstein is not neatly or simply a radical theologian in her identity as a philosopher of religion; yet her pluralist pantheology is resonant with some of the most vital perspectives of what passes for radical theological thinking today. She advocates for a critical radical theology of science that would uncover the ways that our factish world is made, as well as a more "constructive movement of finding those places in which modern science is implicitly, but powerfully, redefining what is meant by 'God.'"[34] Redefining God in more pantheistic ways means thinking about God from more immanent and plural perspectives, which resonates better with the indigenous traditions we started this section with that are usually dubbed polytheistic.

I am affirming Rubenstein's pantheology as a species of radical critical theology, not to discipline or domesticate it but somewhat as a Trojan horse, because her pluralist pantheology works in and against radical theology in transformative ways so that radical theology can become more pantheistic and more pluralist, that is, rhizomatic along the lines of Deleuze and Guattari. This means that radical theology needs to more explicitly reconceive divinity as "immanent, self-exceeding, relational, changing, and multiply perspectival."

Rubenstein argues that when we use the word *God* it usually functions as "the guarantor of the whole structure of Western metaphysics."[35] Western metaphysics underlies the logics of modernity, democracy, and human rights, but also the logics of colonialism, racism, capitalism, and environmental destruction. It is not sufficient to leave this word alone, to cordon it off from everything else, the all of *pan*. We need to change our thinking of and about God, to push god into the pluralist pantheism that affirms a relational naturalism of multiple worlds *without end*, assuming we want to continue to inhabit this one. The classical view of God is static, fixed, immutable, and eternal, but if the concept of God has any use for us today, it must undergo *change*. Rubenstein concludes that "this particular word requires the most change of all, even to the point of *God's being recoded as change*: as the ongoing, intraspecies processes that world and unworld worlds."[36] Herein lies Rubenstein's challenge, which is nothing less than changing everything. All of it.

RELIGION, POLITICS, AND THE EARTH

To attend to theology in a radical sense is to be open to what matters, what makes a difference, and in our current situation in this century the planet is insisting upon us in new and urgent ways. New materialism also opens up to an ecology, a theological ecology that thinks from the Earth as a locus of what Hegel calls "substance becoming subject" in his *Phenomenology of Spirit*. At the same time, this thinking from Earth would be closer to what Deleuze and Guattari call a "Geology of Morals" in *A Thousand Plateaus*. We need the resources of physical, biological, and environmental sciences, anthropology and sociology, and political economy, along with philosophy, fiction, and poetry, if we want to survive in an increasingly inhospitable Anthropocene. In short, we need to assemble the elements for what Keller calls a *Political Theology of the Earth*.

The average cumulus cloud weighs 1.1 million pounds, even though these clouds appear light and fluffy. Clouds are formed by microscopic water vapor molecules that evaporate from the ground and rise as they become warm and gaseous. As they rise, they eventually meet colder air, which causes the water vapor to return to liquid in the form of tiny microdroplets. Eventually the cold slows the molecules down enough so that they begin to bump into one another and stick. It takes about a million microdroplets to form one average size raindrop. As the larger raindrops form, they weigh more, and gravity exerts its pressure, drawing them downward in the form of rain. The faster the transition from warm to cold air, the harder and more intense the rainfall.

Clouds also cool the Earth by reflecting incoming sunlight, as the microdroplets (sometimes in the form of ice particles) scatter 20–90 percent of the sunlight that strikes them. If there were no clouds, the planet would absorb approximately 20 percent more heat from the sun than it does. Clouds also warm the surface of the Earth by absorbing infrared radiation from the sun and reradiating it back down. This process traps heat and slows the rate of cooling of the Earth. Under the current global distribution of clouds, the net effect is about a 5 degree Celcius cooling of the planet, according to some estimates, although these numbers are uncertain and contested. We are even more uncertain about the effects of global warming by and on clouds, and vice versa.

Scientists studying climate change are increasingly drawn to modeling simulations of clouds, because they are one of the most important and most complex regulators of global climate. They contribute to climate feedbacks in ways that are not fully understood. In *Cloud of the Impossible*, Keller quotes a climate scientist, Tapio Schneider, who states: "*the dominant source of uncertainty are cloud feedbacks, which are incompletely understood.*"[37] A *Scientific American* article from early 2019 suggests that cloud modeling is vital for our comprehension of the effects of anthropogenic global warming. One technique, called the "large-eddy situation," has given rise to a study that argues that at a certain level of CO_2 (1,200 ppm), "huge tracts of stratocumulus clouds in the Earth's atmosphere—which help to reflect sunlight away from the planet and cool the climate—could disintegrate."[38] If this happens, global temperatures could skyrocket 8 degrees Celsius or 14 degrees Fahrenheit, on top of whatever global warming has already occurred.

This study comes with important caveats, which shows the uncertainty of such cloud modeling. But it also demonstrates how important these studies are, and researchers are developing projects like the "Climate Machine" and the "Cloud Brain" to better predict the outcomes of models that simulate clouds. Clouds are already key actants, to use Latour's term, in any political theology of the Earth. We are running out of time, even if every estimation of this timing is indeterminate. This book is limited, and we all have other things we need to read and do and be, to go and become. However, as Keller quotes the proponents of the fugitive undercommons Stephano Harvey and Fred Motens: "We owe each other the indeterminate. We owe each other everything."[39] Who are we here, and how can we include the multitudinous forms of life that compose us and the exceptional planet that we call Earth?

One way to comprehend the Trump administration (which was in so many ways incomprehensible as well as reprehensible) is to view it as a desperate gambit of what Keller calls a warrior ethos. Every conquest is about opening up new territory to exploit as a resource. But we are running up against real limits of planetary resources. So the response is denial and confusion. The ground is shifting under our feet, and the effects of global warming, extreme weather events, massive migrations, the explosive inequality of our country and our world, Brexit, Trump, Putin, and Xi, along with the global pandemic caused by the COVID-19 virus, are all linked inextricably together. Even if Biden suggests a return to normalcy and a renewed neoliberalism, our social and ecological fabric is coming undone.

Carl Schmitt originates a certain political theology with his little book and his thesis on sovereignty. It's just a little sentence from Schmitt's famous book on *Political Theology*: "Sovereign is he [sic!] who decides on the exception."[40] The real power is the power to decide what constitutes an exception to the rule, case, or law. For Schmitt, this is a unitary power, concentrated in a personalist ruler, ultimately a Führer. As in Heaven, so on Earth, and vice versa. It's all about locating the ultimate source of power, knowing who is to be "the decider."

In *Political Theology of the Earth*, however, Keller turns Schmitt on his head. Rather than the sovereign exception, she affirms an ecosocial *inception*. She signals an emergence as opposed to an emergency. "In the becomingness of the exception flashes the resistance to each self-declared exception. Freed of any single, sovereign Decider, political theology *divines* another possibility: the multifaceted public embrace of planetary entanglement."[41] This scenario is more messy; planetary entanglement makes a mess. Keller makes a mess of political theology, but she does so as to redeem it for us, for our world, which is all that is the case.

Perhaps God makes a mess too. In the religious cosmology of Jewish Kabbalah, the Infinite gives way to the *sefirot*, the ten vessels that express various qualities of the divine name, YHVH. Divinity proceeds downward from the Crown, *Keter*, to the lowest element of divinity, *Malkhut*, which is called Sovereign. According to the teachings of Isaac Luria, the sixteenth-century Spanish rabbi who landed in Safed, the pure light of spiritual energy breaks the vessels, in particular Malkhut, the last *sefira*, which is shattered and scattered across the Earth.[42] Sovereignty is divine, here, but it is *broken*. This brokenness turns God on his head, or rather hers. Because of course Malkhut is also the *Shechinah*, which is the feminine element of the divine, the immanent presence that dwells upon the earth and within us. The sparks or shells of the Shechinah are scattered everywhere in the universe, and it is up to all of God's people to participate in *tikkun olam*, the healing of the world. What if the breaking of the sovereign power were the true nature of divinity itself, and what if that was not the exception but rather the case? Every single case.

Every exceptional event is not simply, solely, or wholly an exception, because it exists in relationality with everything else. Every difference in degree is a difference in kind, so there is no absolute exception, since everything is an exception to the norm, including us, society, life, bacteria, Earth, Sun, Milky Way, universe, Big Bang—*everything*. Keller affirms the relational ontology of Barad, for whom at the level of quantum physics, specifically quantum field theory, there is an indeterminate *cloud* of intra-activity. There is a weak messianic structure to all matter, everything that we call matter, anything and everything that exists, that makes of it "an enormous entangled multitude." So even matter is a mess, and, furthermore, it is mess-ianic. Keller explains that Barad's cosmology "undermines not just human but animal, and indeed organic, exceptionalism . . . the messianic does not take itself out of matter but inscribes itself at its core."[43]

The messianic inception "flashes up" at every moment, to paraphrase Walter Benjamin's famous "Theses on the Philosophy of History." According to Keller, "a political theology of the earth, forged of entangled difference, calls upon that very multitude [of an infinity of possible relations] for Ecocene solidarity, which is to say, for our self-organization across vast reaches of critical difference."[44] We are all All In (*pan en*), without exception, even God. Nobody gets unscathed. Despite the darkness surrounding us, Keller dares to hope: "Black-draped as we are, we have it in us to get it together. In the fierce urgency of our all too human now, what local planetary solidarity might emerge?"[45] What terrestrial politics is possible, given everything that we have done and have to do? We will surely fail, but perhaps we can fail better. All of us.

We are all energy; being is energy transformation. We don't know what energy is; we can only try to measure what it does. Energy is how we account for change. Energy is also another name for divinity, for spirit, and for materiality. A metaphor to try (and fail) to describe that which is ultimate. As Keller puts it in another essay, "We feel the energy we are" when we feel "the throb of eternal delight." We could describe the affirmation of this energy we are as a kind of love. In *Political Theology of the Earth*, Keller calls it an "amatory spirit," which "does not cease to enliven those who will breathe it in."[46]

We follow this spirit, which "blows through any religion, any irreligion." We cannot avoid being crucified, as us, indeed as any distinct and separate things. Resurrection, if it occurs, is elsewhere; it happens for somebody else. Insurrection happens here, now. Our "failing schematisms of politics, of ecology, and of religion do not merge with each other, but they tangle inseparably."[47] Keller's work allows us to traverse these edges, tracking the apocalypses that have happened and are yet to come.

That is to say, we are not dead yet. So long as we breathe, we manifest this breath, this life, this love, this hope—not for a better world, but for this one, which we are destroying, which is destroying us, which is destroying itself in us. As we live, we think and breathe. We resist, become, and change. And the stake, which is at once theological, philosophical, economic, political, ecological, biological, physical, and spiritual, is the struggle between the Spirit of Capitalism and the Spirit of Earth. Capitalism is based on the exploitation of materials and energy flows as financial resources. Capitalism practices a brutally "creative" destruction, because it destroys territory in what Deleuze and Guattari call deterritorialization. Whatever is deterritorialized, however, gets reterritorialized in terms of financial markets. In their experimental work on *Capitalism and Schizophrenia*, Deleuze and Guattari attempt to push deterritorialization beyond capitalism toward a planetary limit.

In *A Thousand Plateaus*, Deleuze and Guattari famously claim that "God is a lobster," because the conventional understanding of divinity represents a blueprint for a double articulation. Double articulation refers to the symmetry that exists in the universe, on Earth, and on most organisms. This symmetry, of course, is never exact; it is symmetrical only in virtual terms. In actual fact, existence is asymmetrical, as Deleuze states in *Difference and Repetition*. In *A Thousand Plateaus*, Deleuze and Guattari contrast the deterritorialized Earth, which they call the Body without Organs, with the inevitable stratification into layers and belts that takes place in and on the earth. We need to resist this double articulation, at least in conventional terms, because it locks together gears that we desperately want to undo. Double articulation refers to the way that things are brought and thought together, to such an extent that they appear to be essentially linked. It's like how Donald Hebb discovered the rule that cells that fire together get wired together, and this is a fundamental insight into how the brain works. Our responses to repeated phenomena become so inextricably linked that we consistently react in the same ways to the same things, even when they are destroying us.

Deleuze and Guattari also develop a theory of assemblages. An assemblage is an abstract machine that refers to the work of intensities and singularities to generate differences. The assemblage contains the minimal amount of form necessary to function, and it works because it stays in contact with the body without organs, the plane of consistency that allows for creation, differentiation, and individuation. At the same time, the body without organs preserves the minimal distance from its own articulation so as to be available for new processes and becomings. An entire Earth conceived in terms of assemblages rather than their strata correlates for Deleuze and Guattari with an absolute deterritorialization; it is a "Mechanosphere."[48]

I think that Earth's electromagnetic field (its magnetosphere) operates somewhat like what Deleuze and Guattari call a Body without Organs, because Earth's magnetic field emerges from the nuclear and thermodynamic energy processes of gradient reduction that produce geological sedimentation. The Earth can be seen as an egg, as Deleuze suggests in *Difference and Repetition*: "the entire world is an egg" composed of "spatiotemporal dynamisms."[49] Earth is composed of deterritorialized potentialities that generate magnetism, electricity, and life, the magnetosphere functions as an abstract machine to generate magnetic and electric fields, which are spatiotemporal dynamisms required for life on Earth. The extraordinary folding that constitutes life then generates and maintains a complex adaptive self-regulating atmosphere with its bacteria and later multicellular organisms. This is what Lovelock names Gaia, but it is not a unity or unification, rather a multiplicity from which we subtract to form our Terran existence.

At the end of *A Thousand Plateaus*, Deleuze and Guattari assert that an absolute deterritorialization belongs to the Earth. The earth "is deterritorialization par excellence; that is why it belongs to the Cosmos, and presents itself as the material through which human [and nonhuman] beings tap cosmic forces."[50] Perceiving the earth as deterritorialized allows us to glimpse this absolute deterritorialization that operates under and potentially against the superficial global corporate capitalism that is crushing us. To extend deterritorialization to its maximum limit is not a crude accelerationism. It is a more thoughtful, committed, and creative effort to reach the point where deterritorialization "can be called the creator of the earth—of a new land, a new universe, not just a reterritorialization."[51] Deleuze and Guattari envision the creation of a new world, which is a creation of Earth. Not another Earth or a different Earth, but the creation of Earth itself: subject of its own events and humans and other territorial creatures as individuations of this new comprehension of Earth.[52]

There lies in Deleuze and Guattari's philosophy the outline—or the plane of immanence—for a new theological ecology. A theological ecology stages an insurrectionist encounter between theology and ecology that distorts and transforms both based on the gradients of their energy transformation. It is genuinely rhizomatic and risks real Change. The constructive thinking of a new Earth, the composition of a perspective of Earth as a whole, is the positive side of this theological ecology. This positive vision is the flip side of the segmentation, destruction, and expropriation of all of the territories, material resources, and populations of Earth produced by the ravages of global capitalism. In all this cataclysmic destruction and extinction, we are bringing something new into being, but not us, not as us. We, signifying beings, are not the goal of evolution, but we are a kind of witness, and therefore we can testify to the sublime beauty of this creation.

IN CONCLUSION: GOD IS CHANGE, LOVE IS A FORM OF ENERGY

This book has adopted a new materialist perspective to track energy transformations across multiple thresholds, including physics, thermodynamics, biology, evolution, life, consciousness, brain, society, politics, economics, ecology, religion, spirit, and theology. Energy is itself a Deleuzean rhizomatic multiplicity that can only be generated by subtracting it from an abstract potentiality into particular situations, which necessarily introduces entropy. Energy is how we measure change and energy necessarily involves and produces change. Change, as we saw in chapter 3, is always exchange, and exchange occurs among and along all of these plateaus. Exchange is active, interactive, and intra-active; it evokes the relationality of all existence. Exchange is always dynamic and asymmetrical, taking place in open systems that are not at equilibrium. Entropy is always at work, allowing, constraining, and ultimately ruining work in a sovereign fashion, as Bataille says. These constraints also ratchet together in a way that organizes and produces complexity and singularity, giving form, as Malabou describes. This form is plastic, in her terms, which means that it is also explosive and destructive of form, which is again a kind of entropy.

While matter and spirit converge in energy, they do not merge; although spirit is fully physical, it is a rare and singular form of matter. Spirit is how we value and evaluate our energetic material existence, which is always (ex)changing. Energy and Change offers a new materialist ontology and, in a certain sense, a cosmo-theology to help us think about and try to make sense of life in the Anthropocene. Climate change is always occurring, but global warming is accelerating, and these processes press against, and in many cases dissolve, living forms. Dissolution is death, which is part of life. And it gives rise to new forms, organic or inorganic, that continue until their dissipation.

Thermodynamics tells us that energy is infinite; it is always conserved because we do not know how to make sense of change unless we posit the conservation of energy in itself. Energy is degraded as useful work for and as us, except as sustained by continuous flows of available energy. We do not know what energy is, where it comes from or where it goes. We cannot make sense of the origin of the universe in terms of energy and entropy except to characterize it as an overwhelming explosion of energy.

In her science fiction book *Parable of the Sower*, Octavia E. Butler creates a character, Lauren Olamina, who suffers from "hyperempathy," the painful ability to feel others' suffering. Olamina develops a new religion she calls Earthseed that revolves around an understanding of God as Change: "The only lasting Truth is Change. God is Change."[53] Butler sets this science fiction novel in the middle of the 2020s, when the world is unraveling because of economic crises and global warming, and a president who sounds a lot like Trump is being elected. This is a very prescient book.

According to Olamina, we both shape and are shaped by God. God shapes the universe, and the universe shapes God. God is not a person, however; God is Change. Butler writes:

> Everyone knows that change is inevitable. From the second law of thermodynamics to Buddhism's insistence that nothing is permanent and all suffering results from our delusions of permanence to the third chapter of Ecclesiastes ("To everything there is a season......"), change is part of life, of existence, of the common wisdom. But I don't believe we're dealing with all that means. We haven't even begun to deal with it.[54]

This book is an attempt to deal with it. Earthseed attempts to deal with reality, even though Olamina holds onto an illusion of seeing humans leave Earth and travel to the stars. There is no more pervasive power than change, and worship does no good without action that accepts, affirms, and works with this change.

Olamina's hyperempathy is both a disability, brought about by a drug ingested by her mother while pregnant with her, as well as a capacity that gives her tremendous insight into the nature of reality. One way to think about empathy is in the context of love. *Love* is a word that has been bastardized almost beyond recognition by Christianity, Romanticism, and Capitalism. We have set up so many barriers to feeling our own pain and that of others that we have become numb, wrapped up in our own selfish egos, hiding out from the rest of existence. And yet the pain still persists in an ongoing overwhelming rush of suffering, cruelty, and death. We are conditioned to love our pain as ourselves and to keep it aflame. And yet empathy as love, or what Mahayana Buddhism calls compassion (*karuna*), opens us up to others, beyond ourselves.

Love is a complex metastable condition composed of physical and mental energy. It can be the narcissism of ego love and it can be the empathetic compassion of sacrificial love. Love is real as a form of energy that gets generated and sustained under specific dynamic conditions. Entropic love opens beings like us up to these flows of energy, which compose and decompose us.

Why does this matter? When I was a child I thought as a child, and in many ways I later put away these childish thoughts, but they persist at so many levels. Mammals require love and care to survive. Babies who do not receive love at birth die. We live because we are loved, and we possess the capacity to love and to feel and express compassion for others. Love is most obvious as care in signifying mammals, but something like love has to exist for anything to exist. Like spirit, love is a particular manifestation of energy that we may value.

We become conscious of love when we lack it, and this lack spurs us to want to feel and find it, from parents, siblings, friends, teachers and coaches, nurses, and other caregivers, and eventually from ourselves. We feel it in and through our other material needs of sustenance, including breath and food and health and community. Our current mode of social organization cuts us off from so many organic connections in order to monetize and commodify goods, relationships, and experiences. We become isolated inside our own subjectivity, conditioned to desire commodities that will bring us happiness. So many of us become alienated, lonely, anxious, and depressed.

I was born in the wake of the murders of Martin Luther King Jr. and Robert F. Kennedy, during the chaos of the civil rights movement and the Vietnam War. This was the start of a period of contraction following the tumult of the hopeful but desperate struggles for liberation across the world. It was also the beginning of an inflection point in global growth, a diminishing of cheap and readily available forms of energy, and the birth pangs of an ecological consciousness. I didn't know any of this at the time. All I knew was a certain vulnerable stability as a white, male, lower-middle-class suburban child whose parents separated and divorced. I was not raised religious, but at some point I decided that I believed in a generic literalist Protestant Christianity, which lasted until I was exposed to biblical criticism and French existentialism in high school. I was then radicalized politically by the Iran-Contra scandal that dogged the second Reagan administration, but not nearly enough in rhizomatic terms.

College was a time to explore myself and my world in a way that is threatened by the corporatization of the university, and it was made more available to more Americans (including my father) as a result of the GI Bill instituted in the wake of World War II. I studied history and religion, and gradually my interests became more and more theoretical and philosophical. The analytic professional philosophy instantiated at the

College of William and Mary appeared unconnected to life, so I sought more existential and continental resources. Graduate school allowed me to hone my academic skills and learn to read and write and eventually even to teach.

Studying theology at a university that did not have a divinity school or seminary gave me the freedom to engage with radical postmodern theology, and this nondogmatic theology then served as the signpost and excuse for my engagement in other theoretical discourses, including psychoanalytic, political, and scientific ones. I have constantly worked against the hyperspecialization that marks so much of academic knowledge in our research universities. Eventually I assembled the resources, ideas, and knowledge to undertake this project.

Why this foray into an unacademic and seemingly self-indulgent autobiography? One of my teachers, Charles E. Winquist, taught me that everything is personal, even when we construct formal procedures to make it appear impersonal and impartial. This split between personal and impersonal, objective and subjective, pervades our world, with a global capitalist market that appears impersonal and impartial but perpetuates the legacies of modern colonialism, slavery, racism, and oppression along with the ongoing heterosexism and religious fundamentalism that characterizes so many societies. So much of the professional success that I achieved has been due to these unearned privileges, as well as the labor of people who could not benefit from them.

This is not just an apology, however; it is also a labor of love. This book is a rhizomatic book in its presentation and invocation of a unique and yet irreducibly plural multiplicity. In my radical theological journey, I learned that God is not love. Most of our understandings of God perpetuate our own fear and hatred of others who are not like us. God-language provides people with a certain kind of security in an insecure world, but it is also weaponized against those who are not insiders. If God means anything positive today, it has to be Change. The ultimate reality of existence is Change. You can call that God, if you want. Of course, this Change is also irreducibly multiple, which means that God is not One. So we can speak of the gods, along the lines of Neil Gaiman's *American Gods*: the tribal ones, the ancient ones, the modern ones, the cosmic ones, and so on.

When we open ourselves up to the universe, we can embrace the fact that God is Change. For me *love is an energy formation that embraces change*. Love then becomes the awareness and affirmation of the energies that form and dissipate us as us, that drive us in the form of relationships within and beyond ourselves in the search for authentic connection with something that is both like and unlike us. We exist as knots of love-energy that are consolidated into an identity we then try to protect and defend, like all identities. This ultimately fails, and we dissolve what we never were. The ego is a tomb; there is only the death of suffocation and auto-enclosure. Everything that matters is outside.

We cannot expect individual immortality, because there is no life after death for us, as us. That doesn't mean that there is nothing, because energy is always conserved. The best we can hope for is to make a difference with the energy we are, and we are always already making a difference. I have loved and been loved. I have been graced by extraordinary gestures of loving-kindness that have made me who I am and other than who I am. I have tried to open myself up to these moments and these opportunities, even as I have squandered so many of them out of a fear for self-preservation. All this is beyond me, everything is beyond *me*, which is what transcendence means. Not a higher plane of existence, but the crossing of lines, boundaries, and gradients where existence is truly shared, sometimes with intoxicating drugs, sometimes in sexual ecstasy, sometimes in meditative tranquility, sometimes in struggle for justice, hope, or peace—or just a breath, a pause (out) of time. Before we go.

NOTES

INTRODUCTION

1. Cara New Daggett, *The Birth of Energy: Fossil Fuels, Thermodynamics, and the Politics of Work* (Durham: Duke University Press, 2019), p. 3. See also Michael Marder, *Energy Dreams: Of Actuality* (New York: Columbia University Press, 2017), with which I engage in chapter 1; *Energy Humanities: An Anthology*, ed. Imre Szeman and Dominic Boyer (Baltimore: Johns Hopkins University Press, 2017); Alan Stoekl, *Bataille's Peak: Energy, Religion, and Sustainability* (Minneapolis: University of Minnesota Press, 2007); *Materialism and the Critique of Energy*, ed. Brent Ryan Bellamy and Jeff Diamanti (Chicago: MCM', 2018); Terra Schwerin Rowe, *Of Modern Extraction: Gender, Theology, and Energy* (London: Bloomsbury, 2022); and Luce Irigaray, *A New Culture of Energy: Beyond East and West*, trans. Stephen Seely et al.TK (New York: Columbia University Press, 2021).
2. Alfred North Whitehead, *Process and Reality*, corrected ed., ed. by David Ray Griffin and Donald Sherburne (New York: Free Press, 1978), p. 309.
3. Maurice Merleau-Ponty, *Phenomenology of Perception*, trans. Collin Smith (London: Routledge, 1958), p. 380.
4. Diana Coole, "The Inertia of Matter and the Generativity of Flesh," in *New Materialisms: Ontology, Agency, and Politics*, ed. Diana Coole and Samantha Frost (Durham, NC: Duke University Press, 2010), pp. 92–115, quote p. 93.
5. See Gilles Deleuze, *Difference and Repetition*, trans. Paul Patton (New York: Columbia University Press, 1994), p. 64.
6. Deleuze, p. 117.
7. "Interview with Rosi Braidotti," in Rick Dolphijn and Iris van der Tuin, *New Materialism: Interviews and Cartographies* (Ann Arbor: Open Humanities, 2012), p. 21.

8. Rosi Braidotti, *Metamorphoses: Towards a Materialist Theory of Becoming* (Cambridge: Polity, 2002), p. 63.
9. Christopher Watkin provides a helpful chart of NM thinkers, French and otherwise, available at https://christopherwatkindotcom.files.wordpress.com/2014/11/new-materialist-thinkers-ordered-alphabetically.jpg. See also his book, *French Philosophy Today: New Figures of the Human in Badiou, Meillassoux, Malabou, Serres, and Latour* (Edinburgh: Edinburgh University Press, 2016).
10. James K. Feibleman, *The New Materialism* (The Hague: Martinus Nihoff, 1970), p. 42.
11. Feibleman, p. 149.
12. Pheng Cheah, "Nondialectical Materialism," in *New Materialisms*, ed. Coole and Frost, pp. 70–91, quote p. 86.
13. Manuel DeLanda, *Intensive Science and Virtual Philosophy* (London: Continuum, 2002), p. 187.
14. John Bellamy Foster, *Marx's Ecology: Materialism and Nature* (New York: Monthly Review Press, 2000), p. 35.
15. Foster, p. 54.
16. Foster, p. 112.
17. Foster, p. 117.
18. Louis Althusser, *Philosophy of the Encounter: Later Writings, 1978–1987*, ed. François Matheron and Oliver Corpet, trans. G. M. Goshgarian (London: Verso, 2006), p. 167 (emphasis in original).
19. Althusser, pp. 167–168.
20. Althusser, p. 169.
21. Vladimir Ilych Lenin, *What Is to Be Done?: Burning Questions for Our Movement*, trans. Joe Fineberg and George Hanna. Available from Marxists Internet Archive: https://www.marxists.org/archive/lenin/works/1901/witbd/.
22. Intergovernmental Panel on Climate Change AR 6 Working Group I Report, "Summary for Policy Makers," p. 42, https://www.ipcc.ch/report/ar6/wg1/downloads/report/IPCC_AR6_WGI_SPM.pdf.
23. NOAA, "It's Official: July 2021 Was Earth's Hottest Month on Record," August 13, 2021, https://www.noaa.gov/news/its-official-july-2021-was-earths-hottest-month-on-record.
24. See Déborah Danowski and Eduardo Viveiros de Castro, *The Ends of the World*, trans. Rodrigo Nunes (Cambridge: Polity, 2017), p. 102.
25. See Elizabeth Kolbert, *The Sixth Extinction: An Unnatural History* (New York: Picador, 2015).
26. Vandana Shiva, *Making Peace with the Earth* (London: Pluto, 2013), p. 9.
27. See Peter Brannen, *The Ends of the World: Volcanic Apocalypses, Lethal Oceans, and Our Quest to Understand the Earth's Past Mass Extinctions* (New York: HarperCollins, 2017), pp. 263–264.
28. See Naomi Klein, *This Changes Everything: Capitalism vs. the Climate* (New York: Simon and Schuster, 2014), p. 21.

29. Michael T. Klare, *The Race for What's Left: The Global Scramble for the World's Last Resources* (New York: Metropolitan, 2012), p. 18.
30. See Christian Marazzi, *The Violence of Financial Capitalism*, trans. Kristina Lebedeva and Jason Francis McGimsey (New York: Semiotext(e), 2011).
31. David Harvey, *Seventeen Contradictions and the End of Capitalism* (Oxford: Oxford University Press, 2014), p. 240.
32. See *Anthropocene or Capitalocene?: Nature, History, and the Crisis of Capitalism*, ed. Jason W. Moore (Oakland: PM, 2016).
33. See Jared Diamond, *Collapse: How Societies Choose to Fail or Succeed* (New York: Penguin, 2005).
34. Richard Feynman, *Lectures on Physics*, quoted in Vaclav Smil, *Energy: A Beginner's Guide* (London: Oneworld, 2017), p. 8 (emphasis in original).
35. Smil, p. 10.
36. See Isabelle Stengers, *Cosmopolitics I (Posthumanities)*, trans. Robert Bononno (Minneapolis: University of Minnesota Press, 2010).

1. ENERGY AND THE DYNAMICS OF NATURE

1. *Aristotle's Physics, Books I and II*, trans. William Charleton (Oxford: Oxford University Press, 1970), p. 2 (184a, 12–13).
2. *Aristotle's Physics, Books III and IV*, trans. Edward Hussey (Oxford: Oxford University Press, 1983), p. 1 (200b, 12–14).
3. *Aristotle's Physics Books I and II*, p. 38 (198b).
4. On these topics, see Sarah Waterlow, *Nature, Change, and Agency in Aristotle's Physics* (Oxford: Oxford University Press, 1982); and Chelsea C. Harry, *Chronos in Aristotle's Physics: On the Nature of Time* (New York: Springer, 2015).
5. Aristotle, *Metaphysics*, in *The Basic Works of Aristotle*, ed. Richard McKeon (New York: Random House, 2001), p. 823 (1047a, 30–33).
6. Aristotle, p. 828 (1049b, 5).
7. Aristotle, p. 829 (1050a, 9–10).
8. Gilles Deleuze, *Difference and Repetition*, trans. Paul Patton (New York: Columbia University Press, 1994), p. 250.
9. See Naomi Klein's discussion and critique of geoengineering as a solution to climate change in *This Changes Everything: Capitalism vs. the Climate* (New York: Simon and Schuster, 2014), chapter 8, "Dimming the Sun," pp. 256–290.
10. See Ray Kurzweil, *The Singularity Is Near: When Humans Transcend Biology* (New York: Penguin, 2006).
11. See Robert J. Gordon, "Is US Economic Growth Over? Faltering Innovation Confronts the Six Headwinds," Centre for Economic Policy Research, *Policy Insight* no. 63, September 2012. Available at www.cepr.org.
12. Michael Marder, *Energy Dreams: Of Actuality* (New York: Columbia University Press, 2017), p. ix.

13. Marder, p. xi (emphasis in original).
14. Marder, p. 7.
15. Marder, p. 15.
16. Marder, p. 147.
17. Marder.
18. Marder, p. 13.
19. Marder, p. 150.
20. Nick Land, *Fanged Noumena: Collected Writings, 1987–2007*, ed. Robin Mackay and Ray Brassier (Falmouth, UK: Urbanomic, 2011), p. 47. On contemporary accelerationism, see Alex Williams and Nick Srnicek, "#ACCELERATE Manifesto for a Radical Politics," *Critical Legal Thinking: Law and the Political*, May 14, 2013, available at http://criticallegalthinking.com/2013/05/14/accelerate-manifesto-for-an-accelerationist-politics/; and *#Accelerate: The Accelerationist Reader*, ed. Robin Mackay and Armen Avanessian (Falmouth, UK: Urbanomic, 2014).
21. Land, *Fanged Noumena*, p. 47.
22. Marder, *Energy Dreams*, p. 75.
23. Aristotle, *Metaphysics*, p. 839 (1054a, 30–31).
24. Aristotle, p. 841 (1055a, 5).
25. Aristotle, p. 912 (1087a, 36-1087b, 1).
26. Deleuze, *Difference and Repetition*, p. 30.
27. Jennifer Coopersmith, *Energy, The Subtle Concept: The Discovery of Feynman's Blocks From Leibniz to Einstein* (Oxford: Oxford University Press, 2015), p. 337.
28. Coopersmith, p. 315.
29. Coopersmith, p. 262.
30. Coopersmith, p. 35.
31. Coopersmith.
32. See Alain Badiou, *Deleuze: The Clamor of Being*, trans. Louise Burchill (Minneapolis: University of Minnesota Press, 2000).
33. Deleuze, *Difference and Repetition*, p. 304.
34. Gilles Deleuze, *Spinoza: Practical Philosophy*, trans. Robert Hurley (San Francisco, City Lights, 1988), p. 128.
35. Cara Daggett, *The Birth of Energy: Fossil Fuels, Thermodynamics, and the Politics of Work* (Durham: Duke University Press, 2019), p. 16.
36. See Coopersmith, *Energy*, p. 40.
37. Coopersmith, p. 82.
38. Coopersmith, p. 118.
39. Coopersmith, p. 112.
40. See Coopersmith, p. 182.
41. Peter Atkins, *The Laws of Thermodynamics: A Very Short Introduction* (Oxford: Oxford University Press, 2010), p. 5.
42. Coopersmith, *Energy*, p. 183.
43. Atkins, *The Laws of Thermodynamics*, p. 22.
44. Atkins, p. 19 (emphasis in original).

45. Sadi Carnot, *Reflections on the Motive Power of Fire*, ed. E. Mendoza, trans. R. H. Thurston (Mineola, NY: Dover, 1988 [1960]), p. 6.
46. Carnot, p. 7.
47. An ideal heat engine also depends on volume and pressure, because while the temperature gradients need to be maximized, they also need to be as small as possible, so that they can be seen as practically, if not theoretically reversible. An ideal heat engine would need to have infinitesimal temperature gradients, which is not possible, but acts as an ideal limit. See Coopersmith, *Energy*, pp. 209–210.
48. Coopersmith, p. 209.
49. Atkins, *The Laws of Thermodynamics*, p. 35.
50. Atkins, p. 37 (emphasis in original).
51. Atkins, p. 82. The formula as written by Clausius is $\Delta U = \Delta Q + \Delta W$, where U is the internal energy, Q is the total heat, and W is the total work accomplished. See Coopersmith, *Energy*, p. 283.
52. See Coopersmith, *Energy*, p. 278.
53. Atkins, *The Laws of Thermodynamics*, p. 41. Thomson's equation for the second law is formulated in terms of a complete ideal cycle, which is impossible in reality: $\Sigma (Q/T) = 0$ (complete reversible cycle). This is the summation of Q, the total heat, over T, the temperature. See Coopersmith, *Energy*, p. 286.
54. Atkins, *The Laws of Thermodynamics*, p. 42. For Clausius, S, or entropy, $= \int dQ/T > 0$ (complete cycle, real transfers). See Coopersmith, *Energy*, p. 290.
55. Coopersmith, *Energy*, p. 285.
56. Atkins, *The Laws of Thermodynamics*, pp. 42, 47 (emphasis in original).
57. William Thomson, "On a Universal Tendency in Nature to the Dissipation of Mechanical Energy," quoted in Coopersmith, *Energy*, p. 287.
58. Coopersmith, *Energy*, p. 308 (emphasis in original). Boltzmann formulated the equation for entropy as: $S + k \log W$, where W is the statistical weight of the particles, and k is a specific constant, called Boltzmann's constant.
59. See Coopersmith, p. 318.
60. Rod Swenson, "Autocatakinetics, Evolution, and the Law of Maximum Energy Production: A Principled Foundation Towards the Study of Human Ecology," *Advances in Human Ecology* 6 (1997), available online at http://www.spontaneous order.net/human eco2.html. See also Clayton Crockett, "Entropy," in *The Future of Continental Philosophy of Religion*, ed. Clayton Crockett, B. Keith Putt, and Jeffrey W. Robbins (Bloomington: Indiana University Press, 2014), from which this discussion partly draws.
61. Swenson, "Autocatakinetics, Evolution."
62. Swenson.
63. See Jeffrey S. Wicken, *Evolution, Dynamics, and Information: Extending the Darwinian Program* (Oxford: Oxford University Press, 1987).
64. Eric D. Schneider and Dorion Sagan, *Into the Cool: Energy Flow, Thermodynamics and Life* (Chicago: University of Chicago Press, 2005), p. 6.
65. Schneider and Sagan, p. 112.
66. Schneider and Sagan, p. 127.

266 1. ENERGY AND THE DYNAMICS OF NATURE

67. Schneider and Sagan, p. 129.
68. Schneider and Sagan, p. 123.
69. Schneider and Sagan, p. 80.
70. Schneider and Sagan, p. 81.
71. Schneider and Sagan, p. 81.
72. Gilles Deleuze, *Difference and Repetition*, trans. Paul Patton (New York: Columbia University Press, 1994), p. 117.
73. Deleuze, *Difference and Repetition*, p. 117. Deleuze's discussion of the differentiator in chapter 2 of *Difference and Repetition* comes before his distinction between differentiation as a virtual difference and differenciation as an actual difference in chapter 5. I am using Patton's translation of *differentiation* or *differentiator* with a *t* here, which acknowledges that here it incorporates both modes of differentiation that Deleuze later distinguishes.
74. See Karen Barad, *Meeting the Universe Halfway: Quantum Physics and the Entanglement of Matter and Meaning* (Durham: Duke University Press, 2007), p. 72.
75. Deleuze, *Difference and Repetition*, p. 119.
76. Deleuze, p. 117.
77. Deleuze, p. 222.
78. Deleuze, p. 223.
79. Deleuze.
80. Deleuze, p. 224.
81. Deleuze, p. 228.
82. Deleuze.
83. Deleuze, p. 229 (emphasis in original).
84. Deleuze, p. 234.
85. Deleuze.
86. Deleuze.
87. Manuel DeLanda, *Intensive Science and Virtual Philosophy* (London: Continuum, 2002), p. 5.
88. James Gleick, *Chaos: Making a New Science* (New York: Penguin, 1987), p. 311.
89. Ilya Prigogine and Isabelle Stengers, *Order Out of Chaos: Man's New Dialogue with Nature* (New York: Bantam, 1984), p. xxix.
90. Prigogine and Stengers, p. 161.
91. Prigogine and Stengers, p. 141.
92. Prigogine and Stengers, p. 287 (emphasis in original).
93. Harold J. Morowitz, *Energy Flow in Biology* (Woodbridge, CT: Oxbow, 1979 [1968]), p. 3.
94. Morowitz, p. 19.
95. Albert Einstein, *Investigations on the Theory of the Brownian Movement*, trans. A. D. Cowper (New York: Dover, 1956), p. 3.
96. Carlo Rovelli, *Reality Is Not What It Seems: The Journey to Quantum Gravity*, trans. Simon Carnell and Erica Segre (New York: Riverhead, 2017), p. 123.
97. Rovelli, p. 124.
98. Rovelli, p. 109.
99. Rovelli, p. 119.

100. Gilles Deleuze, *Cinema 2: The Time-Image*, trans. Hugh Tomlinson and Robert Galeta (Minneapolis: University of Minnesota Press, 1989), p. 179.
101. Deleuze, pp. 179–180.
102. Barad, *Meeting the Universe Halfway*, p. 85.
103. Barad, p. 102.
104. Barad, p. 106.
105. Barad, p. 307.
106. Barad, p. 309.
107. Karen Barad, "Quantum Entanglements and Hauntological Relations of Inheritance: Dis/continuities, SpaceTime Enfoldings, and Justice-to-Come," *Derrida Today* 3, no. 2, (2010): 240–268 (quote p. 251).
108. Barad, p. 251.
109. Barad, p. 264.
110. Barad, p. 210.
111. Barad, p. 210.
112. Quoted in Barad, p. 212.
113. Barad, p. 210.
114. Another philosopher whose work needs more engagement is François Laruelle, particularly in connection with quantum physics. See Francois Laruelle, *Philosophie Non-Standard: Générique, Quantique, Philo-Fiction* (Paris: Kimé, 2010).
115. Rovelli, *Reality Is Not What It Seems*, p. 251.
116. Rovelli, p. 247.
117. Rovelli, pp. 246–247.
118. Gleick, *The Information*, p. 219.
119. Gleick, p. 362.
120. Gleick, p. 365 (emphasis in original).
121. Luciano Floridi, *The Philosophy of Information* (Oxford: Oxford University Press, 2011), p. 30 (emphases in original).
122. Coopersmith, *Energy, the Subtle Concept*, p. 131.
123. Coopersmith, p. 232.
124. Coopersmith, p. 232.
125. Rovelli, *Reality Is Not What It Seems*, p. 251.
126. Richard Feynman, *Six Not-So-Easy Pieces: Einstein's Relativity, Symmetry, and Space-Time* (Cambridge, MA: Perseus, 1997), p. 66 (emphasis in original).
127. Morowitz, *Energy Flow in Biology*, p. 17.

2. VITAL MATTERS: BIOENERGETICS AND LIFE

1. Catherine Malabou, *The Future of Hegel: Plasticity, Temporality and Dialectic*, trans. Lisabeth During (London: Routledge, 2005), p. 9.
2. Catherine Malabou, *What Should We Do with Our Brain?*, trans. Sebastian Rand (New York: Fordham University Press, 2008), p. 16.

3. Malabou, p. 76.
4. Malabou, p. 79.
5. Brenna Bhandar and Jonathan Goldberg-Hiller, "Introduction," *Plastic Materialities: Politics, Legality, and Metamorphosis in the Work of Catherine Malabou* (Durham: Duke University Press, 2015), p. 3.
6. Catherine Malabou, *Plasticity at the Dusk of Writing: Dialectic, Destruction, Deconstruction*, trans. Carolyn Shread (New York: Columbia University Press, 2010), p. 61 (emphasis in original).
7. Jane Bennett, *Vibrant Matters: A Political Ecology of Things* (Durham: Duke University Press, 2010), p. ix.
8. Malabou, *What Should We Do with Our Brain?*, p. 73.
9. Catherine Malabou, *The Heidegger Change: On the Fantastic in Philosophy*, trans. Peter Skafish (New York: State University of New York Press, 2012), p. 21.
10. Malabou, p. 157.
11. Malabou, p. 277.
12. Malabou, p. 278.
13. Malabou, p. 279.
14. Malabou, *What Should We Do with Our Brain?*, p. 68.
15. Malabou, p. 73.
16. Malabou, p. 74.
17. Catherine Malabou, "Darwin and the Social Destiny of Natural Selection," in "Plastique: The Dynamics of Catherine Malabou," *theory@buffalo* 16, 2012, pp. 144–156 (quote pp. 144–145).
18. Malabou, p. 153.
19. Malabou.
20. Catherine Malabou, *Changing Difference: The Feminine and the Question of Philosophy*, trans. Carolyn Shread (Cambridge: Polity, 2011), p. 138.
21. Malabou, p. 34.
22. Malabou, p. 140.
23. Malabou, p. 35.
24. Malabou, p. 36.
25. Malabou, p. 37.
26. Malabou, p. 39.
27. Malabou, pp. 39–40.
28. Malabou, pp. 140–141.
29. Malabou, p. 141.
30. See Eric D. Schneider and Dorion Sagan, *Into the Cool: Energy Flow, Thermodynamics, and Life* (Chicago: University of Chicago Press, 2005), p. 13.
31. Schneider and Sagan, p. 18.
32. Schneider and Sagan, p. 145.
33. Harold J. Morowitz, *Energy Flow in Biology* (Woodbridge, CT: Oxbow, 1979 [1968]), p. 5 (emphasis in original).
34. Morowitz, p. 46.

2. VITAL MATTERS: BIOENERGETICS AND LIFE   269

35. Morowitz, p. 50.
36. Nick Lane, *The Vital Question: Energy, Evolution, and the Origins of Complex Life* (New York: Norton, 2015), p. 13.
37. Schneider and Sagan, *Into the Cool*, p. 164.
38. Schneider and Sagan, p. 178.
39. Schneider and Sagan, p. 180.
40. Lane, *The Vital Question*, p. 113.
41. Lane, p. 119.
42. Lane, p. 80.
43. Lane, p. 96.
44. Lane, p. 57 (emphasis in original).
45. Lane, p. 64.
46. Lane, p. 65 (emphasis in original).
47. Morowitz, *Energy Flow in Biology*, p. 55.
48. See Lane, *The Vital Question*, pp. 65–66. The formula is ADP + P_i + energy → ATP.
49. Lane, p. 69.
50. Lane, p. 71 (emphasis in original).
51. Lane, p. 73.
52. Morowitz, *Energy Flow in Biology*, p. 138.
53. Lynn Margulis, *Symbiotic Planet: A New Look at Evolution* (New York: Basic Books, 1998), p. 77.
54. Lane, *The Vital Question*, p. 81.
55. Lane, pp. 35–36.
56. Nick Lane, *Power, Sex, Suicide: Mitochondria and the Meaning of Life* (Oxford: Oxford University Press, 2005), p. 47.
57. See Lane, pp. 52–54.
58. Lane, p. 57.
59. Lane, p. 59.
60. Lane, p. 61.
61. Lane, pp. 125–126.
62. Lane, p. 153.
63. Charles Darwin, *On the Origin of Species: A Facsimile of the First Edition* (Cambridge, MA: Harvard University Press, 1964), p. 81.
64. Stephen Jay Gould, *Ever Since Darwin: Reflections in Natural History* (New York: Norton, 1977), p. 13.
65. John Bellamy Foster, *Marx's Ecology: Materialism and Nature* (New York: Monthly Review, 2000), p. 190.
66. Foster, p. 197.
67. Stephen Jay Gould, *The Structure of Evolutionary Theory* (Cambridge, MA: Harvard University Press, 2002), p. 674.
68. Gould, p. 766.
69. Gould, p. 922.
70. Gould, p. 925.

71. Gould, p. 929.
72. Gould, p. 1216.
73. Gould, p. 1217.
74. Gould, p. 1218.
75. See Gould, p. 1232.
76. Gould, p. 1247.
77. Gould, p. 1252.
78. Gould, p. 505.
79. Gould, p. 900.
80. Gould, p. 898.
81. Gould, p. 808.
82. Lane, *Power, Sex, and Suicide*, p. 224.
83. Lane, p. 225.
84. Lane, p. 261 (emphasis in original).
85. Margulis, *Symbiotic Planet*, p. 88.
86. Margulis, p. 89.
87. Margulis, p. 6.
88. See Margulis, p. 22.
89. Lynn Margulis and Dorion Sagan, *Dazzle Gradually: Reflections on the Nature of Nature* (Whiteriver Junction, VT: Chelsea Green, 2007), p. 45.
90. Gould, *The Structure of Evolutionary Theory*, p. 622.
91. Gould, p. 622.
92. See Bruce Bagemihl, *Biological Exuberance: Animal Homosexuality and Natural Diversity* (New York: Stonewall Inn, 2000). What is striking is not so much the detailed accounts of same-sex sexual activity in the nonhuman animal world, but the extent to which previous scientists have gone to neglect, overlook, and edit out these prevalent phenomena.
93. Richard Dawkins, *The Selfish Gene* (New York: Oxford University Press, 1976), p. 12.
94. Gould, *The Structure of Evolutionary Theory*, p. 621.
95. Gould, p. 615.
96. Nessa Carey, *The Epigenetic Revolution: How Modern Biology Is Rewriting Our Understanding of Genetics, Disease, and Inheritance* (New York: Columbia University Press, 2012), p. 184 (emphasis in original).
97. Gould, *The Structure of Evolutionary Theory*, p. 1271.
98. Carey, *The Epigenetic Revolution*, p. 7.
99. Carey, p. 26.
100. Carey, p. 41.
101. Carey, p. 57.
102. Carey, p. 68.
103. Carey, p. 72.
104. Carey, p. 101.
105. See Carey, p. 102.
106. Carey, pp. 108–109.

107. Eva Jablonka and Marion J. Lamb, *Evolution in Four Dimensions: Genetic, Epigenetic, Behavioral, and Symbolic Variation in the History of Life* (Cambridge, MA: MIT Press, 2005), p. 1.
108. Jablonka and Lamb, p. 144.
109. Jablonka and Lamb, p. 145.
110. Jablonka and Lamb, p. 166.
111. Jablonka and Lamb, pp. 219–220.
112. Jablonka and Lamb, p. 221 (emphasis in original).
113. Jablonka and Lamb, p. 248.
114. Malabou, *What Should We Do with Our Brain?*, p. 5.
115. Quentin Meillassoux, *After Finitude: An Essay on the Necessity of Contingency*, trans. Ray Brassier (London: Continuum, 2008), p. 10.
116. See Meillassoux, pp. 103–105.
117. Catherine Malabou, *Before Tomorrow: Epigenesis and Rationality*, trans. Carolyn Shread (Cambridge: Polity, 2016), p. 16 (emphasis in original).
118. Malabou, p. 81.
119. Malabou, p. 89.
120. Malabou, p. 161 (emphasis in original).
121. Malabou, p. 183 (emphasis in original).
122. Malabou (emphasis in original).
123. Malabou, p. 175.
124. Malabou, *Before Tomorrow*, p. 78.
125. See Carey, *The Epigenetics Revolution*, pp. 250–255.
126. Peter Godfrey-Smith, *Other Minds: The Octopus, the Sea, and the Deep Origins of Consciousness* (New York: Farrar, Straus and Giroux, 2016), p. 22 (emphasis in original).
127. Godfrey-Smith, p. 34.
128. Lynn Margulis, "Prejudice and Bacterial Consciousness," in Margulis and Sagan, *Dazzle Gradually*, p. 37.
129. Margulis, p. 39.
130. Godfrey-Smith, *Other Minds*, p. 23.
131. Richard Wrangham, *Catching Fire: How Cooking Made Us Human* (New York: Basic Books, 2009), p. 109.
132. Wrangham, p. 111.
133. Ed Yong, *I Contain Multitudes: The Microbes Within Us and a Grander View of Life* (New York: HarperCollins, 2016), p. 17.
134. Yong, p. 52.
135. See Sam Mickey, *Coexistentialism and the Unbearable Intimacy of Ecological Emergency* (Lanham, MD: Lexington, 2016), p. 13: "Coexistentialism can foster a democratic politics of care for all beings folded into the mesh of ecological coexistence."
136. Jean-Pierre Changeux, *Neuronal Man: The Biology of Mind*, trans. Laurence Garey (Princeton: Princeton University Press, 1985), p. 249 (emphasis in original).
137. Joseph LeDoux, *The Synaptic Self: How Our Brains Become Who We Are* (New York: Penguin, 2002), p. 323.

138. LeDoux, pp. 310, 315.
139. LeDoux, p. 317.
140. Malabou, *What Should We Do with Our Brain?*, p. 11 (emphasis in original).
141. Malabou, p. 74.
142. Gilles Deleuze and Félix Guattari, *What Is Philosophy?*, trans. Hugh Tomlinson and Graham Burchell (New York: Columbia University Press, 1994), p. 210.
143. Deleuze and Guattari.
144. Godfrey-Smith, *Other Minds*, p. 39.
145. See Godfrey-Smith, pp. 81–97.
146. Godfrey-Smith, p. 144 (emphasis mine).
147. Godfrey-Smith, p. 211.
148. Godfrey-Smith, p. 211.
149. Godfrey-Smith, p. 207.
150. N. Katherine Hayles, *Unthought: The Powers of the Cognitive Unconscious* (Chicago: University of Chicago Press, 2017), p. 22 (emphasis in original).
151. Hayles, p. 2 (emphasis in original).
152. See Bernard Stiegler, *States of Shock: Stupidity and Knowledge in the Twenty-first Century* (London: Polity, 2015).
153. Hayles, *Unthought*, p. 7.
154. Terrence W. Deacon, *Incomplete Nature: How Mind Emerged from Matter* (New York: Norton, 2012), p. 216. This book has created some controversy, as Deacon has been charged with poaching or even plagiarizing the work of Alicia Juarrero and Evan Thompson, or at least of not properly citing them. See http://www.chronicle.com/blogs/percolator/stolen-ideas-or-great-minds-thinking-alike/29306.
155. Deacon, p. 253.
156. Deacon, p. 317.
157. Deacon.
158. Malabou, *Before Tomorrow*, p. 183 (emphasis in original).
159. Gould, *Ever Since Darwin*, p. 67 (emphasis in original).
160. Jeffrey W. Robbins, *Radical Theology: A Vision for Change* (Bloomington: Indiana University Press, 2016), p. 152.
161. See Lisa Zyga, "Physicists Confirm Thermodynamic Irreversibility in a Quantum System," *Phys.org*, December 1, 2015, available at https://phys.org/news/2015-12-physicists-thermodynamic-irreversibility-quantum.html#jCp.
162. Natalie Wolchover, "A New Physics Theory of Life," *Quanta Magazine*, January 22, 2014, Available at https://www.quantamagazine.org/a-new-thermodynamics-theory-of-the-origin-of-life-20140122.
163. Wolchover.
164. Wolchover.
165. Elizabeth Grosz, *Becoming Undone: Darwinian Reflections on Life, Politics, and Art* (Durham: Duke University Press, 2011), p. 33.
166. Grosz, p. 85.

3. POLITICAL ECONOMY AND POLITICAL ECOLOGY

1. Plato, *The Last Days of Socrates*, trans. Hugh Tredennick and Harrold Tarrant (New York: Penguin, 1993), p. 121.
2. Plato, p. 172.
3. Plato, p. 185.
4. https://editors.eol.org/eoearth/wiki/Anthropocene.
5. See Robinson Meyer, "Geologists' Timekeepers are Feuding," *The Atlantic*, July 20, 2018. https://www.theatlantic.com/science/archive/2018/07/anthropocene-holocene-geology-drama/565628/.
6. Roy Scranton, *Learning to Die in the Anthropocene: Reflections on the End of a Civilization* (San Francisco: City Lights, 2015), p. 21.
7. Scranton, p. 23.
8. Scranton, p. 68.
9. Elizabeth Kolbert, *The Sixth Extinction: An Unnatural History* (New York: Picador, 2015).
10. Center for Biological Diversity, "The Extinction Crisis." https://www.biologicaldiversity.org/programs/biodiversity/elements_of_biodiversity/extinction_crisis/
11. Scranton, *Learning to Die in the Anthropocene*, p. 94.
12. Scranton, p. 56.
13. I owe this conception of environmental care as hospice to Whitney A. Bauman. See his *Religion and Ecology: Developing a Planetary Ethic* (New York: Columbia University Press, 2014).
14. Jason W. Moore, "Introduction," in *Anthropocene of Capitalocene?: Nature, History, and the Crisis of Capitalism*, ed. Jason W. Moore (Oakland: PM Press, 2016), p. 4.
15. Naomi Klein, *This Changes Everything: Capitalism vs the Climate* (New York: Simon and Schuster, 2014), p. 21.
16. Klein, p. 5.
17. Naomi Klein, "How Science Is Telling Us to Revolt, *New Statesman*, October 29, 2013, https://www.newstatesman.com/2013/10/science-says-revolt.
18. James A. Caporaso and David P. Levine, *Theories of Political Economy* (Cambridge: Cambridge University Press, 1992), p. 1.
19. Caporaso and Levine, p. 28.
20. Andreas Malm, *Fossil Capital: The Rise of Steam Power and the Roots of Global Warming* (London: Verso, 2016), p. 13.
21. Malm, p. 19.
22. Cara New Daggett, *The Birth of Energy: Fossil Fuels, Thermodynamics, and the Politics of Work* (Durham: Duke University Press, 2019), p. 16.
23. Daggett, p. 11.
24. Malm, *Fossil Capital*, p. 124 (emphasis in original).
25. Timothy Mitchell, *Carbon Democracy: Political Power in the Age of Oil* (London: Verso, 2011), p. 19.

26. Mitchell, p. 205.
27. Mitchell, p. 233.
28. See Edward E. Baptist, *The Half Has Never Been Told: Slavery and the Making of American Capitalism* (New York: Basic Books, 2016).
29. Antti Salminen and Tere Vadén, *Energy and Experience: An Essay in Nafthology* (Chicago: MCM, 2016), p. 1.
30. Salminen and Vadén, p. 20.
31. See Thom Hartmann, *The Last Hours of Ancient Sunlight: The Fate of the World and What We Can Do Before it's Too Late* (New York: Three Rivers Press, 1999).
32. Malm, Fossil Capital, p. 314 (emphasis in original).
33. Mitchell, *Carbon Democracy*, p. 125.
34. See Philip Mirowski, *More Heat Than Light: Economics as Social Physics, Physics as Nature's Economics* (Cambridge: Cambridge University Press, 1989), pp. 306–307.
35. See Thomas Picketty, *Capital in the Twenty-First Century*, trans. Arthur Goldhammer (Cambridge, MA: Harvard University Press, 2014), pp. 146–149.
36. Picketty, p. 297.
37. David Harvey, *Seventeen Contradictions and the End of Capitalism* (Oxford: Oxford University Press, 2014), p. 240.
38. See Naomi Klein, *The Shock Doctrine: The Rise of Disaster Capitalism* (New York: Metropolitan, 2007).
39. For a good overview of energy, economics and military power in the twentieth century, including how nuclear energy is interconnected with fossil fuels, see Adam Broinowki, "Nuclear Power and Oil Capital in the Long Twentieth Century," in *Materialism and the Critique of Energy*, ed. Brent Ryan Bellamy and Jeff Diamanti (Chicago: MCM, 2018), pp. 197–240.
40. Mike Davis, *Planet of Slums* (London: Verso, 2006), p. 1.
41. Davis, p. 15.
42. See Samir Amin, *The Liberal Virus: Permanent War and the Americanization of the World* (New York: Monthly Review, 2004), p. 39.
43. Samir Amin, *The Implosion of Contemporary Capitalism* (New York: Monthly Review, 2013), p. 40.
44. Mirowski, *More Heat Than Light*, p. 66.
45. Mirowski, p. 68.
46. Mirowski, p. 74.
47. Mirowski, p. 195.
48. Nicolas Georgescu-Roegen, *The Entropy Law and the Economic Process* (Cambridge, MA: Harvard University Press, 1971), p. 6 (emphasis in original).
49. Georgescu-Roegen, p. 9.
50. Georgescu-Roegen, p. 10.
51. Georgescu-Roegen, p. 223.
52. Georgescu-Roegen, p. 4.
53. Georgescu-Roegen, p. 4.

3. POLITICAL ECONOMY AND POLITICAL ECOLOGY

54. Georgescu-Roegen, p. 284.
55. Karl Marx, *Grundrisse: Foundations of the Critique of Political Economy*, trans. Martin Nicholaus (New York: Penguin, 1973), p. 143.
56. Marx, p. 200 (emphasis in original).
57. Marx, p. 260 (emphasis in original).
58. Geoffrey Ingham, *The Nature of Money* (Cambridge: Polity, 2004), p. 12 (emphasis in original).
59. David Graeber, *Debt: The First 5,000 Years* (New York: Melville House, 2011), p. 40.
60. Ingham, *The Nature of Money*, p. 122.
61. Ingham, p. 74 (emphasis in original).
62. Graeber, *Debt*, p. 391.
63. Graeber, p. 98.
64. Graeber, p. 103.
65. Graeber, p. 109.
66. Pierre Klossowski, *Living Currency*, ed. Vernon W. Cisney, Nicolae Morar, and Daniel W. Smith (London: Bloomsbury Academic, 2017), p. 48.
67. Klossowski, p. 67.
68. Klossowski, p. 67.
69. Klossowski, p. 60.
70. Klossowski, p. 69 (emphasis in original).
71. Klossowski, p. 69.
72. Klossowski, p. 75.
73. See Jacques Lacan, *Seminar XVII: The Other Side of Psychoanalysis*, trans. Russell Grigg (New York: Norton, 2007); and Jean-François Lyotard, *Libidinal Economy*, trans. Iain Hamilton Grant (London: Bloomsbury Academic, 2015).
74. Klossowski, *Living Currency*, p. 61.
75. Georges Bataille, *The Accursed Share: An Essay on General Economy*, vol. 1: *Consumption*, trans. Robert Hurley (New York: Zone, 1991), p. 9.
76. Kojin Karatani, *The Structure of World History: From Modes of Production to Modes of Exchange*, trans. Michael K. Bourdaghs (Durham: Duke University Press, 2014), p. 1.
77. Karatani, p. 4.
78. Karatani, p. 9.
79. Jacques Derrida, *Rogues: Two Essays on Reason*, trans. Pascale-Anne Brault and Michael Naas (Stanford: Stanford University Press, 2005), p. 87.
80. Karatani, *The Structure of World History*, p. 134.
81. Karatani, p. 198.
82. Bataille, *The Accursed Share*, 1:67.
83. Bataille, 1:67 (emphasis in original).
84. Bataille, 1:68.
85. Karatani, *The Structure of World History*, p. 33.
86. Karatani, p. 42.
87. Karatani, p. 43.

88. Karatani, p. 44.
89. Karatani, p. 40.
90. Karatani, p. 41.
91. Karatani, p. 83.
92. Karatani, p. 51.
93. Karatani, p. 48.
94. Georges Bataille, *The Accursed Share*, vols. 2 and 3, trans. Robert Hurley (New York: Zone, 1991), p. 47.
95. Bataille, p. 47.
96. Bataille, p. 41 (emphasis in original).
97. See Daniel L. Pals, *Eight Theories of Religion*, 2d ed. (New York: Oxford University Press, 2006), pp. 250–251.
98. Karatani, *The Structure of World History*, p. 44.
99. Karatani, p. 49.
100. Bataille, *The Accursed Share*, 1:19.
101. Bataille, 1:21.
102. Bataille, 1:28.
103. Bataille, p. 29.
104. Bataille, p. 21.
105. Bataille, p. 30.
106. Bataille, p. 33.
107. Bataille, p. 33.
108. Bataille, p. 39.
109. Bataille, p. 22.
110. Bataille, p. 23.
111. Bataille, p. 59.
112. See Gilles Deleuze, *Difference and Repetition*, trans. Paul Patton (New York: Columbia University Press, 1994), p. 242.
113. Allan Stoekl, *Bataille's Peak: Energy, Religion, and Postsustainability* (Minneapolis: University of Minnesota Press, 2007), p. xiii.
114. Stoekl, p. xx (emphasis in original).
115. Bataille, *The Accursed Share*, 1:23.
116. Bataille, 1:24.
117. Stoekl, *Bataille's Peak*, p. 138.
118. Stoekl,, p. 144.
119. Stoekl, p. 25.
120. Stoekl, p. 148.
121. Donna J. Haraway, *Staying with the Trouble: Making Kin in the Chthulucene* (Durham: Duke University Press, 2016), p. 1.
122. Haraway, p. 2.
123. Haraway, p. 14.
124. Haraway, p. 126 (emphasis in original).

3. POLITICAL ECONOMY AND POLITICAL ECOLOGY   277

125. Haraway (emphasis in original).
126. Haraway, p. 127 (emphasis in original).
127. Haraway (emphasis in original).
128. Haraway, p. 147 (emphasis in original).
129. Haraway (emphasis in original).
130. Haraway, p. 176.
131. Haraway, p. 276.
132. Haraway, p. 277. On the connection between Marx and Heidegger, see also the work of Gianni Vattimo and Santiago Zabala, *Hermeneutic Communism: From Heidegger to Marx* (New York: Columbia University Press, 2011).
133. Haraway, p. 278 (emphasis in original).
134. Haraway, p. 279.
135. See Isabelle Stengers, *In Catastrophic Times: Resisting the Coming Barbarism*, trans. Andrew Goffey (London: Open Humanities, 2015), pp. 4, 20.
136. Michel Serres, *The Natural Contract*, trans. Elizabeth MacArthur and William Paulson (Ann Arbor: University of Michigan Press, 1995), p. 3.
137. Serres, p. 25.
138. Bruno Latour, *Politics of Nature: How to Bring the Sciences Into Democracy*, trans. Catherine Porter (Cambridge, MA: Harvard University Press, 2004), pp. 18–19.
139. Latour, p. 21.
140. Latour, p. 59.
141. Bruno Latour, *Facing Gaia: Eight Lectures on the New Climatic Regime*, trans. Catherine Porter (Cambridge: Polity, 2017), pp. 51–53.
142. Clare Taylor, "Why Mississippi and Atchafalaya River Flooding Is Likely to Happen More Often, Experts Say," *Acadiana Advocate*, June 1, 2019, https://www.theadvocate.com/acadiana/news/article_f6ef23cc-82f2-11e9-96d2-576c3fafa0a7.html. On the Yazoo Pumps, see Phil MacCausland and Alex Rozier, "Mississippi Residents Flooded Out for Four Months Say the EPA Could Save Them but Won't," *Mississippi Today*, June 13, 2019, https://www.nbcnews.com/news/us-news/mississippi-residents-flooded-out-four-months-say-epa-could-save-n1014856.
143. Latour, *Facing Gaia*, p. 70.
144. Latour, p. 35.
145. Latour, p. 57.
146. Bruno Latour, *Down to Earth: Politics in the New Climatic Regime*, trans. Catherine Porter (Cambridge: Polity, 2018), p. 1.
147. Latour, p. 19 (emphasis in original).
148. Latour, p. 33.
149. Latour, p. 40 (emphasis in original).
150. Latour, p. 82.
151. Latour, *Facing Gaia*, p. 87 (emphasis in original).
152. Latour, p. 219 (emphasis in original).
153. Michel Serres, *Biogea*, trans. Randolph Burks (Minneapolis: Univocal, 2012), pp. 28, 34.

154. Serres, p. 172.
155. Serres, pp. 199–200.
156. Serres, p. 200.

4. OF SPIRIT IN AMERINDIAN, VODOU, AND CHINESE TRADITIONS

1. Mark Rifkin, *Beyond Settler Time: Temporal Sovereignty and Indigenous Self-Determination* (Durham: Duke University Press, 2017), p. 29. This important study of indigenous temporality does not explicitly reference energy, but Rifkin does cite Einstein's special relativity as a way to comprehend the interaction of different frames of reference (p. 20).
2. Kojin Karatani, *Isonomia and the Origins of Philosophy*, trans. Joseph A. Murphy (Durham: Duke University Press, 2017), p. 10.
3. Peter Sloterdijk, *You Must Change Your Life: On Anthropotechnics*, trans. Wieland Hoban (Cambridge: Polity, 2013), p. 3.
4. Sloterdijk, p. 39.
5. Sloterdijk, p. 207.
6. Sloterdijk, p. 300.
7. Sloterdijk, p. 444.
8. See Dipesh Chakrabarty, *Provincializing Europe: Postcolonial Thought and Historical Difference* (Princeton: Princeton University Press, 2000), p. 254.
9. The quote is from Fredric Jameson, "Future City," *New Left Review* 21 (May-June 2003); see https://newleftreview.org/issues/II21/articles/fredric-jameson-future-city.
10. Eduardo Viveiros de Castro, *The Relative Native: Essays on Indigenous Conceptual Worlds* (Chicago: Hau, 2015), p. 59.
11. Eduardo Viveiros de Castro, *Cannibal Metaphysics: For a Post-structural Anthropology*, trans. Peter Skafish (Minneapolis: Univocal, 2014), p. 55.
12. Viveiros de Castro, *The Relative Native*, p. 356.
13. Viveiros de Castro, p. 246.
14. Viveiros de Castro, *Cannibal Metaphysics*, p. 74 (emphasis in original).
15. Viveiros de Castro, p. 258 (emphasis in original).
16. Déborah Danowski and Eduardo Viveiros de Castro, *The Ends of the World*, trans. Rodrigo Nunes (Cambridge: Polity, 2017), p. 67.
17. Danowski and Viveiros de Castro, p. 70.
18. Danowski and Viveiros de Castro, p. 63 (emphasis in original).
19. Viveiros de Castro, *The Relative Native*, p. 149.
20. Viveiros de Castro, p. 280.
21. Viveiros de Castro, p. 281.
22. Viveiros de Castro, p. 292 (emphasis in original).
23. See Mary-Jane Rubenstein, *Pantheologies: Gods, Worlds, Monsters* (New York: Columbia University Press, 2018).

4. OF SPIRIT IN AMERINDIAN, VODOU, AND CHINESE TRADITIONS   279

24. Danowski and Viveiros de Castro, *The Ends of the World*, p. 14.
25. Danowski and Viveiros de Castro, p. 96.
26. Danowski and Viveiros de Castro, p. 99.
27. Danowski and Viveiros de Castro, p. 98.
28. Danowski and Viveiros de Castro, p. 78 (emphasis in original).
29. Danowski and Viveiros de Castro, p. 107.
30. See Charles C. Mann, *1491: New Revelations of the Americas Before Columbus* (New York: Random House, 2006), p. 108.
31. Danowski and Viveiros de Castro, *The Ends of the World*, p. 105 (emphasis in original).
32. Danowski and Viveiros de Castro, p. 105 (emphasis in original).
33. Danowski and Viveiros de Castro, p. 123 (emphasis in original).
34. Robin Wall Kimmerer, *Braiding Sweetgrass: Indigenous Wisdom, Scientific Knowledge, and the Teachings of Plants* (Minneapolis: Milkweed, 2013), p. 9.
35. Mary L. Keller, "The Indigeneity of Spirit Possession," in *Spirit Possession: Multidisciplinary Approaches to a Worldwide Phenomenon* (Budapest: Central European Press, 2022), p. 197.
36. Walter D. Mignolo, *The Darker Side of Western Modernity: Global Futures, Decolonial Options* (Durham: Duke University Press, 2011), p. 8.
37. *Basic Call to Consciousness*, ed. Akwesane Notes (Summertown, TN: Native Voices, 2005), p. 98.
38. Mignolo, *The Darker Side of Western Modernity*, p. 9.
39. Mann, *1491*, p. 356.
40. Mann, p. 363.
41. Mann, p. 363.
42. The proposed date has been associated with a solar eclipse that took place in either 1142 or 1451 CE. Scholars have not been able to settle on which date is more plausible.
43. Mann, *1491*, p. 382.
44. Mann, pp. 386–387.
45. Roxanne Dunbar-Ortiz, *An Indigenous Peoples' History of the United States* (Boston: Beacon, 2014), p. 26. See also Jack Weatherford, *Indian Givers: How Native Americans Transformed the World* (New York: Three Rivers, 1988), chapter 8, "The Founding Indian Fathers."
46. Mann, *1491*, p. 388.
47. *Basic Call to Consciousness*, p. 129.
48. *Basic Call to Consciousness*, p. 85.
49. *Basic Call to Consciousness*, p. 86.
50. *Basic Call to Consciousness*, p. 90.
51. *Basic Call to Consciousness*, p. 121.
52. *Basic Call to Consciousness*, p. 122.
53. Laurent Dubois, *Avengers of the New World: The Story of the Haitian Revolution* (Cambridge, MA: Belknap, 2004), p. 40. See also the classic but still persuasive account by C. L. R. James, *The Black Jacobins* (New York: Vintage, 1963).

280   4. OF SPIRIT IN AMERINDIAN, VODOU, AND CHINESE TRADITIONS

54. Bruno Latour, *Facing Gaia: Eight Lectures on the New Climatic Regime*, trans. Catherine Porter (Cambridge: Polity, 2017), p. 58.
55. The philosophy of "Object-Oriented Ontology" is a way to describe the complexity of objects in nonsubjective terms. As a response to the subjective biases that permeate Western philosophy and culture, it can read as a corrective tonic; as a full-fledged ontology, however, it is deeply naive and problematic for many reasons, including its rejection of any form of subjectivity. See Graham Harman, *Object-Oriented Ontology: A New Theory of Everything* (New Orleans: Pelican, 2018).
56. Dubois, *Avengers of the New World*, p. 100.
57. On the construction of the categories and criteria of world religions in the late nineteenth and early twentieth centuries, see Tomoko Masuzawa, *The Invention of World Religions* (Chicago: University of Chicago Press, 2005).
58. Patrick Bellegarde-Smith, *Haiti: The Breached Citadel*, 2d ed. (Toronto: Canadian Scholars' Press, 2004), p. 24.
59. Mambo Chita Tann, *Haitian Vodou: An Introduction to Haiti's Indigenous Spiritual Tradition* (Woodbury MN: Llewellyn, 2012), p. 93.
60. Tann, p. 52.
61. Anthony B. Pinn, *Varieties of African-American Religious Experience* (Minneapolis: Fortress, 1998), p. 33.
62. Tann, *Haitian Vodou*, p. 150.
63. Philip P. Arnold, *Eating Landscape: Aztec and European Occupation of Tlalocan* (Boulder: University Press of Colorado, 2001), pp.105–111.
64. Susan Buck-Morss, *Hegel, Haiti, and Universal History* (Pittsburgh: University of Pittsburgh Press, 2009), p. 50.
65. Jacques Derrida, *Rogues: Two Essays on Reason*, trans. Pascale-Anne Brault and Michael Naas (Stanford: Stanford University Press, 2005), p. 37.
66. Patrick Bellegarde-Smith, "Resisting Freedom: Cultural Factors in Democracy—the Case for Haiti," in *Invisible Powers: Vodou in Haitian Life and Culture*, ed. Claudine Michel and Patrick Bellegarde-Smith (New York: Palgrave-Macmillan, 2006), p. 112.
67. Jean-Bertrand Aristide, *Eyes of the Heart: Seeking a Path for the Poor in an Age of Globalization* (Monroe, ME: Common Courage, 2000), p. 36.
68. See Jacques Derrida, "Force of Law: The Mystical Foundation of Authority, in *Acts of Religion*, ed. Gil Anidjar (New York: Routledge, 2002), pp. 228–298.
69. Derrida, *Rogues*, p. 110.
70. Derrida, p. 111.
71. Paola Marrati, *Gilles Deleuze: Cinema and Philosophy*, trans. Alisa Hartz (Baltimore: Johns Hopkins University Press, 2008), p. 55.
72. Gilles Deleuze, *Cinema 2: The Time-Image*, trans. Hugh Tomlinson and Robert Galeta (Minneapolis: University of Minnesota Press, 1989), p. 17. See also my initial engagement with Vodou in the context of an interpretation of Deleuze in Clayton Crockett, *Deleuze Beyond Badiou: Ontology, Multiplicity, and Event* (New York: Columbia University Press, 2013), chapter 10, "Vodou Economics: Haiti and the Future of Democracy."
73. Deleuze, *Cinema 2*, p. 155.

4. OF SPIRIT IN AMERINDIAN, VODOU, AND CHINESE TRADITIONS   281

74. Deleuze, p. 179.
75. Deleuze, pp. 179–180.
76. Deleuze, p. 80.
77. Deleuze, p. 211.
78. Deleuze, p. 213.
79. Deleuze, p. 215.
80. For an example of a veve of Papa Legba, see https://commons.wikimedia.org/wiki/File:VeveLegba.svg#/media/File:VeveLegba.svg.
81. Deleuze, *Cinema 2*, p. 216.
82. Deleuze, p. 220.
83. Neil Roberts, *Freedom as Marronage* (Chicago: University of Chicago Press, 2015), p. 8.
84. Roberts, p. 9.
85. Tu Wei-Ming, *Confucian Thought: Selfhood as Creative Transformation* (Albany: State University of New York Press, 1985), p. 37.
86. See Eiho Baba, "Li as Emergent Patterns of Qi: A Nonreductive Interpretation," in *Returning to Zhu Xi: Emerging Patterns Within the Supreme Polarity*, ed. David Jones and Jinli He (Albany: SUNY Press, 2015), pp. 197–228.
87. Ira Kasoff, *The Thought of Chang Tsai (1020–1077)* (Cambridge: Cambridge University Press, 1984), p. 148. Unfortunately, Kasoff uses the more traditional Wade-Giles system of transliteration of Chinese characters, whereas most contemporary scholars use the later Pinyin version. For Kasoff, Zhang is written Chang, and qi is written as ch'i.
88. Kasoff, p. 153.
89. See Kasoff, p. 145.
90. Chang Tsai (Zhang Zai), *Correcting Youthful Ignorance*, in *A Source Book in Chinese Philosophy*, trans. Wing-Tsit Chan (Princeton: Princeton University Press, 1963), p. 501.
91. Kasoff, *The Thought of Chang Tsai*, p. 36.
92. Kasoff, p. 36.
93. Chang, *Correcting Youthful Ignorance*, p. 501.
94. Kasoff, *The Thought of Chang Tsai*, p. 41.
95. Kasoff, p. 43.
96. Kasoff, p. 36.
97. Jung-Yeup Kim, *Zhang Zai's Philosophy of Qi: A Practical Understanding* (Lanham, MD: Lexington, 2015), p. 2.
98. Kim, p. 2.
99. Kim, p. 62.
100. Kim, p. 65.
101. Chang, *Correcting Youthful Ignorance*, pp. 500–501.
102. Kasoff, *The Thought of Chang Tsai*, p. 61.
103. Kasoff, p. 24–25.
104. Kasoff, p. 25.
105. Hyo-Dong Lee, *Spirit, Qi, and Multitude: A Comparative Theology for the Democracy of Creation* (New York: Fordham University Press, 2014), p. 148.

106. See Chou Tun-I (Zhou Dunyi), "An Explanation of the Diagram of the Great Ultimate," in Wing-Tsit Chan, *A Sourcebook in Chinese Philosophy* (Princeton: Princeton University Press, 1963), pp. 463–464. In addition, in the bodily practice of *taiji qaun*, the practitioner begins by experiencing the body-mind as Wuji or unlimited and moves toward the Taiji as the manifestation of the Great Ultimate as integrated harmoniously into the person. As related by Adam Frank, personal communication.
107. I owe this interpretation of *neng* to my interactions and conversations with the contemporary Chinese philosopher Dai Zhaoguo, of Anhui Normal University.
108. We can also attend the expressions of qi in the Japanese philosophy of Kaibara Ekken (1630–1714), as well as in the Korean philosophy of *ki* in Sŏ Kyŏngdŏk (1489–1546). See Kim, *Zhang Zai's Philosophy of Qi*, pp. 95–103, and Kaibara Ekken, *The Philosophy of Qi: The Record of Great Doubts*, trans. Mary Evelyn Tucker (New York: Columbia University Press, 2007).
109. Wang Fu-Chih, selections from the *Ch'uan-shan i-shu*, in *A Source Book of Chinese Philosophy*, p. 697.
110. Wang Fu-Chih, p. 698.
111. Wang Fu-Chih, p. 694.
112. Nicholas S. Brasovan, *Neo-Confucian Ecological Humanism: An Engagement with Wang Fuzhi* (Albany: SUNY Press, 2017), pp. 63, 65.
113. Peter Atkins, *The Laws of Thermodynamics: A Very Short Introduction* (Oxford: Oxford University Press, 2010), p. 37.
114. See Richard J. Smith, *The I Ching: A Biography* (Princeton: Princeton University Press, 2012).
115. See Daniel Cunha, "The Anthropocene as Fetishism," in *Materialism and the Critique of Energy*, ed. Brent Ryan Bellamy and Jeff Diamanti (Chicago: MCM, 2018), pp. 51–70.
116. See Jeffrey W. Robbins, *Radical Theology: A Vision for Change* (Bloomington: Indiana University Press, 2016).

5. RADICAL THEOLOGY AND THE NATURE OF GOD

1. Gilles Deleuze and Félix Guattari, *A Thousand Plateaus: Capitalism and Schizophrenia*, trans. Brian Massumi (Minneapolis: University of Minnesota Press, 1987), p. 5.
2. Deleuze and Guattari, p. 5.
3. Deleuze and Guattari, p. 6 (emphasis in original). This method of subtraction is also that of Alain Badiou and Slavoj Žižek, although they ignore the existence of subtraction in Deleuze and Guattari's work.
4. Deleuze and Guattari, p. 6.
5. Deleuze and Guattari, p. 7.
6. Deleuze and Guattari, p. 8.
7. Gilles Deleuze and Félix Guattari, *What Is Philosophy?*, trans. Hugh Tomlinson and Graham Burchell (New York: Columbia University Press, 1994), p. 36.

5. RADICAL THEOLOGY AND THE NATURE OF GOD 283

8. See Thomas J. J. Altizer and William Hamilton, *Radical Theology and the Death of God* (Indianapolis: Bobbs Merrill, 1968). This book was dedicated to the memory of Paul Tillich.
9. Thomas J. J. Altizer, *The Gospel of Christian Atheism* (Philadelphia: Westminster, 1966), p. 10.
10. See Paul Tillich, *Theology of Culture*, ed. Robert C. Kimball (Oxford: Oxford University Press, 1959).
11. Michael Grimshaw, "Did God Die in *The Christian Century*?," *Journal for Cultural and Religious Theory* 6, no. 3 (2005): 11.
12. James Cone, *The Cross and the Lynching Tree* (Maryknoll, NY: Orbis, 2011), p. 160.
13. Mary Daly, *Beyond God the Father* (Boston: Beacon, 1972), p. 127.
14. Christopher D. Rodkey, "The Nemesis Hex," in *Retrieving the Radical Tillich: His Legacy and Contemporary Importance*, ed. Russell Re Manning (New York: Palgrave Macmillan, 2015), p. 66.
15. Marcella Althaus-Reid, *Indecent Theology: Theological Perversions in Sex, Gender, and Politics* (London: Routledge, 2000), p. 88.
16. See Stephanie Marie Gray, "A Break in Time: Revolutionizing Temporalities from the Margins," M.A. thesis, Global Center for Advanced Studies, www.gcas.ie, chapter 2.
17. Althaus-Reid, *Indecent Theology*, p. 22. Another Argentine theologian who has radicalized Liberation Theology is Ivan Petrella. See his *Beyond Liberation Theology: A Polemic* (London: SCM, 2008).
18. Althaus-Reid, *Indecent Theology*, p. 173.
19. Miguel A. de la Torre, *Embracing Hopelessness* (Minneapolis: Fortress, 2017), p. 139.
20. De la Torre, p. 149 (emphasis in original).
21. See Jeffrey W. Robbins, "Terror and the Postmodern Condition: Toward a Radical Political Theology," in *Religion and Violence in a Secular World: Toward a New Political Theology*, ed. Clayton Crockett (Charlottesville: University of Virginia Press, 2006, pp. 187–205.
22. See Clayton Crockett, *Radical Political Theology: Religion and Politics After Liberalism* (New York: Columbia University Press, 2011); and Jeffrey W. Robbins, *Radical Democracy and Political Theology* (New York: Columbia University Press, 2011).
23. Creston Davis, "Introduction: Holy Saturday or Insurrection Sunday? Staging an Unlikely Debate," in Slavoj Žižek and John Milbank, *The Monstrosity of Christ: Paradox or Dialectic?*, ed. Creston Davis (Cambridge, MA: MIT Press, 2009), p. 3.
24. Alfred North Whitehead, *Process and Reality*, corrected ed., ed. David Ray Griffin and Donald W. Sherburne (New York: Free Press, 1978), p. 348.
25. John B. Cobb, Jr., *A Christian Natural Theology: Based on the Thought of Alfred North Whitehead* (Philadelphia: Westminster, 1965), p. 190.
26. Catherine Keller, *The Face of the Deep: A Theology of Becoming* (New York: Routledge, 2002), p. 219.
27. Keller, p. 33.
28. Mary-Jane Rubenstein, *Pantheologies: Gods, Worlds, Monsters* (New York: Columbia University Press, 2018), p. 24.

29. Rubenstein, p. 99.
30. Rubenstein, p. 127.
31. Rubenstein, p. 173.
32. Rubenstein, p. 173.
33. Mary-Jane Rubenstein, "Science," in *The Palgrave Handbook of Radical Theology*, ed. Christopher Rodkey and Jordan E. Miller (New York: Palgrave Macmillan, 2018), pp. 747–756; quote p. 751 (emphasis in original).
34. Rubenstein, p. 752.
35. Rubenstein, *Pantheologies*, p. 187.
36. Rubenstein, p. 187 (emphasis mine).
37. Catherine Keller, *Cloud of the Impossible: Negative Theology and Planetary Entanglement* (New York: Columbia University Press, 2014), p. 276 (emphasis mine).
38. Chelsea Harvey, "Clouds May Hold the Key to Future Warming," *Scientific American*, February 27, 2019, https://www.scientificamerican.com/article/clouds-may-hold-the-key-to-future-warming/.
39. Catherine Keller, *Political Theology of Earth* (New York: Columbia University Press, 2018), p. 32.
40. Carl Schmitt, *Political Theology: Four Chapters on the Concept of Sovereignty*, trans. George Schwab (Chicago: University of Chicago Press, 2006), p. 5.
41. Keller, *Political Theology of the Earth*, p. 44.
42. See *The Tree of Life: The Palace of Adam Kadmon—Chayyam Vital's Introduction to the Kabbalah of Isaac Luria*, trans. Donald Wilder Menzi and Zwe Padeh (New York: Arizal, 2008).
43. Keller, *Political Theology of the Earth*, p. 101.
44. Keller, p. 102.
45. Keller, p. 180.
46. Keller, p. 158.
47. Keller, p. 158.
48. Deleuze and Guattari, p. 514.
49. Gilles Deleuze, *Difference and Repetition*, trans. Paul Patton (New York: Columbia University Press, 1994), p. 216.
50. Deleuze and Guattari, p. 509.
51. Deleuze and Guattari, p. 509.
52. Deleuze and Guattari's new creation of Earth understood in terms of an absolute deterritorialization at the end of *A Thousand Plateaus* should also be read as a response to Carl Schmitt's *The Nomos of the Earth: In the International Law of the Jus Publicum Europaeum*, trans. G. L. Ulmen (New York: Telos, 2006).
53. Octavia E. Butler, *Parable of the Sower* (New York: Grand Central, 2000), p. 3.
54. Butler, p. 26.

INDEX

Accelerationism, 34–35, 255
Agamben, Giorgio, 237
Agential, 23, 70, 180–181, 186–187, 194–195, 199, 206, 244; agential realism, 34, 186
Ahmed, Sarah, 6
Aleatory materialism, 10
Althaus-Reid, Marcella, 235–236
Althusser, Louis, 9–10, 97
Altizer, Thomas J.J., 229, 232–233
Amazonians, 185, 192–193, 222
Amerindian, 23, 185–187, 191–195, 197–203, 222–223, 226, 230, 247
Amin, Samir, 147
An Yountae, 248
Animism, 23, 185, 193–194, 239, 246
Anthropocene, 11, 22, 133–135, 173, 178, 200, 214, 226, 249, 256
Aristide, Jean-Baptiste, 210, 215
Aristotle, 2, 18, 20, 26–30, 32–39, 41, 76
Archaea, 91, 93, 100–102
Assemblages, 122, 186, 198, 214–216, 229, 246, 254
Atkins, Peter, 42–43, 46, 225
Aspect, Alain, 69
ATP (adenosine triphosphate), 18, 89–91, 93

Baba, Eiho, 217
Bacteria, 91–93, 99, 101–102, 114–115, 254
Badiou, Alain, 37, 77, 110
Bak, Per, 96
Barad, Karen, 6, 8, 23, 34, 66–71, 75, 102, 186, 194, 204, 231, 239, 252
Baron Samedi, 208
Barreiro, José, 202
Bataille, Georges, 21, 34–35, 137, 159, 162–163, 165–175, 178, 184, 189, 194, 256
Batalhão, Tiago, 129
Bateson, Gregory, 2
Bellgarde-Smith, Patrick, 207, 210
Bénard, Henri, 53; Bénard cells, 53–54
Benjamin, Walter, 252
Bennett, Charles, 72–73
Bennett, Jane, 6, 79
Bernouilli, Daniel, 40
Bezos, Jeff, 12
Bell, John, 69
Biden, Joe, 12, 189, 251
Bioenergetics, 21, 86
Biogea, 183–184
Black, Joseph, 40
Bohr, Neils, 64, 67–69

Boltzmann, Ludwig, 19, 48–49, 54, 63, 72
Boukman, 206
Braidotti, Rosi, 5–6
Brain, 77–78, 81, 110, 113, 115–121, 215, 230, 254–255; building a brain, 211–213; cloud brain, 254; increased energy needed for the brain, 19, 117; evolution of the brain, 113–115, 120
Brasovan, Nicholas S., 225
Bray, Karen, 248
Buck-Morss, Susan, 209
Buddhism, 22, 216–217, 222, 257
Burroughs, William S., 229
Butler, Judith, 6, 82
Butler, Octavia E., 1, 256–257

Cambrian, 113
Cantor, Georg, 110
Capitolocene, 135–136, 173
Caputo, John D., 248
Carey, Nessa, 104–107
Carnot, Sadi, 18, 40, 44–47, 51, 90
Cesaire, Aimé, 215
Chakrabarty, Dipesh, 190
Changeux, Jean-Pierre, 115–116
Cheah, Pheng, 6–7
Chen, Mel, 6
Cheng Hao, 217–218, 224
Cheng Yi, 217–218, 224
Christianity, 2, 207–208, 227, 236, 257–258
Chthulucene, 173
Clausius, Rudolf, 19, 46–47, 67
Cobb, John B., 232, 241–242
Coles, Donald, 53
Colonialism, 3, 137–139, 199–200, 203–204, 209–210, 236, 248, 259
Columbus, Christopher, 197, 200 204
Cone, James, 234
Connolly, William, 6, 246
Consciousness, 5, 27, 114, 117, 119, 121, 123–125, 127–128, 165, 198, 202–203, 205, 207, 209, 213–214, 255, 258
Coole, Diana, 5

Coopersmith, Jennifer, 37, 40, 45, 74
COVID-19, 12, 146, 189, 251
Cox, Harvey, 233
Crooks, Gavin, 129
Crutzen, Paul, 133

Daggett, Cara New, 3, 39, 140–141
Dalton, John, 48, 63
Daly, Mary, 234–235
Damasio, Antonio, 115
Danowski, Déborah, 193, 196–198, 203–204
Daoism, 217
Dark energy, 19–20
Darwin, Charles, 48, 81, 94–99, 101–104, 111–112
Davis, Creston, 237
Davis, Mike, 146
Dawkins, Richard, 103–104, 109, 118
Deacon, Terrence, 124–127, 129–131, 152
Decolonial, 200, 236
Deganawidah, 201
DeLanda, Manuel, 6–7, 59,
Deleuze, Gilles, 4–6, 21,23, 31, 35–38, 55–59, 65–66, 71, 74, 77, 79, 81, 117–122, 155, 171, 186, 192, 198, 209, 211–215, 230–232, 253–255; Deleuze and Guattari, 2, 6, 34, 108, 117–118, 214–215, 228–231, 248–249, 253–255
Democritus, 8
Dennett, Daniel, 103
Derrida, Jacques, 6, 10, 21, 77, 79, 84, 160, 209–210, 237
Deterritorialization, 253–255
Diamond, Jared, 17
Differentiator, 5, 56
Diffraction Pattern, 23, 56, 186
Dirac, Paul, 64
Dissipative systems, 20, 39, 50–51, 125
DNA methylation, 105–107, 109, 113
Dobbyns, Henry F., 197
Dobzhansky, Theodosius, 98
Dolphijn, Rick, 6

Du Weiming, 216
Duns Scotus, 37

Efference copy, 119–120
Einstein, Albert, 3, 33, 39, 48, 62–64, 67–69, 71, 74, 84, 148, 245
Eldridge, Niles, 95–96
Energeia, 2, 18, 29, 31–36, 41
Energy humanities, 3–4
England, Jeremy, 129–130
Entropy, 18–21, 46–55, 57–61, 64–65, 71–76, 84–85, 87–90, 124–131, 135, 137, 170–171, 173, 185, 223–224, 256; economics and, 147, 149–152, 155, 159, information and, 71–74, 130; law of, 18, 49, 51–52; negative or negentropy, 51, 84, 126
Epigenesis, 84, 109–113
Epigenetics, 21, 81–82, 103–113, 115–116
Epicurus, 8, 10, 60, 65, 94
EPR paradox, 69
Eukaryotes, 91–93, 99–102, 114
Evans-Pritchard, E. E., 166
Evolution, 21, 51–52, 60, 64, 72–73, 77, 85–86, 91–92, 94–99, 101–104, 107–109, 111–112, 114–115, 120, 128, 168, 193, 255
Exaptation, 97–98, 104
Exchange, 8, 22–23, 80, 101, 137, 153–155, 157, 159–168, 170–171, 173–178, 182–183, 189–194; being as exchange, 22, 80–81, 83, 175, 206, 227, 256; exchange value, 152–154; systems or modes of exchange, 22, 101, 159–168, 183, 186–187, 190–191

Fanmi Lavalas, 215
Feibleman, James K., 7
Feminist theology, 232, 234–235, 242, 244, 246
Feuerbach, Ludwig, 9
Feynman, Richard, 17, 79
Fisher, R. A., 98
Floridi, Luciano, 72–73
Floyd, George, 12
Foster, John Bellamy, 8–10, 94–95
Fourier, Charles, 155–157

Gaia, 86, 178, 180, 183, 246–248, 254
Gaiman, Neil, 259
Gell-Mann, Murray, 71
Geoengineering, 31–32
Georgescu-Roegen, Nicolas, 21, 150–152, 154–155, 159, 178
Gibbs, Josiah Willard, 48–49, 54
Gilkey, Langdon, 234
Gleick, James, 60, 72
Glissant, Édouard, 215
Global warming, 3, 12–13, 19, 31–32, 147, 189, 196, 250–251, 256–257
Godfrey-Smith, Peter, 113–114, 119–120
Golding, William, 183
Gould, Stephen Jay, 9, 21, 94–99, 101–194, 108–109, 128
Gradients, 39, 50–54, 58–59, 61–64, 73–74, 85–89, 91, 96, 124–125, 131, 136, 141, 183, 187–188, 204, 255, 260; gradient reduction, 50–52, 54–59, 64, 66, 73–75, 88–89, 150–151, 254
Graeber, David, 154–155, 157, 160–162
Great Acceleration, 15, 133, 135, 143–144, 237
Great Depression, 15, 143, 217
Grimshaw, Michael, 234
Grosz, Elizabeth, 6, 130
Gutiérrez, Gustavo, 235

Hadot, Pierre, 189
Haldane, J. B. S., 98
Hamilton, William Rowan, 73, 148
Hamiltonian function, 73, 148–149
Haraway, Donna J., 173, 178, 183, 246
Harris, Sam, 103
Hartshorne, Charles, 232, 241
Harvey, David, 16, 144
Harvey, Stephano, 251
Haudenosaunee, 185, 198, 201–203, 210
Hayles, N. Katherine, 121–124
Heat engines, 18, 40–41, 44–46, 85–86, 90
Hebb, Donald, 254
Heidegger, Martin, 5–6, 10, 37, 56, 79–80, 83–84, 132–133, 172–177, 210

Heisenberg, Werner, 64
Hegel, G. W. F., 6, 8, 78–79, 84, 159, 199, 209, 233, 249
Heraclitus, 1
Hesiod, 183
Hierarchy (in biology), 108, 122
Hitchens, Christopher, 103
Hobbes, Thomas, 10
Holocene, 133
Homeodynamics, 124
Hu Ganfu, 224
Huxley, Julian, 98
Hydrogen hypothesis, 92–93
Hysteresis, 53, 97

Immanence, 6, 220, 232, 238, 245–246
Indigenous, 23, 139, 142, 162, 187–188, 191–192, 194–199, 201–207, 210, 213–214, 226, 231, 247–248
Industrial Revolution, 2, 15, 19, 39–40, 133, 135–136, 139–140, 155–156, 204
Information, 20, 49, 71–74, 85, 106, 108–109, 116, 121, 124, 126, 148, 184; entropy and information, 64, 71–72, 130, 150; genes and information, 86, 104
Ingram, Geoffrey, 154–155
Intensity, 5, 31, 37, 55–59, 212
Intergovenmental Panel on Climate Change (IPCC), 13
Interstice, 65–66, 186, 211–212
Intra-activity, 8, 34, 75, 204, 252, 256
Irigaray, Luce, 5–6, 82, 84

Jablonka, Eva, 21, 107–109, 111
James, C. L. R., 215
Jameson, Fredric, 191
Jarzynski, Chris, 129
Johnson, Lyndon, 145
Joule, James Prescott, 46
Joyce, James, 229

Kabbalah, 251
Kant, Immanuel, 110–112, 127

Karatani, Kojin, 22, 159–167, 171, 173, 175–176, 178, 182, 186–187, 190–191, 194, 203, 209
Kasoff, Ira, 217, 219, 221
Kay, James, 52
Keller, Catherine, 24, 231, 238, 242–245, 248–253
Keller, Mary L., 199
Kennedy, Robert F., 145
Keynes, John Maynard, 143, 158
Kim Jeung-Yeup, 219–220, 224
Kimmerer, Robin Wall
Kinetic energy, 2, 30, 35, 37, 39–40
King, Martin Luther, 145
Klare, Michael T., 14
Klein, Naomi, 14, 136–137, 145
Klossowski, Pierre, 155–159, 168, 178
Kolbert, Elizabeth, 134
Kurtzweil, Ray, 32

Lacan, Jacques, 158
Lagrange, Joseph-Louis, 73, 148
Lamb, Marion J., 21, 107–109, 111
Land, Nick, 35
Lane, Nick, 87–89, 91–93, 99–101
Lateral gene transfer, 101
Latour, Bruno, 23, 27, 178, 180–183, 186, 194, 196–198, 204, 206, 239, 246–248, 250
LeDoux, Joseph, 115–116
Leibniz, G. W., 30, 39–40, 153, 192
Lenin, V. I., 11
Leucippus, 8
Lévi-Strauss, Claude, 165
Levins, Richard, 9
Lewontin, R. C., 9
Liberation theology, 234–236
Living currency, 158, 165, 168
Lovelock, James, 86, 183, 246, 254
Lucretius, 8, 10, 60, 65, 94, 97
Lwa (Loa), 23, 205–208, 211, 213–214

Machiavelli, Niccolo, 10
Malabou, Catherine, 6, 21–22, 77–85, 109–113, 115–117, 128, 173–177, 182, 189, 194, 227, 256

INDEX   289

Malm, Andreas, 139–141, 143, 155, 178
Mandelbrot, Benoit, 96
Mann, Charles, 200–201, 203
Marder, Michael, 32–37
Margulis, Lynn, 21, 52, 86, 90–91, 98–99, 101–102, 114–115, 246
Marrati, Paola, 211
Marrazi, Christian, 16
Marx, Karl, 8–10, 19, 80, 94–95, 97, 103, 135–136, 138, 146, 152–155, 157, 159–160, 177, 192, 227
Massumi, Brian, 6
Mauss, Marcel, 161, 174–175
Mechanical materialism, 8, 10, 71, 220
Meillassoux, Quentin, 6, 77, 110, 112
Mendel, Gregor, 98
Merleau-Ponty, Maurice, 4–5, 79
Metabolic rift, 9, 136, 146
Metaphyiscs, 20, 26–27, 30, 80–81, 83, 176, 217, 229, 248; Western, 1–2, 24, 248
Metastable, 14, 20, 54, 57, 60–61, 76, 85, 96, 183, 185, 202, 257
Mignolo, Walter, 199–200, 236
Milbank, John, 237
Miller, D. G., 54
Miller, Jordan E., 248
Mirowski, Philip, 143, 147–150
Mitchell, Timothy, 141–143, 178
Mitochondria, 19, 89–90, 92–93, 100–102
Moise, Juvenal, 215
Moore, Jason W., 135
Morphodynamics, 124–127, 129
Morowitz, Harold J., 61, 74, 85–86, 89–90, 151
Morton, Timothy, 27
Motens, Fred, 251
Multiculturalism, 23, 187, 190, 192
Multinaturalism, 23, 187, 191–194, 244, 247
Multiplicity, 24, 181, 186, 191–192, 220, 222–224, 226, 229–231, 234, 244–247, 254, 256, 259
Multiverse, 193, 195, 245
Musk, Elon, 12

Napoleon, 205
Neng, 223–224
Neoclassical economics, 138–139, 143, 147, 149, 158–159
Neo-Confucianism, 23, 185–186, 216–218, 220. 231
Neoliberalism, 3, 11–12, 136, 144–147, 170, 180, 237, 251, 242, 249
New materialism, 1, 4–10, 17, 22–24, 79, 81, 83, 97, 122, 124, 183, 185, 220, 225–226, 231
Newton, Isaac, 6, 40, 44
Nietzsche, Friedrich, 24, 37–38, 81, 97, 171, 188, 192, 233
Nixon, Richard, 145
Nonequilibrium thermodynamics, 18, 21, 39, 42, 39, 50–52, 54–56, 59, 60–62, 64, 71, 85, 90, 124, 129–130, 151, 159, 169–170, 176, 185, 220, 224, 226–227
Nonlinear systems, 7, 20, 55, 59, 124, 148, 151, 246

Obama, Barack, 189
Object-oriented ontology, 110
Onsager, Lars, 54–55
Ozu, Yasujiro, 211

Panentheism, 24, 238, 243–245
Pantheism, 24, 195, 238, 243, 245–247, 249
Papa Legba, 205, 207
Parmendides, 1, 37
Penrose, Roger, 72
Perrin, Jean, 48, 63
Perspectivism, 186, 190–193, 195, 226, 247
Petrella, Ivan, 236
Picketty, Thomas, 143
Pinn, Anthony, 208
Plane of immanence, 7, 38, 231, 255
Planck, Max, 62
Plasticity, 77–84, 109, 129, 175, 177, 227; neuroplasticity, 78, 82, 84, 110, 115–117
Plato, 1–2, 28, 76, 132
Polanyi, Karl, 165
Polytheism, 195, 239, 247

Postructuralism, 6, 21, 77; the poststructural, 21, 96–98, 194
Postsustainability, 172–173
Potential energy, 2, 18, 29–30, 32–33, 35–37, 39–40, 195, 223
Prigogine, Ilya, 50–51, 55, 60–62, 90, 96, 125, 170
Process theology, 232, 236–238, 241–242
Prokaryotes, 91–93, 99–102
Putin, Vladimir, 251

Qi, 24, 185–186, 216–225, 231
Quantum physics 7, 20, 34, 39, 60, 62–73, 84, 129, 147–148, 239, 245; quantum entanglement, 69–70; quantum field theory 34, 66, 70, 75, 245; quantum superposition, 68–69; quantum thermodynamics, 62, 129–130
Quijano, Anibal, 199, 236

Radical theology, 24, 195, 227–233, 235–238, 245, 247–248
Ray, Thomas, 96
Relativity, 7, 62–65, 71, 74, 147; general relativity, 62, 64; special relativity, 3, 62, 148
Rhizome, 228–231, 248, 255–256, 258–259
Rifkin, Mark, 185
Robbins, Jeffrey W., 128, 227, 231, 237, 248
Rockefeller, John D., 141
Rodkey, Christopher D., 235, 248
Rousseau, Jean-Jacques, 10, 198
Rovelli, Carlo, 64–66, 72–73
Rubenstein, Mary-Jane, 24, 195, 231, 238, 243, 245–249
Rubenstein, Richard, 232–233
Russell, Bertrand, 239

Sade, Marquis de, 155–156, 158
Sagan, Dorion, 52–53, 64, 85
Salminen, Antti, 142
Schmitt, Carl, 237, 251
Schneider, Eric D., 52–56, 85, 125, 129

Schneider, Tapio, 250
Schrödinger, Erwin, 51, 67–68, 73, 84
Scranton, Roy, 134–135
Segwalise, 202–203
Self-organization, 7, 54, 96, 116, 128, 252
Selme, Léon, 57
Serres, Michel, 179, 183–184
Shannon, Claude, 72
Shechinah, 252
Shen, 221
Shenzhong, 218
Shiva, Vandana, 13
Singularity, 20, 32, 38, 96, 101, 256
Skafish, Peter, 83
Sloterdijk, Peter, 187–189, 192, 196, 199
Smil, Vaclav, 17
Smolin, Lee, 72
Socrates, 132
Speculative realism, 6, 110
Spinoza, 37
Stengers, Isabelle, 25, 60–62, 178, 246
Stiegler, Bernard, 122
Stoekl, Allan, 171–173
Swenson, Rod, 51–52, 55, 64, 125
Symbiogenesis, 92, 101, 246
Synapses, 112, 116–117, 119, 212

Taiji, 219, 222–223, 225
Tainos, 204–206, 208, 213
Taixu, 218–219
Tann, Mambo Chita, 208
Taylor, Geoffrey Ingram, 53; Taylor vortices, 53–54
Teilhard de Chardin, Pierre, 32
Teleodynamics, 125–127, 129–130
Terrans, 196–199, 214, 254
Thermodynamics, 2–4, 18, 20–21, 30, 33, 37, 39–41, 43–45, 48–53, 57–58, 60, 62–65, 71–72, 85, 89, 124, 128–130, 136, 140, 147, 150–151, 170, 176, 221, 225, 255–256; laws of thermodynamics, 18, 41–43, 45–48, 52, 57, 61, 74, 85, 88–89, 129, 218, 223, 257; statistical thermodynamics, 49, 63

Thom, René, 96
Thomson, William (Lord Kelvin), 46–48
Tillich, Paul, 233–236
Time-image, 23, 65–66, 118–121, 186, 211–216
Transcendental, 110–112, 127–128
Trouillot, Michel-Rolphe, 215
Trump, Donald, 12, 180, 189, 251, 257
Turing, Alan, 72

Utility, 97, 104, 149, 158–159, 166–171, 175; disutility, 158–159; marginal utility, 149

Vadén, Tere, 142
Vahanian, Gabriel, 232–233
Vahanian, Noëlle, 248
Van Buren, Paul, 233
Veve, 213–214
Vitalism, 4, 21, 77, 185
Viveiros de Castro, Eduardo, 23, 187, 191–200, 202–204, 222–223, 226, 244, 247
Vodou, 23, 185–186, 204–209, 213–216, 226
Voluptuous emotion, 155–158

Waddington, Conrad, 105
Wang An-shih, 217
Wang Fuzhi, 224
Wheeler, John, 72
Whitehead, Alfred North, 4, 7, 10, 79, 114, 232, 237–243
Whitlaw, Emma, 107
Wicken, Jeffrey, 52
Winquist, Charles E., 259
Wittig, Monique, 6
Woese, Carl, 99
Wrangham, Richard, 114
Wynter, Sylvia, 215

Xi Jinping, 251

Yong, Ed, 115
Young, Thomas, 41

Zhang Zai, 24, 217–225
Zhou Dunyi, 218, 222–225
Zhu Xi, 217–219, 224
Žižek, Slavoj, 191, 237

INSURRECTIONS: CRITICAL STUDIES IN RELIGION, POLITICS, AND CULTURE

Slavoj Žižek, Clayton Crockett, Creston Davis, Jeffrey W. Robbins, Editors

After the Death of God, John D. Caputo and Gianni Vattimo, edited by Jeffrey W. Robbins

The Politics of Postsecular Religion: Mourning Secular Futures, Ananda Abeysekara

Nietzsche and Levinas: "After the Death of a Certain God," edited by Jill Stauffer and Bettina Bergo

Strange Wonder: The Closure of Metaphysics and the Opening of Awe, Mary-Jane Rubenstein

Religion and the Specter of the West: Sikhism, India, Postcoloniality, and the Politics of Translation, Arvind Mandair

Plasticity at the Dusk of Writing: Dialectic, Destruction, Deconstruction, Catherine Malabou

Anatheism: Returning to God After God, Richard Kearney

Rage and Time: A Psychopolitical Investigation, Peter Sloterdijk

Radical Political Theology: Religion and Politics After Liberalism, Clayton Crockett

Radical Democracy and Political Theology, Jeffrey W. Robbins

Hegel and the Infinite: Religion, Politics, and Dialectic, edited by Slavoj Žižek, Clayton Crockett, and Creston Davis

What Does a Jew Want? On Binationalism and Other Specters, Udi Aloni

A Radical Philosophy of Saint Paul, Stanislas Breton, edited by Ward Blanton, translated by Joseph N. Ballan

Hermeneutic Communism: From Heidegger to Marx, Gianni Vattimo and Santiago Zabala

Deleuze Beyond Badiou: Ontology, Multiplicity, and Event, Clayton Crockett

Self and Emotional Life: Philosophy, Psychoanalysis, and Neuroscience, Adrian Johnston and Catherine Malabou

The Incident at Antioch: A Tragedy in Three Acts / L'Incident d'Antioche: Tragédie en trois actes, Alain Badiou, translated by Susan Spitzer

Philosophical Temperaments: From Plato to Foucault, Peter Sloterdijk

To Carl Schmitt: Letters and Reflections, Jacob Taubes, translated by Keith Tribe

Encountering Religion: Responsibility and Criticism After Secularism, Tyler Roberts

Spinoza for Our Time: Politics and Postmodernity, Antonio Negri, translated by William McCuaig

Force of God: Political Theology and the Crisis of Liberal Democracy, Carl A. Raschke

Factory of Strategy: Thirty-Three Lessons on Lenin, Antonio Negri, translated by Arianna Bove

Cut of the Real: Subjectivity in Poststructuralism Philosophy, Katerina Kolozova

A Materialism for the Masses: Saint Paul and the Philosophy of Undying Life, Ward Blanton

Our Broad Present: Time and Contemporary Culture, Hans Ulrich Gumbrecht

Wrestling with the Angel: Experiments in Symbolic Life, Tracy McNulty

Cloud of the Impossible: Negative Theology and Planetary Entanglements, Catherine Keller

What Does Europe Want? The Union and Its Discontents, Slavoj Žižek and Srećko Horvat

Harmattan: A Philosophical Fiction, Michael Jackson

Nietzsche Versus Paul, Abed Azzam

Christo-Fiction: The Ruins of Athens and Jerusalem, François Laruelle

Paul's Summons to Messianic Life: Political Theology and the Coming Awakening, L. L. Welborn

Reimagining the Sacred: Richard Kearney Debates God with James Wood, Catherine Keller, Charles Taylor, Julia Kristeva, Gianni Vattimo, Simon Critchley, Jean-Luc Marion, John Caputo, David Tracy, Jens Zimmermann, and Merold Westphal, edited by Richard Kearney and Jens Zimmermann

A Hedonist Manifesto: The Power to Exist, Michel Onfray

An Insurrectionist Manifesto: Four New Gospels for a Radical Politics, Ward Blanton, Clayton Crockett, Jeffrey W. Robbins, and Noëlle Vahanian

The Intimate Universal: The Hidden Porosity Among Religion, Art, Philosophy, and Politics, William Desmond

Heidegger: His Life and His Philosophy, Alain Badiou and Barbara Cassin, translated by Susan Spitzer

The Work of Art: Rethinking the Elementary Forms of Religious Life, Michael Jackson

Sociophobia: Political Change in the Digital Utopia, César Rendueles, translated by Heather Cleary

There's No Such Thing as a Sexual Relationship: Two Lessons on Lacan, Alain Badiou and Barbara Cassin, translated by Susan Spitzer and Kenneth Reinhard

Unbearable Life: A Genealogy of Political Erasure, Arthur Bradley

GPSR Authorized Representative: Easy Access System Europe, Mustamäe tee
50, 10621 Tallinn, Estonia, gpsr.requests@easproject.com

www.ingramcontent.com/pod-product-compliance
Lightning Source LLC
Chambersburg PA
CBHW031235290426
44109CB00012B/300